INFORMATION SYSTEMS

Kruger Brentt
Publishers

INFORMATION SYSTEMS

York Science Group

Kruger Brentt
Publishers

2 0 2 3

Kruger Brentt Publishers UK. LTD.
Company Number 9728962

Regd. Office: 68 St Margarets Road, Edgware, Middlesex HA8 9UU

© 2023 AUTHOR

ISBN: 978-1-78715-098-0

For information on all our publications visit our website at http://krugerbrentt.com/

Information is data that has been processed into a form that is meaningful to the user. An information system (IS) is an organized combination of people, hardware, software, communications network, and data resources that collects, transforms and disseminates information in an organization. Information systems and technologies have become a vital component of businesses and organizations. People rely on information systems to communicate with each other using a variety of physical devices (hardware), information processing instructions and procedures (software), communication channels (networks), and stored data (data resources). Information can be classified into facts, opinions, concepts, procedures, processes, principles, primary information, and secondary information. Apart from this, it can also be classified into several types based on its nature, usage, creation, application, structure, and form. Primary data collection refers to collecting original data or collecting data directly from the source. Secondary data collection refers to collecting data from secondary sources such as books, journals, research reports, online databases, Internet, etc. The user should check whether this data has been updated before analyzing the data and drawing conclusions. The transmission of information between one person and another, takes place with the help of the communications system. Summarization and message routing are the two methods that increase the sending and receiving efficiency of the system. Individuals tend to exercise discretion over the content or distribution of information by message delay, message modification or filtering, inference or uncertainty absorption, and presentation bias. The benefits of information in organizations include – it helps in management control, it helps in decision-making, and it helps to build models, backgrounds, and motivation. Quality of information is also a vital issue. The term 'quality' is subjective in nature and hence its parameters should be clearly defined in order to judge the quality of information. The various parameters of quality are validity, consistency, reliability, impartiality, and age.

Errors and bias occur as a result of giving too much importance and preference to the quantity of information rather than the quality. An IS accepts data resources as input and processes it and delivers information products as output. Information systems consist of people resources (end users and IS specialists), hardware resources (machines and media), software (programs and procedures), data (data and knowledge bases), and networks (communications media and network support) to perform input, processing, output, storage, and control activities that convert data resources into information products. Some of the important activities performed by an IS are processing of data into information, storage of data resources and control of system performance. Information systems perform three vital roles in any type of organization. They support business operations, support managerial decision- making, and provide strategic competitive advantage to the organization. Information systems are classified into different classes according to their use in a business.

The present book contains 14-chapters namely Setting the Stage: The Modern Enterprise and Technology, Technique and Strategy: Concepts and Frameworks for Understanding What Separates Winners from Losers, Zara: Savvy Systems' Fast Fashion, Netflix: The Making of an E-commerce Giant and Atoms to Bits' Uncertain Future, Moore's Law: What Fast, Affordable Computing Means for the Manager, NETWORK EFFECTS: AN OVERVIEW, Web 2.0, social media, and peer production, Facebook: Making the Business from the Social Graph, Software comprehension: A Manager's Guide, Software in Flux: Partly Cloudy and Partly Cloudy and Occasionally Free, The Data Asset Business intelligence, databases, and competitive advantage, The Internet and Telecommunications: A Manager's Guide, Barbarians at the Information Security Gateway (and Just About Everywhere Else), Google: Online Advertising, Search, and More. It is written in a lucid style with the most recent advances, and with theoretical discussions being supplemented with illustrations, and tables for easy understanding of the subject. This book provides technological and research advances in information system development with extensive coverage of methodologies, techniques and tools. The text explains the fundamental principles and practices required to use and manage information, and illustrates how information systems can create, or obstruct, opportunities within various organizations. This book is highly useful for academics, researchers, and advanced students of information technology, cyber law and also to the practitioners in the related field.

We are grateful to all those persons as well as various books, manuals, periodicals, magazines, journals etc. that helped in the preparation of this book. In spite of the best efforts, it is possible that some errors may have occurred into the compilation and editing of the book. Further queries, constructive suggestions and criticisms for the improvement of the book are always welcomed and shall be thankfully acknowledged.

York Science Group

CONTENTS

PREFACE V

1. SETTING THE STAGE: THE MODERN ENTERPRISE AND TECHNOLOGY 1

    1.1 Tech's Tectonic Shift: Radically Changing Business Landscapes   *1*

    1.2 It's Your Revolution   *2*

    References   *10*

2. TECHNIQUE AND STRATEGY: CONCEPTS AND FRAMEWORKS FOR UNDERSTANDING WHAT SEPARATES WINNERS FROM LOSERS 13

    2.1 Introduction: An Overview   *13*

    2.2 Effective Resources   *19*

    2.3 Entry-level Obstacles, Technology, and Timing   *26*

    References   *29*

3. ZARA: SAVVY SYSTEMS' FAST FASHION 33

    3.1 Introduction: An Overview   *33*

    3.2 Moving Forward   *40*

    References   *41*

4. NETFLIX: THE MAKING OF AN E-COMMERCE GIANT AND ATOMS TO BITS' UNCERTAIN FUTURE 43

    4.1 Introduction: An Overview   *43*

    4.2 Tech and Timing: Making Killer Assets   *44*

    4.3 Atoms to Bits: Opportunity or Threat?   *53*

    References   *58*

5. MOORE'S LAW: WHAT FAST, AFFORDABLE COMPUTING MEANS FOR THE MANAGER 61

    5.1 Introduction: An Overview   *61*

    5.2 The Demise of Moore's Law?   *67*

5.3 Bringing Together Brains: Supercomputing and Grid Computing Information Systems   69

5.4 The Negative Side of Moore's Law: E-Waste   72

References   75

6.   NETWORK EFFECTS: AN OVERVIEW **77**

6.1 Introduction: An Overview   77

6.2 What's the Source of All That Value??   77

6.3 One-Sided or Two-Sided Markets?   79

6.4 How Are These Markets Different?   80

6.5 The Role of Network Effects in Competition   82

References   88

7.   WEB 2.0, SOCIAL MEDIA, AND PEER PRODUCTION **91**

7.1 Introduction: An Overview   91

7.2 Blogs (short for Web logs)   96

7.3 Wikis   99

7.4 Digital Social Networks   102

7.5 Other Key Web 2.0 Terms and Concepts   109

7.6 The Wisdom of the Crowd and Prediction Markets   114

7.7 Crowdsourcing: An Overview   116

7.8 Creating the Team   119

References   128

8.   FACEBOOK: MAKING THE BUSINESS FROM THE SOCIAL GRAPH.............. **133**

8.1 Introduction: An Overview   133

8.2 Big Deal   135

8.3 Graph of Social Media   136

8.4 Facebook Feeds: Data Flows' Ebola   137

8.5 A Platform for Facebook   138

8.6 A Work in Progress: Social Networks and Advertising   140

8.7 Privacy Peril: Beacon and the TOS Debacle   144

8.8 Predators and Privacy   147

8.9 One Graph to Rule Them All: Facebook Dominates the Web   147

8.10 Facebook: Is It Worth It   150

References   152

9.   SOFTWARE COMPREHENSION: A MANAGER'S GUIDE **157**

9.1 Introduction: An Overview   157

9.2 Operating Systems   159

Contents

9.3 Application Software 160

9.4 Distributed Computing 164

9.5 Writing Software 168

9.6 Total Cost of Ownership (TCO): Tech Costs Go Way beyond the Price Tag 170

References 172

10. SOFTWARE IN FLUX: PARTLY CLOUDY AND PARTLY CLOUDY AND OCCASIONALLY FREE 175

10.1 Open Source 175

10.2 Why Open Source? 176

10.3 Open Source Software: Examples 178

10.4 Cloud computing: Is it a Scam or a Hope? 180

10.5 The Software Cloud: Why Purchase Software When You Can Rent? 181

10.6 The Benefits of SaaS 183

10.7 SaaS: Not free from risks 185

10.8 The Hardware Cloud: The Cousins of Utility Computing 187

10.9 Impact of Clouds on the Technology Sector 189

10.10 Virtualization: Software That Makes One Computer Act Like Many 190

10.11 Make, Buy, or Rent 191

10.12 Introduction 193

References 194

11. THE DATA ASSET BUSINESS INTELLIGENCE, DATABASES, AND COMPETITIVE ADVANTAGE 197

11.1 Introduction: An Overview 197

11.2 Data, Information, and Knowledge 198

11.3 What Sources Do Data Come From? 201

11.4 Data Rich, Information Poor 203

11.5 The utilisation of data marts and warehouses 204

11.6 A toolkit for business intelligence 206

11.7 Data Asset in Action: The Rise of Wal-Mart and Technology 210

11.8 Data Asset in Use: Harrah's Solid Gold CRM for the Service Sector 213

References 218

12. THE INTERNET AND TELECOMMUNICATIONS: A MANAGER'S GUIDE 221

12.1 Introduction: An Overview 221

12.2 Internet 101: Understanding the Operation of the Internet 221

13.3 Getting Where You Want To Go 226

11.4 Last Mile: Greater Access and Speed 229

References 237

13. BARBARIANS AT THE INFORMATION SECURITY GATEWAY (AND JUST ABOUT EVERYWHERE ELSE) 241

13.1 Introduction: An Overview 241

13.2 Why Is This Happening? Who Is Doing It? And What's Their Motivation? 242

13.3 Where Are Vulnerabilities? Understanding the Weaknesses 245

13.4 Taking Action 254

References 262

14. GOOGLE: ONLINE ADVERTISING, SEARCH, AND MORE 265

14.1 Introduction: An Overview 265

14.2 Search Understanding 267

14.3 Understanding the Rise in Online Ad Spending 268

14.4 Online Search Marketing 269

14.5 Beyond Search Distribution through Ad Networks 273

14.6 More ad types and payment options 276

14.7 Targeting by behaviour and customer profiling 277

14.8 What do you mean by Profiling and Privacy? 280

14.9 Fraud, ad networks, and search engines 281

14.10 The Battle Starts to Take Shape 284

References 290

INDEX 293

CHAPTER 1

SETTING THE STAGE: THE MODERN ENTERPRISE AND TECHNOLOGY

1.1 TECH'S TECTONIC SHIFT: RADICALLY CHANGING BUSINESS LANDSCAPES

This book is written for a world that has changed radically in the past decade.

At the start of the prior decade, Google barely existed and well-known strategists dismissed Internet advertising models (Porter, 2001). By decade's end, Google brought in more advertising revenue than any firm, online or off, and had risen to become the most profitable media company on the planet. Today billions in advertising dollars flee old media and are pouring into digital efforts, and this shift is reshaping industries and redefining skills needed to reach today's consumers.

A decade ago the iPod also didn't exist and Apple was widely considered a tech-industry has-been. By spring 2010 Apple had grown to be the most valuable tech firm in the United States, selling more music and generating more profits from mobile device sales than any firm in the world.

Moore's Law and other factors that make technology faster and cheaper have thrust computing and telecommunications into the hands of billions in ways that are both empowering the poor and poisoning the planet.

Social media barely warranted a mention a decade ago, but today, Facebook's user base is larger than any nation, save for China and India. Firms are harnessing social media for new product ideas and for millions in sales. But with promise comes peril. When mobile phones are cameras just a short hop from YouTube, Flickr, and Twitter, every ethical lapse can be captured, every customer service flaw graffiti-tagged on the permanent record that is the Internet. The service and ethics bar for today's manager has never been higher.

Speaking of globalization, China started the prior decade largely as a nation unplugged and offline. But today China has more Internet users than any other country and has spectacularly launched several publicly traded Internet firms including Baidu, Tencent, and Alibaba. By 2009, China Mobile was more valuable than any firm in the United States except for Exxon Mobil and Wal-Mart. Think the United States holds the number one ranking in home broadband access? Not even close—the United States is ranked fifteenth (Shankland, 2010).

The way we conceive of software and the software industry is also changing radically. IBM, HP, and Oracle are among the firms that collectively pay thousands of programmers to write code that is then given away for free. Today, open source software powers most of the Web sites you visit. And the rise of open source has rewritten the revenue models for the computing industry and lowered computing costs for start-ups to blue chips worldwide.

Cloud computing and software as a service is turning sophisticated, high-powered computing into a utility available to even the smallest businesses and nonprofits.

Data analytics and business intelligence are driving discovery and innovation, redefining modern marketing, and creating a shifting knife-edge of privacy concerns that can shred corporate reputations if mishandled.

And the pervasiveness of computing has created a set of security and espionage threats unimaginable to the prior generation.

As the last ten years have shown, tech creates both treasure and tumult. These disruptions aren't going away and will almost certainly accelerate, impacting organizations, careers, and job functions throughout your lifetime. It's time to place tech at the center of the managerial playbook.

1.2 IT'S YOUR REVOLUTION

The intersection where technology and business meet is both terrifying and exhilarating. But if you're under the age of thirty, realize that this is *your* space. While the fortunes of any individual or firm rise and fall over time, it's abundantly clear that many of the world's most successful technology firms—organizations that have had tremendous impact on consumers and businesses across industries—were created by young people. Consider just a few:

Bill Gates was an undergraduate when he left college to found Microsoft—a firm that would eventually become the world's largest software firm and catapult Gates to the top of the *Forbes* list of world's wealthiest people (enabling him to also become the most generous philanthropist of our time).

Michael Dell was just a sophomore when he began building computers in his dorm room at the University of Texas. His firm would one day claim the top spot among PC manufacturers worldwide.

Mark Zuckerberg founded Facebook as a nineteen-year-old college sophomore. Steve Jobs was just twenty-one when he founded Apple.

Tony Hsieh proved his entrepreneurial chops when, at twenty-four, he sold LinkExchange to Microsoft for over a quarter of a billion dollars (Chafkin, 2009). He'd later serve as CEO of Zappos, eventually selling that firm to Amazon for $900 million (Lacy, 2009).

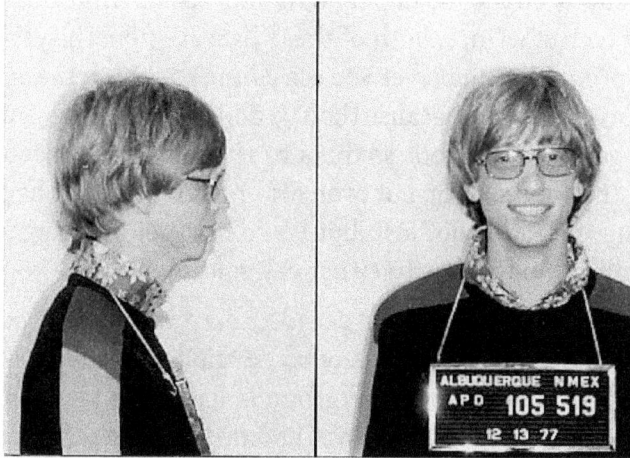

Figure 1.1 Young Bill Gates appears in a mug shot for a New Mexico traffic violation. Microsoft, now headquartered in Washington State, had its roots in New Mexico when Gates and partner Paul Allen moved there to be near early PC maker Altair.

Sergey Brin and Larry Page were both twenty-something doctoral students at Stanford University when they founded Google. So were Jerry Yang and David Filo of Yahoo! All would become billionaires.

If you want to go a little older, Kevin Rose of Digg and Steve Chen and Chad Hurley of YouTube were all in their late twenties when they launched their firms. Jeff Bezos hadn't yet reached thirty when he began working on what would eventually become Amazon.

Of course, those folks would seem downright ancient to Catherine Cook, who founded MyYearbook.com, a firm that at one point grew to become the third most popular social network in the United States. Cook started the firm when she was a sophomore—in high school.

But you don't have to build a successful firm to have an impact as a tech revolutionary. Shawn Fanning's Napster, widely criticized as a piracy playground, was written when he was just nineteen. Fanning's code was the first significant salvo in the tech-fueled revolution that brought about an upending of the entire music industry. Finland's Linus Torvals wrote the first version of the Linux operating system when he was just twenty-one. Today Linux has grown to be the most influential component of the open source arsenal, powering everything from cell phones to supercomputers.

BusinessWeek regularly runs a list of America's Best Young Entrepreneurs—the top twenty-five aged twenty- five and under. *Inc.* magazine's list of the Coolest Young Entrepreneurs is subtitled the "30 under 30" (Fenn, 2009). While not exclusively filled with the ranks of tech start-ups, both of these lists are nonetheless dominated with technology entrepreneurs. Whenever you see young people on the cover of a business magazine, it's almost certainly because they've done something groundbreaking with technology. The generals and foot soldiers of the technology revolution are filled with the ranks of the young, some not even old enough to legally have a beer. For the old-timers reading this, all is not lost, but you'd best get cracking with technology, quick. Junior might be on the way to either eat your lunch or be your next boss.

Shortly after the start of the prior decade, there was a lot of concern that tech jobs would be outsourced, leading many to conclude that tech skills carried less value and that workers with tech backgrounds had little to offer. Turns out this thinking was stunningly wrong. Tech jobs boomed, and as technology pervades all other management disciplines, tech skills are becoming more important, not less. Today, tech knowledge can be a key differentiator for the job seeker. It's the worker without tech skills that needs to be concerned.

As we'll present in depth in a future chapter, there's a principle called Moore's Law that's behind fast, cheap computing. And as computing gets both faster and cheaper, it gets "baked into" all sorts of products and shows up everywhere: in your pocket, in your vacuum, and on the radio frequency identification (RFID) tags that track your luggage at the airport.

Well, there's also a sort of Moore's Law corollary that's taking place with people, too. As technology becomes faster and cheaper and developments like open source software, cloud computing, software as a service (SaaS), and outsourcing push technology costs even lower, tech skills are being embedded inside more and more job functions. What this means is that even if you're not expecting to become the next Tech Titan, your career will doubtless be shaped by the forces of technology. Make no mistake about it—there isn't a single modern managerial discipline that isn't being deeply and profoundly impacted by tech.

Finance

Many business school students who study finance aspire to careers in investment banking. Many i-bankers will work on IPOs, or initial public stock offerings, in effect helping value companies the first time these firms wish to sell their stock on the public markets. IPO markets need new firms, and the tech industry is a fertile ground that continually sprouts new businesses like no other. Other i-bankers will be involved in valuing merger and acquisition (M&A) deals, and tech firms are active in this space, too. Leading tech firms are flush with cash and constantly on the hunt for new firms to acquire. Cisco bought forty-eight firms in the prior decade; Oracle bought five firms in 2009 alone. And even in nontech industries, technology impacts nearly every endeavor as an opportunity catalyst or a disruptive wealth destroyer. The aspiring investment banker who doesn't understand he role of technology in firms and industries can't possibly provide an accurate guess at how much a company is worth.

Table 1.1 Top Acquirers of VC-Backed Companies 2000–2009

Acquiring Company	Acquisitions
Cisco	48
IBM	35
Microsoft	30
EMC Corporation	25
Oracle Corp.	23
Broadcom	18
Symantec	18
Hewlett-Packard	18
Google	17
Sun Microsystems	16

Source: VentureSource.

Those in other finance careers will be lending to tech firms and evaluating the role of technology in firms in an investment portfolio. Most of you will want to consider tech's role as part of your personal investments. And modern finance simply wouldn't exist without tech. When someone arranges for a bridge to be built in Shanghai, those funds aren't carried over in a suitcase—they're digitally transferred from bank to bank. And forces of technology blasted open the two-hundred-year-old floor trading mechanism of the New York Stock Exchange, in effect forcing the NYSE to sell shares in itself to finance the acquisition of technology-based trading platforms that were threatening to replace it. As another example of the importance of tech in finance, consider that Boston- based Fidelity Investments, one of the nation's largest mutual fund firms, spends roughly $2.8 billion a year on technology. Tech isn't a commodity for finance—it's the discipline's lifeblood.

Accounting

If you're an accountant, your career is built on a foundation of technology. The numbers used by accountants are all recorded, stored, and reported by information systems, and the reliability of any audit is inherently tied to the reliability of the underlying technology. Increased regulation, such as the heavy executive penalties tied to the **Sarbanes-Oxley Act** in the United States, have ratcheted up the importance of making sure accountants (and executives) get their numbers right. Negligence could mean jail time. This means the link between accounting and tech have never been tighter, and the stakes for ensuring systems accuracy have never been higher.

Business students might also consider that while accounting firms regularly rank near the top of *BusinessWeek*'s "Best Places to Start Your Career" list, many of the careers at these firms are highly tech-centric. Every major accounting firm has spawned a tech-focused consulting practice, and in many cases, these firms have grown to be larger than the accounting services functions from which they sprang. Today, Deloitte's tech-centric consulting division is larger than the firm's audit, tax, and risk practices. At the time of its spin-off, Accenture was larger than the accounting practice at former parent Arthur Andersen (Accenture executives are also grateful they split before Andersen's collapse in the wake of the prior decade's accounting scandals). Now, many accounting firms that had previously spun off technology practices are once again building up these functions, finding strong similarities between the skills of an auditor and skills needed in emerging disciplines such as information security and privacy.

Marketing

Technology has thrown a grenade onto the marketing landscape, and as a result, the skill set needed by today's marketers is radically different from what was leveraged by the prior generation. Online channels have provided a way to track and monitor consumer activities, and firms are leveraging this insight to understand how to get the right product to the right customer, through the right channel, with the right message, at the right price, at the right time. The success or failure of a campaign can often be immediately assessed base on online activity such as Web site visit patterns and whether a campaign results in an online purchase.

The ability to track customers, analyze campaign results, and modify tactics has amped up the return on investment of marketing dollars, with firms increasingly shifting spending from tough-to-track media such as print, radio, and television to the Web (Pontin 2009). And new channels continue to emerge. Firms as diverse as Southwest Airlines, Starbucks, UPS, and Zara have introduced apps for the iPhone and iPod touch. In less than four years, the iPhone has emerged as a channel capable of reaching over 75 million consumers, delivering location-based messages and services, and even allowing for cashless payment.

The rise of social media is also part of this blown-apart marketing landscape. Now all customers can leverage an enduring and permanent voice, capable of broadcasting word-of-mouth influence in ways that can benefit and harm a firm. Savvy firms are using social media to generate sales, improve their reputations, better serve customers, and innovate. Those who don't understand this landscape risk being embarrassed, blindsided, and out of touch with their customers.

Search engine marketing (SEM), search engine optimization (SEO), customer relationship management (CRM), personalization systems, and a sensitivity to managing the delicate balance between gathering and leveraging data and respecting consumer privacy are all central components of the new marketing toolkit. And there's no looking back—tech's role in marketing will only grow in prominence.

Operations

A firm's operations management function is focused on producing goods and services, and operations students usually get the point that tech is the key to their future. Quality programs, process redesign, supply chain management, factory automation, and service operations are all tech-centric. These points are underscored in this book as we introduce several examples of how firms have designed fundamentally different ways of conducting business (and even entirely different industries), where value and competitive advantage are created through technology-enabled operations.

Human Resources

Technology helps firms harness the untapped power of employees. Knowledge management systems are morphing into social media technologies—social networks, wikis, and Twitter-style messaging systems that can accelerate the ability of a firm to quickly organize and leverage teams of experts. Human resources (HR) directors are using technology for employee training, screening, and evaluation. The accessibility of end-user technology means that every employee can reach the public, creating an imperative for firms to set policy on issues such as firm representation and disclosure and to continually monitor and enforce policies as well as capture and push out best practices. The successful HR manager recognizes that technology continually changes an organization's required skill sets, as well as employee expectations.

The hiring and retention practices of the prior generation are also in flux. Recruiting hasn't just moved online; it's now grounded in information systems that scour databases for specific skill sets, allowing recruiters to cast a wider talent net than ever before. Job seekers are writing résumés with keywords in mind, aware that the first cut is likely made by a database search program, not a human being. The rise of professional social networks also puts added pressure on employee satisfaction and retention. Prior HR managers fiercely guarded employee directories for fear that a headhunter or competitive firm might raid top talent. Now the equivalent of a corporate directory can be easily pulled up via LinkedIn, a service complete with discrete messaging capabilities that can allow competitors to rifle-scope target your firm's best and brightest. Thanks to technology, the firm that can't keep employees happy, engaged, and feeling valued has never been more vulnerable.

The Law

And for those looking for careers in corporate law, many of the hottest areas involve technology. Intellectual property, patents, piracy, and privacy are all areas where activity has escalated dramatically in recent years. The number of U.S. patent applications waiting approval has tripled in the past decade, while China saw a threefold increase in patent applications in just five years (Schmid & Poston, 2009). Firms planning to leverage new inventions and business methods need legal teams with the skills to sleuth out whether a firm can legally do what it plans to. Others will need legal expertise to help them protect proprietary methods and content, as well as to help enforce claims in the home country and abroad.

Careers in Information Systems

While the job market goes through ebbs and flows, recent surveys have shown there to be more IT openings than in any field except health care1. *Money* magazine ranked tech jobs as two of the top five "Best Jobs in America."[2] *BusinessWeek* ranks consulting (which heavily hires tech grads) and technology as the second and third highest paying industries for recent college graduates (Gerdes, 2008). Technology careers have actually 11 Information Systems ranked among the safest careers to have during the most recent downturn (Kaneshige, 2009). And *Fortune*'s ranks of the "Best Companies to Work For" is full of technology firms and has been topped by a tech business for four years straight[3].

Students studying technology can leverage skills in ways that range from the highly technical to those that emphasize a tech-centric use of other skills. Opportunities for programmers abound, particularly for those versed in new technologies, but there are also roles for experts in areas such as user-interface design (who work to make sure systems are easy to use), process design (who leverage technology to make firms more efficient), and strategy (who specialize in technology for competitive advantage). Nearly every large organization has its own information systems department. That group not only ensures that systems get built and keep running but also increasingly takes on strategic roles targeted at proposing solutions for how technology can give the firm a competitive edge. Career paths allow for developing expertise in a particular technology (e.g., business intelligence analyst, database administrator, social media manager), while project management careers leverage skills in taking projects from conception through deployment.

Even in consulting firms, careers range from hard-core programmers who "build stuff" to analysts who do no programming but might work identifying problems and developing a solutions blueprint that is then turned over to another team to code. Careers at tech giants like Apple, Google, and Microsoft don't all involve coding end- user programs either. Each of these firms has their own client-facing staff that works with customers and partners to implement solutions. Field engineers at these firms may work as part of a sales team to show how a given company's software and services can be used. These engineers often put together prototypes that are then turned over to a client's in-house staff for further development. An Apple field engineer might show how a firm can leverage podcasting in its organization, while a Google field engineer can help a firm incorporate search, banner, and video ads into its online efforts. Careers that involve consulting and field engineering are often particularly attractive for those who enjoy working with an ever-changing list of clients and problems across various industries and in many different geographies.

Upper-level career opportunities are also increasingly diverse. Consultants can become partners who work with the most senior executives of client firms, helping identify opportunities for those organizations to become more effective. Within a firm, technology specialists can rise to be chief information officer or chief technology officer—positions focused on overseeing a firm's information systems development and deployment. And many firms are developing so-called *C-level* specialties in emerging areas with a technology focus, such as chief information security officer (CISO), and chief privacy officer (CPO). Senior technology positions may also be a ticket to the chief executive's suite. A recent *Fortune* article pointed out how the prominence of technology provides a training ground for executives to learn the breadth and depth of a firm's operations and an understanding of the ways in which firms are vulnerable to attack and where it can leverage opportunities for growth (Fort, 2009).

Your Future

With tech at the center of so much change, realize that you may very well be preparing for careers that don't yet exist. But by studying the intersection of business and technology today, you develop a base to build upon and critical thinking skills that will help evaluate new, emerging technologies. Think you can afford to wait on tech study, then quickly get up to speed? Think about it. Whom do you expect to have an easier time adapting and leveraging a technology like social media—today's college students who are immersed in technology or their parents who are embarrassingly dipping their toes into the waters of Facebook? Those who put off an understanding of technology risk being left in the dust.

Consider the nontechnologists who have tried to enter the technology space these past few years. Newscorp head Rupert Murdoch piloted his firm to the purchase of MySpace only to see this one-time leader lose share to rivals (Malik, 2010). Former Warner executive Terry Semel presided over Yahoo!'s malaise as Google blasted past it (Thaw, 2007). Barry Diller, the man widely credited with creating the Fox Network, led InterActive Corp (IAC) in the acquisition of a slew of tech firms ranging from Expedia to Ask.com, only to break the empire up as it foundered. And Time Warner head Jerry Levin presided over the acquisition of AOL, executing what many consider to be one of the most disastrous mergers in U.S. business history (Quinn, 2009). Contrast these guys against the technology-centric successes of Mark Zuckerberg (Facebook), Steve Jobs (Apple), and Sergey Brin and Larry Page (Google).

While we'll make it abundantly clear that a focus solely on technology is a recipe for disaster, a business perspective that lacks an appreciation for tech's role is also likely to be doomed. At this point in history, technology and business are inexorably linked, and those not trained to evaluate and make decisions in this ever- shifting space risk irrelevance, marginalization, and failure.

REFERENCES

Brynjolfsson, E., A. McAfee, M. Sorell, and F. Zhu, "Scale without Mass: Business Process Replication and Industry Dynamics," *SSRN*, September 30, 2008.

Chafkin, M. "The Zappos Way of Managing," *Inc.*, May 1, 2009.

Fortt, J., "Tech Execs Get Sexy," *Fortune*, February 12, 2009.

Fenn, D. "30 Under 30: For Young Entrepreneurs, Safety in Numbers," *Inc.*, October 1, 2009. Lacy, S. "Amazon Buys Zappos; The Price Is $928m., Not $847m.," *TechCrunch*, July 22, 2009.

Gerdes, L., "The Best Places to Launch a Career," *BusinessWeek*, September 15, 2008. Technology careers have actually ranked among the safest careers to have during the most recent downturn.

Kaneshige, T., "Surprise! Tech Is a Safe Career Choice Today," *InfoWorld*, February 4, 2009. Malik, O., "MySpace, R.I.P.," *GigaOM*, February 10, 2010.

McAfee A. and E. Brynjolfsson, "Dog Eat Dog," *Sloan Management Review*, April 27, 2007.

Pontin, J., "But Who's Counting?" *Technology Review*, March/April 2009.

Porter, M., "Strategy and the Internet," *Harvard Business Review* 79, no. 3 (March 2001): 62–78. Shankland, S., "Google to Test Ultrafast Broadband to the Home," *CNET*, February 10, 2010.

Quinn, J., "Final Farewell to Worst Deal in History—AOL-Time Warner," *Telegraph* (UK), November 21, 2009. Schmid, J. and B. Poston, "Patent Backlog Clogs Recovery," *Milwaukee Journal Sentinel*, August 15, 2009.

Thaw, J., "Yahoo's Semel Resigns as Chief amid Google's Gains," *Bloomberg*, June 18, 2007.

TECHNIQUE AND STRATEGY: CONCEPTS AND FRAMEWORKS FOR UNDERSTANDING WHAT SEPARATES WINNERS FROM LOSERS

2.1 INTRODUCTION: AN OVERVIEW

Managers are confused, and for good reason. Management theorists, consultants, and practitioners often vehemently disagree on how firms should craft tech-enabled strategy, and many widely read articles contradict one another. Headlines such as "Move First or Die" compete with "The First-Mover Disadvantage." A leading former CEO advises, "destroy your business," while others suggest firms focus on their "core competency" and "return to basics." The pages of the *Harvard Business Review* declare, "IT Doesn't Matter," while a *New York Times* bestseller hails technology as the "steroids" of modern business.

Theorists claiming to have mastered the secrets of strategic management are contentious and confusing. But as a manager, the ability to size up a firm's strategic position and understand its likelihood of sustainability is one of the most valuable and yet most difficult skills to master. Layer on thinking about technology—a key enabler to nearly every modern business strategy, but also a function often thought of as easily "outsourced"—and it's no wonder that so many firms struggle at the intersection where strategy and technology meet. The business landscape is littered with the corpses of firms killed by managers who guessed wrong.

Developing strong strategic thinking skills is a career-long pursuit—a subject that can occupy tomes of text, a roster of courses, and a lifetime of seminars. While this chapter can't address the breadth of strategic thought, it is meant as a primer on developing the skills for strategic thinking about technology. A manager that understands issues presented in this chapter should be able to see through seemingly conflicting assertions about best practices more clearly; be better prepared to recognize opportunities and risks; and be more adept at successfully brainstorming new, tech-centric approaches to markets.

The Risk of Dependence on Technology

Firms strive for **sustainable competitive advantage**, financial performance that consistently outperforms their industry peers. The goal is easy to state, but hard to achieve. The world is so dynamic, with new products and new competitors rising seemingly overnight, that truly sustainable advantage might seem like an impossibility.

New competitors and copycat products create a race to cut costs, cut prices, and increase features that may benefit consumers but erode profits industry-wide. Nowhere is this balance more difficult than when competition involves technology. The fundamental strategic question in the Internet era is, *"How can I possibly compete when everyone can copy my technology and the competition is just a click away?"* Put that way, the pursuit of sustainable competitive advantage seems like a lost cause.

But there are winners—big, consistent winners—empowered through their use of technology. How do they do it? In order to think about how to achieve sustainable advantage, it's useful to start with two concepts defined by Michael Porter. A professor at the Harvard Business School and father of the *value chain* and the *five forces* concepts (see the sections later in this chapter), Porter is justifiably considered one of the leading strategic thinkers of our time.

According to Porter, the reason so many firms suffer aggressive, margin-eroding competition is because they've defined themselves according to operational effectiveness rather than strategic positioning. **Operational effectiveness** refers to performing the same tasks better than rivals perform them. Everyone wants to be better, but the danger in operational effectiveness is "sameness." This risk is particularly acute in firms that rely on technology for competitiveness. After all, technology can be easily acquired. Buy the same stuff as your rivals, hire students from the same schools, copy the look and feel of competitor Web sites, reverse engineer their products, and you can match them. The **fast follower problem** exists when savvy rivals watch a pioneer's efforts, learn from their successes and missteps, then enter the market quickly with a comparable or superior product at a lower cost.

Since tech can be copied so quickly, followers can be fast, indeed. Several years ago while studying the Web portal industry (Yahoo! and its competitors), a colleague and I found that when a firm introduced an innovative feature, at least one of its three major rivals would match that feature in, on average, only one and a half months (Gallaugher & Downing, 2000). When technology can be matched so quickly, it is rarely a source of competitive advantage. And this phenomenon isn't limited to the Web.

Tech giant EMC saw its stock price appreciate more than any other firm during the decade of the 1990s. However, when IBM and Hitachi entered the high-end storage market with products comparable to EMC's Symmetrix unit, prices plunged 60 percent the first year and another 35 percent the next (Engardio & Keenan, 2002). Needless to say, EMC's stock price took a comparable beating. TiVo is another example. At first blush, it looks like this first mover should be a winner since it seems to have established a leading brand; TiVo is now a verb for digitally recording TV broadcasts. But despite this, TiVo has largely been a money loser, going years without posting an annual profit. And while 1.5 million TiVos have been sold, there are over thirty million digital video recorders (DVRs) in use (DiMeo, 2010). Rival devices offered by cable and satellite companies appear the same to consumers, and are offered along with pay television subscriptions—a critical distribution channel for reaching customers that TiVo doesn't control.

Operational effectiveness is critical. Firms must invest in techniques to improve quality, lower cost, and generate design-efficient customer experiences. But for the most part, these efforts can be matched. Because of this, operational effectiveness is usually not sufficient enough to yield sustainable dominance over the competition. In contrast to operational effectiveness, **strategic positioning** refers to performing different activities from those of rivals, or the same activities in a different way. While technology itself is often very easy to replicate, technology is essential to creating and enabling novel approaches to business that are defensibly different from those of rivals and can be quite difficult for others to copy.

Different Is Good: Fresh Direct Redefines the NYC Grocery Landscape

For an example of the relationship between technology and strategic positioning, consider FreshDirect. The New York City–based grocery firm focused on the two most pressing problems for Big Apple shoppers: selection is limited and prices are high. Both of these problems are a function of the high cost of real estate in New York. The solution? Use technology to craft an ultraefficient model that makes an end-run around stores.

The firm's "storefront" is a Web site offering one-click menus, semiprepared specials like "meals in four minutes," and the ability to pull up prior grocery lists for fast reorders—all features that appeal to the time-strapped Manhattanites who were the firm's first customers. (The Web's not the only channel to reach customers—the firm's iPhone app was responsible for 2.5 percent of sales just weeks after launch) (Schneiderman, 2010). Next- day deliveries are from a vast warehouse the size of five football fields located in a lower-rent industrial area of Queens. At that size, the firm can offer a fresh goods selection that's over five times larger than local supermarkets. Area shoppers—many of whom don't have cars or are keen to avoid the traffic-snarled streets of the city—were quick to embrace the model. The service is now so popular that apartment buildings in New York have begun to redesign common areas to include secure freezers that can accept FreshDirect deliveries, even when customers aren't there (Croghan, 2006).

Figure 2.1 The FreshDirect Web Site and the Firm's Tech-Enabled Warehouse Operation

The FreshDirect model crushes costs that plague traditional grocers. Worker shifts are highly efficient, avoiding the downtime lulls and busy rush hour spikes of storefronts. The result? Labor costs that are 60 percent lower than at traditional grocers. FreshDirect buys and prepares what it sells, leading to less waste, an advantage that the firm claims is "worth 5 percentage points of total revenue in terms of savings" (Fox, 2009). Overall perishable inventory at FreshDirect turns 197 times a year versus 40 times a year at traditional grocers (Schonfeld, 2004). Higher inventory turns mean the firm is selling product faster, so it collects money quicker than its rivals do. And those goods are fresher since they've been in stock for less time, too. Consider that while the average grocer may have seven to nine days of seafood inventory, FreshDirect's seafood stock turns each day. Stock is typically purchased direct from the docks in order to fulfill orders placed less than twenty-four hours earlier (Laseter, et. al., 2003).

Artificial intelligence software, coupled with some seven miles of fiber-optic cables linking systems and sensors, supports everything from baking the perfect baguette to verifying orders with 99.9 percent accuracy (Black, 2002; Sieber & Mitchell, 2002). Since it lacks the money-sucking open-air refrigerators of the competition, the firm even saves big on energy (instead, staff bundle up for shifts in climate-controlled cold rooms tailored to the specific needs of dairy, deli, and produce). And a new initiative uses recycled biodiesel fuel to cut down on delivery costs.

Fresh Direct buys directly from suppliers, eliminating middlemen wherever possible. The firm also offers suppliers several benefits beyond traditional grocers, all in exchange for more favorable terms. These include offering to carry a greater selection of supplier products while eliminating the "slotting fees" (payments by suppliers for prime shelf space) common in traditional retail, cobranding products to help establish and strengthen supplier brand, paying partners in days rather than weeks, and sharing data to help improve supplier sales and operations. Add all these advantages together and the firm's big, fresh selection is offered at prices that can undercut the competition by as much as 35 percent (Green, 2003). And FreshDirect does it all with margins in the range of 20 percent (to as high as 45 percent on many semiprepared meals), easily dwarfing the razor-thin 1 percent margins earned by traditional grocers.

Today, FreshDirect serves a base of some 600,000 paying customers. That's a population roughly the size of metro-Boston, serviced by a single grocer with no physical store. The privately held firm has been solidly profitable for several years. Even in recession-plagued 2009, the firm's CEO described 2009 earnings as "pretty spectacular," while 2010 revenues are estimated to grow to roughly $300 million (Schneiderman, 2010).

Technology is critical to the FreshDirect model, but it's the collective impact of the firm's differences when compared to rivals, this tech-enabled strategic positioning, that delivers success. Operating for more than half a decade, the firm has also built up a set of strategic assets that not only address specific needs of a market but are now extremely difficult for any upstart to compete against. Traditional grocers can't fully copy the firm's delivery business because this would leave them **straddling** two markets (low-margin storefront and high-margin delivery), unable to gain optimal benefits from either. Entry costs for would-be competitors are also high (the firm spent over $75 million building infrastructure before it could serve a single customer), and the firm's complex and highly customized software, which handles everything from delivery scheduling to orchestrating the preparation of thousands of recipes, continues to be refined and improved each year (Valerio, 2009). On top of all this comes years of customer data used to further refine processes, speed reorders, and make helpful recommendations. Competing against a firm with such a strong and tough-to-match strategic position can be brutal. Just five years after launch there were one-third fewer supermarkets in New York City than when FreshDirect first opened for business (Shulman, 2008).

But What Kinds of Differences?

The principles of operational effectiveness and strategic positioning are deceptively simple. But while Porter claims strategy is "fundamentally about being different," how can you recognize whether your firm's differences are special enough to yield sustainable competitive advantage (Porter, 1996)?

An approach known as the **resource-based view of competitive advantage** can help. The idea here is that if a firm is to maintain sustainable competitive advantage, it must control a set of exploitable resources that have four critical characteristics. These resources must be (1) *valuable*, (2) *rare*, (3) *imperfectly imitable* (tough to imitate), and (4) *nonsubstitutable*. Having all four characteristics is key. Miss value and no one cares what you've got. Without rareness, you don't have something unique. If others can copy what you have, or others can replace it with a substitute, then any seemingly advantageous differences will be undercut.

Strategy isn't just about recognizing opportunity and meeting demand. Resource-based thinking can help you avoid the trap of carelessly entering markets simply because growth is spotted. The telecommunications industry learned this lesson in a very hard and painful way. With the explosion of the Internet it was easy to see that demand to transport Web pages, e-mails, MP3s, video, and everything else you can turn into ones and zeros, was skyrocketing.

Most of what travels over the Internet is transferred over long-haul fiber-optic cables, so telecom firms began digging up the ground and laying webs of fiberglass to meet the growing demand. Problems resulted because firms laying long-haul fiber didn't fully appreciate that their rivals and new upstart firms were doing the exact same thing. By one estimate there was enough fiber laid to stretch from the Earth to the moon some 280 times (Kahney, 2000)! On top of that, a technology called **dense wave division multiplexing (DWDM)** enabled existing fiber to carry more transmissions than ever before. The end result—these new assets weren't rare and each day they seemed to be less valuable.

For some firms, the transmission prices they charged on newly laid cable collapsed by over 90 percent. Established firms struggled, upstarts went under, and WorldCom became the biggest bankruptcy in U.S. history. The impact was felt throughout all industries that supplied the telecom industry. Firms like Sun, Lucent, and Nortel, whose sales growth relied on big sales to telecom carriers, saw their value tumble as orders dried up. Estimates suggest that the telecommunications industry lost nearly $4 trillion in value in just three years, much of it due to executives that placed big bets on resources that weren't strategic (Endlich, 2004).

2.2 EFFECTIVE RESOURCES

Management has no magic bullets. There is no exhaustive list of key resources that firms can look to in order to build a sustainable business. And recognizing a resource doesn't mean a firm will be able to acquire it or exploit it forever. But being aware of major sources of competitive advantage can help managers recognize an organization's opportunities and vulnerabilities, and can help them brainstorm winning strategies. And these assets rarely exist in isolation. Oftentimes, a firm with an effective strategic position can create an arsenal of assets that reinforce one another, creating advantages that are particualrly difficult for rivals to successfully challenge.

Imitation-Resistant Value Chains

While many of the resources below are considered in isolation, the strength of any advantage can be far more significant if firms are able to leverage several of these resources in a way that makes each stronger and makes the firm's way of doing business more difficult for rivals to match. Firms that craft an **imitation-resistant value chain** have developed a way of doing business that others will struggle to replicate, and in nearly every successful effort of this kind, technology plays a key enabling role. The *value chain* is the set of interrelated activities that bring products or services to market (see below). When we compare FreshDirect's value chain to traditional rivals, there are differences across every element. But most importantly, the elements in FreshDirect's value chain work together to create and reinforce competitive advantages that others cannot easily copy. Incumbents would be *straddled* between two business models, unable to reap the full advantages of either. And late-moving pure-play rivals will struggle, as FreshDirect's lead time allows the firm to develop brand, scale, data, and other advantages that newcomers lack (see below for more on these resources).

Brand

A firm's **brand** is the symbolic embodiment of all the information connected with a product or service, and a strong brand can also be an exceptionally powerful resource for competitive advantage. Consumers use brands to *lower search costs*, so having a strong brand is particularly vital for firms hoping to be the first online stop for consumers. Want to buy a book online? Auction a product? Search for information? Which firm would you visit first? Almost certainly Amazon, eBay, or Google. But how do you build a strong brand? It's *not* just about advertising and promotion. First and foremost, customer experience counts. A strong brand *proxies quality* and *inspires trust*, so if consumers can't rely on a firm to deliver as promised, they'll go elsewhere. As an upside, tech can play a critical role in rapidly and cost-effectively strengthening a brand. If a firm performs well, consumers can often be enlisted to promote a product or service (so-called **viral marketing**). Consider that while scores of dot-coms burned through money on Super Bowl ads and other costly promotional efforts, Google, Hotmail, Skype, eBay, MySpace, Facebook, Twitter, YouTube, and so many other dominant online properties built multimillion member followings before committing any significant spending to advertising.

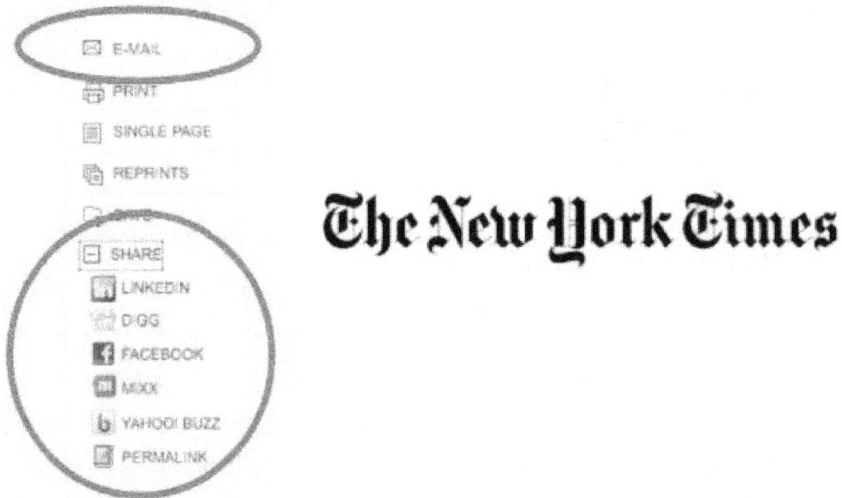

Figure 2.2 The "E-mail" and "Share" links at the New York Times Web site enlist customers to spread the word about products and services, user to user, like a virus.

Early customer accolades for a novel service often mean that positive press (a kind of free advertising) will also likely follow.

But show up late and you may end up paying much more to counter an incumbent's place in the consumer psyche. In recent years, Amazon has spent no money on television advertising, while rivals Buy.com and Overstock.com spent millions. Google, another strong brand, has become a verb, and the cost to challenge it is astonishingly high. Yahoo! and Microsoft's Bing each spent $100 million on Google-challenging branding campaigns, but the early results of these efforts seemed to do little to grow share at Google's expense. Branding is difficult, but if done well, even complex tech products can establish themselves as killer brands. Consider that Intel has taken an ingredient product that most people don't understand, the microprocessor, and built a quality-conveying name recognized by computer users worldwide.

Scale

Many firms gain advantages as they grow in size. Advantages related to a firm's size are referred to as **scale advantages**. Businesses benefit from **economies of scale** when the cost of an investment can be spread across increasing units of production or in serving a growing customer base. Firms that benefit from scale economies as they grow are sometimes referred to as being *scalable*. Many Internet and tech-leveraging businesses are highly scalable since, as firms grow to serve more customers with their existing infrastructure investment, profit margins improve dramatically.

Consider that in just one year, the Internet firm BlueNile sold as many diamond rings with just 115 employees and one Web site as a traditional jewelry retailer would sell through 116 stores. And with lower operating costs, BlueNile can sell at prices that brick-and-mortar stores can't match, thereby attracting more customers and further fueling its scale advantages. Profit margins improve as the cost to run the firm's single Web site and operate its one warehouse is spread across increasing jewelry sales.

A growing firm may also gain *bargaining power with its suppliers or buyers.* As Dell grew larger, the firm forced suppliers wanting in on Dell's growing business to make concessions such as locating close to Dell plants. Similarly, for years eBay could raise auction fees because of the firm's market dominance. Auction sellers who left eBay lost pricing power since fewer bidders on smaller, rival services meant lower prices.

The scale of technology investment required to run a business can also act as a barrier to entry, discouraging new, smaller competitors. Intel's size allows the firm to pioneer cutting-edge manufacturing techniques and invest $7 billion on next-generation plants. And although Google was started by two Stanford students with borrowed computer equipment running in a dorm room, the firm today runs on an estimated 1.4 million servers. The investments being made by Intel and Google would be cost-prohibitive for almost any newcomer to justify.

Switching Costs and Data

Switching costs exist when consumers incur an expense to move from one product or service to another. Tech firms often benefit from strong switching costs that cement customers to their firms. Users invest their time learning a product, entering data into a system, creating files, and buying supporting programs or manuals. These investments may make them reluctant to switch to a rival's effort.

Similarly, firms that seem dominant but that don't have high switching costs can be rapidly trumped by strong rivals. Netscape once controlled more than 80 percent of the market share in Web browsers, but when Microsoft began bundling Internet Explorer with the Windows operating system and (through an alliance) with America Online (AOL), Netscape's market share plummeted. Customers migrated with a mouse click as part of an upgrade or installation. Learning a new browser was a breeze, and with the Web's open standards, most customers noticed no difference when visiting their favorite Web sites with their new browser.

It is critical for challengers to realize that in order to win customers away from a rival, a new entrant must not only demonstrate to consumers that an offering provides more value than the incumbent, they have to ensure that their value added exceeds the incumbent's value *plus* any perceived customer switching costs (see Figure 2.3). If it's going to cost you and be inconvenient, there's no way you're going to leave unless the benefits are overwhelming.

Data can be a particularly strong switching cost for firms leveraging technology. A customer who enters her profile into Facebook, movie preferences into Netflix, or grocery list into FreshDirect may be unwilling to try rivals—even if these firms are cheaper—if moving to the new firm means she'll lose information feeds, recommendations, and time savings provided by the firms that already know her well. Fueled by scale over time, firms that have more customers and have been in business longer can gather more data, and many can use this data to improve their value chain by offering more accurate demand forecasting or product recommendations.

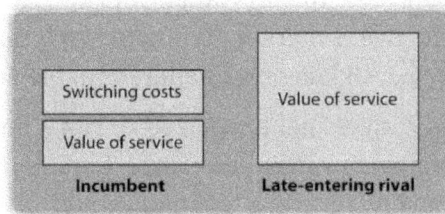

Figure 2.3 In order to win customers from an established incumbent, a late-entering rival must offer a product or service that not only exceeds the value offered by the incumbent but also exceeds the incumbent's value and any customer switching costs.

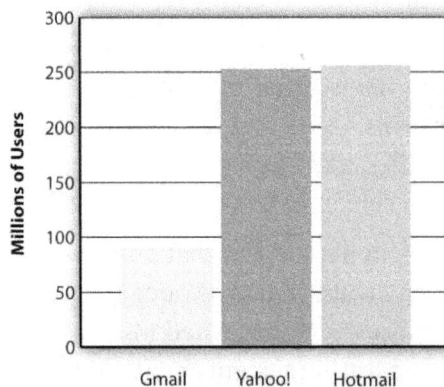

Figure 2.4 E-mail Market Share in Millions of Users

Differentiation

Commodities are products or services that are nearly identically offered from multiple vendors. Consumers buying commodities are highly price-focused since they have so many similar choices. In order to break the commodity trap, many firms leverage technology to *differentiate* their goods and services. Dell gained attention from customers not only because of its low prices, but also because it was one of the first PC vendors to build computers based on customer choice. Want a bigger hard drive? Don't need the fast graphics card? Dell will oblige.

Technology has allowed Lands' End to take this concept to clothing. Now 40 percent of the firm's chino and jeans orders are for custom products, and consumers pay a price markup of one-third or more for the tailored duds. This kind of tech-led differentiation creates and reinforces other assets. While rivals also offer custom products, Lands' End has established a switching cost with its customers, since moving to rivals would require twenty minutes to reenter measurements and preferences versus two minutes to reorder from LandsEnd.com. The firm's reorder rates are 40 to 60 percent on custom clothes, and Lands' End also gains valuable information on more accurate sizing—critical because current clothes sizes provided across the U.S. apparel industry comfortably fit only about one-third of the population.

Data is not only a switching cost, it also plays a critical role in differentiation. Each time a visitor returns to Amazon, the firm uses browsing records, purchase patterns, and product ratings to present a custom home page featuring products that the firm hopes the visitor will like. Customers value the experience they receive at Amazon so much that the firm received the highest score ever recorded on the University of Michigan's American Customer Satisfaction Index (ACSI). The score was not just the highest performance of any online firm, it was the highest ranking that any service firm in any industry had ever received.

Capital One has also used data to differentiate its offerings. The firm mines data and runs experiments to create risk models on potential customers. Because of this, the credit card firm aggressively pursued a set of customers that other lenders considered too risky based on simplistic credit scoring. Technology determined that these underserved customers not properly identified by conventional techniques were actually good bets. Finding profitable new markets that others ignored allowed Capital One to grow its EPS (earnings per share) 20 percent a year for seven years, a feat matched by less than 1 percent of public firms.

Network Effects

AOL's instant messaging client, AIM, has the majority of instant messaging users in the United States. Microsoft Windows has a 90 percent market share in operating systems. EBay has an 80 percent share of online auctions. Why are these firms so dominant? Largely due to the concept of **network effects** (see Chapter 6 "Understanding Network Effects"). Network effects (sometimes called *network externalities* or *Metcalfe's Law*) exist when a product or service becomes more valuable as more people use it. If you're the first person with an AIM account, then AIM isn't very valuable. But with each additional user, there's one more person to chat with. A firm with a big network of users might also see value added by third parties. Sony's PlayStation 2 dominated the prior generation of video game consoles in large part because it had more games than its rivals, and most of these games were provided by firms other than Sony. Third-party add-on products, books, magazines, or even skilled labor are all attracted to networks of the largest number of users, making dominant products more valuable.

Switching costs also play a role in determining the strength of network effects. Tech user investments often go far beyond simply the cost of acquiring a technology. Users spend time learning a product; they buy add-ons, create files, and enter preferences. Because no one wants to be stranded with an abandoned product and lose this additional investment, users may choose a technically inferior product simply because the product has a larger user base and is perceived as having a greater chance of being offered in the future. The virtuous cycle of network₁ effects doesn't apply to all tech products, and it can be a particularly strong asset for firms that can control and leverage a leading standard (think Apple's iPhone and iPad with their closed systems versus Netscape, which was almost entirely based on open standards), but in some cases where network effects are significant, they can create winners so dominant that firms with these advantages enjoy a near-monopoly hold on a market.

Distribution Channels

If no one sees your product, then it won't even get considered by consumers. So **distribution channels**—the path through which products or services get to customers—can be critical to a firm's success. Again, technology opens up opportunities for new ways to reach customers.

Users can be recruited to create new distribution channels for your products and services (usually for a cut of the take). You may have visited Web sites that promote books sold on Amazon.com. Web site operators do this because Amazon gives them a percentage of all purchases that come in through these links. Amazon now has over 1 million of these "associates" (the term the firm uses for its **affiliates**), yet it only pays them if a promotion gains a sale. Google similarly receives some 30 percent of its ad revenue not from search ads, but from advertisements distributed within third-party sites ranging from lowly blogs to the *New York Times.*

In recent years, Google and Microsoft have engaged in bidding wars, trying to lock up distribution deals that would bundle software tools, advertising, or search capabilities with key partner offerings. Deals with partners such as Dell, MySpace, and Verizon Wireless have been valued at up to $1 billion each.

The ability to distribute products by bundling them with existing offerings is a key Microsoft advantage. But beware—sometimes these distribution channels can provide firms with such an edge that international regulators have stepped in to try to provide a more level playing field. Microsoft was forced by European regulators to unbundle the Windows Media Player, for fear that it provided the firm with too great an advantage when competing with the likes of RealPlayer and Apple's QuickTime (see Chapter 6 "Understanding Network Effects").

What about Patents?

Intellectual property protection can be granted in the form of a patent for those innovations deemed to be useful, novel, and nonobvious. In the United States, technology and (more controversially) even business models can be patented, typically for periods of twenty years from the date of patent application. Firms that receive patents have some degree of protection from copycats that try to identically mimic their products and methods.

The patent system is often considered to be unfairly stacked against start-ups. U.S. litigation costs in a single patent case average about $5 million, and a few months of patent litigation can be enough to sink an early stage firm. Large firms can also be victims. So-called patent trolls hold intellectual property not with the goal of bringing novel innovations to market but instead in hopes that they can sue or extort large settlements from others. BlackBerry maker Research in Motion's $612 million settlement with the little-known holding company NTP is often highlighted as an example of the pain trolls can inflict.

Even if an innovation is patentable, that doesn't mean that a firm has bulletproof protection. Some patents have been nullified by the courts upon later review (usually because of a successful challenge to the uniqueness of the innovation). Software patents are also widely granted, but notoriously difficult to defend. In many cases, coders at competing firms can write substitute algorithms that aren't the same, but accomplish similar tasks. For example, although Google's PageRank search algorithms are fast and efficient, Microsoft, Yahoo! and others now offer their own noninfringing search that presents results with an accuracy that many would consider on par with PageRank. Patents do protect tech-enabled operations innovations at firms like Netflix and Harrah's (casino hotels), and design innovations like the iPod click wheel. But in a study of the factors that were critical in enabling firms to profit from their innovations, Carnegie Mellon professor Wes Cohen found that patents were only the fifth most important factor. Secrecy, lead time, sales skills, and manufacturing all ranked higher.

2.3 ENTRY-LEVEL OBSTACLES, TECHNOLOGY, AND TIMING

Some have correctly argued that the barriers to entry for many tech-centric businesses are low. This argument is particularly true for the Internet where rivals can put up a competing Web site seemingly overnight. But it's absolutely critical to understand that market entry is *not* the same as building a sustainable business and just showing up doesn't guarantee survival.

Platitudes like "follow, don't lead" can put firms dangerously at risk, and statements about low entry barriers ignore the difficulty many firms will have in matching the competitive advantages of successful tech pioneers (Carr 2003). Should Blockbuster have waited while Netflix pioneered? In a year where Netflix profits were up seven-fold, Blockbuster lost more than $1 billion (Economist 2003). Should Sotheby's have dismissed seemingly inferior eBay? Sotheby's lost over $6 million in 2009; eBay earned nearly $2.4 billion in profits. Barnes & Noble waited seventeen months to respond to Amazon.com. Amazon now has twelve times the profits of its offline rival and its market cap is over forty-eight times greater.[1] Today's Internet giants are winners because in most cases, they were the first to move with a profitable model and they were able to quickly establish resources for competitive advantage. With few exceptions, established offline firms have failed to catch up to today's Internet leaders.

Timing and technology alone will not yield sustainable competitive advantage. Yet both of these can be *enablers* for competitive advantage. Put simply, it's not the time lead or the technology; it's what a firm *does* with its time lead and technology. True strategic positioning means that a firm has created differences that cannot be easily matched by rivals. Moving first pays off when the time lead is used to create critical resources that are valuable, rare, tough to imitate, and lack substitutes. Anything less risks the arms race of operational effectiveness. Build resources like brand, scale, network effects, switching costs, or other key assets and your firm may have a shot. But guess wrong about the market or screw up execution and failure or direct competition awaits. It is true that most tech can be copied—there's little magic in eBay's servers, Intel's processors, Oracle's databases, or Microsoft's operating systems that past rivals have not at one point improved upon. But the lead that each of these tech-enabled firms had was leveraged to create network effects, switching costs, data assets, and helped build solid and well-respected brands.

KeyStructure: The Five Forces of Competitive Advantage in Industry

Professor and strategy consultant Gary Hamel once wrote in a *Fortune* cover story that "the dirty little secret of the strategy industry is that it doesn't have any theory of strategy creation" (Hamel, 1997). While there is no silver bullet for strategy creation, strategic frameworks help managers describe the competitive environment a firm is facing. Frameworks can also be used as brainstorming tools to generate new ideas for responding to industry competition. If you have a model for thinking about competition, it's easier to understand what's happening and to think creatively about possible solutions.

One of the most popular frameworks for examining a firm's competitive environment is **Porter's five forces**, also known as the *Industry and Competitive Analysis*. As Porter puts it, "analyzing [these] forces illuminates an industry's fundamental attractiveness, exposes the underlying drivers of average industry profitability, and provides insight into how profitability will evolve in the future." The five forces this framework considers are (1) the intensity of rivalry among existing competitors, (2) the threat of new entrants, (3) the threat of substitute goods or services, (4) the bargaining power of buyers, and (5) the bargaining power of suppliers (see Figure 2.5 "The Five Forces of Industry and Competitive Analysis").

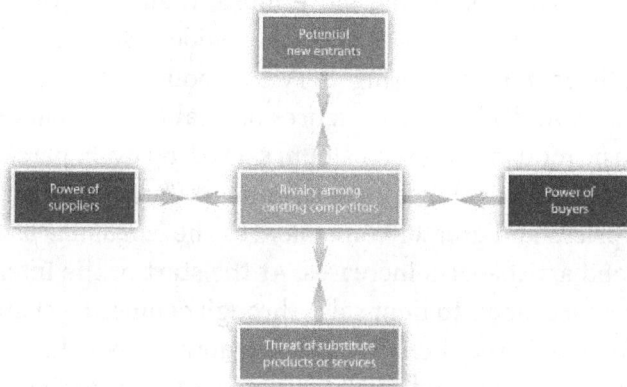

Figure 2.5 The Five Forces of Industry and Competitive Analysis

New technologies can create jarring shocks in an industry. Consider how the rise of the Internet has impacted the five forces for music retailers. Traditional music retailers like Tower and Virgin found that customers were seeking music online. These firms scrambled to invest in the new channel out of what is perceived to be a necessity. Their *intensity of rivalry* increases because they not only compete based on the geography of where brick-and-mortar stores are physically located, they now compete online as well. Investments online are expensive and uncertain, prompting some firms to partner with *new entrants* such as Amazon. Free from brick-and-mortar stores, Amazon, the dominant new entrant, has a highly scalable cost structure. And in many ways the online buying experience is superior to what customers saw in stores. Customers can hear samples of almost all tracks, selection is seemingly limitless (the *long tail* phenomenon—see this concept illuminated in Chapter 4 "Netflix: The Making of an E- commerce Giant and the Uncertain Future of Atoms to Bits"), and data is leveraged using *collaborative filtering* software to make product recommendations and assist in music discovery[1]. Tough competition, but it gets worse because CD sales aren't the only way to consume music. The process of buying a plastic disc now faces *substitutes* as digital music files become available on commercial music sites. Who needs the physical atoms of a CD filled with ones and zeros when you can buy the bits one song at a time? Or don't buy anything and subscribe to a limitless library instead.

From a sound quality perspective, the *substitute good* of digital tracks purchased online is almost always inferior to their CD counterparts. To transfer songs quickly and hold more songs on a digital music player, tracks are encoded in a smaller file size than what you'd get on a CD, and this smaller file contains lower playback fidelity. But the additional tech-based market shock brought on by digital music players (particularly the iPod) has changed listening habits. The convenience of carrying thousands of songs trumps what most consider just a slight quality degradation. ITunes is now responsible for selling more music than any other firm, online or off. Most alarming to the industry is the other widely adopted substitute for CD purchases—theft. Illegal music "sharing" services abound, even after years of record industry crackdowns. And while exact figures on real losses from online piracy are in dispute, the music industry has seen album sales drop by 45 percent in less than a decade (Barnes, 2009). All this choice gives consumers (buyers) *bargaining power*. They demand cheaper prices and greater convenience. The *bargaining power of suppliers*— the music labels and artists—also increases. At the start of the Internet revolution, retailers could pressure labels to limit sales through competing channels. Now, with many of the major music retail chains in bankruptcy, labels have a freer hand to experiment, while bands large and small have new ways to reach fans, sometimes in ways that entirely bypass the traditional music labels.

While it can be useful to look at changes in one industry as a model for potential change in another, it's important to realize that the changes that impact one industry do not necessarily impact other industries in the same way. For example, it is often suggested that the Internet increases bargaining power of buyers and lowers the bargaining power of suppliers. This suggestion is true for some industries like auto sales and jewelry where the products are commodities and the **price transparency** of the Internet counteracts a previous **information asymmetry** where customers often didn't know enough information about a product to bargain effectively. But it's not true across the board.

In cases where network effects are strong or a seller's goods are highly differentiated, the Internet can strengthen supplier bargaining power. The customer base of an antique dealer used to be limited by how many likely purchasers lived within driving distance of a store. Now with eBay, the dealer can take a rare good to a global audience and have a much larger customer base bid up the price. Switching costs also weaken buyer bargaining power. Wells Fargo has found that customers who use online bill pay (where switching costs are high) are 70 percent less likely to leave the bank than those who don't, suggesting that these switching costs help cement customers to the company even when rivals offer more compelling rates or services.

Tech plays a significant role in shaping and reshaping these five forces, but it's not the only significant force that can create an industry shock. Government deregulation or intervention, political shock, and social and demographic changes can all play a role in altering the competitive landscape. Because we live in an age of constant and relentless change, mangers need to continually visit strategic frameworks to consider any market- impacting shifts. Predicting the future is difficult, but ignoring change can be catastrophic.

REFERENCES

Album Sales Fizzle for '08," USA Today, January 4, 2009. Hamel, G., "Killer Strategies that Make Shareholders Rich," Fortune, June 23, 1997.

Black, J., "Can FreshDirect Bring Home the Bacon?" BusinessWeek, September 24, 2002. Croghan, L., "Food Latest Luxury Lure," New York Daily News, March 12, 2006.

Carr, N. "IT Doesn't Matter," Harvard Business Review 81, no. 5 (May 2003): 41–49. "Movies to Go," Economist, July 9, 2005.

Davenport, T., and J. Harris, Competing on Analytics: The New Science of Winning (Boston: Harvard Business School Press, 2007).

DiMeo, N., "TiVo's Goal with New DVR: Become the Google of TV," Morning Edition, National Public Radio, April 7, 2010.

Edwards, J., "JWT's $100 Million Campaign for Microsoft's Bing Is Failing," BNET, July 16, 2009.

Endlich, L., Optical Illusions: Lucent and the Crash of Telecom (New York: Simon & Schuster, 2004). Engardio, P. and F. F. Keenan, "The Copycat Economy," BusinessWeek, August 26, 2002.

Feld, B., "Why the Decks Are Stacked against Software Startups in Patent Litigation," Technology Review, April 12, 2009.

Flatley, J., "Intel Invests $7 Billion in Stateside 32nm Manufacturing," Engadget, February 10, 2009.

Fox, P., "Interview with FreshDirect Co-Founder Jason Ackerman," Bloomberg Television, June 17, 2009.

Friscia, T., K. O'Marah, D. Hofman, and J. Souza, "The AMR Research Supply Chain

Top 25 for 2009," AMR Research, May 28, 2009, http://www.amrresearch.com/Content/View.aspx?compURI=tcm:7-43469.

Gallaugher, J. and C. Downing, "Portal Combat: An Empirical Study of Competition in the Web Portal Industry,"

Google Fourth Quarter 2008 Earnings Summary, http://investor.google.com/earnings.html.

Graham, J., "E-mail Carriers Deliver Gifts of Nifty Features to Lure, Keep Users," USA Today, April 16, 2008. Katz, R., "Tech Titans Building Boom," IEEE Spectrum 46, no. 2 (February 1, 2009): 40–43.

Journal of Information Technology Management 11, no. 1–2 (2000): 13–24. Green, H., "FreshDirect," BusinessWeek, November 24, 2003.

Kahney, L., "Net Speed Ain't Seen Nothin' Yet," Wired News, March 21, 2000.

Laseter, T., B. Berg, and M. Turner, "What FreshDirect Learned from Dell," Strategy+Business, February 12, 2003.

M. Porter, "Strategy and the Internet," Harvard Business Review 79, no. 3 (March 2001): 62–78. Mullaney T., and S. Ante, "InfoWars," BusinessWeek, June 5, 2000.

Mullaney, T., "Jewelry Heist," BusinessWeek, May 10, 2004.

Porter, M., "Strategy and the Internet," Harvard Business Review 79, no. 3 (March 2001): 62–78. Schlosser, J., "Cashing In on the New World of Me," Fortune, December 1, 2004.

Porter, M., "What Is Strategy?" Harvard Business Review 74, no. 6 (November–December 1996): 61 78. Schneiderman, R. M., "FreshDirect Goes to Greenwich," Wall Street Journal, April 6, 2010.

Schonfeld, E., "The Big Cheese of Online Grocers Joe Fedele's Inventory-Turning Ideas May Make FreshDirect the First Big Web Supermarket to Find Profits," Business 2.0, January 1, 2004.

Shapiro, C., and H. Varian, (Adapted from) "Locked In, Not Locked Out," Industry Standard, November 2–9, 1998.

Shulman, R., "Groceries Grow Elusive for Many in New York City," Washington Post, February 19, 2008.

Sieber, S. and J. Mitchell, "FreshDirect: Online Grocery that Actually Delivers!" IESE Insight, 2007; D. Kirkpatrick, "The Online Grocer Version 2.0," Fortune, November 25, 2002.

Valerio, C., "Interview with FreshDirect Co-Founder Jason Ackerman," Venture, Bloomberg Television, September 18, 2009.

Wingfield, N., "Microsoft Wins Key Search Deals," Wall Street Journal, January 8, 2009.

Wu, T., "Weapons of Business Destruction," Slate, February 6, 2006; R. Kelley, "BlackBerry Maker, NTP Ink

ZARA: SAVVY SYSTEMS' FAST FASHION | 3

3.1 INTRODUCTION: AN OVERVIEW

The poor, ship-building town of La Coruña in northern Spain seems an unlikely home to a tech-charged innovator in the decidedly ungeeky fashion industry, but that's where you'll find "The Cube," the gleaming, futuristic central command of the Inditex Corporation (Industrias de Diseño Textil), parent of game-changing clothes giant, Zara. The blend of technology-enabled strategy that Zara has unleashed seems to break all of the rules in the fashion industry. The firm shuns advertising and rarely runs sales. Also, in an industry where nearly every major player outsources manufacturing to low-cost countries, Zara is highly vertically integrated, keeping huge swaths of its production process in-house. These counterintuitive moves are part of a recipe for success that's beating the pants off the competition, and it has turned the founder of Inditex, Amancio Ortega, into Spain's wealthiest man and the world's richest fashion executive.

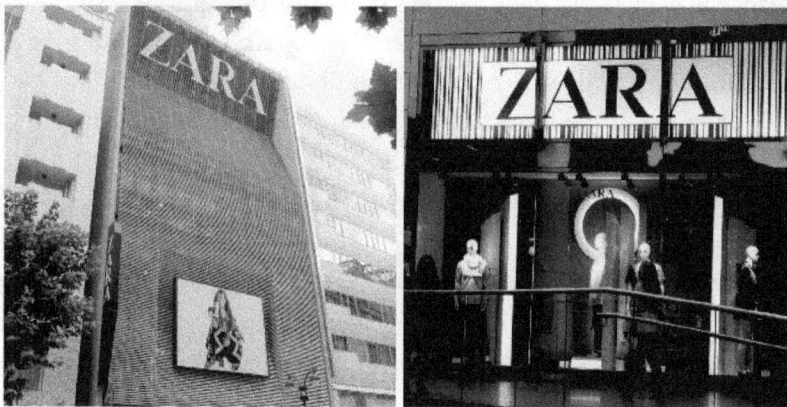

Figure 3.1 Zara's operations are concentrated in Spain, but they have stores around the world like these in Tokyo and Canada. Alberto Garcia – Zara – CC BY-SA 2.0; bargainmoose – Zara Store Canada – CC BY 2.0.

The firm tripled in size between 1996 and 2000, then its earnings skyrocketed from $2.43 billion in 2001 to $13.6 billion in 2007. By August 2008, sales edged ahead of Gap, making Inditex the world's largest fashion retailer (Hall, 2008).Table 3.1 "Gap versus Inditex at a Glance" compares the two fashion retailers. While Inditex supports eight brands, Zara is unquestionably the firm's crown jewel and growth engine, accounting for roughly two-thirds of sales (Murphy, 2008).

Table 3.1 Gap versus Inditex at a Glance

	Gap	Inditex
Revenue	$14.5 billion	$14.7 billion
Net Income	$967 million	$1.68 billion
Number of Stores	3,149	4,359
Number of Countries	6	73
Biggest Brand	Gap	Zara
Number of Other Brads	4	7
Based in	San Francisco, USA	Arteixo (near La Coruña), Spain
First Store Opened	1969	1975

Sources: http://www.gapinc.com; http://www.inditex.com; http://www.marketwatch.com; updated from C. Rohwedder, "Zara Grows as Retail Rivals Struggle," Wall Street Journal, March 26, 2009.

Why Study Zara?

While competitors falter, Zara is undergoing one of the fastest global expansions the fashion world has ever seen, opening one store per day and entering new markets worldwide—seventy-three countries so far. The chain's profitability is among the highest in the industry (Sull & Turconi, 2008). The fashion director for luxury goods maker LVMH calls Zara "the most innovative and devastating retailer in the world" (Surowiecki, 2000).

Zara's duds look like high fashion but are comparatively inexpensive (average item price is $27, although prices vary by country)(Rohwedder, 2009). A Goldman analyst has described the chain as "Armani at moderate prices," while another industry observer suggests that while fashions are more "Banana Republic," prices are more "Old Navy" (Folpe, 2000). Legions of fans eagerly await "Z-day," the twice-weekly inventory delivery to each Zara location that brings in the latest clothing lines for women, men, and children.

In order to understand and appreciate just how counterintuitive and successful Zara's strategy is, and how technology makes all of this possible, it's important to first examine the conventional wisdom in apparel retail. To do that we'll look at former industry leader—Gap.

Gap: An Icon in Crisis

Most fashion retailers place orders for a seasonal collection months before these lines make an appearance in stores. While overseas contract manufacturers may require hefty lead times, trying to guess what customers want months in advance is a tricky business. In retail in general and fashion in particular, there's a saying: inventory equals death. Have too much unwanted product on hand and you'll be forced to mark down or write off items, killing profits. For years, Gap sold most of what it carried in stores. Micky Drexler, a man with a radar-accurate sense of style and the iconic CEO who helped turn Gap's button-down shirts and khakis into America's business casual uniform, led the way. Drexler's team had spot-on tastes throughout the 1990s, but when sales declined in the early part of the following decade, Drexler was left guessing on ways to revitalize the brand, and he guessed wrong—disastrously wrong. Chasing the youth market, Drexler filled Gap stores with miniskirts, low-rise jeans, and even a much-ridiculed line of purple leather pants (Boorstein, 2006). The throngs of teenagers he sought to attract never showed up, and the shift in offerings sent Gap's mainstay customers to retailers that easily copied the styles that Gap had made classic.

The inventory hot potato Drexler was left with crushed the firm. Gap's same-store sales declined for twenty-nine months straight. Profits vanished. Gap founder and chairman Dan Fisher lamented, "It took us thirty years to get to $1 billion in profits and two years to get to nothing" (Sellers, 2003). The firm's debt was downgraded to junk status. Drexler was out and for its new head the board chose Paul Pressler, a Disney executive who ran theme parks and helped rescue the firm's once ailing retail effort.

Pressler shut down hundreds of stores, but the hemorrhaging continued largely due to bad bets on colors and styles (Lee, 2007). During one holiday season, Gap's clothes were deemed so off target that the firm scrapped its advertising campaign and wrote off much of the inventory. The marketing model used by Gap to draw customers in via big-budget television promotion had collapsed. Pressler's tenure saw same-store sales decline in eighteen of twenty-four months (Boorstein, 2006). A *Fortune* article on Pressler's leadership was titled "Fashion Victim." *BusinessWeek* described his time as CEO as a "Total System Failure," and Wall Street began referring to him as DMW for Dead Man Walking. In January 2007, Pressler resigned, with Gap hoping its third chief executive of the decade could right the ailing giant (Lee, 2007).

Don't Guess, Collect Data

Having the wrong items in its stores hobbled Gap for nearly a decade. But how do you make sure stores carry the kinds of things customers want to buy? Try asking them. Zara's store managers lead the intelligence-gathering effort that ultimately determines what ends up on each store's racks. Armed with **personal digital assistants (PDAs)**—handheld computing devices meant largely for mobile use outside an office setting—to gather customer input, staff regularly chat up customers to gain feedback on what they'd like to see more of. A Zara manager might casually ask, "What if this skirt were in a longer length?" "Would you like it in a different color?" "What if this V-neck blouse were available in a round neck?" Managers are motivated because they have skin in the game. The firm is keen to reward success—as much as 70 percent of salaries can come from commissions (Capell, 2008).

Another level of data gathering starts as soon as the doors close. Then the staff turns into a sort of investigation unit in the forensics of trendspotting, looking for evidence in the piles of unsold items that customers tried on but didn't buy. Are there any preferences in cloth, color, or styles offered among the products in stock (Sull & Turconi, 2008)?

PDAs are also linked to the store's **point-of-sale (POS) system**—a transaction process that captures customer purchase information—showing how garments rank by sales. In less than an hour, managers can send updates that combine the hard data captured at the cash register with insights on what customers would like to see (Rohwedder & Johnson, 2008). All this valuable data allows the firm to plan styles and issue rebuy orders based on feedback rather than hunches and guesswork. The goal is to improve the frequency and quality of decisions made by the design and planning teams.

Design

Rather than create trends by pushing new lines via catwalk fashion shows, Zara designs follow evidence of customer demand. Data on what sells and what customers want to see goes directly to "The Cube" outside La Coruña, where teams of some three hundred designers crank out an astonishing thirty thousand items a year versus two to four thousand items offered up at big chains like H&M (the world's third largest fashion retailer) and Gap (Pfeifer, 2007)[1]. While H&M has offered lines by star designers like Stella McCartney and Karl Lagerfeld, as well as celebrity collaborations with Madonna and Kylie Minogue, the Zara design staff consists mostly of young, hungry *Project Runway* types fresh from design school. There are no prima donnas in "The Cube." Team members must be humble enough to accept feedback from colleagues and share credit for winning ideas. Individual bonuses are tied to the success of the team, and teams are regularly rotated to cross-pollinate experience and encourage innovation.

Manufacturing and Logistics

In the fickle world of fashion, even seemingly well-targeted designs could go out of favor in the months it takes to get plans to contract manufacturers, tool up production, then ship items to warehouses and eventually to retail locations. But getting locally targeted designs quickly onto store shelves is where Zara really excels. In one telling example, when Madonna played a set of concerts in Spain, teenage girls arrived to the final show sporting a Zara knockoff of the outfit she wore during her first performance[1]. The average time for a Zara concept to go from idea to appearance in store is fifteen days versus their rivals who receive new styles once or twice a season. Smaller tweaks arrive even faster. If enough customers come in and ask for a round neck instead of a V neck, a new version can be in stores with in just ten days (Tagliabue, 2003). To put that in perspective, Zara is *twelve times* faster than Gap despite offering roughly *ten times* more unique products (Helft, 2002)! At H&M, it takes three to five months to go from creation to delivery—and they're considered one of the best. Other retailers need an average of six months to design a new collection and then another three months to manufacture it. VF Corp (Lee, Wrangler) can take nine months just to design a pair of jeans, while J. Jill needs a year to go from concept to store shelves (Sullivan, 2005). At Zara, most of the products you see in stores didn't exist three weeks earlier, not even as sketches (Surowiecki, 2000).

The firm is able to be so responsive through a competitor-crushing combination of **vertical integration** and technology-orchestrated coordination of suppliers, just-in-time manufacturing, and finely tuned logistics. Vertical integration is when a single firm owns several layers in its **value chain**. While H&M has nine hundred suppliers and no factories, nearly 60 percent of Zara's merchandise is produced in-house, with an eye on leveraging technology in those areas that speed up complex tasks, lower cycle time, and reduce error. Profits from this clothing retailer come from blending math with a data-driven fashion sense. Inventory optimization models help the firm determine how many of which items in which sizes should be delivered to each specific store during twice-weekly shipments, ensuring that each store is stocked with just what it needs Gentry, 2007). Outside the distribution center in La Coruña, fabric is cut and dyed by robots in twenty-three highly automated factories. Zara is so vertically integrated, the firm makes 40 percent of its own fabric and purchases most of its dyes from its own subsidiary. Roughly half of the cloth arrives undyed so the firm can respond as any midseason fashion shifts occur. After cutting and dying, many items are stitched together through a network of local cooperatives that have worked with Inditex so long they don't even operate with written contracts. The firm does leverage contract manufacturers (mostly in Turkey and Asia) to produce staple items with longer shelf lives, such as t-shirts and jeans, but such goods account for only about one-eighth of dollar volume (Tokatli, 2008).

All of the items the firm sells end up in a five-million-square-foot distribution center in La Coruña, or a similar facility in Zaragoza in the northeast of Spain. The La Coruña facility is some nine times the size of Amazon's warehouse in Fernley, Nevada, or about the size of ninety football fields Helft (2002). The facilities move about two and a half million items every week, with no item staying in-house for more than seventy-two hours. Ceiling-mounted racks and customized sorting machines patterned on equipment used by overnight parcel services, and leveraging Toyota-designed logistics, whisk items from factories to staging areas for each store. Clothes are ironed in advance and packed on hangers, with security and price tags affixed. This system means that instead of wrestling with inventory during busy periods, employees in Zara stores simply move items from shipping box to store racks, spending most of their time on value-added functions like helping customers find what they want. Efforts like this help store staff regain as much as three hours in prime selling time (Rohwedder & Johnson, 2008; Capell, 2008).

Trucks serve destinations that can be reached overnight, while chartered cargo flights serve farther destinations within forty-eight hours (Capell, 2008). The firm recently tweaked its shipping models through Air France–KLM Cargo and Emirates Air so flights can coordinate outbound shipment of all Inditex brands with return legs loaded with raw materials and half-finished clothes items from locations outside of Spain. Zara is also a pioneer in going green. In fall 2007, the firm's CEO unveiled an environmental strategy that includes the use of renewable energy systems at **logistics** centers including the introduction of biodiesel for the firm's trucking fleet.

Stores

Most products are manufactured for a limited production run. While running out of bestsellers might be seen as a disaster at most retailers, at Zara the practice delivers several benefits.

First, limited runs allow the firm to cultivate the exclusivity of its offerings. While a Gap in Los Angeles carries nearly the same product line as one in Milwaukee, each Zara store is stocked with items tailored to the tastes of its local clientele. A Fifth Avenue shopper quips, "At Gap, everything is the same," while a Zara shopper in Madrid says, "You'll never end up looking like someone else" (Capell, 2006). Upon visiting a Zara, the CEO of the National Retail Federation marveled, "It's like you walk into a new store every two weeks" (Helft, 2002).

Second, limited runs encourage customers to buy right away and at full price. Savvy Zara shoppers know the newest items arrive on black plastic hangers, with store staff transferring items to wooden ones later on. Don't bother asking when something will go on sale; if you wait three weeks the item you wanted has almost certainly been sold or moved out to make room for something new. Says one twenty-three year-old Barcelona shopper, "If you see something and don't buy it, you can forget about coming back for it because it will be gone" (Capell, 2006) A study by consulting firm Bain & Company estimated that the industry average markdown ratio is approximately 50 percent, while Zara books some 85 percent of its products at full price (Sull & Turconi, 2008; Capell, 2006).

The constant parade of new, limited-run items also encourages customers to visit often. The average Zara customer visits the store seventeen times per year, compared with only three annual visits made to competitors (Kumar & Linguri, 2006). Even more impressive—Zara puts up these numbers with almost no advertising. The firm's founder has referred to advertising as a "pointless distraction." The assertion carries particular weight when you consider that during Gap's collapse, the firm increased advertising spending but sales dropped (Bhatnagar, 2004). Fashion retailers spend an average of 3.5 percent of revenue promoting their products, while ad spending at Inditex is just 0.3 percent[3].

Finally, limited production runs allow the firm to, as Zara's CEO once put it, "reduce to a minimum the risk of making a mistake, and we do make mistakes with our collections" (Vitzthum, 2001). Failed product introductions are reported to be just 1 percent, compared with the industry average of 10 percent (Kumar & Linguri, 2006). So even though Zara has higher manufacturing costs than rivals, Inditex gross margins are 56.8 percent compared to 37.5 percent at Gap (Rohwedder, 2009; Capell, 2008).

While stores provide valuable front-line data, headquarters plays a major role in directing in-store operations. Software is used to schedule staff based on each store's forecasted sales volume, with locations staffing up at peak times such as lunch or early evening. The firm claims these more flexible schedules have shaved staff work hours by 2 percent. This constant refinement of operations throughout the firm's value chain has helped reverse a prior trend of costs rising faster than sales (Rohwedder & Johnson, 2008).

Even the store displays are directed from "The Cube," where a basement staging area known as "Fashion Street" houses a Potemkin village of bogus storefronts meant to mimic some of the chain's most exclusive locations throughout the world. It's here that workers test and fine-tune the chain's award-winning window displays, merchandise layout, and even determine the in-store soundtrack. Every two weeks, new store layout marching orders are forwarded to managers at each location (Rohwedder & Johnson, 2008).

3.2 MOVING FORWARD

The holy grail for the strategist is to craft a sustainable competitive advantage that is difficult for competitors to replicate. And for nearly two decades Zara has delivered the goods. But that's not to say the firm is done facing challenges.

Consider the limitations of Zara's Spain-centric, just-in-time manufacturing model. By moving all of the firm's deliveries through just two locations, both in Spain, the firm remains hostage to anything that could create a disruption in the region. Firms often hedge risks that could shut down operations—think weather, natural disaster, terrorism, labor strife, or political unrest—by spreading facilities throughout the globe. If problems occur in northern Spain, Zara has no such fallback.

In addition to the **operations** vulnerabilities above, the model also leaves the firm potentially more susceptible to financial vulnerabilities during periods when the euro strengthens relative to the dollar. Many low-cost manufacturing regions have currencies that are either pegged to the dollar or have otherwise fallen against the euro. This situation means Zara's Spain-centric costs rise at higher rates compared to competitors, presenting a challenge in keeping profit margins in check. Rising transportation costs are another concern. If fuel costs rise, the model of twice-weekly deliveries that has been key to defining the Zara experience becomes more expensive to maintain.

Still, Zara is able to make up for some cost increases by raising prices overseas (in the United States, Zara items can cost 40 percent or more than they do in Spain). Zara reports that all North American stores are profitable, and that it can continue to grow its presence, serving forty to fifty stores with just two U.S. jet flights a week (Tagliabue, 2003). Management has considered a logistics center in Asia, but expects current capacity will suffice until 2013 (Rohwedder & Johnson, 2008). Another possibility might be a center in the Maquiladora region of northern Mexico, which could serve the U.S. markets via trucking capacity similar to the firm's Spain-based access to Europe, while also providing a regional center to serve expansion throughout the Western Hemisphere.

Rivals have studied the Zara recipe, and while none have attained the efficiency of Amancio Ortega's firm, many are trying to learn from the master. There is precedent for contract firms closing the cycle time gap with vertically integrated competitors that own their own factories. Dell (a firm that builds its own PCs while nearly all its competitors use contract labor) has recently seen its manufacturing advantage from vertical integration fall as the partners that supply rivals have mimicked its techniques and have become far more efficient (Friscia, et. al., 2009). In terms of the number of new models offered, clothing is actually more complex than computing, suggesting that Zara's value chain may be more difficult to copy. Still, H&M has increased the frequency of new items in stores, Forever 21 and Uniqlo get new looks within six weeks, and Renner, a Brazilian fast fashion rival, rolls out mini collections every two months (Pfeifer, 2007; Rohwedder & Johnson, 2008). Rivals have a keen eye on Inditex, with the CFO of luxury goods firm Burberry claiming the firm is a "fantastic case study" and "we're mindful of their techniques" (Rohwedder & Johnson, 2008).

Finally, firm financial performance can also be impacted by broader economic conditions. When the economy falters, consumers simply buy less and may move a greater share of their wallet to less-stylish and lower-cost offerings from deep discounters like Wal-Mart . Zara is particularly susceptible to conditions in Spain, since the market accounts for nearly 40 percent of Inditex sales (Hall, 2008), as well as to broader West European conditions (which with Spain make up 79 percent of sales) (Rohwedder, 2009). Global expansion will provide the firm with a mix of locations that may be better able to endure downturns in any single region . Recent Spanish and European financial difficulties have made clear the need to decrease dependence on sales within one region.

Zara's winning formula can only exist through management's savvy understanding of how information systems can enable winning strategies (many tech initiatives were led by José Maria Castellano, a "technophile" business professor who became Ortega's right-hand man in the 1980s) (Rohwedder & Johnson, 2008). It is technology that helps Zara identify and manufacture the clothes customers want, get those products to market quickly, and eliminate costs related to advertising, inventory missteps, and markdowns. A strategist must always scan the state of the market as well as the state of the art in technology, looking for new opportunities and remaining aware of impending threats. With systems so highly tuned for success, it may be unwise to bet against "The Cube."

REFERENCES

Bhatnagar, P., "How Do You Ad(dress) the Gap?" Fortune, October 11, 2004. Capell, K., "Fashion Conquistador," BusinessWeek, September 4, 2006.

Boorstein, J., "Fashion Victim," Fortune, April 13, 2006.

Capell, K., "Zara Thrives by Breaking All the Rules," BusinessWeek, October 9, 2008.

Cho, E., "Gap: Report of Kids' Sweatshop 'Deeply Disturbing,'" CNN.com, October 29, 2007, http://www.cnn.com/2007/WORLD/asiapcf/10/29/gap.labor/index.html#cnnSTCVideo.

Folpe, J., "Zara Has a Made-to-Order Plan for Success," Fortune, September 4, 2000. Hall, J., "Zara Is Now Bigger Than Gap," Telegraph, August 18, 2008.

Friscia, T., K. O'Marah, D. Hofman, and J. Souza, "The AMR Research Supply Chain Top 25 for 2009," AMR Research, May 28, 2009, http://www.amrresearch.com/Content/View.aspx?compURI=tcm:7-43469.

Gentry, C., "European Fashion Stores Edge Past U.S. Counterparts," Chain Store Age, December 2007. Helft, M., "Fashion Fast Forward," Business 2.0, May 2002.

Hall, J., "Zara Is Now Bigger Than Gap," Telegraph, August 18, 2008. Pfeifer, M., "Fast and Furious," Latin Trade, September 2007

Kumar N., and S. Linguri, "Fashion Sense," Business Strategy Review, Summer 2006. Lindsay, G., "Prada's High-Tech Misstep," Business 2.0, March 1, 2004.

Lee, L., "Paul Pressler's Fall from The Gap," BusinessWeek, February 26, 2007. Murphy, R., "Expansion Boosts Inditex Net," Women's Wear Daily, April 1, 2008.

Pfeifer, M., "Fast and Furious," Latin Trade, September 2007

Rohwedder C. and K. Johnson, "Pace-Setting Zara Seeks More Speed to Fight Its Rising Cheap-Chic Rivals,"

Rohwedder C. and K. Johnson, "Pace-Setting Zara Seeks More Speed to Fight Its Rising Cheap-Chic Rivals,"

Rohwedder, C., "Zara Grows as Retail Rivals Struggle," Wall Street Journal, March 26, 2009. Sellers, P., "Gap's New Guy Upstairs," Fortune, April 14, 2003.

Sanchenko, A., "Foundations of Information Systems in Business" (lecture, October 13, 2007), http://www.scribd.com/doc/396076/Foundations-of-Information-Systems-in-Business.

Sull D. and S. Turconi, "Fast Fashion Lessons," Business Strategy Review, Summer 2008. Sullivan, L., "Designed to Cut Time," InformationWeek, February 28, 2005.

Sull D. and S. Turconi, "Fast Fashion Lessons," Business Strategy Review, Summer 2008. Surowiecki, J., "The Most Devastating Retailer in the World," New Yorker, September 18, 2000.

Tagliabue, J., "A Rival to Gap That Operates Like Dell," New York Times, May 30, 2003.

Tagliabue, J., "A Rival to Gap That Operates Like Dell," New York Times, May 30, 2003.

Tokatli, N., "Global Sourcing: Insights from the Global Clothing Industry—The Case of Zara, a Fast Fashion Retailer," Journal of Economic Geography 8, no. 1 (2008): 21–38.

Vitzthum, C., "Zara's Success Lies in Low-Cost Lines and a Rapid Turnover of Collections," Wall Street Journal, May 18, 2001.

Wall Street Journal, February 20, 2008.

NETFLIX: THE MAKING OF AN E-COMMERCE GIANT AND ATOMS TO BITS' UNCERTAIN FUTURE

4

4.1 INTRODUCTION: AN OVERVIEW

Entrepreneurs are supposed to want to go public. When a firm sells stock for the first time, the company gains a ton of cash to fuel expansion and its founders get rich. Going public is the dream in the back of the mind of every tech entrepreneur. But in 2007, Netflix founder and CEO Reed Hastings told *Fortune* that if he could change one strategic decision, it would have been to delay the firm's **initial public stock offering (IPO)**: "If we had stayed private for another two to four years, not as many people would have understood how big a business this could be" (Boyle, 2007). Once Netflix was a public company, financial disclosure rules forced the firm to reveal that it was on a money-minting growth tear. Once the secret was out, rivals showed up.

Hollywood's best couldn't have scripted a more menacing group of rivals for Hastings to face. First in line with its own DVD-by-mail offering was Blockbuster, a name synonymous with video rental. Some 40 million U.S. families were already card-carrying Blockbuster customers, and the firm's efforts promised to link DVD-by-mail with the nation's largest network of video stores. Following close behind was Wal-Mart—not just *a* big *Fortune* 500 company but *the* largest firm in the United States ranked by sales. In Netflix, Hastings had built a great firm, but let's face it, his was a dot-com, an Internet **pure play** without a storefront and with an overall customer base that seemed microscopic compared to these behemoths.

Before all this, Netflix was feeling so confident that it had actually raised prices. Customers loved the service, the company was dominating its niche, and it seemed like the firm could take advantage of a modest price hike, pull in more revenue, and use this to improve and expand the business. But the firm was surprised by how quickly the newcomers mimicked Netflix with cheaper rival efforts. This new competition forced Netflix to cut prices even lower than where they had been before the price increase. To keep pace, Netflix also upped advertising at a time when online ad rates were increasing. Big competitors, a price war, spending on the rise—how could Netflix possibly withstand this onslaught? Some Wall Street analysts had even taken to referring to Netflix's survival prospects as "The Last Picture Show" (Conlin, 2007).

Fast-forward a year later and Wal-Mart had cut and run, dumping their experiment in DVD-by-mail. Blockbuster had been mortally wounded, hemorrhaging billions of dollars in a string of quarterly losses. And Netflix? Not only had the firm held customers, it grew bigger, recording record profits. The dot-com did it. Hastings, a man who prior to Netflix had already built and sold one of the fifty largest public software firms in the United States, had clearly established himself as one of America's most capable and innovative technology leaders. In fact, at roughly the same time that Blockbuster CEO John Antioco resigned, Reed Hastings accepted an appointment to the Board of Directors of none other than the world's largest software firm, Microsoft. Like the final scene in so many movies where the hero's face is splashed across the news, *Time* named Hastings as one of the "100 most influential global citizens."

Why Study Netflix?

Studying Netflix gives us a chance to examine how technology helps firms craft and reinforce a competitive advantage. We'll pick apart the components of the firm's strategy and learn how technology played a starring role in placing the firm atop its industry. We also realize that while Netflix emerged the victorious underdog at the end of the first show, there will be at least one sequel, with the final scene yet to be determined. We'll finish the case with a look at the very significant challenges the firm faces as new technology continues to shift the competitive landscape.

4.2 TECH AND TIMING: MAKING KILLER ASSETS

To understand Netflix's strengths, it's important to view the firm as its customers see it. And for the most part, what they see they like—a lot! Netflix customers are rabidly loyal and rave about the service. The firm repeatedly ranks at the top of customer satisfaction surveys. Ratings agency ForeSee has named Netflix the number one e-commerce site in terms of customer satisfaction nine times in a row (placing it ahead of Apple and Amazon, among others). Netflix has also been cited as the best at satisfying customers by Nielsen and *Fast Company*, and was also named the Retail Innovator of the Year by the National Retail Federation.

Building a great brand, especially one online, starts with offering exceptional value to the customer. Don't confuse branding with advertising. During the dot-com era, firms thought brands could be built through Super Bowl ads and expensive television promotion. Advertising can build awareness, but *brands are built through customer experience.* This is a particularly important lesson for online firms. Have a bad experience at a burger joint and you might avoid that location but try another of the firm's outlets a few blocks away. Have a bad experience online and you're turned off by the firm's one and only virtual storefront. If you click over to an online rival, the offending firm may have lost you forever. But if a firm can get you to stay through quality experience, switching costs and data-driven value might keep you there for a long, long time, even when new entrants try to court you away.

If brand is built through customer experience, consider what this means for the Netflix subscriber. They expect the firm to offer a huge selection, to be able to find what they want, for it to arrive on time, for all of this to occur with no-brainer ease of use and convenience, and at a fair price. Technology drives all of these capabilities, so tech is at the very center of the firm's brand building efforts. Let's look at how the firm does it.

Selection: The Long Tail in Action

Customers have flocked to Netflix in part because of the firm's staggering selection. A traditional video store (and Blockbuster had some 7,800 of them) stocks roughly three thousand DVD titles on its shelves. For comparison, Netflix is able to offer its customers a selection of over one hundred thousand DVD titles, and rising! At traditional brick-and-mortar retailers, shelf space is the biggest constraint limiting a firm's ability to offer customers what they want when they want it. Just which films, documentaries, concerts, cartoons, TV shows, and other fare make it inside the four walls of a Blockbuster store is dictated by what the average consumer is most likely to be interested in. To put it simply, Blockbuster stocks blockbusters.

Finding the right product mix and store size can be tricky. Offer too many titles in a bigger storefront and there may not be enough paying customers to justify stocking less popular titles (remember, it's not just the cost of the DVD—firms also pay for the real estate of a larger store, the workers, the energy to power the facility, etc.). You get the picture—there's a breakeven point that is arrived at by considering the geographic constraint of the number of customers that can reach a location, factored in with store size, store inventory, the payback from that inventory, and the cost to own and operate the store. Anyone who has visited a video store only to find a title out of stock has run up against the limits of the physical store model.

But many online businesses are able to run around these limits of geography and shelf space. Internet firms that ship products can get away with having just a few highly automated warehouses, each stocking just about all the products in a particular category. And for firms that distribute products digitally (think songs on iTunes), the efficiencies are even greater because there's no warehouse or physical product at all (more on that later).

Offer a nearly limitless selection and something interesting happens: there's actually *more money* to be made selling the obscure stuff than the hits. Music service Rhapsody makes more from songs outside of the top ten thousand than it does from songs ranked above ten thousand. At Amazon.com, roughly 60 percent of books sold are titles that aren't available in even the biggest Borders or Barnes & Noble Superstores (Anderson, 2004). And at Netflix, roughly 75 percent of DVD titles shipped are from back-catalog titles, not new releases (at Blockbuster outlets the equation is nearly flipped, with some 70 percent of business coming from new releases) (McCarthy, 2009). Consider that Netflix sends out forty-five thousand different titles each day. That's *fifteen times* the selection available at your average video store! Each quarter, roughly 95 percent of titles are viewed—that means that every few weeks Netflix is able to find a customer for nearly *every* DVD title that has *ever* been commercially released.

This phenomenon whereby firms can make money by selling a near-limitless selection of less-popular products is known as the **long tail**. The term was coined by Chris Anderson, an editor at *Wired* magazine, who also wrote a best-selling business book by the same name. The "tail" (see Figure 4.1 "The Long Tail") refers to the demand for less popular items that aren't offered by traditional brick-and-mortar shops. While most stores make money from the area under the curve from the vertical axis to the dotted line, long tail firms can also sell the less popular stuff. Each item under the right part of the curve may experience less demand than the most popular products, but someone somewhere likely wants it. And as demonstrated from the examples above, the total demand for the obscure stuff is often much larger than what can be profitably sold through traditional stores alone. While some debate the size of the tail (e.g., whether obscure titles collectively are more profitable for most firms), two facts are critical to keep above this debate: (1) selection attracts customers, and (2) the Internet allows large-selection inventory efficiencies that offline firms can't match.

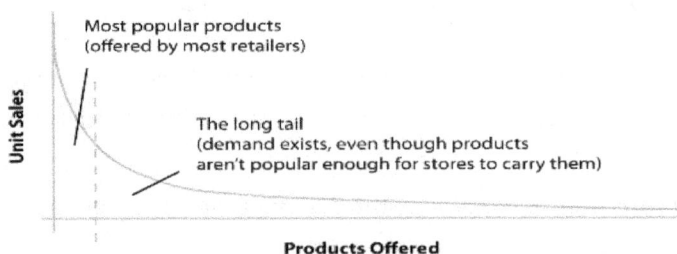

Most popular products
(offered by most retailers)

Unit Sales

The long tail
(demand exists, even though products
aren't popular enough for stores to carry them)

Products Offered

Figure 4.1 The Long Tail

The long tail works because the cost of production and distribution drop to a point where it becomes economically viable to offer a huge selection. For Netflix, the cost to stock and ship an obscure foreign film is the same as sending out the latest

Will Smith blockbuster. The long tail gives the firm a selection advantage (or one based on scale) that traditional stores simply cannot match.

For more evidence that there is demand for the obscure stuff, consider Bollywood cinema—a term referring to films produced in India. When ranked by the number of movies produced each year, Bollywood is actually bigger than Hollywood, but in terms of U.S. demand, even the top-grossing Hindi film might open in only one or two American theaters, and few video stores carry many Bollywood DVDs. Again, we see the limits that geography and shelf space impose on traditional stores. As Anderson puts it, when it comes to traditional methods of distribution, "an audience too thinly spread is the same as no audience at all (Anderson, 2004)." While there are roughly 1.7 million South Asians living in the United States, Bollywood fans are geographically disbursed, making it difficult to offer content at a physical storefront. Fans of foreign films would often find the biggest selection at an ethnic grocery store, but even then, that wouldn't be much. Enter Netflix. The firm has found the U.S. fans of South Asian cinema, sending out roughly one hundred thousand Bollywood DVDs a month. As geographic constraints go away, untapped markets open up!

The power of Netflix can revive even well-regarded work by some of Hollywood's biggest names. In between *The Godfather* and *The Godfather Part II*, director Francis Ford Coppola made *The Conversation*, a film starring Gene Hackman that, in 1975, was nominated for a Best Picture Academy Award. Coppola has called *The Conversation* the finest film he has ever made (Leonhardt, 2006), but it was headed for obscurity as the ever-growing pipeline of new releases pushed the film off of video store shelves. Netflix was happy to pick up *The Conversation* and put it in the long tail. Since then, the number of customers viewing the film has tripled, and on Netflix, this once underappreciated gem became the thirteenth most watched film from its time period.

For evidence on Netflix's power to make lucrative markets from nonblockbusters, visit the firm's "Top 100 page."[1] You'll see a list loaded with films that were notable for their *lack* of box office success. As of this writing the number one rank had been held *for over five years in a row*, not by a first-run mega-hit, but by the independent film *Crash* (an Oscar winner, but box office weakling) (Elder, 2009).

Netflix has used the long tail to its advantage, crafting a business model that creates close ties with film studios. In most cases, studios earn a percentage of the subscription revenue for every disk sent out to a Netflix customer. In exchange, Netflix gets DVDs at a very low cost. The movie business is characterized by large fixed costs up front. Studio marketing budgets are concentrated on films when they first appear in theaters, and when they're first offered on DVD. After that, studios are done promoting a film, focusing instead on their most current titles. But Netflix is able to find an audience for a film without the studios spending a dime on additional marketing. Since so many of the titles viewed on Netflix are in the long tail, revenue sharing is all gravy for the studios—additional income they would otherwise be unlikely to get. It's a win-win for both ends of the supply chain. These supplier partnerships grant Netflix a sort of soft bargaining power that's distinctly opposite the strong-arm price bullying that giants like Wal-Mart are often accused of.

Cinematch: A data asset is produced by technology and produces profits.

Netflix proves there's both demand and money to be made from the vast back catalog of film and TV show content. But for the model to work best, the firm needed to address the biggest inefficiency in the movie industry—"audience finding," that is, matching content with customers. To do this, Netflix leverages some of the industry's most sophisticated technology, a proprietary recommendation system that the firm calls Cinematch.

Each time a customer visits Netflix after sending back a DVD, the service essentially asks "So, how did you like the movie?" With a single click, each film can be rated on a scale of one to five stars. If you're new to Netflix, the service can prompt you with a list of movies (or you can search out and rate titles on your own). Love *Rushmore* but hate *The Life Aquatic*? Netflix wants to know.

The magic of Cinematch happens not by offering a gross average user rating—user tastes are too varied and that data's too coarse to be of significant value. Instead, Cinematch develops a map of user ratings and steers you toward titles preferred by people with tastes that are most like yours. Techies and marketers call this trick **collaborative filtering**. The term refers to a classification of software that monitors trends among customers and uses this data to personalize an individual customer's experience. Input from collaborative filtering software can be used to customize the display of a Web page for each user so that an individual is greeted only with those items the software predicts they'll most likely be interested in. The kind of data mining done by collaborative filtering isn't just used by Netflix; other sites use similar systems to recommend music, books, even news stories. While other firms also employ collaborative filtering, Netflix has been at this game for years, and is constantly tweaking its efforts. The results are considered the industry gold standard.

Collaborative filtering software is powerful stuff, but is it a source of competitive advantage? Ultimately it's just math. Difficult math, to be sure, but nothing prevents other firms from working hard in the lab, running and refining tests, and coming up with software that's as good, or perhaps one day even better than Netflix's offering. But what the software has created for the early-moving Netflix is an enormous data advantage that is valuable, results yielding, and impossible for rivals to match. Even if Netflix gave Cinematch to its competitors, they'd be without the over 3 billion ratings that the firm has amassed (according to the firm, users add about a million new ratings to the system each day). More ratings make the system seem smarter, and with more info to go on, Cinematch can make more accurate recommendations than rivals.

Evidence suggests that users trust and value Cinematch. Recommended titles make up over 60 percent of the content users place in their queues—an astonishing penetration rate. Compare that to how often you've received a great recommendation from the sullen teen behind the video store counter. While data and algorithms improve the service and further strengthen the firm's brand, this data is also a switching cost. Drop Netflix for Blockbuster and the average user abandons the two hundred or more films they've rated. Even if one is willing to invest the time in recreating their ratings on Blockbuster's site, the rival will still make less accurate recommendations because there are fewer users and less data to narrow in on similarities across customers.

One way to see how strong these switching costs are is to examine the Netflix **churn rate**. Churn is a marketing term referring to the rate at which customers leave a product or service. A low churn is usually key to profitability because it costs more to acquire a customer than to keep one. And the longer a customer stays with the firm, the more profitable they become and the less likely they are to leave. If customers weren't completely satisfied with the Netflix experience, many would be willing to churn out and experiment with rivals offering cheaper service. However, the year after Blockbuster and Wal-Mart launched with copycat efforts, the rate at which customers left Netflix actually *fell* below 4 percent, an all-time low. And the firm's churn rates have continued to fall over time. By the middle of 2008, rates for customers in Netflix most active regions of the country were below 3 percent, meaning fewer than three in one hundred Netflix customers canceled their subscriptions each year[2]. To get an idea of how enviable the Netflix churn rates are, consider that a year earlier the mobile phone industry had a churn rate of 38.6 percent, while roughly one in four U.S. banking customers defected that year[3].

All of this impacts marketing costs, too. Happy customers refer friends (free marketing from a source consumers trust more than a TV commercial). Ninety-four percent of Netflix subscribers say they have recommended the service to someone else, and 71 percent of new subscribers say an existing subscriber has encouraged them to sign up. It's no wonder subscriber acquisition costs have been steadily falling, further contributing to the firm's overall profitability.

A Look at Operations

Tech also lies at the heart of the warehouse operations that deliver customer satisfaction and enhance brand value. As mentioned earlier, brand is built through customer experience, and a critical component of customer experience is for subscribers to get their DVDs as quickly as possible. In order to do this, Netflix has blanketed the country with a network of fifty-eight ultrahigh-tech distribution centers that collectively handle in excess of 1.8 million

DVDs a day. These distribution centers are purposely located within driving distance of 119 U.S. Postal Service (USPS) processing and distribution facilities.

By 4:00 a.m. each weekday, Netflix trucks collect the day's DVD shipments from these USPS hubs and returns the DVDs to the nearest Netflix center. DVDs are fed into custom-built sorters that handle disc volume on the way in and the way out. That same machine fires off an e-mail as soon as it detects your DVD was safely returned (now rate it via Cinematch). Most DVDs never hit the restocking shelves. Scanners pick out incoming titles that are destined for other users and place these titles into a sorted outbound pile with a new, appropriately addressed red envelope. Netflix not only helps out the postal service by picking up and dropping off the DVDs at its hubs, it presorts all outgoing mail for faster delivery. This extra effort has a payoff—Netflix gets the lowest possible postal rates for first-class mail delivery. And despite the high level of automation, 100 percent of all discs are inspected by hand so that cracked ones can be replaced, and dirty ones can be given a wipe down (McCarthy, 2009). Total in and out turnaround time for a typical Netflix DVD is just eight hours (Kenny, 2009)!

First-class mail takes only one day to be delivered within a fifty-mile radius, so the warehouse network allows Netflix to service over 97 percent of its customer base within a two-day window—one day is allotted for receipt; early the next morning the next item in their queue is processed; and the new title arrives at the customer's address by that afternoon. And in 2009, the firm added Saturday processing. All this means a customer with the firm's most popular "three disc at a time" plan could watch a movie a day and never be without a fresh title.

Figure 4.2 A Proprietary Netflix Sorting Machine

Warehouse processes don't exist in a vacuum; they are linked to Cinematch to offer the firm additional operational advantages. The software recommends movies that are likely to be in stock so users aren't frustrated by a wait.

Everyone on staff is expected to have an eye on improving the firm's processes. Every warehouse worker gets a free DVD player and Netflix subscription so that they understand the service from the customer's perspective and can provide suggestions for improvement. Quality management features are built into systems supporting nearly every process at the firm, allowing Netflix to monitor and record the circumstances surrounding any failures. When an error occurs, a tiger team of quality improvement personnel swoops in to figure out how to prevent any problems from recurring. Each phone call is a cost, not a revenue enhancement, and each error increases the chance that a dissatisfied customer will bolt for a rival.

By paying attention to process improvements and designing technology to smooth operations, Netflix has slashed the number of customer representatives even as subscriptions ballooned. In the early days, when the firm had one hundred and fifteen thousand customers, Netflix had one-hundred phone support reps. By the time the customer base had grown thirtyfold, errors had been reduced to the point where only forty-three reps were needed (mcGregor, 2005). Even more impressive, because of the firm's effective use of technology to drive the firm's operations, fulfillment costs as a percentage of revenue have actually dropped even though postal rates have increased and Netflix has cut prices.

Recap of Killer Asset: Understanding Scale

Netflix executives are quite frank that the technology and procedures that make up their model can be copied, but they also realize the challenges that any copycat rival faces. Says the firm's VP of Operations Andy Rendich, "Anyone can replicate the Netflix operations if they wish. It's not going to be easy. It's going to take a lot of time and a lot of money."[2]

While we referred to Netflix as David to the Goliaths of Wal-Mart and Blockbuster, within the DVD-by-mail segment Netflix is now the biggest player by far, and this size gives the firm significant scale advantages. The yearly cost to run a Netflix-comparable nationwide delivery infrastructure is about $300 million (Reda & Schulz, 2008). Think about how this relates to economies of scale. In Chapter 2 "Strategy and Technology: Concepts and Frameworks for Understanding What Separates Winners from Losers", we said that firms enjoy *scale economies* when they are able to leverage the cost of an investment across increasing units of production. Even if rivals have identical infrastructures, the more profitable firm will be the one with more customers (see Figure 4.3). And the firm with better scale economies is in a position to lower prices, as well as to spend more on customer acquisition, new features, or other efforts. Smaller rivals have an uphill fight, while established firms that try to challenge Netflix with a copycat effort are in a position where they're straddling markets, unable to gain full efficiencies from their efforts.

NETFLIX

Subscribers:
14 million

vs.

Cost to run the effort:
$300 million

BLOCKBUSTER

Subscribers:
2.2 million

Cost to run the effort:
$300 million

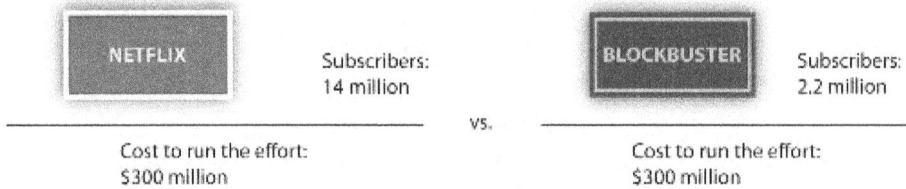

Figure 4.3 Running a nationwide sales network costs an estimated $300 million a year. But Netflix has several times more subscribers than Blockbuster. Which firm has economies of scale?4

For Blockbuster, the arrival of Netflix plays out like a horror film where it is the victim. For several years now, the in-store rental business has been a money loser. Things got worse in 2005 when Netflix pressure forced Blockbuster to drop late fees, costing it about $400 million (Mullaney, 2006). The Blockbuster store network once had the advantage of scale, but eventually its many locations were seen as an inefficient and bloated liability. Between 2006 and 2007, the firm shuttered over 570 stores (Farrell, 2007). By 2008, Blockbuster had been in the red for ten of the prior eleven years. During a three-year period that included the launch of its Total Access DVD-by-mail effort, Blockbuster lost over $4 billion (MacDonald, 2008). The firm tried to outspend Netflix on advertising, even running Super Bowl ads for Total Access in 2007, but a money loser can't outspend its more profitable rival for long, and it has since significantly cut back on promotion. Blockbuster also couldn't sustain subscription rates below Netflix's, so it has given up its price advantage. In early 2008, Blockbuster even briefly pursued a merger with another struggling giant, Circuit City, a strategy that has left industry experts scratching their heads. A Viacom executive said about the firm, "Blockbuster will certainly not survive and it will not be missed" (Epstein, 2006).

For Netflix, what delivered the triple scale advantage of the largest selection; the largest network of distribution centers; the largest customer base; and the firm's industry-leading strength in brand and data assets? Moving first. Timing and technology don't always yield sustainable competitive advantage, but in this case, Netflix leveraged both to craft what seems to be an extraordinarily valuable pool of assets that continue to grow and strengthen over time. To be certain, competing against a wounded giant like Blockbuster will remain difficult. The latter firm has few options and may spend itself into oblivion, harming Netflix in its collapsing gasp. And as we'll see in the next section, while technology shifts helped Netflix attack Blockbuster's once-dominant position, even newer technology shifts may threaten Netflix. As they like to say in the mutual fund industry "Past results aren't a guarantee of future returns."

4.3 ATOMS TO BITS: OPPORTUNITY OR THREAT?

Nicholas Negroponte, the former head of MIT's Media Lab and founder of the One Laptop per Child effort, wrote a now-classic essay on the shift from atoms to bits. Negroponte pointed out that most media products are created as bits—digital files of ones and zeros that begin their life on a computer. Music, movies, books, and newspapers are all created using digital technology. When we buy a CD, DVD, or even a "dead tree" book or newspaper, we're buying physical atoms that are simply a container for the bits that were created in software—a sound mixer, a video editor, or a word processor.

The shift from atoms to bits is realigning nearly every media industry. Newspapers struggle as readership migrates online and once-lucrative classified ads and job listings shift to the bits-based businesses of Craigslist, Monster.com, and LinkedIn. Apple dominates music sales, selling not a single "atom" of physical CDs, while most of the atom-selling "record store" chains of a decade ago are bankrupt. Amazon has even begun delivering digital books, developing the Kindle digital reader. Who needs to kill a tree, spill ink, fill a warehouse, and roll a gas-guzzling truck to get you a book? Kindle can slurp your purchases through the air and display them on a device lighter than any college textbook. When Amazon CEO Bezos unveiled the Kindle DX at a press event at Pace University in Spring 2009, he indicated that Kindle book sales were accounting for 35 percent of sales for the two hundred and seventy-five thousand titles available for the device—a jaw-dropping impact for a device many had thought to be an expensive, niche product for gadget lovers (Penenberg, 2009).

Video is already going digital, but Netflix became a profitable business by handling the atoms of DVDs. The question is, will the atoms to bits shift crush Netflix and render it as irrelevant as Hastings did Blockbuster? Or can Reed pull off yet another victory and recast his firm for the day that DVDs disappear?

Concerns over the death of the DVD and the relentless arrival of new competitors are probably the main cause for Netflix's stock volatility these past few years. Through the first half of 2010, the firm's growth, revenue, and profit graphs all go up and to the right, but the stock has experienced wild swings as pundits have mostly guessed wrong about the firm's imminent demise (one well-known Silicon Valley venture capitalist even referred to the firm as "an ice cube in the sun," a statement Netflix countered with five years of record-breaking growth and profits) (Copeland, 2008). The troughs on the Netflix stock graph have proven great investment opportunities for the savvy. The firm broke all previous growth and earnings records and posted its lowest customer churn ever, even as a deep recession and the subprime crisis hammered many other firms. The firm continued to enjoy its most successful quarters as a public company, and subscriber growth rose even as DVD sales fell. But even the most bullish investor knows there's no stopping the inevitable shift from atoms to bits, and the firm's share price swings continue. When the DVD dies, the high-tech shipping and handling infrastructure that Netflix has relentlessly built will be rendered worthless.

Reed Hastings clearly knows this, and he has a plan: "We named the company Netflix for a reason; we didn't name it DVDs-by-mail" (Boyle, 2007). But he also prepared the public for a first-cut service that was something less than we'd expect from the long tail poster child. When speaking about the launch of the firm's Internet video streaming offering in January 2007, Hastings said it would be "underwhelming." The two biggest limitations of this initial service? As we'll see below, not enough content, and figuring out how to squirt the bits to a television.

Content Access

First the content. Three years after the launch of Netflix streaming option (enabled via a "Watch Now" button next to movies that can be viewed online), only 17,000 videos were offered, just 17 percent of the firm's long tail. And not the best 17 percent. Why so few titles? It's not just studio reluctance or fear of piracy. There are often complicated legal issues involved in securing the digital distribution rights for all of the content that makes up a movie. Music, archival footage, and performer rights may all hold up a title from being available under "Watch Now." The 2007 Writers Guild strike occurred largely due to negotiations over digital distribution, showing just how troublesome these issues can be.

Add to that the exclusivity contracts negotiated by key channels, in particular the so-called *premium* television networks. Film studios release their work in a system called **windowing**. Content is available to a given distribution channel (in theaters, through hospitality channels like hotels and airlines, on DVD, via pay-per-view, via pay cable, then broadcast commercial TV) for a specified time window, usually under a different revenue model (ticket sales, disc sales, license fees for broadcast). Pay television channels in particular have negotiated exclusive access to content as they strive to differentiate themselves from one another. This exclusivity means that even when a title becomes available for streaming by Netflix, it may disappear when a pay TV window opens up. If HBO or Showtime has an exclusive for a film, it's pulled from the Netflix streaming service until the exclusive pay TV time window closes. A 2008 partnership with the Starz network helped provide access to some content locked up inside pay television windows, and deals with Disney and CBS allow for streaming of current-season shows (Portnoy, 2008). But the firm still has a long way to go before the streaming tail seems comparably long when compared against its disc inventory.

While studios embrace the audience-finding and revenue-sharing advantages of Netflix, they also don't want to undercut higher-revenue early windows. Fox, Universal, and Warner have all demanded that Netflix delay sending DVDs to customers until twenty-eight days after titles go on sale. In exchange, Netflix has received guarantees that these studios will offer more content for digital streaming.

There's also the influence of the king of DVD sales: Wal-Mart. The firm accounts for about 40 percent of DVD sales—a scale that delivers a lot of the bargaining power it has used to "encourage" studios to hold content from competing windows or to limit offering digital titles at competitive pricing during the peak new release period (Grover, 2006). Apparently, Wal-Mart isn't ready to yield ground in the shifts from atoms to bits, either. In February 2010, the retail giant spent an estimated $100 million to buy the little-known video streaming outfit VUDU (Stone, 2010). Wal-Mart's negotiating power with studios may help it gain special treatment for VUDU. As an example, VUDU was granted exclusive high-definition streaming rights for the hit movie *Avatar*, offering the title online the same day the DVD appeared for sale (Jacobson, 2010).

Studios may also be wary of the increasing power Netflix has over product distribution, and as such, they may be motivated to keep rivals around. Studios have granted Blockbuster more favorable distribution terms than Netflix. In many cases, Blockbuster can now distribute DVDs the day of release instead of waiting nearly a month, as Netflix does (Birchall, 2010). Studios are likely concerned that Netflix may be getting so big that it will one day have Wal-Mart-like negotiating leverage.

Taken together, all these factors make it clear that shifting the long tail from atoms to bits will be significantly more difficult than buying DVDs and stacking them in a remote warehouse.

But How Does It Get to the TV?

The other major problem lies in getting content to the place where most consumers want to watch it: the living room TV. Netflix's "Watch Now" button first worked only on Windows PCs. Although the service was introduced in January 2007, the months before were fueled with speculation that the firm would partner with TiVo. Just one month later, TiVo announced its partner—Amazon.com. At that point Netflix found itself up against a host of rivals that all had a path to the television: Apple had its own hardware solution in Apple TV (not to mention the iPod and iPhone for portable viewing), the cable companies delivered OnDemand through their set-top boxes, and now Amazon had TiVo.

An internal team at Netflix developed a prototype set top box that Hastings himself supported offering. But most customers aren't enthusiastic about purchasing yet another box for their set top, the consumer electronics business is brutally competitive, and selling hardware would introduce an entirely new set of inventory, engineering, marketing, distribution, and competitive complexities.

The solution Netflix eventually settled on was to think beyond one hardware alternative and instead recruit others to provide a wealth of choice. The firm developed a software platform and makes this available to firms seeking to build Netflix access into their devices. Today, Netflix streaming is baked into televisions and DVD players from LG, Panasonic, Samsung, Sony, Toshiba, and Vizio, among others. It's also available on all major video game consoles. A Netflix app for Apple's iPad was available the day the device shipped. Even TiVo now streams Netflix. And that internally developed Netflix set-top box? The group was spun out to form Roku, an independent firm that launched their own $99 Netflix streamer.

The switch to Blu-ray movies may offer the most promise. Blu-ray players are on the fast track to commoditization. If consumer electronics firms incorporate Netflix access into their players as a way to attract more customers with an additional, differentiating feature, Hastings's firm could end up with more living room access than either Amazon or Apple. There are 73 million households in the United States that have a DVD player and an Internet connection. Should a large portion of these homes end up with a Netflix-ready Blu-ray player, Hastings will have built himself an enviable base through which to grow the video streaming business.

Who's going to win the race for delivering bits to the television is still very much an uncertain bet. The models all vary significantly. Apple's early efforts were limited, with the firm offering only video purchases for Apple TV, but eventually moving to online "rentals" that can also play on the firm's entire line of devices. Movie studios are now all in Apple's camp, although the firm did temporarily lose NBC's television content in a dispute over pricing. Amazon and Microsoft also have online rentals and purchase services, and can get their content to the television via TiVo and Xbox, respectively (yes, this makes Microsoft both a partner and a sort of competitor, a phenomenon often referred to as **coopetition,** or *frenemies* (Brandenberger & Nalebuff, 1997; Johnson, 2008). Hulu, a joint venture backed by NBC, Fox, and other networks, is free, earning money from ads that run like TV commercials. While Hulu has also received glowing reviews, the venture has lagged in offering a method to get streaming content to the television. Netflix pioneered "all-you-can-eat" subscription streaming. Anyone who has at least the $8.99 subscription plan can view an unlimited number of video streams. And Blockbuster isn't dead yet. It also streams over TiVo and has other offerings in the works.

There's a clear upside to the model when it shifts to streaming: it will eliminate a huge chunk of costs associated with shipping and handling. Postage represents one-third of the firm's expenses. A round-trip DVD mailing, even at the deep discounts Netflix receives from the U.S. Postal Service, runs about eighty cents. The bandwidth and handling costs to send bits to a TV set are around a nickel (McCarthy, 2009). At some point, if postage goes away, Netflix may be in a position to offer even greater profits to its studio suppliers, and to make more money itself, too.

Wrangling licensing costs presents a further challenge. Estimates peg Netflix 2009 streaming costs at about $100 million, up 250 percent in three years. But these expenses still deliver just a fraction of the long tail. Streaming licensing deals are tricky because they're so inconsistent even when titles are available. Rates vary, with some offered via a flat rate for unlimited streams, a per-stream rate, a rate for a given number of streams, and various permutations in between. Some vendors have been asking as much as four dollars per stream for more valuable content (Rayburn, 2009) —a fee that would quickly erase subscriber profits, making any such titles too costly to add to the firm's library. Remember, Netflix doesn't charge more for streaming—it's built into the price of its flat-rate subscriptions.

Any extra spending doesn't come at the best time. The switch to Blu-ray movies means that Netflix will be forced into the costly proposition of carrying two sets of video inventory: standard and high-def. Direct profits may not be the driver. Rather, the service may be a feature that attracts new customers to the firm and helps prevent subscriber flight to rival video-on-demand efforts. The stealth arrival of a Netflix set-top box, in the form of upgraded Blu- ray players, might open even more customer acquisition opportunities to the firm. Bought a Blu-ray player? For just nine dollars per month you can get a ticket to the all-you-can-eat Netflix buffet. And more customers ready to watch content streamed by Netflix may prime the pump for studios to become more aggressive in licensing more of their content. Many TV networks and movie studios are leery of losing bargaining power to a dominant firm, having witnessed how Apple now dictates pricing terms to music labels. The goodwill Netflix has earned over the years may pay off if it can become the studios' partner of first choice.

While one day the firm will lose the investment in its warehouse infrastructure, nearly all assets have a limited lifespan. That's why corporations depreciate assets, writing their value down over time. The reality is that the shift from atoms to bits won't flick on like a light switch; it will be a hybrid transition that takes place over several years. If the firm can grab long-tail content, grow its customer base, and lock them in with the switching costs created by Cinematch (all big "ifs"), it just might emerge as a key player in a bits-only world.

Is the hybrid strategy a dangerous straddling gambit or a clever ploy to remain dominant? Netflix really doesn't have a choice but to try. Hastings already has a long history as one of the savviest strategic thinkers in tech. As the networks say, stay tuned!

REFERENCES

Boyle, M., "Questions for...Reed Hastings," Fortune, May 23, 2007. Conlin, M., "Netflix: Flex to the Max," BusinessWeek, September 24, 2007.

Birchall, J., "Blockbuster Strikes Deal to Ensure DVD Supply," Financial Times, April 8, 2010. Boyle, M., "Questions for...Reed Hastings," Fortune, May 23, 2007.

Brandenberger A. and B. Nalebuff, Co-opetition: A Revolution Mindset that Combines Competition and Cooperation: The Game Theory Strategy That's Changing the Game of Business (New York: Broadway Business, 1997)

Copeland, M., "Netflix Lives! Video Downloads Haven't Made the DVD-by-Mail Business Obsolete," Fortune, April 21, 2008.

Gallaugher, J., "E-Commerce and the Undulating Distribution Channel," Communications of the ACM, July 2002. Grover, R., "Wal-Mart and Apple Battle for Turf," BusinessWeek, August 31, 2006.

Jacobson, J., "VUDU/Wal-Mart Gets Avatar HD Streaming Exclusive," Electronic House, April 22, 2010. Johnson, J., "The Frenemy Business Relationship," Fast Company, November 25, 2008.

McCarthy, B., "Netflix, Inc." (remarks, J. P. Morgan Global Technology, Media, and Telecom Conference, Boston, May 18, 2009).

Penenberg, A., "Amazon Taps Its Inner Apple," Fast Company, July 1, 2009.

Portnoy, S., "Netflix News: Starz Catalog Added to Online Service, Streaming to PS3, Xbox 360 through PlayOn Beta Software," ZDNet, October 2, 2008, http://blogs.zdnet.com/home-theater/?p=120

Rayburn, D., "Netflix Streaming Costs," Streaming Media, June/July 2009.

Rich M. and B. Stone, "Publisher Wins Fight with Amazon over E-Books," New York Times, January 31, 2010. Stone, B., "Wal-Mart Adds Clout to Streaming," New York Times, February 22, 2010.

Breen, B., "Living in Dell Time," Fast Company, November 24, 2004. Copeland, M., "How to Ride the Fifth Wave," Business 2.0, July 1, 2005.

Corbett, S., "Can the Cellphone Help End Global Poverty?" New York Times Magazine, April 13, 2008. Ewing, J., "Upwardly Mobile in Africa," BusinessWeek, September 24, 2007, 64–71.

Huggins, J., "How Much Data Is That?" Refrigerator Door, August 19, 2008.

Landau, E., "Tattletale Pills, Bottles Remind You to Take Your Meds," CNN, February 2, 2010. Lawton, C., "The X.O. Laptop Two Years Later," Wired, June 19, 2009.

Miller, J., "Goodbye G.U.I? Ambient Orb a Computer 'Mood Ring,'" Mass High Tech, February 10, 2003. Moore, G., "Cramming More Components onto Integrated Circuits," Electronics Magazine, April 19, 1965.

Rose, D., presentation as part of "From Disruption to Innovation" at the MIT Enterprise Forum, Cambridge, MA, June 23, 2010.

Schonfeld,E., "For Books Available on Kindle, Sales Are Now Tracking at 35 Percent of Print Sales," TechCrunch, May 6, 2009.

Schuman, E., "At Wal-Mart, World's Largest Retail Data Warehouse Gets Even Larger," eWeek, October 13, 2004.

MOORE'S LAW: WHAT FAST, AFFORDABLE COMPUTING MEANS FOR THE MANAGER

5

5.1 INTRODUCTION: AN OVERVIEW

Faster and cheaper—those two words have driven the computer industry for decades, and the rest of the economy has been along for the ride. Today it's tough to imagine a single industry not impacted by more powerful, less expensive computing. Faster and cheaper puts mobile phones in the hands of peasant farmers, puts a free video game in your Happy Meal, and drives the drug discovery that may very well extend your life.

Definitions

This phenomenon of "faster, cheaper" computing is often referred to as **Moore's Law**, after Intel cofounder, Gordon Moore. Moore didn't show up one day, stance wide, hands on hips, and declare "behold my law," but he did write a four-page paper for *Electronics Magazine* in which he described how the process of chip making enabled more powerful chips to be manufactured at cheaper prices (Moore, 1965).

Moore's friend, legendary chip entrepreneur and CalTech professor Carver Mead, later coined the "Moore's Law" moniker. That name sounded snappy, plus as one of the founders of Intel, Moore had enough geek cred for the name to stick. Moore's original paper offered language only a chip designer would love, so we'll rely on the more popular definition: *chip performance per dollar doubles every eighteen months* (Moore's original paper assumed two years, but many sources today refer to the *eighteen*-month figure, so we'll stick with that).

Moore's Law applies to chips—broadly speaking, to *processors*, or the electronics stuff that's made out of silicon[1]. The **microprocessor** is the brain of a computing device. It's the part of the computer that executes the instructions of a computer program, allowing it to run a Web browser, word processor, video game, or virus. For processors, Moore's Law means that next generation chips should be twice as fast in *eighteen* months, but cost the same as today's models (or from another perspective, in a year and a half, chips that are same speed as today's models should be available for half the price).

Random-access memory (RAM) is chip-based memory. The RAM inside your personal computer is **volatile memory**, meaning that when the power goes out, all is lost that wasn't saved to **nonvolatile memory** (i.e., a more permanent storage media like a hard disk or flash memory). Think of RAM as temporary storage that provides fast access for executing computer programs and files. When you "load" or "launch" a program, it usually moves from your hard drive to those RAM chips, where it can be more quickly executed by the processor.

Cameras, MP3 players, USB drives, and mobile phones often use **flash memory** (sometimes called *flash RAM*). It's not as fast as the RAM used in most traditional PCs, but holds data even when the power is off (so flash memory is also nonvolatile memory). You can think of flash memory as the chip-based equivalent of a hard drive. In fact, flash memory prices are falling so rapidly that several manufactures including Apple and the One Laptop per Child initiative (see the "Tech for the Poor" sidebar later in this section) have begun offering chip-based, nonvolatile memory as an alternative to laptop hard drives. The big advantage? Chips are **solid state electronics** (meaning no moving parts), so they're less likely to fail, and they draw less power. The solid state advantage also means that chip-based MP3 players like the iPod nano make better jogging companions than hard drive players, which can skip if jostled. For RAM chips and flash memory, Moore's Law means that in *eighteen* months you'll pay the same price as today for twice as much storage.

Computer chips are sometimes also referred to as **semiconductors** (a substance such as silicon dioxide used inside most computer chips that is capable of enabling as well as inhibiting the flow of electricity). So if someone refers to the *semiconductor industry*, they're talking about the chip business[2].

Strictly speaking, Moore's Law does not apply to other technology components. But other computing components are also seeing their price versus performance curves skyrocket exponentially. Data storage doubles every twelve months. Networking speed is on a tear, too. With an equipment change at the ends of the cables, the amount of data that can be squirted over an **optical fiber line** can double every nine months[3]. These numbers should be taken as rough approximations and shouldn't be expected to be strictly precise over time. However, they are useful as rough guides regarding future computing price/performance trends. Despite any fluctuation, it's clear that the price/performance curve for many technologies is exponential, offering astonishing improvement over time.

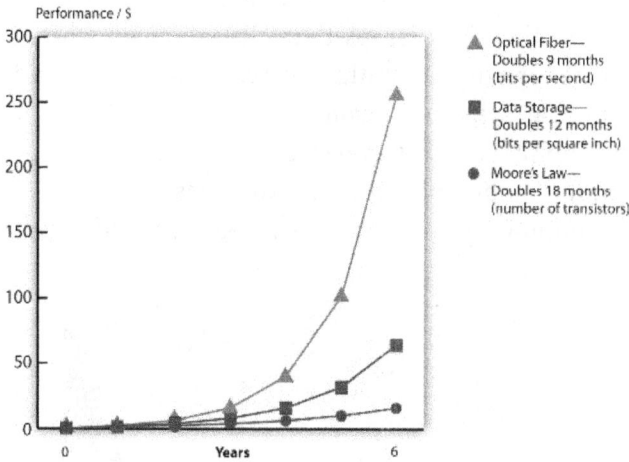

Figure 5.1 Advancing Rates of Technology (Silicon, Storage, Telecom)

Get Out Your Crystal Ball

Faster and cheaper makes possible the once impossible. As a manager, your job will be about predicting the future. First, consider how the economics of Moore's Law opens new markets. When technology gets cheap, **price elasticity** kicks in. Tech products are highly *price elastic*, meaning consumers buy more products as they become cheaper[4]. And it's not just that existing customers load up on more tech; entire *new markets* open up as firms find new uses for these new chips.

Just look at the *five waves of computing* we've seen over the previous five decades (Copeland, 2005). In the *first wave* in the 1960s, computing was limited to large, room-sized mainframe computers that only governments and big corporations could afford. Moore's Law kicked in during the 1970s for the *second wave*, and minicomputers were a hit. These were refrigerator-sized computers that were as speedy as or speedier than the prior generation of mainframes, yet were affordable by work groups, factories, and smaller organizations. The 1980s brought *wave three* in the form of PCs, and by the end of the decade nearly every white-collar worker in America had a fast and cheap computer on their desk. In the 1990s *wave four* came in the form of Internet computing—cheap servers and networks made it possible to scatter data around the world, and with more power, personal computers displayed graphical interfaces that replaced complex commands with easy-to-understand menus accessible by a mouse click. At the close of the last century, the majority of the population in many developed countries had home PCs, as did most libraries and schools.

Now we're in *wave five*, where computers are so fast and so inexpensive that they have become ubiquitous—woven into products in ways few imagined years before. Silicon is everywhere! It's in the throwaway radio frequency identification (RFID) tags that track your luggage at the airport. It provides the smarts in the world's billion-plus mobile phones. It's the brains inside robot vacuum cleaners, next generation Legos, and the table lamps that change color when the stock market moves up or down. These digital shifts can rearrange entire industries. Consider that today the firm that sells more cameras than any other is Nokia, a firm that offers increasingly sophisticated chip-based digital cameras as a giveaway as part of its primary product, mobile phones. This shift has occurred with such sweeping impact that former photography giants Pentax, Konica, and Minolta have all exited the camera business.

One of the most agile surfers of this *fifth wave* is Apple, Inc.—a firm with a product line that is now so broad that in January 2007, it dropped the word "Computer" from its name. Apple's breakout resurgence owes a great deal to the iPod. At launch, the original iPod sported a 5 GB hard drive that Steve Jobs declared would "put 1,000 songs in your pocket." Cost? $399. Less than six years later, Apple's highest-capacity iPod sold for fifty dollars less than the original, yet held *forty times* the songs. By that time the firm had sold over one hundred fifty million iPods—an adoption rate faster than the original Sony Walkman. Apple's high-end models have morphed into Internet browsing devices capable of showing maps, playing videos, and gulping down songs from Starbucks' Wi-Fi while waiting in line for a latte.

The original iPod has also become the jumping-off point for new business lines including the iPhone, Apple TV, iPad, and iTunes. As an online store, iTunes is always open. ITunes regularly sells tens of millions of songs on Christmas Day alone, a date when virtually all of its offline competition is closed for the holiday. In a short five years after its introduction, iTunes has sold over 4 billion songs and has vaulted past retail giants Wal-Mart, Best Buy, and Target to become the number one music retailer in the world. Today's iTunes is a digital media powerhouse, selling movies, TV shows, games, and other applications. And with podcasting, Apple's iTunes University even lets students at participating schools put their professors' lectures on their gym playlist for free. Surfing the fifth wave has increased the value of Apple stock sixteenfold six years after the iPod's launch. Ride these waves to riches, but miss the power and promise of Moore's Law and you risk getting swept away in its riptide. Apple's rise occurred while Sony, a firm once synonymous with portable music, sat on the sidelines unwilling to get on the surfboard. Sony's stock stagnated, barely moving in six years. The firm has laid off thousands of workers while ceding leadership in digital music (and video) to Apple.

Table 5.1 Top U.S. Music Retailers

1992	2005	2006	2008
1. Musicland	1. Wal-Mart	1. Wal-Mart	1. iTunes
2. The Handleman	2. Best Buy	2. Best Buy	2. Wal-Mart
3. Tower Records	3. Target	3. Target	3. Best Buy
4. Trans World Music	7. iTunes	4. iTunes, Amazon tie	4. Amazon, Target tie
Moore's Law restructures industries. The firms that dominated music sales when you were born are now bankrupt, while one that had never sold a physical music CD now sells more than anyone else.			

Source: Michelle Quinn and Dawn C. Chmielewski, "Top Music Seller's Store Has No Door," Los Angeles Times, April 4, 2008.

While the change in hard drive prices isn't directly part of Moore's Law (hard drives are magnetic storage, not silicon chips), as noted earlier, the faster and cheaper phenomenon applies to storage, too. Look to Amazon as another example of jumping onto a once-impossible opportunity courtesy of the price/performance curve. When Amazon.com was founded in 1995, the largest corporate database was one terabyte, or TB (see Note 5.14 "Bits and Bytes" below) in size. In 2003, the firm offered its "Search Inside the Book" feature, digitizing the images and text from thousands of books in its catalog. "Search Inside the Book" lets customers peer into a book's contents in a way that's both faster and more accurate than browsing a physical bookstore. Most importantly for Amazon and its suppliers, titles featured in "Search Inside the Book" enjoyed a 7 percent sales increase over nonsearchable books. When "Search Inside the Book" launched, the database to support this effort was 20 TB in size. In just eight years, the firm found that it made good business sense to launch an effort that was a full *twenty times* larger than anything used by *any* firm less than a decade earlier. And of course, all of these capacities seem laughably small by today's standards. (See Chapter 11 "The Data Asset: Databases, Business Intelligence, and Competitive Advantage".) For Amazon, the impossible had not just become possible; it became good business. By 2009, digital books weren't just for search; they were for sale. Amazon's Kindle reader (a Moore's Law marvel sporting a microprocessor and flash storage) became the firm's top-selling product in terms of both unit sales and dollar volume. The real business opportunity for Amazon isn't Kindle as a consumer electronics device but as an ever-present, never-closing store, which also provides the firm with a migration path from atoms to bits. (For more on that topic, see Chapter 4 "Netflix: The Making of an E-commerce Giant and the Uncertain Future of Atoms to Bits".) By 2009, Amazon (by then the largest book retailer in North America) reported, "For books that are available on the Kindle, sales are already 35 percent of the same books in print" (Schonfeld, 2009). Apple's 2010 introduction of the iPad, complete with an iBook store, shows how Moore's Law rewrites the boundaries of competition—bringing a firm that started as a computer retailer and a firm that started as an online bookstore in direct competition with one another.

Here's another key implication—if you are producing products with a significant chip-based component, the chips inside that product rapidly fall in value. That's great when it makes your product cheaper and opens up new markets for your firm, but it can be deadly if you overproduce and have excess inventory sitting on shelves for long periods of time. Dell claims its inventory depreciates as much as a single percentage point in value each week (Breen, 2004). That's a big incentive to carry as little inventory as possible, and to unload it, fast!

While the strategic side of tech may be the most glamorous, Moore's Law impacts mundane management tasks, as well. From an accounting and budgeting perspective, as a manager you'll need to consider a number of questions: How long will your computing equipment remain useful? If you keep upgrading computing and software, what does this mean for your capital expense budget? Your training budget? Your ability to make well-reasoned predictions regarding tech's direction will be key to answering these questions.

5.2 THE DEMISE OF MOORE'S LAW?

Moore simply observed that we're getting better over time at squeezing more stuff into tinier spaces. Moore's Law is possible because the distance between the pathways inside silicon chips gets smaller with each successive generation. While chip plants (semiconductor fabrication facilities, or **fabs**) are incredibly expensive to build, each new generation of fabs can crank out more chips per **silicon wafer**. And since the pathways are closer together, electrons travel shorter distances. If electronics now travel half the distance to make a calculation, that means the chip is twice as fast.

But the shrinking can't go on forever, and we're already starting to see three interrelated forces—*size*, *heat*, and *power*—threatening to slow down the Moore's Law gravy train. When you make processors smaller, the more tightly packed electrons will heat up a chip—so much so that unless today's most powerful chips are cooled down, they will melt inside their packaging. To keep the fastest computers cool, most PCs, laptops, and video game consoles need fans, and most corporate data centers have elaborate and expensive air conditioning and venting systems to prevent a meltdown. A trip through the Facebook data center during its recent rise would show that the firm was a "hot" start-up in more ways than one. The firm's servers ran so hot that the Plexiglas sides of the firm's server racks were warped and melting (McGirt, 2007)! The need to cool modern data centers draws a lot of power and that costs a lot of money.

The chief eco officer at Sun Microsystems has claimed that computers draw 4 to 5 percent of the world's power. Google's chief technology officer has said that the firm spends more to power its servers than the cost of the servers themselves (Kirkpatrick, 2007). Microsoft, Yahoo! and Google have all built massive data centers in the Pacific Northwest, away from their corporate headquarters, specifically choosing these locations for access to cheap hydroelectric power. Google's location in The Dalles, Oregon, is charged a cost per kilowatt hour of two cents by the local power provider, less than one-fifth of the eleven-cent rate the firm pays in Silicon

Valley (Mehta, 2006)[1]. This difference means big savings for a firm that runs more than a million servers.

And while these powerful shrinking chips are getting hotter and more costly to cool, it's also important to realize that chips can't get smaller forever. At some point Moore's Law will run into the unyielding laws of nature. While we're not certain where these limits are, chip pathways certainly can't be shorter than a single molecule, and the actual physical limit is likely larger than that. Get too small and a phenomenon known as quantum tunneling kicks in, and electrons start to slide off their paths. Yikes!

Buying Time

One way to overcome this problem is with **multicore microprocessors**, made by putting two or more lower power processor cores (think of a core as the calculating part of a microprocessor) on a single chip. Philip Emma, IBM's Manager of Systems Technology and Microarchitecture, offers an analogy. Think of the traditional fast, hot, single-core processors as a three hundred-pound lineman, and a dual-core processor as two 160-pound guys. Says Emma, "A 300-pound lineman can generate a lot of power, but two 160-pound guys can do the same work with less overall effort" (Ashton, 2005). For many applications, the multicore chips will outperform a single speedy chip, while running cooler and drawing less power. Multicore processors are now mainstream.

Today, most PCs and laptops sold have at least a two-core (dual-core) processor. The Microsoft Xbox 360 has three cores. The PlayStation 3 includes the so-called *cell processor* developed by Sony, IBM, and Toshiba that runs nine cores. By 2010, Intel began shipping PC processors with eight cores, while AMD introduced a twelve- core chip. Intel has even demonstrated chips with upwards of fifty cores.

Multicore processors can run older software written for single-brain chips. But they usually do this by using only one core at a time. To reuse the metaphor above, this is like having one of our 160-pound workers lift away, while the other one stands around watching. Multicore operating systems can help achieve some performance gains. Versions of Windows or the Mac OS that are aware of multicore processors can assign one program to run on one core, while a second application is assigned to the next core. But in order to take full advantage of multicore chips, applications need to be rewritten to split up tasks so that smaller portions of a problem are executed simultaneously inside each core.

Writing code for this "divide and conquer" approach is not trivial. In fact, developing software for multicore systems is described by Shahrokh Daijavad, software lead for next-generation computing systems at IBM, as "one of the hardest things you learn in computer science" (Ashton, 2005). Microsoft's chief research and strategy officer has called coding for these chips "the most conceptually different [change] in the history of modern computing" (Copeland, 2008). Despite this challenge, some of the most aggressive adaptors of multicore chips have been video game console manufacturers. Video game applications are particularly well-suited for multiple cores since, for example, one core might be used to render the background, another to draw objects, another for the "physics engine" that moves the objects around, and yet another to handle Internet communications for multiplayer games.

Another approach to breathing life into Moore's Law is referred to as **stacked or three-dimensional semiconductors**. In this approach, engineers slice a flat chip into pieces, then reconnect the pieces vertically, making a sort of "silicon sandwich." The chips are both faster and cooler since electrons travel shorter distances. What was once an end-to-end trip on a conventional chip might just be a tiny movement up or down on a stacked chip. But stacked chips present their own challenges. In the same way that a skyscraper is more difficult and costly to design and build than a ranch house, 3-D semiconductors are tougher to design and manufacture. IBM has developed stacked chips for mobile phones, claiming the technique improves power efficiency by up to 40 percent. HP Labs is using a technology called *memristors*, or memory resistors, to improve on conventional transistors and speed the transition to 3-D chips, yielding significant improvement over 2-D offerings (Markoff, 2010).

5.3 BRINGING TOGETHER BRAINS: SUPERCOMPUTING AND GRID COMPUTING INFORMATION SYSTEMS

As Moore's Law makes possible the once impossible, businesses have begun to demand access to the world's most powerful computing technology. **Supercomputers** are computers that are among the fastest of any in the world at the time of their introduction[1]. Supercomputing was once the domain of governments and high-end research labs, performing tasks such as simulating the explosion of nuclear devices, or analyzing large-scale weather and climate phenomena. But it turns out with a bit of tweaking, the algorithms used in this work are profoundly useful to business. Consider perhaps the world's most well-known supercomputer, IBM's Deep Blue, the machine that rather controversially beat chess champion Garry Kasparov. While there is not a burning need for chess-playing computers in the world's corporations, it turns out that the computing algorithms to choose the best among multiple chess moves are similar to the math behind choosing the best combination of airline flights.

One of the first customers of Deep Blue technologies was United Airlines, which gained an ability to examine three hundred and fifty thousand flight path combinations for its scheduling systems—a figure well ahead of the previous limit of three thousand. Estimated savings through better yield management? Over $50 million! Finance found uses, too. An early adopter was CIBC (the Canadian Imperial

Bank of Commerce), one of the largest banks in North America. Each morning CIBC uses a supercomputer to run its portfolio through Monte Carlo simulations that aren't all that different from the math used to simulate nuclear explosions. An early adopter of the technology, at the time of deployment, CIBC was the only bank that international regulators allowed to calculate its own capital needs rather than use boilerplate ratios. That cut capital on hand by hundreds of millions of dollars, a substantial percentage of the bank's capital, saving millions a year in funding costs. Also noteworthy: the supercomputer-enabled, risk-savvy CIBC was relatively unscathed by the subprime crisis.

Modern supercomputing is typically done via a technique called **massively parallel** processing (computers designed with many microprocessors that work together, simultaneously, to solve problems). The fastest of these supercomputers are built using hundreds of microprocessors, all programmed to work in unison as one big brain. While supercomputers use special electronics and software to handle the massive load, the processors themselves are often of the off-the-shelf variety that you'd find in a typical PC. Virginia Tech created what at the time was the world's third-fastest supercomputer by using chips from 1,100 Macintosh computers lashed together with off- the-shelf networking components. The total cost of the system was just $5.2 million, far less than the typical costfor such burly hardware. The Air Force recently issued a request-for-proposal to purchase 2,200 PlayStation 3 systems in hopes of crafting a supercheap, superpowerful machine using off-the-shelf parts.

Another technology, known as **grid computing**, is further transforming the economics of supercomputing. With grid computing, firms place special software on its existing PCs or servers that enables these computers to work together on a common problem. Large organizations may have thousands of PCs, but they're not necessarily being used all the time, or at full capacity. With grid software installed on them, these idle devices can be marshaled to attack portions of a complex task as if they collectively were one massively parallel supercomputer. This technique radically changes the economics of high-performance computing. *BusinessWeek* reports that while a middle-of-the-road supercomputer could run as much as $30 million, grid computing software and services to perform comparable tasks can cost as little as twenty-five thousand dollars, assuming an organization already has PCs and servers in place.

An early pioneer in grid computing is the biotech firm Monsanto. Monsanto enlists computers to explore ways to manipulate genes to create crop strains that are resistant to cold, drought, bugs, pesticides, or that are more nutritious. Previously with even the largest computer Monsanto had in-house, gene analysis was taking six weeks and the firm was able to analyze only ten to fifty genes a year. But by leveraging grid computing, Monsanto has reduced gene analysis to less than a day. The fiftyfold time savings now lets the firm consider thousands of genetic combinations in a year (Schwartz, et. al., 2006). Lower R&D time means faster time to market—critical to both the firm and its customers.

Grids are now everywhere. Movie studios use them to create special effects and animated films. Proctor & Gamble has used grids to redesign the manufacturing process for Pringles potato chips. GM and Ford use grids to simulate crash tests, saving millions in junked cars and speeding time to market. Pratt and Whitney test aircraft engine designs on a grid. And biotech firms including Aventis, GlaxoSmithKline, and Pfizer push their research through a quicker pipeline by harnessing grid power. JP Morgan Chase even launched a grid effort that mimics CIBC's supercomputer, but at a fraction of the latter's cost. By the second year of operation, the JPMorgan Chase grid was saving the firm $5 million per year.

You can join a grid, too. SETI@Home turns your computer screen saver into a method to help "search for extraterrestrial intelligence," analyzing data from the Arecibo radio telescope system in Puerto Rico (no E.T. spotted yet). FightAids@Home will enlist your PC to explore AIDS treatments. And Folding@Home is an effort by Stanford researchers to understanding the science of protein-folding within diseases such as Alzheimer's, cancer, and cystic fibrosis. A version of Folding@Home software for the PlayStation 3 had enlisted over half a million consoles within months of release. Having access to these free resources is an enormous advantage for researchers. Says the director of Folding@Home, "Even if we were given all of the NSF supercomputing centers combined for a couple of months, that is still fewer resources than we have now" (Johnson, 2002).

Multicore, massively parallel, and grid computing are all related in that each attempts to lash together multiple computing devices so that they can work together to solve problems. Think of multicore chips as having several processors in a single chip. Think of massively parallel supercomputers as having several chips in one computer, and think of grid computing as using existing computers to work together on a single task (essentially a computer made up of multiple computers). While these technologies offer great promise, they're all subject to the same limitation: software must be written to divide existing problems into smaller pieces that can be handled by each core, processor, or computer, respectively. Some problems, such as simulations, are easy to split up, but for problems that are linear (where, for example, step two can't be started until the results from step one are known), the multiple-brain approach doesn't offer much help.

Massive clusters of computers running software that allows them to operate as a unified service also enable new service-based computing models, such as **software as a service (SaaS)** and **cloud computing**. In these models, organizations replace traditional software and hardware that they would run in-house with services that are delivered online. Google, Microsoft, Salesforce.com, and Amazon are among the firms that have sunk billions into these Moore's Law–enabled **server farms**, creating entirely new businesses that promise to radically redraw the software and hardware landscape while bringing gargantuan computing power to the little guy. (See Chapter 10 "Software in Flux: Partly Cloudy and Sometimes Free".)

Moore's Law will likely hit its physical limit in your lifetime, but no one really knows if this "Moore's Wall" is a decade away or more. What lies ahead is anyone's guess. Some technologies, such as still-experimental quantum computing, could make computers that are more powerful than all the world's conventional computers combined. Think strategically—new waves of innovation might soon be shouting "surf's up!"

5.4 THE NEGATIVE SIDE OF MOORE'S LAW: E-WASTE

We should celebrate the great bounty Moore's Law and the tech industry bestow on our lives. Costs fall, workers become more productive, innovations flourish, and we gorge at a buffet of digital entertainment that includes music, movies, and games. But there is a dark side to this faster and cheaper advancement. A PC has an expected lifetime of three to five years. A cell phone? Two years or less. Rapid obsolescence means the creation of ever-growing mountains of discarded tech junk, known as electronic waste or **e-waste**. According to the U.S. Environmental Protection Agency (EPA), in 2007 the United States alone generated over 2.5 million tons of e- waste[1], and the results aren't pretty. Consumer electronics and computing equipment can be a toxic cocktail that includes cadmium, mercury, lead, and other hazardous materials. Once called the "effluent of the affluent," e- waste will only increase with the rise of living standards worldwide.

The quick answer would be to recycle this stuff. Not only does e-waste contain mainstream recyclable materials we're all familiar with, like plastics and aluminum, it also contains small bits of increasingly valuable metals such as silver, platinum, and copper. In fact, there's more gold in one pound of discarded tech equipment than in one pound of mined ore (Kovessy, 2008). But as the sordid record of e-waste management shows, there's often a disconnect between consumers and managers who *want* to do good and those efforts that are *actually* doing good. The complexities of the modern value chain, the vagaries of international law, and the nefarious actions of those willing to put profits above principle show how difficult addressing this problem will be.

The process of separating out the densely packed materials inside tech products so that the value in e-waste can be effectively harvested is extremely labor intensive, more akin to reverse manufacturing than any sort of curbside recycling efforts. Sending e-waste abroad can be ten times cheaper than dealing with it at home

(Bodeen, 2007), so it's not surprising that up to 80 percent of the material dropped off for recycling is eventually exported (Royte, 2006). Much of this waste ends up in China, South Asia, or sub-Saharan Africa, where it is processed in dreadful conditions.

Consider the example of Guiyu, China, a region whose poisoning has been extensively chronicled by organizations such as the Silicon Valley Toxics Coalition, the Basel Action Network (BAN), and Greenpeace. Workers in and around Guiyu toil without protective equipment, breathing clouds of toxins generated as they burn the plastic skins off of wires to get at the copper inside. Others use buckets, pots, or wok-like pans (in many cases the same implements used for cooking) to sluice components in acid baths to release precious metals—recovery processes that create even more toxins. Waste sludge and the carcasses of what's left over are most often dumped in nearby fields and streams. Water samples taken in the region showed lead and heavy metal contamination levels some four hundred to six hundred times greater than what international standards deem safe (Grossman, 2006). The area is so polluted that drinking water must be trucked in from eighteen miles away. Pregnancies are six times more likely to end in miscarriage, and 70 percent of the kids in the region have too much lead in their blood[2].

Figure 5.2 Photos from Guiyu, China (Biggs, 2008)

China cares about its environment. The nation has banned the importing of e-waste since 2000 (Grossman, 2006). But corruption ensures that e-waste continues to flow into the country. According to one exporter, all that's required to get e-waste past customs authorities is to tape a one-hundred-dollar bill on the side of the container (Bodeen, 2007). Well-meaning U.S. recyclers, as well as those attempting to collect technology for reuse in poorer countries, are often in the dark as to where their products end up.

The trade is often brokered by middlemen who mask the eventual destination and fate of the products purchased. BAN investigators in Lagos, Nigeria, documented mountains of e-waste with labels from schools, U.S. government agencies, and even some of the world's largest corporations. And despite Europe's prohibition on exporting e-waste, many products originally labeled for repair and reuse end up in toxic recycling efforts. Even among those products that gain a second or third life in developing nations, the inevitable is simply postponed, with e-waste almost certain to end up in landfills that lack the protective groundwater barriers and environmental engineering of their industrialized counterparts. The reality is that e-waste management is extraordinarily difficult to monitor and track, and loopholes are rampant.

Thinking deeply about the ethical consequences of a firm's business is an imperative for the modern manager. A slip up (intentional or not) can, in seconds, be captured by someone with a cell phone, uploaded to YouTube, or offered in a blog posting for the world to see. When Dell was caught using Chinese prison labor as part of its recycling efforts, one blogger chastised the firm with a tweak of its marketing tagline, posting "Dude, you're getting a cell" (Russell, 2003). The worst cases expose firms to legal action and can tarnish a brand for years. Big firms are big targets, and environmentalists have been quick to push the best-known tech firms and retailers to take back their products for responsible recycling and to eliminate the worst toxins from their offerings.

Consider that even Apple (where Al Gore sits on the firm's Board of Directors), has been pushed by a coalition of environmental groups on all of these fronts. Critics have shot back that signaling out Apple is unfair. The firm was one of the first computer companies to eliminate lead-lined glass monitors from its product line, and has been a pioneer of reduced-sized packaging that leverage recyclable materials. And Apple eventually claimed the top in Greenpeace's "Greener Electronics" rankings (Dalrymple, 2010). But if the firm that counts Al Gore among its advisors can get tripped up on green issues, all firms are vulnerable.

Environmentalists see this pressure to deal with e-waste as yielding results: Apple and most other tech firms have continually moved to eliminate major toxins from their manufacturing processes. All this demonstrates that today's business leaders have to be far more attuned to the impact not only of their own actions, but also to those of their suppliers and partners. How were products manufactured? Using which materials? Under what conditions? What happens to items when they're discarded? Who provides collection and disposal? It also shows the futility of legislative efforts that don't fully consider and address the problems they are meant to target.

Which brings us back to Gordon Moore. To his credit, Moore is not just the founder of the world's largest microprocessor firm and first to identify the properties we've come to know as Moore's Law, he has also emerged as one of the world's leading supporters of environmental causes. The generosity of the Gordon and Betty Moore foundation includes, among other major contributions, the largest single gift to a private conservation organization. Indeed, Silicon Valley, while being the birthplace of products that become e-waste, also promises to be at the forefront of finding solutions to modern environmental challenges. The Valley's leading venture capitalists, including Sequoia and Kleiner Perkins (where Al Gore is now a partner), have started multimillion- dollar green investment funds, targeted at funding the next generation of sustainable, environmental initiatives.

REFERENCES

Ashton, A., "More Life for Moore's Law," BusinessWeek, June 20, 2005.

Biggs, J., "Guiyu, the E-waste Capital of China," CrunchGear, April 4, 2008.

Bodeen, C., "In 'E-waste' Heartland, a Toxic China," International Herald Tribune, November 18, 2007. Dalrymple, J., "Apple Ranks Highest among Greenpeace's Top Tech Companies," The Loop, January 7, 2010. Kovessy, P., "How to Trash Toxic Tech," Ottawa Business Journal, May 12, 2008.

Cane, A.,"A Valley By Any Other Name..." Financial Times, December 11, 2006.

Chen, Y. L., J. G. Analytis, J.-H. Chu, Z. K. Liu, S.-K. Mo, X. L. Qi, H. J. Zhang, et al., "Experimental Realization of a Three-Dimensional Topological Insulator, Bi2Te3," Science 325, no. 5937 (July 10, 2009): 178–81.

Copeland, M., "A Chip Too Far?" Fortune, September 1, 2008.

Greene, K., "Intel Looks Beyond Silicon," Technology Review, December 11, 2007.

Grossman, E., "Where Computers Go to Die—and Kill," Salon.com, April 10, 2006, http://www.salon.com/news/ feature/2006/04/10/ewaste.

Johnson, G., "Supercomputing '@Home' Is Paying Off," New York Times, April 23, 2002.

Kaihla, P., "Quantum Leap," Business 2.0, August 1, 2004.

Kirkpatrick, D., "The Greenest Computer Company under the Sun," April 13, 2007. Markoff, J., "HP Sees a Revolution in Memory Chip," New York Times, April 7, 2010. McGirt, E., "Hacker, Dropout, C.E.O.," Fast Company, May 2007.

MacDonald, G., "Don't Recycle 'E-waste' with Haste, Activists Warn," USA Today, July 6, 2008. Royte, E., "E-waste@Large," New York Times, January 27, 2006.

Mehta, S., "Behold the Server Farm," Fortune, August 1, 2006.

Russell, J., "Dell under Attack over Using Prison Labour," Inquirer, January 10, 2003. See also http://laughingmeme.org/2003/03/23/dell-recycling-a-ways-to-go-still.

Schwartz, P., C. Taylor, and R. Koselka, "The Future of Computing: Quantum Leap," Fortune, August 2, 2006.

Schwartz, P., C. Taylor, and R. Koselka, "The Future of Computing: Quantum Leap," Fortune, August 2, 2006.

NETWORK EFFECTS: AN OVERVIEW

6.1 INTRODUCTION: AN OVERVIEW

Network effects are sometimes referred to as "Metcalfe's Law" or "Network Externalities." But don't let the dull names fool you—this concept is rocket fuel for technology firms. Bill Gates leveraged network effects to turn Windows and Office into virtual monopolies and in the process became the wealthiest man in America. Mark Zuckerberg of Facebook, Pierre Omidyar of eBay, Caterina Fake and Stewart Butterfield of Flickr, Kevin Rose of Digg, Evan Williams and Biz Stone of Twitter, Chris DeWolfe and Tom Anderson—the MySpace guys—all of these entrepreneurs have built massive user bases by leveraging the concept. When network effects are present, *the value of a product or service increases as the number of users grows.* Simply, more users = more value. Of course, most products aren't subject to network effects—you probably don't care if someone wears the same socks, uses the same pancake syrup, or buys the same trash bags as you. But when network effects are present they're among *the most important* reasons you'll pick one product or service over another. You may care very much, for example, if others are part of your social network, if your video game console is popular, if the Wikipedia article you're referencing has had prior readers. And all those folks who bought HD DVD players sure were bummed when the rest of the world declared Blu-ray the winner. In each of these examples, network effects are at work.

6.2 WHAT'S THE SOURCE OF ALL THAT VALUE??

The value derived from network effects comes from three sources: exchange, staying power, and complementary benefits.

Exchange

Facebook for one person isn't much fun, and the first guy in the world with a fax machine didn't have much more than a paperweight. But as each new Facebook friend or fax user comes online, a network becomes more valuable because its users can potentially communicate with more people. These examples show the importance of *exchange* in creating value. Every product or service subject to network effects fosters some kind of exchange. For firms leveraging technology, this might include anything you can represent in the ones and zeros of digital storage, such as movies, music, money, video games, and computer programs. And just about any standard that allows things to plug into one another, interconnect, or otherwise communicate will live or die based on its ability to snare network effects.

Staying Power

Users don't want to buy a product or sign up for a service that's likely to go away, and a number of factors can halt the availability of an effort: a firm could bankrupt or fail to attract a critical mass of user support, or a rival may successfully invade its market and draw away current customers. Networks with greater numbers of users suggest a stronger **staying power**. The staying power, or long-term viability, of a product or service is particularly important for consumers of technology products. Consider that when someone buys a personal computer and makes a choice of Windows, Mac OS, or Linux, their investment over time usually greatly exceeds the initial price paid for the operating system. One invests in learning how to use a system, buying and installing software, entering preferences or other data, creating files—all of which mean that if a product isn't supported anymore, much of this investment is lost.

The concept of staying power (and the fear of being stranded in an unsupported product or service) is directly related to **switching costs** (the cost a consumer incurs when moving from one product to another) and switching costs can strengthen the value of network effects as a strategic asset. The higher the value of the user's overall investment, the more they're likely to consider the staying power of any offering before choosing to adopt it. Similarly, the more a user has invested in a product, the less likely he or she is to leave.

Switching costs also go by other names. You might hear the business press refer to products (particularly Web sites) as being "sticky" or creating "friction." Others may refer to the concept of "lock-in." And the elite Boston Consulting Group is really talking about a firm's switching costs when it refers to how well a company can create customers who are "barnacles" (that are tightly anchored to the firm) and not "butterflies" (that flutter away to rivals). The more friction available to prevent users from migrating to a rival, the greater the switching costs. And in a competitive market where rivals with new innovations show up all the time, that can be a very good thing!

Complementary Benefits

Complementary benefits are those products or services that add additional value to the network. These products might include "how-to" books, software add-ons, even labor. You'll find more books on auctioning over eBay, more virtual storefronts in Second Life, and more accountants that know Excel, than on any of their rivals. Why? Book authors, Second Life partners, and accountants invest their time where they're likely to reach the biggest market and get the greatest benefit. In auctions, virtual worlds, and spreadsheet software, eBay, Second Life, and Excel each dwarf their respective competition.

Products and services that encourage others to offer complementary goods are sometimes called **platforms**. Allowing other firms to contribute to your platform can be a brilliant strategy, because those firms will spend *their* time and money to enhance *your* offerings. Consider the billion-dollar hardware ecosystem that Apple has cultivated around the iPod. There are over ninety brands selling some 280 models of iPod speaker systems (Hansell, 2008). Thirty-four auto manufacturers now trumpet their cars as being iPod-ready, many with in-car docking stations and steering wheel iPod navigation systems. Each add-on enhances the value of choosing an iPod over a rival like the Microsoft Zune. And now with the App Store for the iPhone, iPod touch, and iPad, Apple is doing the same thing with software add-ons. Software-based ecosystems can grow very quickly. In less than a year after its introduction, the iTunes App Store boasted over fifty thousand applications, collectively downloaded over one billion times.

These three value-adding sources—*exchange*, *staying power*, and *complementary benefits*—often work together to reinforce one another in a way that makes the network effect even stronger. When users *exchanging* information attract more users, they can also attract firms offering *complementary* products. When developers of complementary products invest time writing software—and users install, learn, and customize these products—switching costs are created that enhance the *staying power* of a given network. From a strategist's perspective this can be great news for dominant firms in markets where network effects exist. The larger your network, the more difficult it becomes for rivals to challenge your leadership position.

6.3 ONE-SIDED OR TWO-SIDED MARKETS?

Network Structure Understanding

To understand the key sources of network value, it's important to recognize the structure of the network. Some networks derive most of their value from a single class of users. An example of this kind of network is instant messaging (IM). While there might be some add-ons for the most popular IM tools, they don't influence most users' choice of an IM system. You pretty much choose one IM tool over another based on how many of your contacts you can reach. Economists would call IM a **one-sided market** (a market that derives most of its value from a single class of users), and the network effects derived from IM users attracting more IM users as being **same-side**

exchange benefits (benefits derived by interaction among members of a single class of participant).

But some markets are comprised of two distinct categories of network participant. Consider video games. People buy a video game console largely based on the number of really great games available for the system. Software developers write games based on their ability to reach the greatest number of paying customers, so they're most likely to write for the most popular consoles first. Economists would call this kind of network a **two-sided market** (network markets comprised of two distinct categories of participant, both of which that are needed to deliver value for the network to work). When an increase in the number of users on one side of the market (console owners, for example) creates a rise in the other side (software developers), that's called a **cross-side exchange benefit**.

6.4 HOW ARE THESE MARKETS DIFFERENT?

When network effects play a starring role, competition in an industry can be fundamentally different than in conventional, nonnetwork industries.

First, network markets experience *early, fierce competition*. The positive-feedback loop inherent in network effects—where the biggest networks become even bigger—causes this. Firms are very aggressive in the early stages of these industries because once a leader becomes clear, *bandwagons* form, and new adopters begin to overwhelmingly favor the leading product over rivals, tipping the market in favor of one dominant firm or standard. This tipping can be remarkably swift. Once the majority of major studios and retailers began to back Blu-ray over HD DVD, the latter effort folded within weeks.

These markets are also often winner-take-all or winner-take-most, *exhibiting monopolistic tendencies* where one firm dominates all rivals. Look at all of the examples listed so far—in nearly every case the dominant player has a market share well ahead of all competitors. When, during the U.S. Microsoft antitrust trial, Judge Thomas Penfield Jackson declared Microsoft to be a **monopoly** (a market where there are many buyers but only one dominant seller), the collective response should have been "of course." Why? The *natural state* of a market where network effects are present (and this includes operating systems and Office software) is for there to be one major player. Since bigger networks offer more value, they can charge customers more. Firms with a commanding network effects advantage may also enjoy substantial bargaining power over partners. For example, Apple, which controls over 75 percent of digital music sales, for years was able to dictate song pricing, despite the tremendous protests of the record labels (Barnes, 2007). In fact, Apple's stranglehold was so strong that it leveraged bargaining power even though the "Big Four" record labels (Universal, Sony, EMI, and Warner) were themselves an **oligopoly** (a market dominated by a small number of powerful sellers) that together provide over 85 percent of music sold in the United States.

Finally, it's important to note that the best product or service doesn't always win. PlayStation 2 dominated the video console market over the original Xbox, despite the fact that nearly every review claimed the Xbox was hands-down a more technically superior machine. Why were users willing to choose an inferior product (PS2) over a superior one (Xbox)? The power of network effects! PS2 had more users, which attracted more developers offering more games.

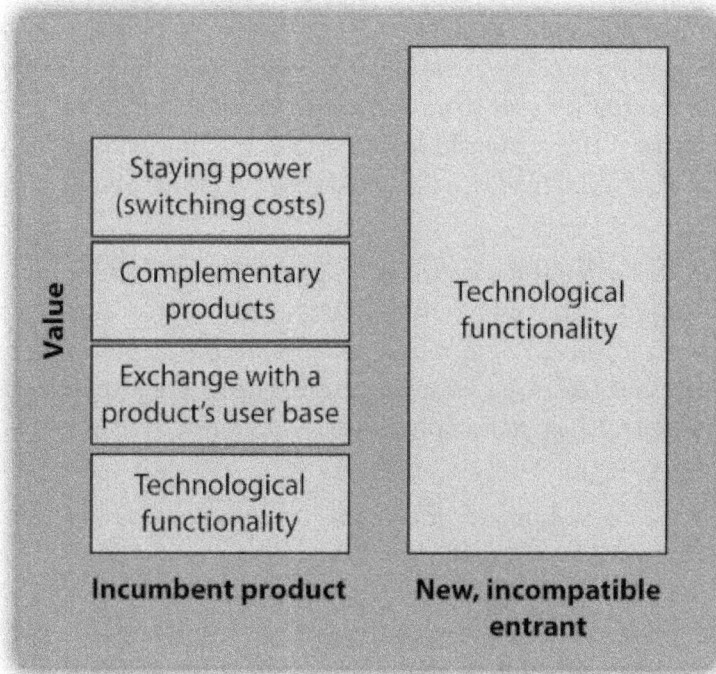

Figure 6.1 Battling a leader with network effects is tough1.

This last note is a critical point to any newcomer wishing to attack an established rival. Winning customers away from a dominant player in a network industry isn't as easy as offering a product or service that is better. Any product that is incompatible with the dominant network has to exceed the value of the technical features of the leading player, plus (since the newcomer likely starts without any users or third-party product complements) the value of the incumbent's exchange, switching cost, and complementary product benefit (see Figure 6.1). And the incumbent must not be able to easily copy any of the newcomer's valuable new innovations; otherwise the dominant firm will quickly match any valuable improvements made by rivals. As such, **technological leapfrogging**, or competing by offering a superior generation of technology, can be really tough (Schilling, 2003).

6.5 THE ROLE OF NETWORK EFFECTS IN COMPETITION

Why do you care whether networks are one-sided, two-sided, or some sort of hybrid? Well, when crafting your plan for market dominance, it's critical to know if network effects exist, how strong they might be, where they come from, and how they might be harnessed to your benefit. Here's a quick rundown of the tools at your disposal when competing in the presence of network effects.

Move Early

In the world of network effects, this is a biggie. Being first allows your firm to start the network effects snowball rolling in your direction. In Japan, worldwide auction leader eBay showed up just five months after Yahoo! launched its Japanese auction service. But eBay was never able to mount a credible threat and ended up pulling out of the market. Being just five months late cost eBay billions in lost sales, and the firm eventually retreated, acknowledging it could never unseat Yahoo!'s network effects lead.

Another key lesson from the loss of eBay Japan? Exchange depends on the ability to communicate! EBay's huge network effects in the United States and elsewhere didn't translate to Japan because most Japanese aren't comfortable with English, and most English speakers don't know Japanese. The language barrier made Japan a "greenfield" market with no dominant player, and Yahoo!'s early move provided the catalyst for victory.

Timing is often critical in the video game console wars, too. Sony's PlayStation 2 enjoyed an eighteen-month lead over the technically superior Xbox (as well as Nintendo's GameCube). That time lead helped to create what for years was the single most profitable division at Sony. By contrast, the technically superior PS3 showed up months after Xbox 360 and at roughly the same time as the Nintendo Wii, and has struggled in its early years, racking up multibillion-dollar losses for Sony (Null, 2008).

Subsidize Adoption

Starting a network effect can be tough—there's little incentive to join a network if there's no one in the system to communicate with. In one admittedly risky strategy, firms may offer to subsidize initial adoption in hopes that network effects might kick in shortly after. Subsidies to adopters might include a price reduction, rebate, or other giveaways. PayPal, a service that allows users to pay one another using credit cards, gave users a modest rebate as a sign-up incentive to encourage adoption of its new effort (in one early promotion, users got back fifteen dollars when spending their first thirty dollars). This brief subsidy paid to early adopters paid off handsomely. EBay later tried to enter the market with a rival effort, but as a late mover its effort was never able to overcome PayPal's momentum. PayPal was eventually purchased by eBay for $1.5 billion, and the business unit is now considered one of eBay's key drivers of growth and profit.

Leverage Viral Promotion

Since all products and services foster some sort of exchange, it's often possible to leverage a firm's customers to promote the product or service. Internet calling service Skype has over five hundred million registered users yet has spent almost nothing on advertising. Most Skype users were recruited by others who shared the word on free and low-cost Internet calls. Within Facebook, feeds help activities to spread virally (see Chapter 8 "Facebook: Building a Business from the Social Graph"). Feeds blast updates on user activities on the site, acting as a catalyst for friends to join groups and load applications that their buddies have already signed up for.

Expand by Redefining the Market

If a big market attracts more users (and in two-sided markets, more complements), why not redefine the space to bring in more users? Nintendo did this when launching the Wii. While Sony and Microsoft focused on the graphics and raw processing power favored by hard-core male gamers, Nintendo chose to develop a machine to appeal to families, women, and age groups that normally shunned alien shoot-'em ups. By going after a bigger, redefined market, Nintendo was able to rack up sales that exceeded the Xbox 360, even though it followed the system by twelve months (Sanchanta, 2007).

Market expansion sometimes puts rivals who previously did not compete on a collision course as markets undergo **convergence** (when two or more markets, once considered distinctly separate, begin to offer similar features and capabilities). Consider the market for portable electronic devices. Separate product categories for media players, cameras, gaming devices, phones, and global positioning systems (GPS) are all starting to merge. Rather than cede its dominance as a media player, Apple leveraged a strategy known as **envelopment**, where a firm seeks to make an existing market a subset of its product offering. Apple deftly morphed the iPod into the iPhone, a device that captures all of these product categories in one device. But the firm went further; the iPhone is Wi-Fi capable, offers browsing, e-mail, and an application platform based on a scaled-down version of the same OS X operating system used in Macintosh computers. As a "Pocket Mac," the appeal of the device broadened beyond just the phone or music player markets, and within two quarters of launch, iPhone become the second-leading smartphone in North America— outpacing Palm, Microsoft, Motorola and every other rival, except RIM's BlackBerry (Kim, 2007).

Alliances and Partnerships

Firms can also use partnerships to grow market share for a network. Sometimes these efforts bring rivals together to take out a leader. In a classic example, consider ATM networks. Citibank was the first major bank in New York City to offer a large ATM network. But the Citi network was initially proprietary, meaning customers of other banks couldn't take advantage of Citi ATMs. Citi's innovation was wildly popular and being a pioneer in rolling out cash machines helped the firm grow deposits fourfold in just a few years. Competitors responded with a partnership. Instead of each rival bank offering another incompatible network destined to trail Citi's lead, competing banks agreed to share their ATM operations through NYCE (New York Cash Exchange). While Citi's network was initially the biggest, after the NYCE launch a Chase bank customer could use ATMs at a host of other banks that covered a geography far greater than Citi offered alone. Network effects in ATMs shifted to the rival bank alliance, Citi eventually joined NYCE and today, nearly every ATM in the United States carries a NYCE sticker.

Google has often pushed an approach to encourage rivals to cooperate to challenge a leader. Its Open Social standard for social networking (endorsed by MySpace, LinkedIn, Bebo, Yahoo! and others) is targeted at offering a larger alternative to Facebook's more closed efforts (see Chapter 8 "Facebook: Building a Business from the Social Graph"), while its Android open source mobile phone operating system has gained commitments from many handset makers that collectively compete with Apple's iPhone.

Leverage Distribution Channels

Firms can also think about novel ways to distribute a product or service to consumers. Sun faced a challenge when launching the Java programming language—no computers could run it. In order for Java to work, computers need a little interpreter program called the Java Virtual Machine (JVM). Most users weren't willing to download the JVM if there were no applications written in Java, and no developers were willing to write in Java if no one could run their code. Sun broke the logjam when it *bundled* the JVM with Netscape's browser. When millions of users downloaded Netscape, Sun's software snuck in, almost instantly creating a platform of millions for would- be Java developers. Today, even though Netscape has failed, Sun's Java remains one of the world's most popular programming languages. Indeed, Java was cited as one of the main reasons for Oracle's 2009 acquisition of Sun, with Oracle's CEO saying the language represented "the single most important software asset we have ever acquired" (Ricadela, 2009).

As mentioned in Chapter 2 "Strategy and Technology: Concepts and Frameworks for Understanding What Separates Winners from Losers", Microsoft is in a particularly strong position to leverage this approach. The firm often bundles its new products into its operating systems, Office suite, Internet Explorer browser, and other offerings. The firm used this tactic to transform once market-leader Real Networks into an also-ran in streaming audio. Within a few years of bundling Windows Media Player (WMP) with its other products, WMP grabbed the majority of the market, while Real's share had fallen to below 10 percent[1] (Eisenmann et. al., 2006).

Caution is advised, however. Regional antitrust authorities may consider product bundling by dominant firms to be anticompetitive. European regulators have forced Microsoft to unbundle Windows Media Player from its operating system and to provide a choice of browsers alongside Internet Explorer.

Seed the Market

When Sony launched the PS3, it subsidized each console by selling at a price estimated at three hundred dollars below unit cost (Null, 2008). Subsidizing consoles is a common practice in the video game industry—game player manufacturers usually make most of their money through royalties paid by game developers. But Sony's subsidy had an additional benefit for the firm—it helped sneak a Blu-ray player into every home buying a PS3 (Sony was backing the Blu-ray standard over the rival HD DVD effort). Since Sony is also a movie studio and manufacturer of DVD players and other consumer electronics, it had a particularly strong set of assets to leverage to encourage the adoption of Blu-ray over rival HD DVD.

Giving away products for half of a two-sided market is an extreme example of this kind of behavior, but it's often used. In two-sided markets, you charge the one who will pay. Adobe gives away the Acrobat reader to build a market for the sale of software that creates Acrobat files. Firms with Yellow Page directories give away countless copies of their products, delivered straight to your home, in order to create a market for selling advertising. And Google does much the same by providing free, ad-supported search.

Encourage the Development of Complementary Goods

There are several ways to motivate others to create complementary goods for your network. These efforts often involve some form of developer subsidy or other free or discounted service. A firm may charge lower royalties or offer a period of royalty-free licensing. It can also offer free software development kits (SDKs), training programs, co-marketing dollars, or even start-up capital to potential suppliers. Microsoft and Apple both allow developers to sell their products online through Xbox LIVE Marketplace and iTunes, respectively. This channel lowers developer expenses by eliminating costs associated with selling physical inventory in brick-and-mortar stores and can provide a free way to reach millions of potential consumers without significant promotional spending.

Venture funds can also prompt firms to create complementary goods. Facebook announced it would spur development for the site in part by administering the fbFund, which initially pledged $10 million in start-up funding (in allotments of up to $250,000 each) to firms writing applications for its platform.

Leverage Backward Compatibility

Those firms that control a standard would also be wise to ensure that new products have **backward compatibility** with earlier offerings. If not, they reenter a market at installed-base zero and give up a major source of advantage—the switching costs built up by prior customers. For example, when Nintendo introduced its 16-bit Super Nintendo system, it was incompatible with the firm's highly successful prior generation 8-bit model. Rival Sega, which had entered the 16-bit market two years prior to Nintendo, had already built up a large library of 16-bit games for its system. Nintendo entered with only its debut titles, and no ability to play games owned by customers of its previous system, so there was little incentive for existing Nintendo fans to stick with the firm (Schilling, 2003).

Backward compatibility was the centerpiece of Apple's strategy to revitalize the Macintosh through its move to the Intel microprocessor. Intel chips aren't compatible with the instruction set used by the PowerPC processor used in earlier Mac models. Think of this as two entirely different languages—Intel speaks French, PowerPC speaks Urdu. To ease the transition, Apple included a free software-based **adaptor**, called Rosetta, that automatically emulated the functionality of the old chip on all new Macs (a sort of Urdu to French translator). By doing so, all new Intel Macs could use the base of existing software written for the old chip; owners of PowerPC Macs were able to upgrade while preserving their investment in old software; and software firms could still sell older programs while they rewrote applications for new Intel-based Macs.

Even more significant, since Intel is the same standard used by Windows, Apple developed a free software adaptor called Boot Camp that allowed Windows to be installed on Macs. Boot Camp (and similar solutions by other vendors) dramatically lowered the cost for Windows users to switch to Macs. Within two years of making the switch, Mac sales skyrocketed to record levels. Apple now boasts a commanding lead in notebook sales to the education market (Seitz, 2008), and a survey by Yankee Group found that 87 percent of corporations were using at least some Macintosh computers, up from 48 percent at the end of the PowerPC era two years earlier (Burrows, 2008).

Rivals: Be Compatible with the Leading Network

Companies will want to consider making new products compatible with the leading standard. Microsoft's Live Maps and Virtual Earth 3D arrived late to the Internet mapping game. Users had already put in countless hours building resources that meshed with Google Maps and Google Earth. But by adopting the same keyhole markup language (KML) standard used by Google, Microsoft could, as TechCrunch put it, "drink from Google's milkshake." Any work done by users for Google in KML could be used by Microsoft. Voilà, an instant base of add-on content!

Incumbents: Close Off Rival Access and Constantly Innovate

Oftentimes firms that control dominant networks will make compatibility difficult for rivals who try to connect with their systems. AOL has been reluctant to open up its instant messaging tool to rivals, and Skype for years had been similarly closed to non-Skype clients.

Firms that constantly innovate make it particularly difficult for competitors to become compatible. Again, we can look to Apple as an example of these concepts in action. While Macs run Windows, Windows computers can't run Mac programs. Apple has embedded key software in Mac hardware, making it tough for rivals to write a software emulator like Boot Camp that would let Windows PCs drink from the Mac milkshake. And if any firm gets close to cloning Mac hardware, Apple sues. The firm also modifies software on other products like the iPhone and iTunes each time wily hackers tap into closed aspects of its systems. And Apple has regularly moved to block third-party hardware, such as Palm's mobile phones, from plugging into iTunes. Even if firms create adaptors that emulate a standard, a firm that constantly innovates creates a moving target that's tough for others to keep up with.

Apple has been far more aggressive than Microsoft in introducing new versions of its software. Since the firm never stays still, would-be cloners never get enough time to create a reliable emulator that runs the latest Apple software.

Large, Well-Known Followers: Preannouncements

Large firms that find new markets attractive but don't yet have products ready for delivery might *preannounce* efforts in order to cause potential adaptors to sit on the fence, delaying a purchasing decision until the new effort rolls out. Preannouncements only work if a firm is large enough to pose a credible threat to current market participants. Microsoft, for example, can cause potential customers to hold off on selecting a rival because users see that the firm has the resources to beat most players (suggesting staying power). Statements from start-ups, however, often lack credibility to delay user purchases. The tech industry acronym for the impact firms try to impart on markets through preannouncements is *FUD* for fear, uncertainty, and doubt.

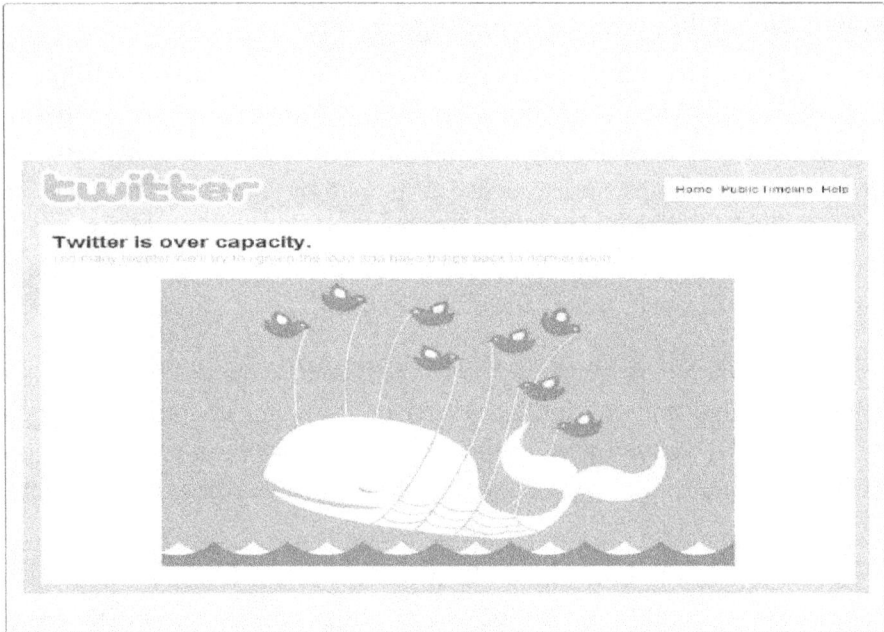

Feel confident! Now you've got a solid grounding in network effects, the key resource leveraged by some of the most dominant firms in technology. And these concepts apply beyond the realm of tech, too. Network effects can explain phenomena ranging from why some stock markets are more popular than others to why English is so widely spoken, even among groups of nonnative speakers. On top of that, the strategies explored in the last half of the chapter show how to use these principles to sniff out, create, and protect this key strategic asset. Go forth, tech pioneer—opportunity awaits!

REFERENCES

Barnes, B., "NBC Will Not Renew iTunes Contract," New York Times, August 31, 2007. Hutheesing, N., "Answer Your Phone, a Videogame Is Calling," Forbes, August 8, 2006.

Burrows, P., "The Mac in the Gray Flannel Suit," BusinessWeek, May 1, 2008.

Eisenmann, T., G. Parker, and M. Van Alstyne, "Strategies for Two-Sided Markets," Harvard Business Review, October 2006.

Eisenmann, T., G. Parker, and M. Van Alstyne, "Strategies for Two-Sided Markets," Harvard Business Review, October 2006.

Fils-Aimé, R., (presentation and discussion, Carroll School of Management, Boston College, Chestnut Hill, MA, April 6, 2009).

Hansell, S., "The iPod Economy and C.E.S.," New York Times, January 7, 2008.

Hansen, E. and D. Becker, "Real Hits Microsoft with $1 Billion Antitrust Suit," CNET, December 18, 2003, http://news.cnet.com/Real-hits-Microsoft-with-1-billion -antitrust-suit/2100-1025_3-5129316.html.

Kim, R., "iPhone No. 2 Smartphone Platform in North America," The Tech Chronicles— The San Francisco Chronicle, December 17, 2007.

Kim, W. C. and R. Mauborgne, Blue Ocean Strategy: How to Create Uncontested Market Space and Make Competition Irrelevant (Cambridge, MA: Harvard Business Press, 2005). See http://www.blueoceanstrategy.com.

Null, C., "Sony's Losses on PS3: $3 Billion and Counting," Yahoo! Today in Tech, June 27, 2008, http://tech.yahoo.com/blogs/null/96355.

Orlowski, A., "Taking Osborne out of the Osborne Effect," The Register, June 20, 2005. Ricadela, A., "Oracle's Bold Java Plans," BusinessWeek, June 2, 2009.

Parsons, M., "Microsoft: 'We'd Have Been Dead a Long Time Ago without Windows APIs," ZDNet UK, April 22, 2004, http://news.zdnet.co.uk/ software/0,1000000121 ,39152686,00.htm.

Sanchanta, M., "Nintendo's Wii Takes Console Lead," Financial Times, September 12, 2007.

Schilling, M., "Technological Leapfrogging: Lessons from the U.S. Video Game Console Industry," California Management Review, Spring 2003.

Schilling, M., "Technological Leapfrogging: Lessons from the U.S. Video Game Console Industry," California Management Review, Spring 2003.

Seitz, P., "An Apple for Teacher, Students: Mac Maker Surges in Education," Investor's Business Daily, August 8, 2008.

Stone, B., "Amid the Gloom, an E-commerce War," New York Times, October 12, 2008. Walker, R., "AntiPod," New York Times, August 8, 2008.

CHAPTER

WEB 2.0, SOCIAL MEDIA, AND PEER PRODUCTION

7

7.1 INTRODUCTION: AN OVERVIEW

Over the past few years a fundamentally different class of Internet services has attracted users, made headlines, and increasingly garnered breathtaking market valuations. Often referred to under the umbrella term "**Web 2.0**," these new services are targeted at harnessing the power of the Internet to empower users to collaborate, create resources, and share information in a distinctly different way from the static Web sites and transaction-focused storefronts that characterized so many failures in the dot-com bubble. Blogs, wikis, social networks, photo and video sharing sites, and tagging systems all fall under the Web 2.0 moniker, as do a host of supporting technologies and related efforts.

The term Web 2.0 is a tricky one because like so many popular technology terms there's not a precise definition. Coined by publisher and pundit Tim O'Reilly in 2003, techies often joust over the breadth of the Web 2.0 umbrella and over whether Web 2.0 is something new or simply an extension of technologies that have existed since the creation of the Internet. These arguments aren't really all that important. What is significant is how quickly the Web 2.0 revolution came about, how unexpected it was, and how deeply impactful these efforts have become. Some of the sites and services that have evolved and their Web 1.0 counterparts are listed in Table 7.1 "Web 1.0 versus Web 2.0"[1].

Table 7.1 Web 1.0 versus Web 2.0

Web 1.0		Web 2.0
DoubleClick	→	Google AdSense
Ofoto	→	Flickr
Akamai	→	BitTorrent
mp3.com	→	Napster
Britannica Online	→	Wikipedia

Web 1.0		Web 2.0
personal Web sites	→	blogging
evite	→	upcoming.org and Eventful
domain name speculation	→	search engine optimization
page views	→	cost per click
screen scraping	→	Web services
publishing	→	participation
content management systems	→	wikis
directories (taxonomy)	→	tagging ("folksonomy")
stickiness	→	syndication
instant messaging	→	Twitter
Monster.com	→	LinkedIn

To underscore the speed with which Web 2.0 arrived on the scene, and the impact of leading Web 2.0 services, consider the following efforts:

⊙ According to a spring 2008 report by Morgan Stanley, Web 2.0 services ranked as seven of the world's top ten most heavily trafficked Internet sites (YouTube, Live.com, MySpace, Facebook, Hi5, Wikipedia, and Orkut); only one of these sites (MySpace) was on the list in 2005 (Stanley, 2008).

⊙ With only seven full-time employees and an operating budget of less than $1 million, Wikipedia has become the Internet's fifth most visited site on the Internet (Kane & Fichman, 2009). The site boasts well over fifteen million articles in over two hundred sixty different languages, all of them contributed, edited, and fact-checked by volunteers.

⊙ Just two years after it was founded, MySpace was bought for $580 million by Rupert Murdoch's News Corporation (the media giant that owns the *Wall Street Journal* and the Fox networks, among other properties). By the end of 2007, the site accounted for some 12 percent of Internet minutes and had repeatedly ranked as the most-visited Web site in the United States (Chmielewski & Guynn, 2008). But rapid rise doesn't always mean a sustained following, and by the start of 2010, some were beginning to write the service's obituary as it failed to keep pace with Facebook (Malik, 2010).

⊙ The population of rival Facebook is now so large that it could be considered the third largest "nation" in the world. Half the site's users log in at least once a day, spending an average of fifty-five minutes a day on the site[2]. A fall 2007 investment from Microsoft pegged the firm's overall value at $15 billion, a number that would have made it the fifth most valuable Internet firm, despite annual revenues at the time of only $150 million (Arrington,

2007). Those revenues have been growing, with the privately held firm expected to bring in from $1.2 to $2 billion in 2010 (Vascellaro, 2010).

◉ Just twenty months after its founding, YouTube was purchased by Google for $1.65 billion. While Google struggles to figure out how to make profitable what is currently a money-losing resource hog (over twenty hours of video are uploaded to YouTube each minute) (Nakashima, 2008) the site has emerged as the Web's leading destination for video, hosting everything from apologies from JetBlue's CEO for service gaffes to questions submitted as part of the 2008 U.S. presidential debates. Fifty percent of YouTube's roughly three hundred million users visit the site at least once a week (Stanley, 2008).

◉ Twitter has emerged as a major force that can break news and shape public opinion. China and Iran are among the governments so threatened by the power of Twitter-fueled data sharing that each has, at times, blocked Twitter access within their borders. At the first Twitter-focused Chirp conference in April 2010, Twitter boasted a population of over one hundred million users who have collectively posted more than ten billion tweets (Twitter messages). By this time, the service had also spawned an ecosystem of over one hundred thousand registered Twitter-supporting apps. In another nod to the service's significance, the U.S. Library of Congress announced plans to archive every tweet ever sent (Bolton, 2010; Shaer, 2010).

◉ Services such as Twitter, Yelp, and the highly profitable TripAdvisor have unleashed the voice of the customer so that it is now often captured and broadcast immediately at the point of service. Reviews are now incorporated into search results and maps, making them the first thing many customers see when encountering a brand online. TripAdvisor, with just five hundred employees, contributes over $150 million in profits to parent company Expedia (at roughly 50 percent margins) (Wash, 2009; Burrows, 2010),

Table 7.2 Major Social Media Tools

	Description	Features	Technology Providers	Use Case Examples
Blogs	Short for "Web log"—an online diary that keeps a running chronology of entries. Readers can comment on posts. Can connect to other blogs through blog rolls or trackbacks. Key uses: Share ideas, obtain feedback, mobilize a community.	Ease of use Reverse chronology Comment threads Persistence Searchability Tags Trackbacks	Blogger (Google) WordPress Six Apart (TypePad and Movable Type) Tumblr	News outlets Google Graco GM Kaiser Permanente Marriott Microsoft
Wikis	A Web site that anyone can edit directly from within the browser. Key uses: Collaborate on common tasks or to create a common knowledge base.	All changes are attributed A complete revision history is maintained, with the ability to roll back changes and revert to earlier versions Automatic notification of updates Searchability Tags Monitoring	Socialtext PBWorks Google Sites WetPaint Microsoft SharePoint Apple OS X Server	Dresdner Kleinwort Wasserstein eBay The FBI, CIA, and other intelligence agencies Intuit Pixar

	Description	Features	Technology Providers	Use Case Examples
Electronic Social Network	Online community that allows users to establish a personal profile, link to other profiles (i.e., friends), share content, and communicate with members via messaging, posts. **Key Uses:** Discover and reinforce affiliations; identify experts; message individuals or groups; virally share media.	• Detailed personal profiles using multimedia • Affiliations with groups • Affiliations with individuals • Messaging and public discussions • Media sharing • "Feeds" of recent activity among members	• Facebook • LinkedIn • MySpace • Ning • SelectMinds • LiveWorld • IBM/Lotus Connections • Salesforce.com • Socialtext	• Barack Obama (campaign and government organizing) • Currensee (foreign exchange trading) • Dell • Deloitte Consulting • Goldman-Sachs • IBM • Reuters • Starbucks
Micro-blogging	Short, asynchronous messaging system. Users send messages to "followers." **Key Uses:** distribute time-sensitive information, share opinions, virally spread ideas, run contests and promotions, solicit feedback, provide customer support, track commentary on firms/products/issues, organize protests.	• 140-character messages sent and received from mobile device • Ability to respond publicly or privately • Can specify tags to classify discussion topics for easy searching and building comment threads • Follower lists	• Twitter • Socialtext Signals • Yammer • Salesforce.com (Chatter)	• Dell • Starbucks • Intuit • Small businesses • Celebrities • Zappos

Millions of users, billions of dollars, huge social impact, and these efforts weren't even on the radar of most business professionals when today's graduating college seniors first enrolled as freshmen. The trend demonstrates that even some of the world's preeminent thought leaders and business publications can be sideswiped by the speed of the Internet.

Consider that when management guru Michael Porter wrote a piece titled "Strategy and the Internet" at the end of the dot-com bubble, he lamented the high cost of building brand online, questioned the power of network effects, and cast a skeptical eye on ad-supported revenue models. Well, it turns out Web 2.0 efforts challenged *all* of these concerns. Among the efforts above, all built brand on the cheap with little conventional advertising, and each owes their hypergrowth and high valuation to their ability to harness the network effect.

While the Web 2.0 moniker is a murky one, we'll add some precision to our discussion of these efforts by focusing on **peer production**, perhaps Web 2.0's most powerful feature, where users work, often collaboratively, to create content and provide services online. Web-based efforts that foster peer production are often referred to as **social media** or *user-generated content* sites. These sites include blogs; wikis; social networks like Facebook and MySpace; communal bookmarking and tagging sites like Del.icio.us; media sharing sites like YouTube and Flickr; and a host of supporting technologies. And it's not just about media. Peer-produced services like Skype and BitTorrent leverage users' computers instead of a central IT resource to forward phone calls and video. This ability saves their sponsors the substantial cost of servers, storage, and bandwidth. Peer production is also leveraged to create much of the open source software that supports many of the Web 2.0 efforts described above. Techniques such as crowdsourcing, where initially undefined groups of users band together to solve problems, create code, and develop services, are also a type of peer production. These efforts often seek to leverage the so-called wisdom of crowds, the idea that a large, diverse group often has more collective insight than a single or small group of trained professionals. These efforts will be expanded on below, along with several examples of their use and impact.

7.2 BLOGS (SHORT FOR WEB LOGS)

Blogs (short for Web logs) first emerged almost a decade ago as a medium for posting online diaries. (In a perhaps apocryphal story, *Wired* magazine claimed the term "Web log" was coined by Jorn Barger, a sometimes homeless, yet profoundly prolific, Internet poster). From humble beginnings, the blogging phenomenon has grown to a point where the number of public blogs tracked by Technorati (the popular blog index) has surpassed one hundred million (Takahashi, 2008). This number is clearly a **long tail** phenomenon, loaded with niche content that remains "discoverable" through search engines and blog indexes. **Trackbacks** (third-party links back to original blog post), and **blog rolls** (a list of a blogger's favorite sites—a sort of shout-out to blogging peers) also help distinguish and reinforce the reputation of widely read blogs.

The most popular blogs offer cutting-edge news and commentary, with postings running the gamut from professional publications to personal diaries. While this cacophony of content was once dismissed, blogging is now a respected and influential medium. Some might say that many of the most popular blogs have grown beyond the term, transforming into robust media enterprises. Consider that the political blog The Huffington Post is now more popular than all but eight newspaper sites and has a valuation higher than many publicly traded papers (Alterman, 2008; Learmonth, 2008). Keep in mind that this is a site without the sports, local news, weather, and other content offered by most papers. Ratings like this are hard to achieve—most bloggers can't make a living off their musings. But among the elite ranks, killer subscriber numbers are a magnet for advertisers. Top blogs operating on shoestring budgets can snare several hundred thousand dollars a month in ad revenue (Zuckerman, 2007). Most start with ad networks like Google AdSense, but the most elite engage advertisers directly for high- value deals and extended sponsorships.

Top blogs have begun to attract well-known journalists away from print media. The Huffington Post hired a former *Washington Post* editor Lawrence Roberts to head the site's investigative unit. The popular blog TechCrunch now features posts by Sarah Lacy (a *BusinessWeek* cover-story writer) and has hired Erick Schonfeld away from Time Warner's business publishing empire. Schonfeld's colleague, Om Malik, has gone on to found another highly ranked tech industry blog, GigaOM.

Senior executives from many industries have also begun to weigh in with online ruminations, going directly to the people without a journalist filtering their comments. Hotel chief Bill Marriott, Paul Levy (CEO of health care quality leader Beth Israel Deaconess Medical Center), Toyota's Akio Toyoda, and Zappos' CEO Tony Hsieh use their blogs for purposes that include a combination of marketing, sharing ideas, gathering feedback, press response, image shaping, and reaching consumers directly without press filtering. Blogs have the luxury of being more topically focused than traditional media, with no limits on page size, word count, or publication deadline. Some of the best examples engage new developments in topic domains much more quickly and deeply than traditional media. For example, it's not uncommon for blogs focused on the law or politics to provide a detailed dissection of a Supreme Court opinion within hours of its release—offering analysis well ahead of, and with greater depth, than via what bloggers call the **mainstream media (MSM)**. As such, it's not surprising that most mainstream news outlets have begun supplementing their content with blogs that can offer greater depth, more detail, and deadline-free timeliness.

The voice of the **blogosphere** can wield significant influence. Examples include leading the charge for Dan Rather's resignation and prompting the design of a new insulin pump. In an example of what can happen when a firm ignores social media, consider the flare-up Ingersoll Rand faced when the online community exposed a design flaw in its Kryptonite bike lock.

Online posts showed the thick metal lock could be broken with a simple ball-point pen. A video showing the hack was posted online. When Ingersoll Rand failed to react quickly, the blogosphere erupted with criticism. Just days after online reports appeared, the mainstream media picked up the story. The *New York Times* ran a piece titled "The Pen Is Mightier Than the Lock" that included a series of photos demonstrating the ballpoint Kryptonite lock pick. The event tarnished the once-strong brand and eventually resulted in a loss of over $10 million.

Like any Web page, blogs can be public, tucked behind a corporate firewall, or password protected. Most blogs offer a two-way dialogue, allowing users to comment on posts (sort of instant "letters to the editor," posted online and delivered directly to the author). The running dialogue can read like an electronic bulletin board, and can be an effective way to gather opinion when vetting ideas. Comments help keep a blogger honest. Just as the "wisdom of crowds" keeps Wikipedia accurate, a vigorous community of commenters will quickly expose a blogger's errors of fact or logic.

Despite this increased popularity, blogging has its downside. Blog comments can be a hothouse for spam and the disgruntled. Ham-handed corporate efforts (such as poor response to public criticism or bogus "praise posts") have been ridiculed. Employee blogging can be difficult to control and public postings can "live" forever in the bowels of an Internet search engine or as content pasted on other Web sites. Many firms have employee blogging and broader Internet posting policies to guide online conduct that may be linked to the firm (see Section 7.9 "Get SMART: The Social Media Awareness and Response Team"). Bloggers, beware—there are dozens of examples of workers who have been fired for what employers viewed as inappropriate posts.

Blogs can be hosted via third-party services (Google Blogger, WordPress, Tumblr, TypePad, Windows Live Spaces), with most offering a combination of free and premium features. Blogging features have also been incorporated into social networks such as Facebook, MySpace, and Ning, as well as corporate social media platforms such as Socialtext. Blogging software can also be run on third-party servers, allowing the developer more control in areas such as security and formatting. The most popular platform for users choosing to host their own blog server is the open source WordPress system.

In the end, the value of any particular blog derives from a combination of technical and social features. The technical features make it easy for a blogger and his or her community to engage in an ongoing conversation on some topic of shared interest. But the social norms and patterns of use that emerge over time in each blog are what determine whether technology features will be harnessed for good or ill. Some blogs develop norms of fairness, accuracy, proper attribution, quality writing, and good faith argumentation, and attract readers that find these norms attractive. Others mix it up with hotly contested debate, one-sided partisanship, or deliberately provocative posts, attracting a decidedly different type of discourse.

7.3 WIKIS

A **wiki** is a Web site anyone can edit directly within a Web browser (provided the site grants the user edit access). Wikis derive their name from the Hawaiian word for "quick." Ward Cunningham, the "wiki father" christened this new class of software with the moniker in honor of the wiki-wiki shuttle bus at the Honolulu airport. Wikis can indeed be one of the speediest ways to collaboratively create content online. Many popular online wikis serve as a shared knowledge repository in some domain.

The largest and most popular wiki is Wikipedia, but there are hundreds of publicly accessible wikis that anyone can participate in. Each attempts to chronicle a world of knowledge within a particular domain, with examples ranging from Wine Wiki for oenophiles to Wookieepedia, the Star Wars wiki. But wikis can be used for any collaborative effort—from meeting planning to project management. And in addition to the hundreds of public wikis, there are many thousand more that are hidden away behind firewalls, used as proprietary internal tools for organizational collaboration.

Like blogs, the value of a wiki derives from both technical and social features. The *technology* makes it easy to create, edit, and refine content; learn when content has been changed, how and by whom; and to change content back to a prior state. But it is the *social motivations of individuals* (to make a contribution, to share knowledge) that allow these features to be harnessed. The larger and more active a wiki community, the more likely it is that content will be up-to-date and that errors will be quickly corrected (again, we see the influence of network effects, where products and services with larger user bases become more valuable). Several studies have shown that large community wiki entries are as or more accurate than professional publication counterparts (Lichter, 2009; Kane, et. al., 2009).

Want to add to or edit a wiki entry? On most sites you just click the "Edit" link. Wikis support **what you see is what you get (WYSIWYG)** editing that, while not as robust as traditional word processors, is still easy enough for most users to grasp without training or knowledge of arcane code or markup language. Users can make changes to existing content and can easily create new pages or articles and link them to other pages in the wiki. Wikis also provide a version history. Click the "History" link on Wikipedia, for example, and you can see when edits were made and by whom. This feature allows the community to **roll back** a wiki to a prior page, in the event that someone accidentally deletes key info, or intentionally defaces a page.

Vandalism is a problem on Wikipedia, but it's more of a nuisance than a crisis. A *Wired* article chronicled how Wikipedia's entry for former U.S. President Jimmy Carter was regularly replaced by a photo of a "scruffy, random unshaven man with his left index finger shoved firmly up his nose" (Pink, 2005). Nasty and inappropriate, to be sure, but the Wikipedia editorial community is now so large and so vigilant that most vandalism is caught and corrected within seconds. Watch-lists for the most active targets (say the Web pages of political figures or controversial topics) tip off the community when changes are made. The accounts of vandals can be suspended, and while mischief-makers can log in under another name, most vandals simply become discouraged and move on. It's as if an army of do-gooders follows a graffiti tagger and immediately repaints any defacement.

Wikis are available both as software (commercial as well as open source varieties) that firms can install on their own computers or as online services (both subscription or ad-supported) where content is hosted off-site by third parties. Since wikis can be started without the oversight or involvement of a firm's IT department, their appearance in organizations often comes from grassroots user initiative. Many wiki services offer additional tools such as blogs, message boards, or spreadsheets as part of their feature set, making most wikis really more full- featured platforms for social computing.

Jump-starting a wiki can be a challenge, and an underused wiki can be a ghost town of orphan, out-of-date, and inaccurate content. Fortunately, once users see the value of wikis, use and effectiveness often snowballs. The unstructured nature of wikis are also both a strength and weakness. Some organizations employ **wikimasters** to "garden" community content; "prune" excessive posts, "transplant" commentary to the best location, and "weed" as necessary. Wikipatterns.com offers a guide to the stages of wiki adoption and a collection of community- building and content-building strategies.

Examples of Wiki Use

Wikis can be vital tools for collecting and leveraging knowledge that would otherwise be scattered throughout an organization; reducing geographic distance; removing boundaries between functional areas; and flattening preexisting hierarchies. Companies have used wikis in a number of ways:

- ⊙ At Pixar, all product meetings have an associated wiki to improve productivity. The online agenda ensures that all attendees can arrive knowing the topics and issues to be covered. Anyone attending the meeting (and even those who can't make it) can update the agenda, post supporting materials, and make comments to streamline and focus in-person efforts.

◉ At European investment bank Dresdner Kleinwort Wasserstein, employees use wikis for everything from setting meeting agendas to building multimedia training for new hires. Six months after launch, wiki use had surpassed activity on the firm's established intranet. Wikis are also credited with helping to reduce Dresdner e-mail traffic by 75 percent (Carlin, 2007).

◉ Sony's PlayStation team uses wikis to regularly maintain one-page overviews on the status of various projects. In this way, legal, marketing, and finance staff can get quick, up-to-date status reports on relevant projects, including the latest projected deadlines, action items, and benchmark progress. Strong security measures are enforced that limit access to only those who must be in the know, since the overviews often discuss products that have not been released.

◉ Employees at investment-advisory firm Manning and Napier use a wiki to collaboratively track news in areas of critical interest. Providing central repositories for employees to share articles and update evolving summaries on topics such as health care legislation, enables the firm to collect and focus what would otherwise be fragmented findings and insight. Now all employees can refer to central pages that each serve as a lightning rod attracting the latest and most relevant findings.

◉ Intellipedia is a secure wiki built on Intelink, a U.S. government system connecting sixteen spy agencies, military organizations, and the Department of State. The wiki is a "magnum opus of espionage," handling some one hundred thousand user accounts and five thousand page edits a day. Access is classified in tiers as "unclassified," "secret," and "top secret" (the latter hosting 439,387 pages and 57,248 user accounts). A page on the Mumbai terror attacks was up within minutes of the event, while a set of field instructions relating to the use of chlorine-based terror bombs in Iraq was posted and refined within two days of material identification—with the document edited by twenty- three users at eighteen locations (Calabrese, 2009).

When brought outside the firewall, corporate wikis can also be a sort of value-generation greenhouse, allowing organizations to leverage input from their customers and partners:

◉ Intuit has created a "community wiki" that encourages the sharing of experience and knowledge not just regarding Intuit products, such as QuickBooks, but also across broader topics its customers may be interested in, such as industry-specific issues (e.g., architecture, nonprofit) or small business tips (e.g., hiring and training employees). The TurboTax maker has also sponsored TaxAlmanac.org, a wiki- based tax resource and research community.

⦿ Microsoft leveraged its customer base to supplement documentation for its Visual Studio software development tool. The firm was able to enter the Brazilian market with Visual Studio in part because users had created product documentation in Portuguese (King, 2007).

⦿ ABC and CBS have created public wikis for the television programs *Lost*, *The Amazing Race*, and *CSI*, among others, offering an outlet for fans, and a way for new viewers to catch up on character backgrounds and complex plot lines.

⦿ Executive Travel, owned by American Express Publishing, has created a travel wiki for its more than one hundred and thirty thousand readers with the goal of creating what it refers to as "a digital mosaic that in theory is more authoritative, comprehensive, and useful" than comments on a Web site, and far more up-to-date than any paper-based travel guide (King, 2007). Of course, one challenge in running such a corporate effort is that there may be a competing public effort already in place. Wikitravel.org currently holds the top spot among travel-based wikis, and network effects suggest it will likely grow and remain more current than rival efforts.

7.4 DIGITAL SOCIAL NETWORKS

Social networks have garnered increasing attention as established networks grow and innovate, new networks emerge, and value is demonstrated. MySpace signed a billion-dollar deal to carry ads from Google's AdSense network. Meanwhile, privately held Facebook has blown past the flagging MySpace. Its leadership in privacy management, offering new features, allowing third-party applications on its platform, and providing sophisticated analytics tools to corporations and other on-site sponsors have helped the firm move beyond its college roots. LinkedIn, which rounds out the big three U.S. public social networks, has grown to the point where its influence is threatening recruiting sites like Monster.com and CareerBuilder (Boyle, 2009). It now offers services for messaging, information sharing, and even integration with the *BusinessWeek* Web site.

Media reports often mention MySpace, Facebook, and LinkedIn in the same sentence. However, while these networks share some common features, they serve very different purposes. MySpace pages are largely for public consumption. Started by musicians, MySpace casts itself as a media discovery tool bringing together users with similar tastes (Johnson, 2010).

Facebook, by contrast, is more oriented towards reinforcing existing social ties between people who already know each other. This difference leads to varying usage patterns. Since Facebook is perceived by users as relatively secure, with only invited "friends" seeing your profile, over a third of Facebook users post their mobile phone numbers on their profile pages.

LinkedIn was conceived from the start as a social network for business users. The site's profiles act as a sort of digital Rolodex that users update as they move or change jobs. Users can pose questions to members of their network, engage in group discussions, ask for introductions through mutual contacts, and comment on others' profiles (e.g., recommending a member). Active members find the site invaluable for maintaining professional contacts, seeking peer advice, networking, and even recruiting. Carmen Hudson, Starbucks manager of enterprise staffing, states LinkedIn is "one of the best things for finding midlevel executives" (King, 2007). Such networks are also putting increasing pressure on firms to work particularly hard to retain top talent. While once HR managers fiercely guarded employee directories for fear that a list of talent may fall into the hands of rivals, today's social networks make it easy for anyone to gain a list of a firm's staff, complete with contact information.

While these networks dominate in the United States, the network effect and cultural differences work to create islands where other social networks are favored by a particular culture or region. The first site to gain traction in a given market is usually the winner. Google's Orkut, Mixi, and Cyworld have small U.S. followings, but are among the largest sites in Brazil, Japan, and South Korea. Research by Ipsos Insight also suggests that users in many global markets, including Brazil, South Korea, and China, are more active social networkers than their U.S. counterparts[1].

Perhaps the most powerful (and controversial) feature of most social networks is the **feed** (or newsfeed). Pioneered by Facebook but now adopted by most services, feeds provide a timely update on the activities of people or topics that an individual has an association with. Feeds can give you a heads-up when someone makes a friend, joins a group, posts a photo, or installs an application.

Feeds are inherently **viral**. By seeing what others are doing on a social network, feeds can rapidly mobilize populations and dramatically spread the adoption of applications. Leveraging feeds, it took just ten days for the Facebook group Support the Monks' Protest in Burma to amass over one hundred and sixty thousand Facebook members. Feeds also helped music app iLike garner three million Facebook users just two weeks after its launch (Lacy, 2008; Nicole, 2007). Its previous Web-based effort took eight months to reach those numbers.

But feeds are also controversial. Many users react negatively to this sort of public broadcast of their online activity, and feed mismanagement can create public relations snafus, user discontent, and potentially open up a site to legal action. Facebook initially dealt with a massive user outcry at the launch of feeds, and faced a subsequent backlash when its Beacon service broadcast user purchases without first explicitly asking their permission, and during attempts to rework its privacy policy and make Facebook data more public and accessible. (See Chapter 8 "Facebook: Building a Business from the Social Graph" for more details.)

Corporate Use of Social Networks

Hundreds of firms have established "fan" pages on Facebook and communites on LinkedIn. These are now legitimate customer- and client-engagement platforms that also support advertising. If a customer has decided to press the "like" button of a firm's Facebook page and become a "fan," corporate information will appear in their newsfeed, gaining more user attention than the often-ignored ads that run on the sides of social networks. (For more on social networks and advertising, see Chapter 8 "Facebook: Building a Business from the Social Graph".)

But social networks have also become organizational productivity tools. Many employees have organized groups using publicly available social networking sites because similar tools are not offered by their firms. *Workforce Management* reported that MySpace had over forty thousand groups devoted to companies or coworkers, while Facebook had over eight thousand (Frauenheim, 2007). Assuming a large fraction of these groups are focused on internal projects, this demonstrates a clear pent-up demand for corporate-centric social networks (and creates issues as work dialogue moves outside firm-supported services).

Many firms are choosing to meet this demand by implementing internal social network platforms that are secure and tailored to firm needs. At the most basic level, these networks have supplanted the traditional employee directory. Social network listings are easy to update and expand. Employees are encouraged to add their own photos, interests, and expertise to create a living digital identity.

Firms such as Deloitte, Dow Chemical, and Goldman Sachs have created social networks for "alumni" who have left the firm or retired. These networks can be useful in maintaining contacts for future business leads, rehiring former employees (20 percent of Deloitte's experienced hires are so-called *boomerangs*, or returning employees), or recruiting retired staff to serve as contractors when labor is tight (King, 2006). Maintaining such networks will be critical in industries like IT and health care that are likely to be plagued by worker shortages for years to come.

Social networking can also be important for organizations like IBM, where some 42 percent of employees regularly work from home or client locations. IBM's social network makes it easier to locate employee expertise within the firm, organize virtual work groups, and communicate across large distances (Bulkley, 2007). As a dialogue catalyst, a social network transforms the public directory into a font of knowledge sharing that promotes organization flattening and value-adding expertise sharing.

While IBM has developed their own social network platforms, firms are increasingly turning to third-party vendors like SelectMinds (adopted by Deloitte, Dow Chemical, and Goldman Sachs) and LiveWorld (adopted by Intuit, eBay, the

NBA, and Scientific American). Ning allows anyone to create a social network and currently hosts over 2.3 million separate online communities (Swisher, 2010).

Firms have also created their own online communities to foster brainstorming and customer engagement. Dell's IdeaStorm.com forum collects user feedback and is credited with prompting line offerings, such as the firm's introduction of a Linux-based laptop (Greenfield, 2008). At MyStarbucksIdea.com, the coffee giant has leveraged user input to launch a series of innovations ranging from splash sticks that prevent spills in to-go cups, to new menu items. Both IdeaStorm and MyStarbucksIdea run on a platform offered by Salesforce.com that not only hosts these sites but also provides integration into Facebook and other services. Starbucks (the corporate brand with the most Facebook "fans") has extensively leveraged the site, using Facebook as a linchpin in the "Free Pastry Day" promotion (credited with generating one million in-store visits in a single day) and promotion of the firm's AIDS-related (Starbucks) RED campaign, which garnered an astonishing three hundred ninety million "viral impressions" through feeds, wall posts, and other messaging (Brandau, 2009).

Twitter and the Rise of Microblogging

Spawned in 2006 as a side project at the now-failed podcasting start-up Odeo (an effort backed by Blogger.com founder Evan Williams), Twitter has been on a rocket ride. The site's user numbers have blasted past both mainstream and new media sites, dwarfing *New York Times*, LinkedIn, and Digg, among others. Reports surfaced of rebuffed buyout offers as high as $500 million (Ante, 2009). By the firm's first developer conference in April 2010, Twitter and its staff of 175 employees had created a global phenomenon embraced by over one hundred million users worldwide.

Twitter is a **microblogging** service that allows users to post 140-character messages (**tweets**) via the Web, **SMS**, or a variety of third-party desktop and smartphone applications. The microblog moniker is a bit of a misnomer. The service actually has more in common with Facebook's status updates and news feeds than it does with traditional blogs. But unlike Facebook, where most users must approve "friends" before they can see status updates, Twitter's default setting allows for asymmetrical following (although it is possible to set up private Twitter accounts and to block followers).

Sure, there's a lot of inane "tweeting" going on—lots of meaningless updates that read, "I'm having a sandwich" or "in line at the airport." But while not every user may have something worthwhile to tweet, many find that Twitter makes for invaluable reading, offering a sense of what friends, customers, thought leaders, and newsmakers are thinking. Twitter leadership has described the service as communicating "The Pulse of the Planet" (Schonfeld, 2009). For many, Twitter is a discovery engine, a taste-making machine, a critical source of market intelligence, a source of breaking news, and an instantaneous way to plug into the moment's zeitgeist.

Many also find Twitter to be an effective tool for quickly blasting queries to friends, colleagues, or strangers who might offer potentially valuable input. Says futurist Paul Saffo, "Instead of creating the group you want, you send it and the group self-assembles" (Miller, 2009). Users can classify comments on a given topic using **hash tags** (keywords preceded by the "#" or "hash" symbol), allowing others to quickly find related tweets (e.g.,

#iranelection, #mumbai, #swineflu, #sxsw). Any user can create a hash tag—just type it into your tweet (you may want to search Twitter first to make sure that the tag is not in use by an unrelated topic and that if it is in use, it appropriately describes how you want your tweet classified).

Twitter users have broken news during disasters, terror attacks, and other major events. Dictators fear the people power Twitter enables, and totalitarian governments worldwide have moved to block citizen access to the service (prompting Twitter to work on censor-evading technology). During the 2009 Iranian election protests, the U.S. State Department even asked Twitter to postpone maintenance to ensure the service would continue to be available to support the voice and activism of Iran's democracy advocates (Ruffini, 2009).

Twitter is also emerging as a legitimate business tool. Consider the following commercial examples:

- ◉ Starbucks uses Twitter in a variety of ways. It has run Twitter-based contests and used the service to spread free samples of new products, such as its VIA instant coffee line. Twitter has also been a way for the company to engage customers in its cause-based marketing efforts, such as (Starbucks) RED, which supports (Product) RED. Starbucks has even recruited staff via Twitter and was one of the first firms to participate in Twitter's advertising model featuring "promoted tweets."

- ◉ Dell used Twitter to uncover an early warning sign indicating poor design of the keyboard on its Mini 9 Netbook PC. After a series of tweets from early adopters indicated that the apostrophe and return keys were positioned too closely together, the firm dispatched design change orders quickly enough to correct the problem when the Mini 10 was launched just three months later. By December 2009, Dell also claimed to have netted $6.5 million in outlet store sales referred via the Twitter account

- ◉ @DellOutlet (more than 1.5 million followers) (Eaton, 2009) and another $1 million from customers who have bounced from the outlet to the new products site (Abel, 2009).

- Brooklyn Museum patrons can pay an additional $20 a year for access to the private, members-only "1stFans" Twitter feed that shares information on special events and exclusive access to artist content.

- Twitter is credited with having raised millions via Text-to-Donate and other fundraising efforts following the Haiti earthquake.

- Twitter can be a boon for sharing time-sensitive information. The True Massage and Wellness Spa in San Francisco tweets last-minute cancellations to tell customers of an unexpected schedule opening. With Twitter, appointments remain booked solid. Gourmet food trucks, popular in many American cities, are also using Twitter to share location and create hipster buzz. Los Angeles's Kogi Korean Taco Truck now has over sixty thousand followers and uses Twitter to reveal where it's parked, ensuring long lines of BBQ-craving foodies. Of the firm's success, owner Roy Choi says, "I have to give all the credit to Twitter" (Romano, 2009).

- Electronics retailer Best Buy has recruited over 2,300 Blue Shirt and Geek Squad staffers to crowdsource Twitter-driven inquiries via @Twelpforce, the firm's customer service Twitter account. Best Buy staffers register their personal Twitter accounts on a separate Best Buy–run site. Then any registered employees tweeting using the #twelpforce, will automatically have those posts echoed through @Twelpforce, with the employee's account credited at the end of the tweet. As of November 2009, Twelpforce had provided answers to over 19,500 customer inquiries[1].=

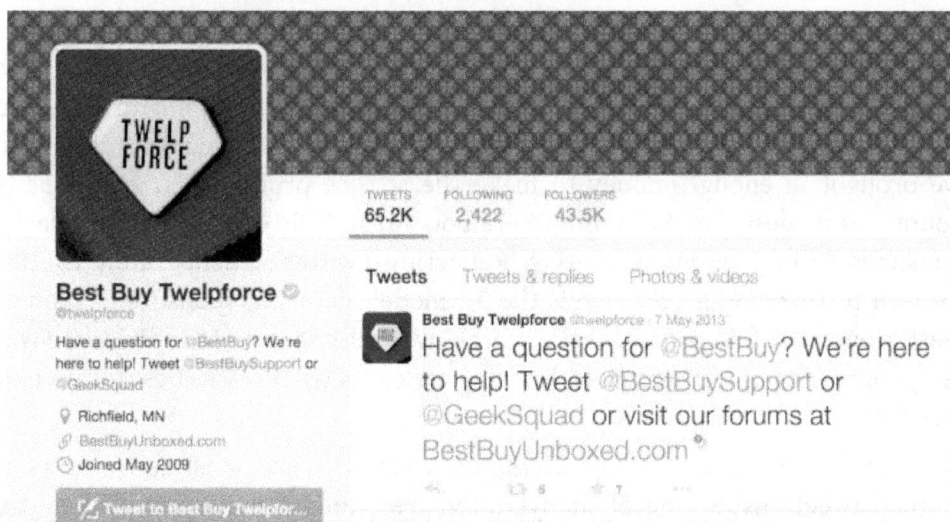

Figure 7.1 A Sampling of Tweets Filtered through Best Buy's @Twelpforce Twitter Account

Surgeons and residents at Henry Ford Hospital have even tweeted during brain surgery (the teaching hospital sees the service as an educational tool). Some tweets are from those so young they've got "negative age." Twitter.com/ kickbee is an experimental fetal monitor band that sends tweets when motion is detected: "I kicked Mommy at 08:52." And savvy hackers are embedding "tweeting" sensors into all sorts of devices. Botanicalls, for example, offers an electronic flowerpot stick that detects when plants need care and sends Twitter status updates to owners (sample post: "URGENT! Water me!").

Organizations are well advised to monitor Twitter activity related to the firm, as it can act as a sort of canary-in- a-coal mine uncovering emerging events. Users are increasingly using the service as a way to form flash protest crowds. Amazon. com, for example, was caught off guard over a spring 2009 holiday weekend when thousands used Twitter to rapidly protest the firm's reclassification of gay and lesbian books (hash tag #amazonfail). Others use the platform for shame and ridicule. BP has endured withering ridicule from the satire account @BPGlobalPR (followed by roughly 200,000 two months after the spill).

For all the excitement, many wonder if Twitter is overhyped. Some reports suggest that many Twitter users are curious experimenters who drop the service shortly after signing up (Martin, 2009). This raises the question of whether Twitter is a durable phenomenon or just a fad.

Pundits also wonder if revenues will ever justify initially high valuations and if rivals could usurp Twitter's efforts with similar features. Thus far, Twitter has been following a "grow-first-harvest-later" approach (Murrell, 2010). The site's rapid rise has allowed it to attract enough start-up capital to enable it to approach revenue gradually and with caution, in the hopes that it won't alienate users with too much advertising (an approach not unlike Google's efforts to nurture YouTube). MIT's *Technology Review* reports that data sharing deals with Google and Bing may have brought in enough money to make the service profitable in 2009, but that amount was modest (just $25 million) (Talbot, 2010). Twitter's advertising platform is expected to be far more lucrative. Reflecting Twitter's "deliberately cautious" approach to revenue development, the ad model featuring sponsored "promoted tweets" rolled out first as part of the search, with distribution to individual Twitter feeds progressing as the firm experiments and learns what works best for users and advertisers.

Another issue—many Twitter users rarely visit the site. Most active users post and read tweets using one of many—often free—applications provided by third parties, such as Seesmic, TweetDeck, and Twhirl. This happens because Twitter made its data available for free to other developers via **API (application programming interface)**. Exposing data can be a good move as it spawned an ecosystem of over one hundred thousand complementary third-party products and services that enhance Twitter's reach and usefulness (generating *network effects* from complementary offerings similar to other "platforms" like Windows, iPhone, and Facebook). There are potential downsides to such openness. If users don't visit Twitter.com, that lessens the impact of any ads running on the site. This creates what is known as the **"free rider problem,"** where users benefit from a service while offering no value in exchange. Encouraging software and service partners to accept ads for a percentage of the cut could lessen the free rider problem (Kafka, 2010).

When users don't visit a service, it makes it difficult to spread awareness of new products and features. It can also create branding challenges and customer frustration. Twitter execs lamented that customers were often confused when they searched for "Twitter" in the iPhone App Store and were presented with scores of offerings but none from Twitter itself (Goldman, 2010). Twitter's purchase of the iPhone app Tweetie (subsequently turned into the free "Twitter for iPhone" app) and the launch of its own URL-shortening service (competing with bit.ly and others) signal that Twitter is willing to move into product and service niches and compete with third parties that are reliant on the Twitter ecosystem.

Microblogging does appear to be here to stay, and the impact of Twitter has been deep, broad, stunningly swift, and at times humbling in the power that it wields. But whether Twitter will be a durable, profit-gushing powerhouse remains to be seen. Speculation on Twitter's future hasn't prevented many firms from commercializing new microblogging services, and a host of companies have targeted these tools for internal corporate use. Salesforce.com's Chatter, Socialtext Signals, and Yammer are all services that have been billed as "Twitter for the Enterprise." Such efforts allow for Twitter-style microblogging that is restricted for participation and viewing by firm-approved accounts.

7.5 OTHER KEY WEB 2.0 TERMS AND CONCEPTS

RSS (an acronym that stands for both "really simple syndication" and "rich site summary") enables busy users to scan the headlines of newly available content and click on an item's title to view items of interest, thus sparing them from having to continually visit sites to find out what's new. Users begin by subscribing to an RSS feed for a Web site, blog, podcast, or other data source. The title or headline of any new content will then show up in an **RSS reader**. Subscribe to the *New York Times* Technology news feed, for example, and you will regularly receive headlines of tech news from the *Times*. Viewing an article of interest is as easy as clicking the title you like. Subscribing is often as easy as clicking on the RSS icon appearing on the home page of a Web site of interest.

Many firms use RSS feeds as a way to mange information overload, opting to distribute content via feed rather than e-mail. Some even distribute corporate reports via RSS. RSS readers are offered by third-party Web sites such as Google and Yahoo! and they have been incorporated into all popular browsers and most e-mail programs. Most blogging platforms provide a mechanism for bloggers to automatically publish a feed when each new post becomes available. Google's FeedBurner is the largest publisher of RSS blog feeds, and offers features to distribute content via e-mail as well.

Folksonomies

Folksonomies (sometimes referred to as social tagging) are keyword-based classification systems created by user communities as they generate and review content. (The label is meant to refer to a people-powered taxonomy.) Bookmarking site Del.icio.us, photo-sharing site Flickr (both owned by Yahoo!), and Twitter's hash tags all make heavy use of folksonomies.

With this approach, classification schemes emerge from the people most likely to understand them—the users. By leveraging the collective power of the community to identify and classify content, objects on the Internet become easier to locate, and content carries a degree of recommendation and endorsement.

Flickr cofounder Stewart Butterfield describes the spirit of folksonomies, saying, "The job of tags isn't to organize all the world's information into tidy categories, it's to add value to the giant piles of data that are already out there" (Terdiman, 2005). The Guggenheim Museum in New York City and the San Francisco Museum of Modern Art, among other museums, are taking a folksonomic approach to their online collections, allowing user-generated categories to supplement the specialized lexicon of curators. Amazon.com has introduced a system that allows readers to classify books, and most blog posts and wiki pages allow for social tagging, oftentimes with hot topics indexed and accessible via a "tag cloud" in the page's sidebar.

Mash-up

Mash-ups are combinations of two or more technologies or data feeds into a single, integrated tool. Some of the best known mash-ups leverage Google's mapping tools. HousingMaps.com combines Craigslist.org listings with Google Maps for a map-based display for apartment hunters. IBM linked together job feeds and Google Maps to create a job-seeker service for victims of Hurricane Katrina. SimplyHired links job listings with Google Maps, LinkedIn listings, and salary data from PayScale.com. And Salesforce.com has tools that allow data from its customer relationship management (CRM) system to be combined with data feeds and maps from third parties.

Mash-ups are made easy by a tagging system called **XML** (for extensible markup language). Site owners publish the parameters of XML data feeds that a service can accept or offer (e.g., an address, price, product descriptions, images). Other developers are free to leverage these public feeds using application programming interfaces (APIs), published instructions on how to make programs call one another, to share data, or to perform tasks. Using APIs and XML, mash-up authors smoosh together seemingly unrelated data sources and services in new and novel ways. Lightweight, browser-friendly software technologies like Ajax and HTML5 can often make a Web site interface as rich as a desktop application, and rapid deployment frameworks like Ruby on Rails will enable and accelerate mash-up creation and deployment.

Location-Based Services

Computing devices increasingly know where you are—and this is creating all sorts of new opportunities for social media. Twitter, Facebook, and Google Buzz are among the many social services that have added location- based options, allowing you to tweet or post a status update attached with a physical location as determined by your phone's **global positioning system (GPS)**, triangulation from nearby cell phone towers, or proximity to neighboring Wi-Fi hotspots. This introduces a whole new way to gather and share information. In a new part of town and curious what folks are saying about the spot? Search for tweets tagged as being posted around that location.

Augmented-reality apps can overlay real data on top of images from a GPS and compass-equipped smartphone. Swivel your iPhone around with Stella Artois's Bar Finder app open, and it'll point you to the nearest Stella-equipped watering hole (it'll also let you text your friends to join you for a drink and call a cab for a safe ride home). Wikitude overlays images appearing through your phone's camera lens with geotagged data from Wikipedia. Point your Yelp app down the street and activate the monocle feature to see starred reviews hover over the top of establishments that appear on screen.

Boston-based SCVNGR (pronounced "scavenger"), a gaming app, has allowed over four hundred clients, including Princeton, MetLife, and Boston's Museum of Fine Arts, to create their own mobile phone-based scavenger hunts. The profitable firm has a 90 percent client return rate and had attracted funding from Google Ventures and Highland Capital Partners all before founder Seth Priebatsch turned twenty-one (Kincaid, 2009).

Perhaps the best known among the location-based pure plays is Foursquare. The service allows players to "check in" at different locations, allowing players to earn "badges" displayed in the app for completing specific achievements ("gym rat" for exercise buffs, "school night" for weeknight bar hoppers). Check into a location more than anyone else and you become that spot's "mayor." Foursquare users can follow public location postings from their friends, discovering when someone's close by and gaining recommendations on new places to explore. Foursquare grew to over one million users roughly one year after the service debuted at the 2009 South by Southwest conference. Firms are now using Foursquare for promotions and to support loyalty programs—offering "mayor specials" or sending out coupons and other incentives when users are nearby. Starbucks, the Bravo television channel, frozen yogurt chain Tasti D-Lite, and the Milwaukee-based burger chain AJ Bombers are among the diverse clients leveraging the service.

Figure 7.2 A Sampling of Location-Aware Apps

Of course, all this public location sharing raises privacy concerns. The Web site PleaseRobMe.com was created to draw attention to the potentially dangerous issues around real-time location sharing. After a brief demonstration period, the site stopped its real-time aggregation of publicly accessible user-location data and now serves as an awareness site warning of the "stalkerish" side of location-based apps. In most cases, though, users remain firmly in control—determining if they want to keep a visit private or release their locale to verified "app friends" or to the broader online space.

Virtual Worlds

In **virtual worlds**, users appear in a computer-generated environment in the form of an **avatar**, or animated character. Users can customize the look of their avatar, interact with others by typing or voice chat, and can travel about the virtual world by flying, teleporting, or more conventional means.

The most popular general-purpose virtual world is Second Life by Linden Labs, although many others exist. Most are free, although game-oriented worlds, such as World of Warcarft (with ten million active subscribers), charge a fee. Many corporations and organizations have established virtual outposts by purchasing "land" in the world of Second Life, while still others have contracted with networks to create their own, independent virtual worlds.

Most organizations have struggled to commercialize these Second Life forays, but activity has been wide-ranging in its experimentation. Reuters temporarily "stationed" a reporter in Second Life, presidential candidates have made appearances in the virtual world, organizations ranging from Sun Microsystems to Armani have set up virtual storefronts, and there's a significant amount of virtual mayhem. Second Life "terrorists" have "bombed" virtual outposts run by several organizations, including ABC News, American Apparel, and Reebok.

Even grade schoolers are heavy virtual world users. Many elementary school students get their first taste of the Web through Webkinz, an online world that allows for an animated accompaniment with each of the firm's plush toys. Webkinz's parent company, privately held Ganz, doesn't release financial figures. But according to Compete.com, by the end of 2008 Webkinz.com had roughly the same number of unique visitors as FoxNews.com. The kiddie set virtual world market is considered so lucrative that Disney acquired ClubPenguin for $350 million with agreements to pay another potential three hundred fifty million if the effort hits growth incentives (Barnes, 2007).

YouTube, Podcasting, and Rich Media

Blogs, wikis, and social networks not only enable sharing text and photos, they also allow for the creation and distribution of audio and video. **Podcasts** are digital audio files (some also incorporate video), provided as a series of programs. Podcasts range from a sort of media blog, archives of traditional radio and television programs, and regular offerings of original online content. While the term podcast derives from Apple's wildly successful iPod, podcasts can be recorded in audio formats such as MP3 that can be played on most portable media players. (In perhaps the ultimate concession to the market leader, even the iPod rival Microsoft Zune refers to serialized audio files as podcasts on its navigation menu).

There are many podcast directories, but Apple's iTunes is by far the largest. Anyone who wants to make a podcast available on iTunes can do so for free. A podcast publisher simply records an audio file, uploads the file to a blog or other hosting server, then sends the RSS feed to Apple (copyrighted material cannot be used without permission, with violators risking banishment from iTunes). Files are discovered in the search feature of the iTunes music store, and listings seamlessly connect the user with the server hosting the podcast. This path creates the illusion that Apple serves the file even though it resides on a publisher's servers.

While blogs have made stars of some unknowns, the most popular podcasts are from mainstream media outlets. A recent visit to the podcasting section of iTunes showed that eight of the top ten most popular podcasts were high-quality productions of mainstream media programs, including offerings from CBS, Comedy Central, NPR, and PBS. Podcasts are also revolutionizing education, with scores of universities "open sourcing" their classrooms and offering lectures for public consumption via Apple's iTunesU.

In contrast to iTunes, YouTube actually hosts video on its own servers, so all you need to do is shoot a video and upload it to the site. YouTube is a bastion of amateur video, with most clips shot and uploaded by nonprofessionals. It's also become a protest site (e.g., "A Comcast Technician Sleeping on my Couch"). However, YouTube has also become a go-to distribution platform for professional content such as ad clips, customer support guides, music videos, TV shows, movies, and more. Much of this **rich media** content can be distributed or streamed within another Web site, blog, or social network profile.

7.6 THE WISDOM OF THE CROWD AND PREDICTION MARKETS

Many social software efforts leverage what has come to be known as the **wisdom of crowds**. In this concept, a group of individuals (the crowd often consists mostly of untrained amateurs), collectively has more insight than a single or small group of trained professionals. Made popular by author James Surowiecki (whose best- selling book was named after the phenomenon), the idea of crowd wisdom is at the heart of wikis, folksonomy tagging systems, and many other online efforts. An article in the journal *Nature* positively comparing Wikipedia to *Encyclopedia Britannica* lent credence to social software's use in harnessing and distilling crowd wisdom (Giles, 2005).

The crowd isn't always right, but in many cases where topics are complex, problems are large, and outcomes are uncertain, a large, diverse group may bring collective insight to problem solving that one smart guy or a professional committee lacks. One technique for leveraging the wisdom of crowds is a **prediction market**, where a diverse crowd is polled and opinions aggregated to form a forecast of an eventual outcome. The concept is not new. The stock market is arguably a prediction market, with a stock price representing collective assessment of the discounted value of a firm's future earnings. But Internet technologies are allowing companies to set up prediction markets for exploring all sorts of problems.

Consider Best Buy, where employees are encouraged to leverage the firm's TagTrade prediction market to make forecasts, and are offered small gifts as incentives for participation. The idea behind this incentive program is simple: the "blue shirts" (Best Buy employees) are closest to customers. They see traffic patterns and buying cycles, can witness customer reactions first hand, and often have a degree of field insight not available to senior managers at the company's Minneapolis headquarters. Harness this collective input and you've got a group brain where, as wisdom of crowds proponents often put it, "the we is greater than the me." When Best Buy asked its employees to predict gift card sales, the "crowd's" collective average answer was 99.5 percent accurate; experts paid to make the prediction were off by 5 percent. Another experiment predicting holiday sales was off by only 1/ 10 of 1 percent. The experts? Off by 7 percent (Dvorak, 2008; Dye, 2008)!

In an article in the *McKinsey Quarterly*, Surowiecki outlined several criteria necessary for a crowd to be "smart" (Dye, 2008). The crowd must

- be *diverse*, so that participants are bringing different pieces of information to the table,

- be *decentralized*, so that no one at the top is dictating the crowd's answer,

- offer *a collective verdict* that summarizes participant opinions,

- be *independent*, so that each focuses on information rather than the opinions of others.

Google, which runs several predictive markets, underscored these principles when it found that predictions were less accurate when users were geographically proximate, meaning folks in the same work group who sat near one another typically thought too much alike (Cowgill, et. al., 2009). Poorer predictive outcomes likely resulted because these relatively homogeneous clusters of users brought the same information to the table (yet another reason why organizations should hire and cultivate diverse teams).

Many firms run predictive markets to aid in key forecasts, and with the potential for real financial payoff. But University of Chicago law professor Todd Henderson warns predictive markets may also hold legal and ethical challenges. The Securities and Exchange Commission may look askance at an employee who gets a heads-up in a predictive market that says a certain drug is going to be approved or fail clinical trials. If she trades on this information is she an insider, subject to prosecution for exploiting proprietary data? Disclosure issues are unclear. Gambling laws are also murky, with Henderson uncertain as to whether certain predictive markets will be viewed as an unregulated form of betting (Dye, 2008).

Publicly accessible prediction markets are diverse in their focus. The Iowa Electronic Market attempts to guess the outcome of political campaigns, with mixed results. Farecast (now part of Microsoft's Bing knowledge engine) claims a 75 percent accuracy rate for forecasting the future price of airline tickets[1]. The Hollywood Stock Exchange allows participants to buy and sell prediction shares of movies, actors, directors, and film-related options. The exchange, now owned by investment firm Cantor Fitzgerald, has picked Oscar winners with 90 percent accuracy (Surowiecki, 2007). And at HedgeStreet.com, participants can make microbets, wagering as little as ten dollars on the outcome of economic events, including predictions on the prices of homes, gold, foreign currencies, oil, and even the economic impact of hurricanes and tropical storms. HedgeStreet is considered a market and is subject to oversight by the Commodity Futures Trading Commission (Lambert, 2006).

7.7 CROWDSOURCING: AN OVERVIEW

The power of Web 2.0 also offers several examples of the democratization of production and innovation. Need a problem solved? Offer it up to the crowd and see if any of their wisdom offers a decent result. This phenomenon, known as **crowdsourcing**, has been defined by Jeff Howe, founder of the blog crowdsourcing.com and an associate editor at *Wired*, as "the act of taking a job traditionally performed by a designated agent (usually an employee) and outsourcing it to an undefined, generally large group of people in the form of an open call" (Howe, 2006).

Can the crowd really do better than experts inside a firm? At least one company has literally struck gold using crowdsourcing. As told by Don Tapscott and Anthony Williams in their book *Wikinomics*, mining firm Goldcorp was struggling to gain a return from its 55,000-acre Canadian property holdings. Executives were convinced there was gold "in them thar hills," but despite years of efforts, the firm struggled to strike any new pay dirt. CEO Rob McEwen, a former mutual fund manager without geology experience who unexpectedly ended up running Goldcorp after a takeover battle, then made what seemed a Hail Mary pass—he offered up all the firm's data, on the company's Web site. Along with the data, McEwen ponied up $575,000 from the firm as prize money for the Goldcorp Challenge to anyone who came up with the best methods and estimates for reaping golden riches. Releasing data was seen as sacrilege in the intensely secretive mining industry, but it brought in ideas the firm had never considered. Taking the challenge was a wildly diverse group of "graduate students, consultants, mathematicians, and military officers." Eighty percent of the new targets identified by entrants yielded "substantial quantities of gold." The financial payoff? In just a few years a one-hundred-million-dollar firm grew into a nine-billion-dollar titan. For Goldcorp, the crowd coughed up serious coin.

Netflix followed Goldcorp's lead, offering anonymous data to any takers, along with a one-million-dollar prize to the first team that could improve the accuracy of movie recommendations by 10 percent. Top performers among the over thirty thousand entrants included research scientists from AT&T Labs, researchers from the University of Toronto, a team of Princeton undergrads, and the proverbial "guy in a garage" (and yes, that was his team name). Frustrated for nearly three years, it took a coalition of four teams from Austria, Canada, Israel, and the United States to finally cross the 10 percent threshold. The winning team represented an astonishing brain trust that Netflix would never have been able to harness on its own (Lohr, 2009).

Other crowdsourcers include Threadless.com, which produces limited run t-shirts with designs users submit and vote on. Marketocracy runs stock market games and has created a mutual fund based on picks from the 100 top- performing portfolios. Just under seven years into the effort, the firm's m100 Index reports a 75 percent return versus 35 percent for the S&P 500. The St. Louis Cardinals baseball team is even crowdsourcing. The club's One for the Birds contest calls for the fans to submit scouting reports on promising players, as the team hopes to broaden its recruiting radar beyond its classic recruiting pool of Division I colleges.

There are several public markets for leveraging crowdsourcing for innovation, or as an alternative to standard means of production. Waltham, Massachusetts–based InnoCentive allows "seekers" to offer cash prizes ranging from ten to one hundred thousand dollars. Over one hundred twenty thousand "solvers" have registered to seek solutions for tasks put forward by seekers that include Dow Chemical, Eli Lilly, and Procter & Gamble. Among the findings offered by the InnoCentive crowd are a biomarker that measures progression of ALS. Amazon.com has even created an online marketplace for crowdsourcing called Mechanical Turk. Anyone with a task to be completed or problem to be solved can put it up for Amazon, setting their price for completion or solution. For its role, Amazon takes a small cut of the transaction. And alpha geeks looking to prove their code chops can turn to TopCoder, a firm that stages coding competitions that deliver real results for commercial clients such as ESPN. By 2009, TopCoder contests had attracted over 175,000 participants from 200 countries[1] (Brandel, 2007; Brandel, 2008).

Not all crowdsourcers are financially motivated. Some benefit by helping to create a better service. Facebook leveraged crowd wisdom to develop versions of its site localized in various languages. Facebook engineers designated each of the site's English words or phrases as a separate translatable object. Members were then invited to translate the English into other languages, and rated the translations to determine which was best. Using this form of crowdsourcing, fifteen hundred volunteers cranked out Spanish Facebook in a month. It took two weeks for two thousand German speakers to draft Deutsch Facebook. How does the Facebook concept of "poke" translate around the world? The Spaniards decided on "dar un toque," Germans settled on "anklopfen," and the French went with "envoyer un poke" (Kirkpatrick, 2008). Vive le crowd!

For an example of how outrage can go viral, consider Dave Carroll[1]. The Canadian singer-songwriter was traveling with his band Sons of Maxwell on a United Airlines flight from Nova Scotia to Nebraska when, during a layover at Chicago's O'Hare International Airport, Carroll saw baggage handlers roughly tossing his guitar case. The musician's $3,500 Taylor guitar was in pieces by the time it arrived in Omaha. In the midst of a busy tour schedule, Carroll didn't have time to follow up on the incident until after United's twenty-four-hour period for filing a complaint for restitution had expired. When United refused to compensate him for the damage, Carroll penned the four-minute country ditty "United Breaks Guitars," performed it in a video, and uploaded the clip to YouTube (sample lyrics: "I should have gone with someone else or gone by car...'cuz United breaks guitars"). Carroll even called out the unyielding United rep by name. Take that, Ms. Irlwig! (Note to customer service reps everywhere: you're always on.)

The clip went viral, receiving 150,000 views its first day and five million more by the next month. Well into the next year, "United Breaks Guitars" remained the top result on YouTube when searching the term "United." No other topic mentioning that word—not "United States," "United Nations," or "Manchester United"—ranked ahead of this one customer's outrage.

Dave Carroll's ode to his bad airline experience, "United Breaks Guitars," went viral, garnering millions of views.

Scarring social media posts don't just come from outside the firm. Earlier that same year employees of Domino's Pizza outlet in Conover, North Carolina, created what they thought would be a funny gross-out video for their friends. Posted to YouTube, the resulting footage of the firm's brand alongside vile acts of food prep was seen by over one million viewers before it was removed. Over 4.3 million references to the incident can be found on Google, and many of the leading print and broadcast outlets covered the story. The perpetrators were arrested, the Domino's storefront where the incident occurred was closed, and the firm's president made a painful apology (on YouTube, of course).

Not all firms choose to aggressively engage social media. As of this writing some major brands still lack a notable social media presence (Apple comes immediately to mind). But your customers are there and they're talking about your organization, its products, and its competitors. Your employees are there, too, and without guidance, they can step on a social grenade with your firm left to pick out the shrapnel. Soon, nearly everyone will carry the Internet in their pocket. Phones and MP3 players are armed with video cameras capable of recording every customer outrage, corporate blunder, ethical lapse, and rogue employee. Social media posts can linger forever online, like a graffiti tag attached to your firm's reputation. Get used to it—that genie isn't going back in the bottle.

As the "United Breaks Guitars" and "Domino's Gross Out" incidents show, social media will impact a firm whether it chooses to engage online or not. An awareness of the power of social media can shape customer support engagement and crisis response, and strong corporate policies on social media use might have given the clueless Domino's pranksters a heads-up that their planned video would get them fired and arrested. Given the power of social media, it's time for all firms to get **SMART**, creating a social media awareness and response team. While one size doesn't fit all, this section details key issues behind SMART capabilities, including creating the social media team, establishing firmwide policies, monitoring activity inside and outside the firm, establishing the social media presence, and managing social media engagement and response.

7.8 CREATING THE TEAM

Firms need to treat social media engagement as a key corporate function with clear and recognizable leadership within the organization. Social media is no longer an ad hoc side job or a task delegated to an intern. When McDonald's named its first social media chief, the company announced that it was important to have someone "dedicated 100% of the time, rather than someone who's got a day job on top of a day job" (York, 2010). Firms without social media baked into employee job functions often find that their online efforts are started with enthusiasm, only to suffer under a lack of oversight and follow-through. One hotel operator found franchisees were quick to create Facebook pages, but many rarely monitored them. Customers later notified the firm that unmonitored hotel "fan" pages contained offensive messages—a racist rant on one, paternity claims against an employee on another.

Organizations with a clearly established leadership role for social media can help create consistency in firm dialogue; develop and communicate policy; create and share institutional knowledge; provide training, guidance, and suggestions; offer a place to escalate issues in the event of a crisis or opportunity; and catch conflicts that might arise if different divisions engage without coordination.

While firms are building social media responsibility into job descriptions, also recognize that social media is a team sport that requires input from staffers throughout an organization. The social media team needs support from public relations, marketing, customer support, HR, legal, IT, and other groups, all while acknowledging that what's happening in the social media space is distinct from traditional roles in these disciplines. The team will hone unique skills in technology, analytics, and design, as well as skills for using social media for online conversations, listening, trust building, outreach, engagement, and response. As an example of the interdisciplinary nature of social media practice, consider that the social media team at Starbucks (regarded by some as the best in the business) is organized under the interdisciplinary "vice president of brand, content, and online[2]."

Also note that while organizations with SMARTs (social media teams) provide leadership, support, and guidance, they don't necessarily drive all efforts. GM's social media team includes representatives from all the major brands. The idea is that employees in the divisions are still the best to engage online once they've been trained and given operational guardrails. Says GM's social media chief, "I can't go in to Chevrolet and tell them 'I know your story better than you do, let me tell it on the Web'" (Barger, 2009)[3]. Similarly, the roughly fifty Starbucks "Idea Partners" who participate in MyStarbucksIdea are specialists. Part of their job is to manage the company's social media. In this way, conversations about the Starbucks Card are handled by card team experts, and merchandise dialogue has a product specialist who knows that business best. Many firms find that the social media team is key for coordination and supervision (e.g., ensuring that different divisions don't overload consumers with too much or inconsistent contact), but the dynamics of specific engagement still belong with the folks who know products, services, and customers best.

Responsibilities and Policy Setting

In an age where a generation has grown up posting shoot-from-the-hip status updates and YouTube is seen as a fame vehicle for those willing to perform sensational acts, establishing corporate policies and setting employee expectations are imperative for all organizations. The employees who don't understand the impact of social media on the firm can do serious damage to their employers and their careers (look to Domino's for an example of what can go wrong).

Many experts suggest that a good social media policy needs to be three things: "short, simple, and clear" (Soat, 2010). Fortunately, most firms don't have to reinvent the wheel. Several firms, including Best Buy, IBM, Intel, The American Red Cross, and Australian telecom giant Telstra, have made their social media policies public.

Most guidelines emphasize the "three Rs": representation, responsibility, and respect.

- ◉ *Representation.* Employees need clear and explicit guidelines on expectations for social media engagement. Are they empowered to speak on behalf of the firm? If they do, it is critical that employees transparently disclose this to avoid legal action. U.S. Federal Trade Commission rules require disclosure of relationships that may influence online testimonial or endorsement. On top of this, many industries have additional compliance requirements (e.g., governing privacy in the health and insurance fields, retention of correspondence and disclosure for financial services firms). Firms may also want to provide guidelines on initiating and conducting dialogue, when to respond online, and how to escalate issues within the organization.

- ◉ *Responsibility.* Employees need to take responsibility for their online actions. Firms must set explicit expectations for disclosure, confidentiality and security, and provide examples of engagement done right, as well as what is unacceptable. An effective social voice is based on trust, so accuracy, transparency, and accountability must be emphasized. Consequences for violations should be clear.

- ◉ *Respect.* Best Buy's policy for its Twelpforce explicitly states participants must "honor our differences" and "act ethically and responsibly." Many employees can use the reminder. Sure customer service is a tough task and every rep has a story about an unreasonable client. But there's a difference between letting off steam around the water cooler and venting online. Virgin Atlantic fired thirteen of the airline's staffers after they posted passenger insults and inappropriate inside jokes on Facebook (Conway, 2008).

Policies also need to have teeth. Remember, a fourth "R" is at stake—reputation (both the firm's and the employee's). Violators should know the consequences of breaking firm rules and policies should be backed by action. Best Buy's policy simply states, "Just in case you are forgetful or ignore the guidelines above, here's what could happen. You could get fired (and it's embarrassing to lose your job for something that's so easily avoided)."

Despite these concerns, trying to micromanage employee social media use is probably not the answer. At IBM, rules for online behavior are surprisingly open. The firm's code of conduct reminds employees to remember privacy, respect, and confidentiality in all electronic communications. Anonymity is not permitted on IBM's systems, making everyone accountable for their actions. As for external postings, the firm insists that employees not disparage competitors or reveal customers' names without permission and asks that any employee posts from IBM accounts or that mention the firm also include disclosures indicating that opinions and thoughts shared publicly are the individual's and not Big Blue's.

Some firms have more complex social media management challenges. Consider hotels and restaurants where outlets are owned and operated by franchisees rather than the firm. McDonald's social media team provides additional guidance so that regional operations can create, for example, a Twitter handle (e.g.,@mcdonalds_cincy) that handle a promotion in Cincinnati that might not run in other regions (York, 2010). A social media team can provide coordination while giving up the necessary control. Without this kind of coordination, customer communication can quickly become a mess.

Training is also a critical part of the SMART mandate. GM offers an intranet-delivered video course introducing newbies to the basics of social media and to firm policies and expectations. GM also trains employees to become "social media proselytizers and teachers." GM hopes this approach enables experts to interact directly with customers and partners, allowing the firm to offer authentic and knowledgeable voices online.

Training should also cover information security and potential threats. Social media has become a magnet for phishing, virus distribution, and other nefarious online activity. Over one-third of social networking users claim to have been sent malware via social networking sites (see Chapter 13 "Information Security: Barbarians at the Gateway (and Just About Everywhere Else)"). The social media team will need to monitor threats and spread the word on how employees can surf safe and surf smart.

Since social media is so public, it's easy to amass examples of what works and what doesn't, adding these to the firm's training materials. The social media team provides a catch point for institutional knowledge and industry best practice; and the team can update programs over time as new issues, guidelines, technologies, and legislation emerge.

The social media space introduces a tension between allowing expression (among employees and by the broader community) and protecting the brand. Firms will fall closer to one end or the other of this continuum depending on compliance requirements, comfort level, and goals. Expect the organization's position to move. Firms will be cautious as negative issues erupt, others will jump in as new technologies become hot and early movers generate buzz and demonstrate results. But it's the SMART responsibility to avoid knee-jerk reaction and to shepherd firm efforts with the professionalism and discipline of other management domains.

Monitoring

Concern over managing a firm's online image has led to the rise of an industry known as **online reputation management**. Firms specializing in this field will track a client firm's name, brand, executives' names, or other keywords, reporting online activity and whether sentiment trends toward the positive or negative.

But social media monitoring is about more than about managing one's reputation; it also provides critical competitive intelligence, it can surface customer support issues, and it can uncover opportunities for innovation and improvement. Firms that are quick to lament the very public conversations about their brands happening online need to embrace social media as an opportunity to learn more.

Resources for monitoring social media are improving all the time, and a number of tools are available for free. All firms can take advantage of Google Alerts, which flag blog posts, new Web pages, and other publicly accessible content, regularly delivering a summary of new links to your mailbox (for more on using Google for intelligence gathering, see Chapter 14 "Google: Search, Online Advertising, and Beyond"). Twitter search and third-party Twitter clients like TweetDeck can display all mentions of a particular term. Tools like Twitrratr will summarize mentions of a phrase and attempt to classify tweets as "positive," "neutral," or "negative."

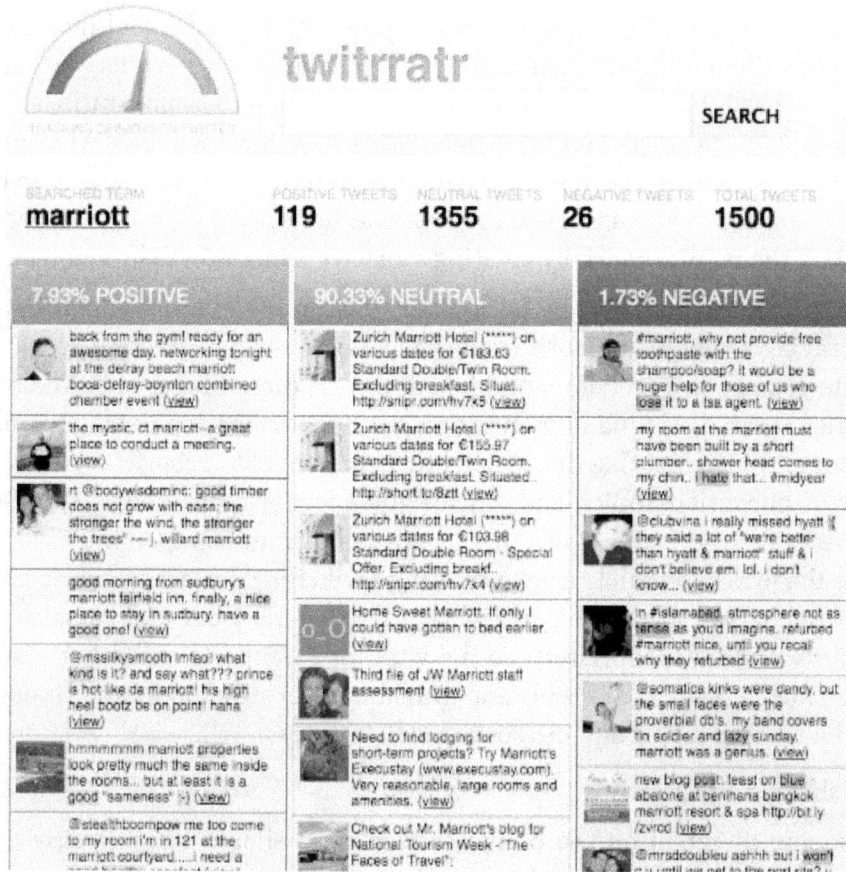

Figure 7.3 Tools like Twitrratr attempt to classify the sentiment behind tweets mentioning a key word or phrase. Savvy firms can mine comments for opportunities to provide thoughtful customer service (like the suggestion at the top right to provide toothpaste for those who lose it in U.S. airport security).

Facebook provides a summary of fan page activity to administrators (including stats on visits, new fans, wall posts, etc.), while Facebook's Insights tool measures user exposure, actions, and response behavior relating to a firm's Facebook pages and ads.

Bit.ly and many other URL-shortening services allow firms to track Twitter references to a particular page. Since bit.ly applies the same shortened URL to all tweets pointing to a page, it allows firms to follow not only if a campaign has been spread through "retweeting" but also if new tweets were generated outside of a campaign. Graphs plot click-throughs over time, and a list of original tweets can be pulled up to examine what commentary accompanied a particular link.

Location-based services like Foursquare have also rolled out robust tools for monitoring how customers engage with firms in the brick-and-mortar world. Foursquare's analytics and dashboard present firms with a variety of statistics, such as who has "checked in" and when, a venue's male-to-female ratio, and which times of day are more active for certain customers. "Business owners will also be able to offer instant promotions to try to engage new customers and keep current ones" (Bolton, 2010). Managers can use the tools to notice if a once-loyal patron has dropped off the map, potentially creating a special promotion to lure her back.

Monitoring should also not be limited to customers and competitors. Firms are leveraging social media both inside their firms and via external services (e.g., corporate groups on Facebook and LinkedIn), and these spaces should also be on the SMART radar. This kind of monitoring can help firms keep pace with employee sentiment and insights, flag discussions that may involve proprietary information or other inappropriate topics, and provide guidance for those who want to leverage social media for the firm's staff—that is, anything from using online tools to help organize the firm's softball league to creating a wiki for a project group. Social media are end-user services that are particularly easy to deploy but that can also be used disastrously and inappropriately, so it's vital for IT experts and other staffers on the social media team to be visible and available, offering support and resources for those who want to take a dip into social media's waters.

Establishing a Presence

Firms hoping to get in on the online conversation should make it easy for their customers to find them. Many firms take an **embassy** approach to social media, establishing presence at various services with a consistent name. Think facebook.com/starbucks, twitter.com/starbucks, youtube.com/starbucks, flickr.com/starbucks, and so on. Corporate e-mail and Web sites can include icons linking to these services in a header or footer. The firm's social media embassies can also be highlighted in physical space such as in print, on bags and packaging, and on store signage. Firms should try to ensure that all embassies carry consistent design elements, so users see familiar visual cues that underscore they are now at a destination associated with the organization.

As mentioned earlier, some firms establish their own communities for customer engagement. Examples include Dell's IdeaStorm and MyStarbucksIdea. Not every firm has a customer base that is large and engaged enough to support hosting its own community. But for larger firms, these communities can create a nexus for feedback, customer-driven innovation, and engagement.

Customers expect an open dialogue, so firms engaging online should be prepared to deal with feedback that's not all positive. Firms are entirely within their right to screen out offensive and inappropriate comments. Noting this, firms might think twice before turning on YouTube comments (described as "the gutter of the Internet" by one leading social media manager) (Nelson, 2010). Such comments could expose employees or customers profiled in clips to withering, snarky ridicule. However, firms engaged in curating their forums to present only positive messages should be prepared for the community to rebel and for embarrassing cries of censorship to be disclosed.

Firms that believe in the integrity of their work and the substance of their message shouldn't be afraid. While a big brand like Starbucks is often a target of criticism, social media also provides organizations with an opportunity to respond fairly to that criticism and post video and photos of the firm's efforts. In Starbucks' case, the firm shares its work investing in poor coffee-growing communities as well as efforts to support AIDS relief. A social media presence allows a firm to share these works without waiting for conventional public relations (PR) to yield results or for journalists to pick up and interpret the firm's story. Starbucks executives have described the majority of comments the company receives through social media as "a love letter to the firm." By contrast, if your firm isn't prepared to be open or if your products and services are notoriously subpar and your firm is inattentive to customer feedback, then establishing a brand-tarring social media beachhead might not make sense. A word to the self-reflective: Customer conversations will happen online even if you don't have any social media embassies. Users can form their own groups, hash tags, and forums. A reluctance to participate may signal that the firm is facing deeper issues around its product and service.

While firms can learn a lot from social media consultants and tool providers, it's considered bad practice to outsource the management of a social media presence to a third-party agency. The voice of the firm should come *from* the firm. In fact, it should come from employees who can provide authentic expertise. Starbucks' primary Twitter feed is managed by Brad Nelson, a former barista, while the firm's director of environmental affairs, Jim Hanna, tweets and engages across social media channels on the firm's green efforts.

Engage and Respond

Having an effective social media presence offers "four Ms" of engagement: it's a *megaphone* allowing for outbound communication; it's a *magnet* drawing communities inward for conversation; and it allows for *monitoring* and *mediation* of existing conversations (Gallaugher & Ransbotham, 2009). This dialogue can happen privately (private messaging is supported on most services) or can occur very publicly (with the intention to reach a wide audience). Understanding when, where, and how to engage and respond online requires a deft and experienced hand.

Many firms will selectively and occasionally retweet praise posts, underscoring the firm's commitment to customer service. Highlighting service heroes also reinforces exemplar behavior to employees who may be following the firm online, too. Users are often delighted when a major brand retweets their comments, posts a comment on their blog, or otherwise acknowledges them online—just be sure to do a quick public profile investigation to make sure your shout-outs are directed at customers you want associated with your firm. Escalation procedures should also include methods to flag noteworthy posts, good ideas, and opportunities that the social media team should be paying attention to. The customer base is often filled with heartwarming stories of positive customer experiences and rich with insight on making good things even better.

Many will also offer an unsolicited apology if the firm's name or products comes up in a disgruntled post. You may not be able to respond to all online complaints, but selective acknowledgement of the customer's voice (and attempts to address any emergent trends) is a sign of a firm that's focused on customer care. Getting the frequency, tone, and cadence for this kind of dialogue is more art than science, and managers are advised to regularly monitor other firms with similar characteristics for examples of what works and what doesn't.

Many incidents can be responded to immediately and with clear rules of engagement. For example, Starbuck issues corrective replies to the often-tweeted urban legend that the firm does not send coffee to the U.S. military because of a corporate position against the war. A typical response might read, "Not true, get the facts here" with a link to a Web page that sets the record straight.

Reaching out to key influencers can also be extremely valuable. Prominent bloggers and other respected social media participants can provide keen guidance and insight. The goal isn't to create a mouthpiece, but to solicit input, gain advice, gauge reaction, and be sure your message is properly interpreted. Influencers can also help spread accurate information and demonstrate a firm's commitment to listening and learning. In the wake of the Domino's gross-out, executives reached out to the prominent blog The Consumerist (Jacques, 2009). Facebook has solicited advice and feedback from MoveOn.org months before launching new features (Stone, 2008). Meanwhile, Kaiser Permanente leveraged advice from well-known health care bloggers in crafting its approach to social media (Kane, et. al., 2009).

However, it's also important to recognize that not every mention is worthy of a response. The Internet is filled with PR seekers, the unsatisfiably disgruntled, axe grinders seeking to trap firms, dishonest competitors, and inappropriate groups of mischief makers commonly referred to as *trolls*. One such group hijacked *Time* Magazine's user poll of the World's Most Influential People, voting their twenty-one-year-old leader to the top of the list ahead of Barack Obama,

Vladimir Putin, and the pope. Prank voting was so finely calibrated among the group that the rankings list was engineered to spell out a vulgar term using the first letter of each nominee's name (Schonfeld, 2009).

To prepare, firms should "war game" possible crises, ensuring that everyone knows their role, and that experts are on call. A firm's social media policy should also make it clear how employees who spot a crisis might "pull the alarm" and mobilize the crisis response team. Having all employees aware of how to respond gives the firm an expanded institutional radar that can lower the chances of being blindsided. This can be especially important as many conversations take place in the so-called dark Web beyond the reach of conventional search engines and monitoring tools (e.g., within membership communities or sites, such as Facebook, where only "friends" have access).

In the event of an incident, silence can be deadly. Consumers expect a response to major events, even if it's just "we're listening, we're aware, and we intend to fix things." When director Kevin Smith was asked to leave a Southwest Airline flight because he was too large for a single seat, Smith went ballistic on Twitter, berating Southwest's service to his thousands of online followers. Southwest responded that same evening via Twitter, posting, "I've read the tweets all night from @ ThatKevinSmith—He'll be getting a call at home from our Customer Relations VP tonight."

In the event of a major crisis, firms can leverage online media outside the social sphere. In the days following the Domino's incident, the gross-out video consistently appeared near the top of Google searches about the firm. When appropriate, companies can buy ads to run alongside keywords explaining their position and, if appropriate, offering an apology (Gregory, 2009). Homeopathic cold remedy Zicam countered blog posts citing inaccurate product information by running Google ads adjacent to these links, containing tag lines such as "Zicam: Get the Facts[4]."

Review sites such as Yelp and TripAdvisor also provide opportunities for firms to respond to negative reviews.

This can send a message that a firm recognizes missteps and is making an attempt to address the issue (follow- through is critical, or expect an even harsher backlash). Sometimes a private response is most effective. When a customer of Farmstead Cheeses and Wines in the San Francisco Bay area posted a Yelp complaint that a cashier was rude, the firm's owner sent a private reply to the poster pointing out that the employee in question was actually hard of hearing. The complaint was subsequently withdrawn and the critic eventually joined the firm's Wine Club (Paterson, 2009) . Private responses may be most appropriate if a firm is reimbursing clients or dealing with issues where public dialogue doesn't help the situation. One doesn't want to train members of the community that public griping gets reward.

For similar reasons, in some cases store credit rather than reimbursement may be appropriate compensation.

It's time to take social media seriously. We're now deep into a revolution that has rewritten the rules of customer- firm communication. There are emerging technologies and skills to acquire, a shifting landscape of laws and expectations, a minefield of dangers, and a wealth of unexploited opportunities. Organizations that professionalize their approach to social media and other Web 2.0 technologies are ready to exploit the upside—potentially stronger brands, increased sales, sharper customer service, improved innovation, and more. Those that ignore the new landscape risk catastrophe and perhaps even irrelevance.

REFERENCES

Abel, J., "Dude—Dell's Making Money Off Twitter!" Wired News, June 12, 2009.

Alterman, E., "Out of Print, the Death and Life of the American Newspaper," New Yorker, March 31, 2008. Learmonth, M., "Huffington Post More Valuable Than Some Newspaper Cos.," DigitalNext, December 1, 2008. Takahashi, D., "Technorati Releases Data on State of the Blogosphere: Bloggers of the World Have United,"

Ante, S., "Facebook's Thiel Explains Failed Twitter Takeover," BusinessWeek, March 1, 2009.

Arrington, M., "Perspective: Facebook Is Now Fifth Most Valuable U.S. Internet Company," TechCrunch, October 25, 2007.

Barger, C., talk at the Social Media Club of Detroit, November 18, 2009. Bolton, N., "Foursquare Introduces New Tools for Businesses," March 9, 2010.

Barnes, B., "Disney Acquires Web Site for Children," New York Times, August 2, 2007.

Bergman, A., "Wikipedia Is Only as Anonymous as your I.P.," O'Reilly Radar, August 14, 2007. Calabrese, M., "Wikipedia for Spies: The CIA Discovers Web 2.0," Time, April 8, 2009.

Bolton, N., "Chirp, Twitter's First Developer Conference, Opens Its Doors," New York Times, April 14, 2010. Burrows, P., "Hot Tech Companies Like Yelp Are Bypassing IPOs," BusinessWeek, February 4, 2010.

Boyle, M., "Recruiting: Enough to Make a Monster Tremble," BusinessWeek, June 25, 2009.

Brandau, M., "Starbucks Brews Up Spot on the List of Top Social Brands in 2008," Nation's Restaurant News, April 6, 2009.

Brandel, M., "Crowdsourcing: Are You Ready to Ask the World for Answers?" Computerworld, March 3, 2008. Brandel, M., "Should Your Company 'Crowdsource' Its Next Project?" Computerworld, December 6, 2007.

Bulkley, W., "Playing Well with Others," Wall Street Journal, June 18, 2007. Frauenheim, E., "Social Revolution," Workforce Management, October 2007. Goetz, T., "Practicing Patients," New York Times Magazine, March 23, 2008.

Carlin, D., "Corporate Wikis Go Viral," BusinessWeek, March 12, 2007. Hansen, E., "Wikipedia Founder Edits Own Bio," Wired, December 19, 2005.

Chmielewski D. and J. Guynn, "MySpace Ready to Prove Itself in Faceoff," Chicago Tribune, June 8, 2008.

Conway, L., "Virgin Atlantic Sacks 13 Staff for Calling Its Flyers 'Chavs,'" The Independent, November 1, 2008.

Cowgill, B., J. Wolfers, and E. Zitzewitz, "Using Prediction Markets to Track Information Flows: Evidence from Google," working paper accessed November 30, 2009, via http://bocowgill.com/ GooglePredictionMarketPaper.pdf.

D. Kirkpatrick, "Help Wanted: Adults on Facebook," Fortune, March 21, 2008.

Dvorak, P., "Best Buy Taps 'Prediction Market,'" Wall Street Journal, September 16, 2008.

Dye, R., "The Promise of Prediction Markets: A Roundtable," McKinsey Quarterly (2008): 83–93.

Eaton, K., "Twitter Really Works: Makes $6.5 Million in Sales for Dell," Fast Company, December 8, 2009. Goldman, D., "Twitter Grows Up: Take a Peek Inside," CNN, April 16, 2010.

Gallaugher J. and S. Ransbotham, "Social Media and Dialog Management at Starbucks" (presented at the MISQE Social Media Workshop, Phoenix, AZ, December 2009).

Giles, J., "Special Report: Internet Encyclopedias Go Head to Head," Nature 438, no. 15 (December 14, 2005): 900–901.

Greenfield, D., "How Companies Are Using I.T. to Spot Innovative Ideas," InformationWeek, November 8, 2008.

Gregory, S., "Domino's YouTube Crisis: 5 Ways to Fight Back," Time, April 18, 2009.

Howe, J., "The Rise of Crowdsourcing," Wired, June 2006.

Jacques, A., "Domino's Delivers during Crisis: The Company's Step-by-Step Response after a Vulgar Video Goes Viral," The Public Relations Strategist, October 24, 2009.

Johnson, B., "MySpace Bosses Battle to Oust Facebook from Social Networking Top Spot," The Guardian, March 15, 2010.

Kafka, P., "Twitter's Ad Plan: Copy Google," AllThingsD, February 25, 2010. Martin, D., "Update: Return of the Twitter Quitters," Nielsen Wire, April 30, 2009. Miller, C., "Putting Twitter's World to Use," New York Times, April 13, 2009.

Kane G. and R. Fichman, "The Shoemaker's Children: Using Wikis for Information Systems Teaching, Research, and Publication," MIS Quarterly, March 2009.

Kane, J., R. Fichman, J. Gallaugher, and J. Glaser, "Community Relations 2.0," Harvard Business Review, November 2009.

Kane, J., R. Fichman, J. Gallaugher, and J. Glaser, "Community Relations 2.0," Harvard Business Review, November 2009.

Kane, J., R. Fichman, J. Gallaugher, and J. Glaser, "Community Relations 2.0," Harvard Business Review, November 2009.

Kincaid, J., "SCVNGR Raises $4 Million from Google Ventures," TechCrunch, December 24, 2009. Terdiman, D., "Folksonomies Tap People Power," Wired, February 1, 2005.

King, R., "No Rest for the Wiki," BusinessWeek, March 12, 2007.

King, R., "No Rest for the Wiki," BusinessWeek, March 12, 2007.

King, R., "Social Networks: Execs Use Them Too," BusinessWeek, November 11, 2006.

Lacy, S., Once You're Lucky, Twice You're Good: The Rebirth of Silicon Valley and the Rise of Web 2.0 (New York: Gotham Books, 2008).

Lambert, E., "Hedging for Dummies," Forbes, March 13, 2006, 70–72. Surowiecki, J., "Crowdsourcing the Crystal Ball," Forbes, October 15, 2007.

Lichter, S. R., Are Chemicals Killing Us? Statistical Assessment Service, May 21, 2009. Pink, D., "The Book Stops Here," Wired, March 2005.

Lohr, S., "And the Winner of the $1 Million Netflix Prize (Probably) Is..." New York Times, June 26, 2009.

Malik, O., "MySpace, R.I.P.," GigaOM, February 10, 2010.

Martin, A., "Whole Foods Executive Used Alias," New York Times, July 12, 2007. Miller, C. C., "Company Settles Case of Reviews It Faked," July 14, 2009.

Murrell, J., "Twitter Treads Gently into Advertising Minefield," San Jose Mercury News, April 13, 2010. Romano, A., "Now 4 Restaurant 2.0," Newsweek, February 28, 2009.

Nakashima, E., "YouTube Ordered to Release User Data," Washington Post, July 4, 2008.

Nelson, B., presentation at the Social Media Conference NW, Mount Vernon, WA, March 25, 2010. Paterson, K., "Managing an Online Reputation," New York Times, July 29, 2009.

Nicole, K., "iLike Sees Exponential Growth with Facebook App," Mashable, June 11, 2007. Schulder, M., "50on50: Saw Blade through Thumb. What Would You Do?" CNN, November 4, 2009.

Popkin, H., "Twitter Gets You Fired in 140 Characters or Less," MSNBC, March 23, 2009. Rathke, L., "Report: Ski Resorts Exaggerate Snowfall Totals," USA Today, January 29, 2010.

Ruffini, C., "State Dept. Asked Twitter to Delay Maintenance," CBS News, June 16, 2009.

Schonfeld, E., "Time Magazine Throws Up Its Hands As It Gets Pawned by 4Chan," TechCrunch, April 27, 2009. Soat, J., "7 Questions Key to Social Networking Success," InformationWeek, January 16, 2010.

Schonfeld, E., "Twitter's Internal Strategy Laid Bare: To Be 'The Pulse of The Planet,'" TechCrunch, July 19, 2009.

Shaer, M., "Google Launches Archive Search for Twitter," Christian Science Monitor, April 15, 2010. Stanley, M., Internet Trends Report, March 2008.

Stone, B., "Facebook Aims to Extend Its Reach across the Web," New York Times, December 2, 2008. York, E., "McDonald's Names First Social-Media Chief," Chicago Business, April 13, 2010.

Swisher, K., "Ning CEO Gina Bianchini to Step Down—Becomes an EIR at Andreessen Horowitz," AllThingsD, March 15, 2010.

Talbot, D., "Can Twitter Make Money?" Technology Review, March/April 2010.

Vascellaro, J., "Facebook CEO in No Rush to 'Friend' Wall Street," Wall Street Journal, March 3, 2010.

VentureBeat, September 28, 2008.

Wash, B., "Double Duty," Colby Magazine, Winter 2009. while Yelp has reportedly turned down acquisition offers valuing it at $700 million.

Williams, I., "Sony Caught Editing Halo 3 Wikipedia Entry," Vnunet.com, September 5, 2007.

Zuckerman, S., "Yes, Some Blogs Are Profitable—Very Profitable," San Francisco Chronicle, October 21, 2007.

FACEBOOK: MAKING THE BUSINESS FROM THE SOCIAL GRAPH

8

8.1 INTRODUCTION: AN OVERVIEW

Here's how much of a Web 2.0 guy Mark Zuckerberg is: during the weeks he spent working on Facebook as a Harvard sophomore, he didn't have time to study for a course he was taking, "Art in the Time of Augustus," so he built a Web site containing all of the artwork in class and pinged his classmates to contribute to a communal study guide. Within hours, the wisdom of crowds produced a sort of custom CliffsNotes for the course, and after reviewing the Web-based crib sheet, he aced the test. Turns out he didn't need to take that exam, anyway. Zuck (that's what the cool kids call him)[1] dropped out of Harvard later that year.

Zuckerberg is known as both a shy, geeky, introvert who eschews parties, and as a brash Silicon Valley bad boy. After Facebook's incorporation, Zuckerberg's job description was listed as "Founder, Master and Commander [and] Enemy of the State" (McGinn, 2004). An early business card read "I'm CEO...Bitch" (Hoffman, 2008). And let's not forget that Facebook came out of drunken experiments in his dorm room, one of which was a system for comparing classmates to farm animals (Zuckerberg, threatened with expulsion, later apologized). For one meeting with Sequoia Capital, the venerable Menlo Park venture capital firm that backed Google and YouTube, Zuckerberg showed up in his pajamas (Hoffman, 2008).

By the age of twenty-three, Mark Zuckerberg had graced the cover of *Newsweek*, been profiled on *60 Minutes*, and was discussed in the tech world with a reverence previously reserved only for Steve Jobs and the Google guys, Sergey Brin and Larry Page. But Mark Zuckerberg's star rose much faster than any of his predecessors. Just two weeks after Facebook launched, the firm had four thousand users. Ten months later it was up to one million. The growth continued, and the business world took notice. In 2006, Viacom (parent of MTV) saw that its core demographic was spending a ton of time on Facebook and offered to buy the firm for three quarters of a billion dollars. Zuckerberg passed (Rosenbush, 2006). Yahoo! offered up a cool billion (twice). Zuck passed again, both times.

As growth skyrocketed, Facebook built on its stranglehold of the college market (over 85 percent of four-year college students are Facebook members), opening up first to high schoolers, then to everyone. Web hipsters started selling shirts emblazoned with "I Facebooked your Mom!" Even Microsoft wanted some of Facebook's magic. In 2006, the firm temporarily locked up the right to broker all banner ad sales that run on the U.S. version of Facebook, guaranteeing Zuckerberg's firm $100 million a year through 2011. In 2007, Microsoft came back, buying 1.6 percent of the firm for $240 million[2].

The investment was a shocker. Do the math and a 1.6 percent stake for $240 million values Facebook at $15 billion (more on that later). That meant that a firm that at the time had only five hundred employees, $150 million in revenues, and was helmed by a twenty-three-year-old college dropout in his first "real job," was more valuable than General Motors. Rupert Murdoch, whose News Corporation owns rival MySpace, engaged in a little trash talk, referring to Facebook as "the flavor of the month" (Morrissey, 2008).

Watch your back, Rupert. Or on second thought, watch Zuckerberg's. By spring 2009, Facebook had more than twice MySpace's monthly unique visitors worldwide (Schonfeld, 2009); by June, Facebook surpassed MySpace in the United States[3]; by July, Facebook was **cash-flow positive**; and by February 2010 (when Facebook turned six), the firm had over four hundred million users, more than doubling in size in less than a year (Gage, 2009). Murdoch, the media titan who stood atop an empire that includes the *Wall Street Journal* and Fox, had been outmaneuvered by "the kid."

Why Examine Facebook?

Looking at the "flavor of the month" and trying to distinguish the reality from the hype is a critical managerial skill. In Facebook's case, there are a lot of folks with a vested interest in figuring out where the firm is headed. If you want to work there, are you signing on to a firm where your *stock options* and *401k* contributions are going to be worth something or worthless? If you're an investor and Facebook **goes public**, should you **short** the firm or increase your holdings? Would you invest in or avoid firms that rely on Facebook's business? Should your firm rush to partner with the firm? Would you extend the firm credit? Offer it better terms to secure its growing business, or worse terms because you think it's a risky bet? Is this firm the next Google (underestimated at first, and now wildly profitable and influential), the next GeoCities (Yahoo! paid $3 billion for it—no one goes to the site today), or the next Skype (deeply impactful with over half a billion accounts worldwide, but not much of a profit generator)? The jury is still out on all this, but let's look at the fundamentals with an eye to applying what we've learned. No one has a crystal ball, but we do have some key concepts that can guide our analysis. There are a lot of broadly applicable managerial lessons that can be gleaned by examining Facebook's successes and missteps. Studying the firm provides a context for examining nework effects, platforms, partnerships, issues in the rollout of new technologies, privacy, ad models, and more.

8.2 BIG DEAL

The prior era's Internet golden boy, Netscape founder Marc Andreessen, has said that Facebook is "an amazing achievement one of the most significant milestones in the technology industry" (Vogelstein, 2007). While still in his twenties, Andreessen founded Netscape, eventually selling it to AOL for over $4 billion. His second firm, Opsware, was sold to HP for $1.6 billion. He joined Facebook's Board of Directors within months of making this comment. Why is Facebook considered such a big deal?

First there's the growth: between December 2008 and 2009, Facebook was adding between six hundred thousand and a million users a day. It was as if every twenty-four hours, a group as big or bigger than the entire city of Boston filed into Facebook's servers to set up new accounts. Roughly half of Facebook users visit the site every single day, (Gage, 2009) with the majority spending fifty-five minutes or more getting their daily Facebook fix[1]. And it seems that Mom really is on Facebook (Dad, too); users thirty-five years and older account for more than half of Facebook's daily visitors and its fastest growing population (Hagel & Brown, 2008; Gage, 2009).

Then there's what these users are doing on the site: Facebook isn't just a collection of personal home pages and a place to declare your allegiance to your friends. The integrated set of Facebook services encroaches on a wide swath of established Internet businesses. Facebook has become the *first-choice* messaging and chat service for this generation. E-mail is for your professors, but Facebook is for friends. In photos, Google, Yahoo! and MySpace all spent millions to acquire photo sharing tools (Picasa, Flickr, and Photobucket, respectively). But Facebook is now the biggest photo-sharing site on the Web, taking in some three billion photos each month[1]. And watch out, YouTube. Facebookers share eight million videos each month. YouTube will get you famous, but Facebook is a place most go to share clips you only want friends to see (Vogelstein, 2009).

Facebook is a kingmaker, opinion catalyst, and traffic driver. While in the prior decade news stories would carry a notice saying, "Copyright, do not distribute without permission," major news outlets today, including the *New York Times*, display Facebook icons alongside every copyrighted story, encouraging users to "share" the content on their profile pages via Facebook's "Like" button, scattering it all over the Web. Like digital photos, video, and instant messaging, link sharing is Facebook's sharp elbow to the competition. Suddenly, Facebook gets space on a page alongside Digg.com and Del.icio.us, even though those guys showed up first.

Facebook Office? Facebook rolled out the document collaboration and sharing service Docs.com in partnership with Microsoft. Facebook is also hard at work on its own e-mail system (Blodget, 2010), music service (Kincaid, 2010), and payments mechanism (Maher, 2010). Look out, Gmail, Hotmail, Pandora, iTunes, PayPal, and Yahoo!—you may all be in Facebook's path!

As for search, Facebook's got designs on that, too. Google and Bing index some Facebook content, but since much of Facebook is private, accessible only among friends, this represents a massive blind spot for Google search. Sites that can't be indexed by Google and other search engines are referred to as the **dark Web**. While Facebook's partnership with Microsoft currently offers Web search results through Bing.com, Facebook has announced its intention to offer its own search engine with real-time access to up-to-the-minute results from status updates, links, and other information made available to you by your friends. If Facebook can tie together standard Internet search with its dark Web content, this just might be enough for some to break the Google habit.

And Facebook is political—in big, regime-threatening ways. The site is considered such a powerful tool in the activist's toolbox that China, Iran, and Syria are among nations that have, at times, attempted to block Facebook access within their borders. Egyptians have used the site to protest for democracy. Saudi women have used it to lobby for driving privileges. ABC News cosponsored U.S. presidential debates with Facebook. And Facebook cofounder Chris Hughes was even recruited by the Obama campaign to create my.barackobama.com, a social media site considered vital in the 2008 U.S. presidential victory (Talbot, 2008; McGirt, 2009).

8.3 GRAPH OF SOCIAL MEDIA

At the heart of Facebook's appeal is a concept Zuckerberg calls the **social graph**, which refers to Facebook's ability to collect, express, and leverage the connections between the site's users, or as some describe it, "the global mapping of everyone and how they're related" (Iskold, 2007). Think of all the stuff that's on Facebook as a node or endpoint that's connected to other stuff. You're connected to other users (your friends), photos about you are tagged, comments you've posted carry your name, you're a member of groups, you're connected to applications you've installed—Facebook links them all (Zeichick, 2008).

While MySpace and Facebook are often mentioned in the same sentence, from their founding these sites were conceived differently. It goes beyond the fact that Facebook, with its neat, ordered user profiles, looks like a planned community compared to the garish, Vegas-like free-for-all of MySpace. MySpace was founded by musicians seeking to reach out to unknown users and make them fans. It's no wonder the firm, with its proximity to Los Angeles and ownership by News Corporation, is viewed as more of a media company. It has cut deals to run network television shows on its site, and has even established a record label. It's also important to note that from the start anyone could create a MySpace identity, and this open nature meant that you couldn't always trust what you saw. Rife with bogus profiles, even News Corporation's Rupert Murdoch has had to contend with the dozens of bogus Ruperts who have popped up on the service (Petrecca, 2006)!

Facebook, however, was established in the relatively safe cocoon of American undergraduate life, and was conceived as a place where you could *reinforce* contacts among those who, for the most part, you already knew. The site was one of the first social networks where users actually identified themselves using their real names. If you wanted to establish that you worked for a certain firm or were a student of a particular university, you had to verify that you were legitimate via an e-mail address issued by that organization. It was this "realness" that became Facebook's distinguishing feature—bringing along with it a degree of safety and comfort that enabled Facebook to become a true social utility and build out a solid social graph consisting of verified relationships. Since "friending" (which is a link between nodes in the social graph) required both users to approve the relationship, the network fostered an incredible amount of trust. Today, many Facebook users post their cell phone numbers and their birthdays, offer personal photos, and otherwise share information they'd never do outside their circle of friends. Because of trust, Facebook's social graph is stronger than MySpace's.

There is also a strong **network effect** to Facebook (see Chapter 6 "Understanding Network Effects"). People are attracted to the service because others they care about are more likely to be there than anywhere else online. Without the network effect Facebook wouldn't exist. And it's because of the network effect that another smart kid in a dorm can't rip off Zuckerberg in any market where Facebook is the biggest fish. Even an exact copy of Facebook would be a virtual ghost town with no social graph (see Note 8.23 "It's Not the Technology" below).

The **switching costs** for Facebook are also extremely powerful. A move to another service means recreating your entire social graph. The more time you spend on the service, the more you've invested in your graph and the less likely you are to move to a rival.

8.4 FACEBOOK FEEDS: DATA FLOWS' EBOLA

While the authenticity and trust offered by Facebook was critical, offering News Feeds concentrated and released value from the social graph. With feeds, each time a user performs an activity in Facebook—makes a friend, uploads a picture, joins a group—

the feed blasts this information to all of your friends in a reverse chronological list that shows up right when they next log on. An individual user's activities are also listed within a mini feed that shows up on their profile. Get a new job, move to a new city, read a great article, have a pithy quote—post it to Facebook—the feed picks it up, and the world of your Facebook friends will get an update.

Feeds are perhaps the linchpin of Facebook's ability to strengthen and deliver user value from the social graph, but for a brief period of time it looked like feeds would kill the company. News Feeds were launched on September 5, 2006, just as many of the nation's undergrads were arriving on campus. Feeds reflecting any Facebook activity (including changes to the relationship status) became a sort of gossip page splashed right when your friends logged in. To many, feeds were first seen as a viral blast of digital nosiness—a release of information they hadn't consented to distribute widely.

And in a remarkable irony, user disgust over the News Feed ambush offered a whip-crack demonstration of the power and speed of the feed virus. Protest groups formed, and every student who, for example, joined a group named Students Against Facebook News Feed, had this fact blasted to their friends (along with a quick link where friends, too, could click to join the group). Hundreds of thousands of users mobilized against the firm in just twenty-four hours. It looked like Zuckerberg's creation had turned on him, Frankenstein style.

The first official Facebook blog post on the controversy came off as a bit condescending (never a good tone to use when your customers feel that you've wronged them). "Calm down. Breathe. We hear you," wrote Zuckerberg on the evening of September 5. The next post, three days after the News Feed launch, was much more contrite ("We really messed this one up," he wrote). In the 484-word open letter, Zuckerberg apologized for the surprise, explaining how users could opt out of feeds. The tactic worked, and the controversy blew over (Vogelstein, 2007). The ability to stop personal information from flowing into the feed stream was just enough to stifle critics, and as it turns out, a lot of people really liked the feeds and found them useful. It soon became clear that if you wanted to use the Web to keep track of your social life and contacts, Facebook was the place to be. Not only did feeds not push users away, by the start of the next semester subscribers had nearly doubled!

8.5 A PLATFORM FOR FACEBOOK

In May 2007, Facebook followed News Feeds with another initiative that set it head and shoulders above its competition. At the firm's first f8 (pronounced "fate") Developers Conference, Mark Zuckerberg stood on stage and announced that he was opening up the screen real estate on Facebook to other application developers. Facebook published a set of **application programming interfaces (APIs)** that specified how programs could be written to run within and interact with Facebook. Now any programmer could write an application that would run inside a user's profile. Geeks of the world, Facebook's user base could be yours! Just write something good.

Developers could charge for their wares, offer them for free, and even run ads. And Facebook let developers keep what they made (Facebook does revenue share with app vendors for some services, such as the Facebook Credits payment service, mentioned later). This was a key distinction; MySpace initially restricted developer revenue on the few products designed to run on their site, at times even blocking some applications. The choice was clear, and developers flocked to Facebook.

To promote the new apps, Facebook would run an Applications area on the site where users could browse offerings. Even better, News Feed was a viral injection that spread the word each time an application was installed. Your best friend just put up a slide show app? Maybe you'll check it out, too. The predictions of $1 billion in social network ad spending were geek catnip, and legions of programmers came calling. Apps could be cobbled together on the quick, feeds made them spread like wildfire, and the early movers offered adoption rates never before seen by small groups of software developers. People began speaking of the Facebook Economy. Facebook was considered a platform. Some compared it to the next Windows, Zuckerberg the next Gates (hey, they both dropped out of Harvard, right?).

And each application potentially added more value and features to the site without Facebook lifting a finger. The initial event launched with sixty-five developer partners and eighty-five applications. There were some missteps along the way. Some applications were accused of spamming friends with invites to install them. There were also security concerns and apps that violated the intellectual property of other firms (see the "Scrabulous" sidebar below), but Facebook worked to quickly remove errant apps, improve the system, and encourage developers. Just one year in, Facebook had marshaled the efforts of some four hundred thousand developers and entrepreneurs, twenty-four thousand applications had been built for the platform, 140 new apps were being added each day, and 95 percent of Facebook members had installed at least one Facebook application. As Sarah Lacy, author of *Once*

You're Lucky, Twice You're Good, put it, "with one masterstroke, Zuck had mobilized all of Silicon Valley to innovate for him."

With feeds to spread the word, Facebook was starting to look like the first place to go to launch an online innovation. Skip the Web, bring it to Zuckerberg's site first. Consider iLike: within the first three months, the firm saw installs of its Facebook app explode to seven million, more than doubling the number of users the firm was able to attract through the Web site it introduced the previous year. ILike became so cool that by September, platinum rocker KT Tunstall was debuting tracks through the Facebook service. A programmer named Mark Pincus wrote a Texas hold 'em game at his kitchen table (Guynn, 2007). Today his social gaming firm, Zynga, is a powerhouse—a profitable firm with over three dozen apps, over 230 million users (MacMillan, 2009), and more than $600 million in annual revenue (Learmonth & Klaasen, 2009; Carlson & Angelova, 2010). Zynga games include MafiaWars, Vampires, and the wildly successful FarmVille, which boasts some twenty times the number of actual farms in the United States. App firm Slide (started by PayPal cofounder Max Levchin) scored investments from Legg Mason, and Fidelity pegged the firm's value at $500 million (Hempel & Copeland, 2008). Playfish, the U.K. social gaming firm behind the Facebook hits Pet Society and Restaurant City, was snapped up by Electronic Arts for $300 million with another $100 million due if the unit hits performance targets. Lee Lorenzen, founder of Altura Ventures, an investment firm exclusively targeting firms creating Facebook apps, said, "Facebook is God's gift to developers. Never has the path from a good idea to millions of users been shorter" (Guynn, 2007).

But legitimate questions remain. Are Facebook apps really a big deal? Just how important will apps be to adding sustained value within Facebook? And how will firms leverage the Facebook framework to extract their own value? A chart from FlowingData showed the top category, Just for Fun, was larger than the next four categories combined. That suggests that a lot of applications are faddish time wasters. Yes, there is experimentation beyond virtual Zombie Bites. Visa has created a small business network on Facebook (Facebook had some eighty thousand small businesses online at the time of Visa's launch). Educational software firm Blackboard offered an application that will post data to Facebook pages as soon as there are updates to someone's Blackboard account (new courses, whether assignments or grades have been posted, etc.). We're still a long way from Facebook as a Windows rival, but the platform helped push Facebook to number one, and it continues to deliver quirky fun (and then some) supplied by thousands of developers off its payroll.

8.6 A WORK IN PROGRESS: SOCIAL NETWORKS AND ADVERTISING

If Facebook is going to continue to give away its services for free, it needs to make money somehow. Right now the bulk of revenue comes from advertising. Fortunately for the firm, online advertising is hot. For years, online advertising has been the only major media category that has seen an increase in spending (see Chapter 14 "Google: Search, Online Advertising, and Beyond"). Firms spend more advertising online than they do on radio and magazine ads, and the Internet will soon beat out spending on cable TV (Sweeney, 2008; Wayne, 2010). But not all Internet advertising is created equal. And there are signs that social networking sites are struggling to find the right ad model.

Google founder Sergey Brin sums up this frustration, saying, "I don't think we have the killer best way to advertise and monetize social networks yet," that social networking ad inventory as a whole was proving problematic and that the "monetization work we were doing [in social media] didn't pan out as well as we had hoped[1]." When Google ad partner Fox Interactive Media (the News Corporation division that contains MySpace) announced that revenue would fall $100 million short of projections, News Corporation's stock tumbled 5 percent, analysts downgraded the company, and the firm's chief revenue officer was dismissed (Stelter, 2008).

Why aren't social networks having the success of Google and other sites? Problems advertising on these sites include **content adjacency**, and user attention. The *content adjacency* problem refers to concern over where a firm's advertisements will run. Consider all of the questionable titles in social networking news groups. Do advertisers really want their ads running alongside conversations that are racy, offensive, illegal, or that may even mock their products? This potential juxtaposition is a major problem with any site offering ads adjacent to free-form social media. Summing up industry wariness, one P&G manager said, "What in heaven's name made you think you could monetize the real estate in which somebody is breaking up with their girlfriend?" (Stone, 2008) An IDC report suggests that it's because of content adjacency that "brand advertisers largely consider user- generated content as low-quality, brand-unsafe inventory" for running ads (Stross, 2008).

Now let's look at the user attention problem.

Attention Major Challenges: The Hunt Versus The Hike

In terms of revenue model, Facebook is radically different from Google and the hot-growth category of search advertising. Users of Google and other search sites are on a *hunt*—a task-oriented expedition to collect information that will drive a specific action. Search users want to learn something, buy something, research a problem, or get a question answered. To the extent that the hunt overlaps with ads, it works. Just searched on a medical term? Google will show you an ad from a drug company. Looking for a toy? You'll see Google ads from eBay sellers and other online shops. Type in a vacation destination and you get a long list of ads from travel providers aggressively courting your spending. Even better, Google only charges text advertisers when a user clicks through. No clicks? The ad runs at no cost to the firm. From a return on investment perspective, this is extraordinarily efficient. How often do users click on Google ads? Enough for this to be the single most profitable activity among *any* Internet firm. In 2009, Google revenue totaled nearly $24 billion. Profits exceeded $6.5 billion, almost all of this from pay-per-click ads (see Chapter 14 "Google: Search, Online Advertising, and Beyond" for more details).

While users go to Google to hunt, they go to Facebook as if they were going on a *hike*—they have a rough idea of what they'll encounter, but they're there to explore and look around, enjoy the sights (or site). They've usually allocated time for fun and they don't want to leave the terrain when they're having conversations, looking at photos or videos, and checking out updates from friends.

These usage patterns are reflected in click-through rates. Google users click on ads around 2 percent of the time (and at a much higher rate when searching for product information). At Facebook, click-throughs are about 0.04 percent (Urstadt, 2008).

Most banner ads don't charge per click but rather **CPM** (cost per thousand) **impressions** (each time an ad appears on someone's screen). But Facebook banner ads performed so poorly that the firm pulled them in early 2010 (McCarthy, 2010). Lookery, a one-time ad network that bought ad space on Facebook in bulk, had been reselling inventory at a CPM of 7.5 cents (note that Facebook does offer advertisers pay-per-click as well as impression- based, or CPM, options). Even Facebook ads with a bit of targeting weren't garnering much (Facebook's Social Ads, which allow advertisers to target users according to location and age, have a floor price of fifteen cents CPM) (Urstadt, 2008; Schonfeld, 2008). Other social networks also suffered. In 2008, MySpace lowered its banner ad rate from $3.25 CPM to less than two dollars. By contrast, information and news-oriented sites do much better, particularly if these sites draw in a valuable and highly targeted audience. The social networking blog Mashable has CPM rates ranging between seven and thirty-three dollars. *Technology Review* magazine boasts a CPM of seventy dollars. *TechTarget*, a Web publisher focusing on technology professionals, has been able to command CPM rates of one hundred dollars and above (an ad inventory that valuable helped the firm go public in 2007).

Getting Creative with Promotions: Does It Work?

Facebook and other social networks are still learning what works. Ad inventory displayed on high-traffic home pages have garnered big bucks for firms like Yahoo! With Facebook offering advertisers greater audience reach than most network television programs, there's little reason to suggest that chunks of this business won't eventually flow to the social networks. But even more interesting is how Facebook and widget sites have begun to experiment with relatively new forms of advertising. Many feel that Facebook has a unique opportunity to get consumers to engage with their brand, and some initial experiments point where this may be heading.

Many firms have been leveraging so-called **engagement ads** by making their products part of the Facebook fun. Using an engagement ad, a firm can set up a promotion where a user can do things such as "Like" or become a fan of a brand, RSVP to an event and invite others, watch and comment on a video and see what your friends have to say, send a "virtual gift" with a personal message, or answer a question in a poll. The viral nature of Facebook allows actions to flow back into the news feed and spread among friends.

COO Sheryl Sandberg discussed Ben & Jerry's promotion for the ice cream chain's free cone day event. To promote the upcoming event, Ben & Jerry's initially contracted to make two hundred and fifty thousand "gift cones" available to Facebook users; they could click on little icons that would gift a cone icon to a friend, and that would show up in their profile. Within a couple of hours, customers had sent all two hundred and fifty thousand virtual cones. Delighted, Ben & Jerry's bought another two hundred and fifty thousand cones. Within eleven hours, half a million people had sent cones, many making plans with Facebook friends to attend the real free cone day. The day of the Facebook promotion, Ben & Jerry's Web site registered fifty-three million impressions, as users searched for store locations and wrote about their favorite flavors (Hardy, 2008). The campaign dovetailed with everything Facebook was good at: it was viral, generating enthusiasm for a promotional event and even prompting scheduling.

In other promotions, Honda gave away three quarters of a million hearts during a Valentine's Day promo (Sandberg, 2009), and the Dr. Pepper Snapple Group offered two hundred and fifty thousand virtual Sunkist sodas, which earned the firm one hundred thirty million brand impressions in twenty-two hours. Says Sunkist's brand manager, "A Super Bowl ad, if you compare it, would have generated somewhere between six to seven million" (Wong, 2008).

Of course, even with this business, Facebook may find that it competes with widget makers. Unlike Apple's App Store (where much of developer-earned revenue comes from selling apps), the vast majority of Facebook apps are free and supported by ads. That means Facebook and its app providers are both running at a finite pot of advertising dollars. Slide's Facebook apps have attracted top-tier advertisers, such as Coke and Paramount Pictures—a group Facebook regularly courts as well. By some estimates, in 2009, Facebook app developers took in well over half a billion dollars—exceeding Facebook's own haul (Learmonth & Klaasen, 2009). And there's controversy. Zynga was skewered in the press when some of its partners were accused of scamming users into signing up for subscriptions or installing unwanted software in exchange for game credits (Zynga has since taken steps to screen partners and improve transparency) (Arrington, 2009).

While these efforts might be innovative, are they even effective? Some of these programs are considered successes; others, not so much. Jupiter Research surveyed marketers trying to create a viral impact online and found that only about 15 percent of these efforts actually caught on with consumers (Cowan, 2008). While the Ben & Jerry's gift cones were used up quickly, a visit to Facebook in the weeks after this campaign saw CareerBuilder,

Wide Eye Caffeinated Spirits, and Coors Light icons lingering days after their first appearance. Brands seeking to deploy their own applications in Facebook have also struggled. *New Media Age* reported that applications rolled out by top brands such as MTV, Warner Bros., and Woolworths were found to have as little as five daily users. Congestion may be setting in for all but the most innovative applications, as standing out in a crowd of over 550,000 applications becomes increasingly difficult[3].

Consumer products giant P&G has been relentlessly experimenting with leveraging social networks for brand engagement, but the results show what a tough slog this can be. The firm did garner fourteen thousand Facebook "fans" for its Crest Whitestrips product, but those fans were earned while giving away free movie tickets and other promos. The *New York Times* quipped that with those kinds of incentives, "a hemorrhoid cream" could have attracted a similar group of "fans." When the giveaways stopped, thousands promptly "unfanned" Whitestrips. Results for Procter & Gamble's "2X Ultra Tide" fan page were also pretty grim. P&G tried offbeat appeals for customer-brand bonding, including asking Facebookers to post "their favorite places to enjoy stain-making moments." But a check eleven months after launch had garnered just eighteen submissions, two from P&G, two from staffers at spoof news site *The Onion*, and a bunch of short posts such as "Tidealicious!" (Stross, 2008)

Efforts around engagement opportunities like events (Ben & Jerry's) or products consumers are anxious to identify themselves with (a band or a movie) may have more success than trying to promote consumer goods that otherwise offer little allegiance, but efforts are so new that metrics are scarce, impact is tough to gauge, and best practices are still unclear.

8.7 PRIVACY PERIL: BEACON AND THE TOS DEBACLE

Conventional advertising may grow into a great business for Facebook, but the firm was clearly sitting on something that was unconventional compared to prior generations of Web services. Could the energy and virulent nature of social networks be harnessed to offer truly useful, consumer information to its users? Word of mouth is considered the most persuasive (and valuable) form of marketing (Kumar, et. al., 2007), and Facebook was a giant word of mouth machine. What if the firm worked with vendors and grabbed consumer activity at the point of purchase to put into the News Feed and post to a user's profile? If you rented a video, bought a cool product, or dropped something in your wish list, your buddies could get a heads-up and they might ask you about it. The person being asked feels like an expert, the person with the question gets a frank opinion, and the vendor providing the data just might get another sale. It looked like a home run.

This effort, named Beacon, was announced in November 2007. Some forty e-commerce sites signed up, including Blockbuster, Fandango, eBay, Travelocity, Zappos, and the *New York Times*. Zuckerberg was so confident of the effort that he stood before a group of Madison Avenue ad executives and declared that Beacon would represent a "once-in-a-hundred-years" fundamental change in the way media works.

Like News Feeds, user reaction was swift and brutal. The commercial activity of Facebook users began showing up without their consent. The biggest problem with Beacon was that it was "opt-out" instead of "opt-in." Facebook (and its partners) assumed users would agree to sharing data in their feeds. A pop-up box did appear briefly on most sites supporting Beacon, but it disappeared after a few seconds (Nakashima, 2007). Many users, blind to these sorts of alerts, either clicked through or ignored the warnings. And well...there are some purchases you might not want to broadcast to the world.

"Facebook Ruins Christmas for Everyone!" screamed one headline from MSNBC. com. Another from *U.S. News and World Report* read "How Facebook Stole Christmas." The *Washington Post* ran the story of Sean Lane, a twenty-eight-year-old tech support worker from Waltham, Massachusetts, who got a message from his wife just two hours after he bought a ring on Overstock.com. "Who is this ring for?" she wanted to know. Facebook had not only posted a feed that her husband had bought the ring, but also that he got it for a 51 percent discount!

Overstock quickly announced that it was halting participation in Beacon until Facebook changed its practice to opt in (Nakashima, 2007).

MoveOn.org started a Facebook group and online petition protesting Beacon. The Center for Digital Democracy and the U.S. Public Interest Research Group asked the Federal Trade Commission to investigate Facebook's advertising programs. And a Dallas woman sued Blockbuster for violating the Video Privacy Protection Act (a 1998 U.S. law prohibiting unauthorized access to video store rental records).

To Facebook's credit, the firm acted swiftly. Beacon was switched to an opt-in system, where user consent must be given before partner data is sent to the feed. Zuckerberg would later say regarding Beacon: "We've made a lot of mistakes building this feature, but we've made even more with how we've handled them. We simply did a bad job with this release, and I apologize for it" (McCarthy, 2007). Beacon was eventually shut down and $9.5 million was donated to various privacy groups as part of its legal settlement (Brodkin, 2009). Despite the Beacon fiasco, new users continued to flock to the site, and loyal users stuck with Zuck. Perhaps a bigger problem was that many of those forty A-list e-commerce sites that took a gamble with Facebook now had their names associated with a privacy screw-up that made headlines worldwide. A manager so burned isn't likely to sign up first for the next round of experimentation.

From the Prada example in Chapter 3 "Zara: Fast Fashion from Savvy Systems" we learned that savvy managers look beyond technology and consider complete information systems—not just the hardware and software of technology but also the interactions among the data, people, and procedures that make up (and are impacted by) information systems. Beacon's failure is a cautionary tale of what can go wrong if users fail to broadly consider the impact and implications of an information system on all those it can touch. Technology's reach is often farther, wider, and more significantly impactful than we originally expect.

Damage to Reputation and Increasing Scrutiny —The Facebook TOS Debacle

Facebook also suffered damage to its reputation, brand, and credibility, further reinforcing perceptions that the company acts brazenly, without considering user needs, and is fast and loose on privacy and user notification. Facebook worked through the feeds outrage, eventually convincing users of the benefits of feeds. But Beacon was a fiasco. And now users, the media, and watchdogs were on the alert.

When the firm modified its terms of service (TOS) policy in Spring 2009, the uproar was immediate. As a cover story in *New York* magazine summed it up, Facebook's new TOS appeared to state, "We can do anything we want with your content, forever," even if a user deletes their account and leaves the service (Grigoriadis, 2009). Yet *another* privacy backlash!

Activists organized, the press crafted juicy, attention-grabbing headlines, and the firm was forced once again to backtrack. But here's where others can learn from Facebook's missteps and response. The firm was contrite and reached out to explain and engage users. The old TOS were reinstated, and the firm posted a proposed new version that gave the firm broad latitude in leveraging user content without claiming ownership. And the firm renounced the right to use this content if a user closed their Facebook account. This new TOS was offered in a way that solicited user comments, and it was submitted to a community vote, considered binding if 30 percent of Facebook users participated. Zuckerberg's move appeared to have turned Facebook into a democracy and helped empower users to determine the firm's next step.

Despite the uproar, only about 1 percent of Facebook users eventually voted on the measure, but the 74 percent to 26 percent ruling in favor of the change gave Facebook some cover to move forward (Smith, 2009). This event also demonstrates that a tempest can be generated by a relatively small number of passionate users. Firms ignore the vocal and influential at their own peril!

In Facebook's defense, the broad TOS was probably more a form of legal protection than any nefarious attempt to exploit all user posts ad infinitum. The U.S. legal environment does require that explicit terms be defined and communicated to users, even if these are tough for laypeople to understand. But a "trust us" attitude toward user data doesn't work, particularly for a firm considered to have committed ham-handed gaffes in the past. Managers must learn from the freewheeling Facebook community. In the era of social media, your actions are now subject to immediate and sustained review. Violate the public trust and expect the equivalent of a high-powered investigative microscope examining your every move, and a very public airing of the findings.

8.8 PREDATORS AND PRIVACY

While spoiling Christmas is bad, sexual predators are far worse, and in October 2007, Facebook became an investigation target. Officials from the New York State Attorney General's office had posed as teenagers on Facebook and received sexual advances. Complaints to the service from investigators posing as parents were also not immediately addressed. These were troubling developments for a firm that prided itself on trust and authenticity.

In a 2008 agreement with forty-nine states, Facebook offered aggressive programs, many of which put it in line with MySpace. MySpace had become known as a lair for predators, and after months of highly publicized tragic incidents, the firm had become very aggressive about protecting minors. To get a sense of the scope of the problem, consider that MySpace claimed that it had found and deleted some twenty-nine thousand accounts from its site after comparing profiles against a database of convicted sex offenders[1]. Following MySpace's lead, Facebook agreed to respond to complaints about inappropriate content within twenty-four hours and to allow an independent examiner to monitor how it handles complaints. The firm imposed age-locking restrictions on profiles, reviewing any attempt by someone under the age of eighteen to change their date of birth. Profiles of minors were no longer searchable. The site agreed to automatically send a warning message when a child is at risk of revealing personal information to an unknown adult. And links to explicit material, the most offensive Facebook groups, and any material related to cyberbullying were banned.

8.9 ONE GRAPH TO RULE THEM ALL: FACEBOOK DOMINATES THE WEB

In spring 2010, the world got a sense of the breadth and depth of Mark Zuckerberg's vision. During the firm's annual f8 Developers Conference, Facebook launched a series of initiatives that placed the company directly at the center of identity, sharing, and personalization—not just on Facebook but also across the Web.

With just a few lines of HTML code, any developer could add a Facebook "Like" button to their site and take advantage of the social network's power of viral distribution. A user clicking that page's "Like" button automatically would then send a link to that page to their news feed, where it has the potential to be seen by all of their friends. No additional sign-in is necessary as long as you logged into

Facebook first (reinforcing Facebook's importance as the first stop in your Internet surfing itinerary). While some sites renamed "Like" to "Recommend" (after all, do you really want to "like" a story about a disaster or tragedy?), the effort was adopted with stunning speed. Facebook's "Like" button served up more than one billion times across the Web in the first twenty-four hours, and over fifty thousand Web sites signed up to add the "Like" button to their content within the first week (Oreskovic, 2010).

Facebook also offered a system where Web site operators can choose to accept a user's Facebook credentials for logging in. Users like this because they can access content without the hurdle of creating a new account. Web sites like it because with the burden of signing up out of the way, Facebook becomes an experimentation lubricant: "Oh, I can use my Facebook ID to sign in? Then let me try this out."

Facebook also lets Web sites embed some Facebook functionality right on their pages. A single line of code added to any page creates a "social toolbar" that shows which of your friends are logged into Facebook, and allows access to Facebook Chat without leaving that site. Site operators who are keen on making it easy for friends to summon friends to their pages can now sprinkle these little bits of Facebook across the Web.

Other efforts allow firms to leverage Facebook data to make their sites more personalized. Firms around the Web can now show if a visitor's friends have "Liked" items on the site, posted comments, or performed other actions. Using this feature, Facebook users logging into Yelp can see a list of restaurants recommended by trusted friends instead of just the reviews posted by a bunch of strangers. Users of the music-streaming site Pandora can have the service customized based on music tastes pulled from their Facebook profile page. They can share stations with friends and have data flow back to update the music preferences listed in their Facebook profile pages. Visit CNN and the site can pull together a list of stories recommended by friends (Valentino-DeVries, 2010). Think about how this strengthens the social graph. While items in the news feed might quickly scroll away and disappear, that data can now be pulled up within a Web site, providing insight from friends when and where you're likely to want it most.

Taken together, these features enlist Web sites to serve as vassal states in the Facebook empire. Each of these ties makes Facebook membership more valuable by enhancing network effects, strengthening switching costs, and creating larger sets of highly personalized data to leverage.

More Privacy Controversy

The decision to launch these new features as "opt-out" instead of "opt-in" immediately drew the concern of lawmakers. Given the Beacon debacle, the TOS controversy, and Google's problems with Buzz (see Chapter 14 "Google: Search, Online Advertising, and Beyond"), you'd think Facebook would have known better. But within a week of Beacon's launch, four U.S. senators contacted the firm, asking why it was so difficult to opt out of the information-sharing platform (Lardinois, 2010). Amid a crush of negative publicity, the firm was forced to quickly roll out simplified privacy management controls.

Facebook's struggles show the tension faced by any firm that wants to collect data to improve the user experience (and hopefully make money along the way). Opt-out guarantees the largest possible audience and that's key to realizing the benefits of network effects, data, and scale. Making efforts opt-in creates the very real risk that not enough users will sign up and that the reach and impact of these kinds of initiatives will be limited (Lardinois, 2010). *Fast Company* calls this the *paradox of privacy*, saying, "We want some semblance of control over our personal data, even if we likely can't be bothered to manage it" (Manjoo, 2010). Evidence suggests that most people are accepting some degree of data sharing as long as they know that they can easily turn it off if they want to. For example, when Google rolled out ads that tracked users across the network of Web sites running Google ads, the service also provided a link in each ad where users could visit an "ad preferences manager" to learn how they were being profiled, to change settings, and to opt out (see Chapter 14 "Google: Search, Online Advertising, and Beyond"). It turns out only one in fifteen visitors to the ad preferences manager ended up opting out completely (Manjoo, 2010). Managers seeking to leverage data should learn from the examples of Facebook and Google and be certain to offer clear controls that empower user choice.

Free Riders and Security Issues

Facebook also allows third-party developers to create all sorts of apps to access Facebook data. Facebook feeds are now streaming through devices that include Samsung, Vizio, and Sony televisions; Xbox 360 and Wii game consoles; Verizon's FiOS pay television service; and the Amazon Kindle. While Facebook might never have the time or resources to create apps that put its service on every gadget on the market, they don't need to. Developers using Facebook's access tools will gladly pick up the slack.

But there are major challenges with a more open approach, most notably a weakening of strategic assets, revenue sharing, and security. First, let's discuss weakened assets. Mark Zuckerberg's geeks have worked hard to make their site the top choice for most of the world's social networkers and social network application developers. Right now, everyone goes to Facebook because everyone else is on Facebook. But as Facebook opens up access to users and content, it risks supporting efforts that undermine the firm's two most compelling sources of competitive advantage: network effects and switching costs. Any effort that makes it easier to pack up your "social self" and move it elsewhere risks undermining vital competitive resources advantages (it still remains more difficult to export contacts, e-mails, photos, and video from Facebook than it does from sites supporting OpenSocial, a rival platform backed by Google and supported by many of Facebook's competitors) (Vogelstein, 2009). This situation also puts more pressure on Facebook to behave. Lower those switching costs at a time when users are disgusted with firm behavior, and it's not inconceivable that a sizable chunk of the population could bolt for a new rival (to Facebook's credit, the site also reached out to prior critics like MoveOn.org, showing Facebook's data-sharing features and soliciting input months before their official release).

Along with asset weakening comes the issue of revenue sharing. As mentioned earlier, hosting content (especially photos and rich media) is a very expensive proposition. What incentive does a site have to store data if it will just be sent to a third-party site that will run ads around this content and not share the take? Too much data portability presents a **free rider problem** where firms mooch off Facebook's infrastructure without offering much in return. Consider services like TweetDeck. The free application allows users to access their Facebook feeds and post status updates—alongside Twitter updates and more—all from one interface. Cool for the user, but bad for Facebook, since each TweetDeck use means Facebook users are "off-site," not looking at ads, and hence not helping Zuckerberg & Co. earn revenue. It's as if the site has encouraged the equivalent of an ad blocker, yet Facebook's openness lets this happen!

Finally, consider security. Allowing data streams that contain potentially private posts and photographs to squirt across the Internet and land where you want them raises all sorts of concerns. What's to say an errant line of code doesn't provide a back door to your address book or friends list? To your messaging account? To let others see photos you'd hoped to only share with family? Security breaches can occur on any site, but once the data is allowed to flow freely, every site with access is, for hackers, the equivalent of a potential door to open or a window to crawl through.

8.10 FACEBOOK: IS IT WORTH IT

It has often been said that the first phase of the Internet was about putting information online and giving people a way to find it. The second phase of the Web is about connecting people with one another. The Web 2.0 movement is big and impactful, but is there much money in it?

While the valuations of private firms are notoriously difficult to pin down due to a lack of financial disclosure, the often-cited $15 billion valuation from the fall of 2007 Microsoft investment was rich, even when made by such a deep-pocketed firm. Using estimates at the time of the deal, if Facebook were a publicly traded company, it would have a price-to-earnings ratio of five hundred; Google's at the time was fifty-three, and the average for the S&P 500 is historically around fifteen.

But the math behind the deal is a bit more complex than was portrayed in most press reports. The deal was also done in conjunction with an agreement that for a time let Microsoft manage the sale of Facebook's banner ads worldwide. And Microsoft's investment was done on the basis of preferred stock, granting the firm benefits beyond common stock, such as preference in terms of asset liquidation (Stone, 2008). Both of these are reasons a firm would be willing to "pay more" to get in on a deal.

Another argument can be made for Microsoft purposely inflating the value of Facebook in order to discourage rival bidders. A fat valuation by Microsoft and a deal locking up ad rights makes the firm seem more expensive, less attractive, and out of reach for all but the richest and most committed suitors. Google may be the only firm that could possibly launch a credible bid, and Zuckerberg is reported to be genuinely uninterested in being absorbed by the search sovereign (Vogelstein, 2009).

Since the fall of 2007, several others have invested private money into Facebook as well, including the Founders Fund and Li Ka-shing, the Hong Kong billionaire behind Hutchison Whampoa. Press reports and court documents suggest that these deals were done at valuations that were lower than what Microsoft accepted. In May 2009 Russian firm Digital Sky paid $200 million for 1.96 percent of the firm, a ten-billion-dollar valuation (also in preferred stock). That's a one-third haircut off the Microsoft price, albeit without the Redmond-specific strategic benefits of the investment (Kirkpatrick, 2008; Ante, 2008). And as the chart in Figure 8.1 "Revenue per User (2009)" shows, Facebook still lags well behind many of its rivals in terms of revenue per user.

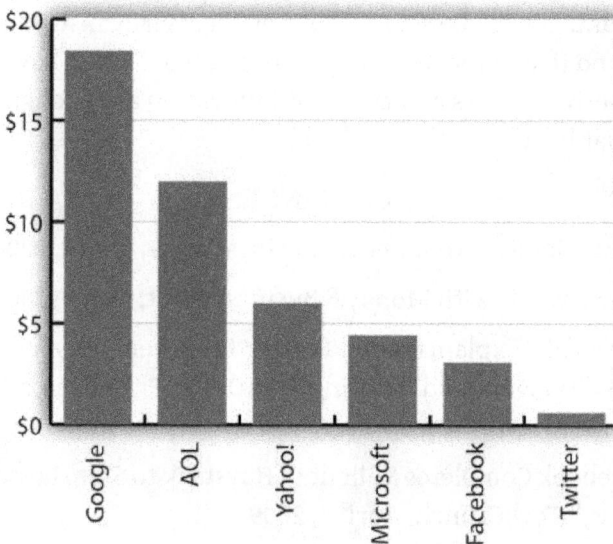

Figure 8.1 Revenue per User (2009)

So despite the headlines, even at the time of the Microsoft investment, Facebook was almost certainly not valued at a pure $15 billion. This isn't to say definitively that Facebook won't be worth $15 billion (or more) someday, but even a valuation at "just" $10 billion is a lot to pay for a then-profitless firm with estimated 2009 revenues of $500 million. Of course, raising more capital enables Zuckerberg to go on the hunt as well. Facebook investor Peter Theil confirmed the firm had already made an offer to buy Twitter (a firm which at the time had zero dollars in revenues and no discernible business model) for a cool half billion dollars (Ante, 2009).

Much remains to be demonstrated for any valuation to hold. Facebook is new. Its models are evolving, and it has quite a bit to prove. Consider efforts to try to leverage friend networks. According to Facebook's own research, "an average Facebook user with 500 friends actively follows the news on only forty of them, communicates with twenty, and keeps in close touch with about ten. Those with smaller networks follow even fewer" (Baker, 2009). That might not be enough critical mass to offer real, differentiable impact, and that may have been part of the motivation behind Facebook's mishandled attempts to encourage more public data sharing. The advantages of leveraging the friend network hinge on increased sharing and trust, a challenge for a firm that has had so many high-profile privacy stumbles. There is promise. Profiling firm Rapleaf found that targeting based on actions within a friend network can increase click-through rates threefold—that's an advantage advertisers are willing to pay for. But Facebook is still far from proving it can consistently achieve the promise of delivering valuable ad targeting.

Steve Rubel wrote the following on his Micro Persuasion blog: "The Internet amber is littered with fossilized communities that once dominated. These former stalwarts include AOL, Angelfire, theGlobe.com, GeoCities, and Tripod." Network effects and switching cost advantages can be strong, but not necessarily insurmountable if value is seen elsewhere and if an effort becomes more fad than "must have." Time will tell if Facebook's competitive assets and constant innovation are enough to help it avoid the fate of those that have gone before them.

REFERENCES

Ante, S., "Facebook: Friends with Money," BusinessWeek, May 9, 2008.

Ante, S., "Facebook: Friends with Money," BusinessWeek, May 9, 2008.

Ante, S., "Facebook's Thiel Explains Failed Twitter Takeover," BusinessWeek, March 1, 2009. Baker, S., "Learning and Profiting from Online Friendships," BusinessWeek, May 21, 2009.

Arrington, A., "Facebook Completes Rollout of Haystack to Stem Losses from Massive Photo Uploads," TechCrunch, April 6, 2009.

Arrington, M., "Zynga Takes Steps to Remove Scams from Games," TechCrunch, November 2, 2009.

Blodget, H., "Facebook's Plan To Build a Real Email System and Attack Gmail Is Brilliant," Business Insider, February 5, 2010.

Blodget, H., "Whoops—Facebook Is Once Again Overhyped," Business Insider, April 26, 2010. Kirkpatrick, D., "Why Microsoft Isn't Buying Facebook," Fortune, May 9, 2008.

Brodkin, J., "Facebook Shuts Down Beacon Program, Donates $9.5 Million to Settle Lawsuit," NetworkWorld, December 8, 2009.

Carlson N. and K. Angelova, "Chart of the Day: FarmVille-Maker Zynga's Revenues Reach $600 Million, Fueled by Social Obligations," April 26, 2010.

Cowan, M., "Marketers Struggle to Get Social," Reuters, June 19, 2008, http://www.reuters.com/news/ video?videoId=84894.

Gage, D., "Facebook Claims 250 Million Users," InformationWeek, July 16, 2009. Hoffman, C., "The Battle for Facebook," Rolling Stone, June 26, 2008, 9.

Gage, D., "Facebook Claims 250 Million Users," InformationWeek, July 16, 2009.

Gaudin, S, "Facebook Rolls Out Storage System to Wrangle Massive Photo Stores," Computerworld, April 1, 2009, http://www.computerworld.com/s/article/9130959/ Facebook_rolls_out_storage_system_to_wrangle_massive_photo_stores.

Grigoriadis, V., "Do You Own Facebook? Or Does Facebook Own You?" New York, April 5, 2009.

Guynn, J., "A Software Industry @ Facebook," Los Angeles Times, September 10, 2007.

Hagel J., and J. S. Brown, "Life on the Edge: Learning from Facebook," BusinessWeek, April 2, 2008. Kincaid, J., "What Is This Mysterious Facebook Music App?" TechCrunch, February 2, 2010.

Hardy, Q., "Facebook Thinks Outside Boxes," Forbes, May 28, 2008.

Hempel J. and M. Copeland, "Are These Widgets Worth Half a Billion?" Fortune, March 25, 2008.

Iskold, A., "Social Graph: Concepts and Issues," ReadWriteWeb, September 12, 2007. Petrecca, L., "If You See These CEOs on MySpace...," USA Today, September 25, 2006. Urstadt, B., "The Business of Social Networks," Technology Review, July/ August 2008. Zeichick, A., "How Facebook Works," Technology Review, July/ August 2008.

Kincaid, J., "A Look at the Future of Facebook Credits," TechCrunch, April 21, 2010.

Kumar, V., J. Andrew Petersen, and Robert Leone, "How Valuable Is Word of Mouth?" Harvard Business Review 85, no. 10 (October 2007): 139–46.

Lardinois, F., "Is It Time for Facebook to Make Opt-In the Default?" Read Write Web, April 27, 2010. Manjoo, F., "Does Privacy on Facebook, Google, and Twitter Even Matter?" Fast Company, May 1, 2010. McCarthy, C., "Facebook to Developers: Get Ready for Credits," CNET, February 25, 2010.

Learmonth M. and A. Klaasen, "Facebook Apps Will Make More Money Than Facebook in 2009," Silicon Alley Insider, May 18, 2009.

Learmonth M., and A. Klaasen, "Facebook Apps Will Make More Money Than Facebook in 2009," Silicon Alley Insider, May 18, 2009. Some of Zynga's revenues come from apps that run on MySpace or other networks, too. Also see N. Carolson, "The Profitable, $100 Million-a-Year Startup You've Never Heard Of," Business Insider, July 27, 2009.

MacMillan, D., "Zynga Enlarges Its War Chest," BusinessWeek, December 17, 2009.

Maher, R., "Facebook's New Payment System Off to Great Start, Could Boost Revenue by $250 Million in 2010," TBI Research, February 1, 2010.

McCarthy, C., "Facebook's Zuckerberg: 'We Simply Did a Bad Job' Handling Beacon," CNET, December 5, 2007.

McCarthy, C., "More Social, Please: Facebook Nixes Banner Ads," CNET, February 5, 2010. Sandberg, S., "Sheryl Sandberg on Facebook's Future," BusinessWeek, April 8, 2009.

McGinn, T., "Online Facebooks Duel over Tangled Web of Authorship," Harvard Crimson, May 28, 2004. Morrissey, B., "Murdoch: Facebook Is 'Flavor of the Month,'" Media Week, June 20, 2008.

McGirt, E., "How Chris Hughes Helped Launch Facebook and the Barack Obama Campaign," Fast Company, March 17, 2009, http://www.fastcompany.com/magazine/134/boy-wonder.html.

Miller C. and B. Stone, "Virtual Goods Start Bringing Real Paydays," New York Times, November 6, 2009. Nuttall, C., "Facebook Credits Bank of the Web," Financial Times, April 23, 2010.

Nakashima, E., "Feeling Betrayed, Facebook Users Force Site to Honor Their Privacy," Washington Post, November 30, 2007.

Oreskovic, A., "Facebook Efforts Hint at Growing Ad Clout," The Guardian, April 30, 2010.

Rosenbush, S., "Facebook's on the Block," BusinessWeek, March 28, 2006. Schonfeld, E., "Dear Owen, Good Luck with That," TechCrunch, April 24, 2009.

Schonfeld, E., "Are Facebook Ads Going to Zero? Lookery Lowers Its Guarantee to 7.5-cent CMPs," TechCrunch, July 22, 2008.

Sentementes, G., "'Hire Me' Nation: Using the Web & Social Media to Get a Job," Baltimore Sun, July 15, 2009; and E. Liebert, Facebook Fairytales (New York: Skyhorse, 2010).

Smith, J., "Facebook TOS Voting Concludes, Users Vote for New Revised Documents," Inside Facebook, April 23, 2009.

Stelter, B., "MySpace Might Have Friends, but It Wants Ad Money," New York Times, June 16, 2008. Stone, B., "Facebook Aims to Extends Its Reach across Web," New York Times, December 1, 2008. Stross, R., "Advertisers Face Hurdles on Social Networking Sites," New York Times, December 14, 2008. Sweeney, M., "Internet Ad Spending Will Overtake Television in 2009," Guardian, May 19, 2008.

Stone B., and M. Helft, "In Developing Countries, Web Grows without Profit," New York Times, April 27, 2009.

Stone, B., "Facebook Aims to Extends Its Reach across Web," New York Times, December 1, 2008. Vogelstein, F., "The Great Wall of Facebook," Wired, July 2009.

Talbot, D., "How Obama Really Did It," Technology Review, September/October 2008.

Timmons, H., "Online Scrabble Craze Leaves Game Sellers at Loss for Words," New York Times, March 2, 2008.

Urstadt, B., "The Business of Social Networks," Technology Review, July/August 2008. Rates quoted in this piece seem high, but a large discrepancy between site rates holds across reported data.

Valentino-DeVries, J., "Facebook CEO Zuckerberg on Plans to Dominate the Web," Wall Street Journal, April 21, 2010.

Vogelstein, F., "How Mark Zuckerberg Turned Facebook into the Web's Hottest Platform," Wired, September 6, 2007.

Vogelstein, F., "How Mark Zuckerberg Turned Facebook into the Web's Hottest Platform," Wired, September 6, 2007.

Vogelstein, F., "Mark Zuckerberg: The Wired Interview," Wired, June 29, 2009. Zeichick, A., "How Facebook Works," Technology Review, July/August 2008.

Vogelstein, F., "The Great Wall of Facebook," Wired, July 2009.

Wayne, T., "A Milestone for Internet Ad Revenue," New York Times, April 25, 2010.

Womack B. and C. Valerio, "Facebook Says Credits Won't Pay Off Soon, Adds 'Like' Feature," BusinessWeek, April 22, 2010.

Wong, E., "Ben & Jerry's, Sunkist, Indy Jones Unwrap Facebook's 'Gift of Gab,'" Brandweek, June 1, 2008.

SOFTWARE COMPREHENSION: A MANAGER'S GUIDE

9.1 INTRODUCTION: AN OVERVIEW

We know **computing hardware** is getting faster and cheaper, creating all sorts of exciting and disruptive opportunities for the savvy manager. But what's really going on inside the box? It's **software** that makes the magic of computing happen. Without software, your PC would be a heap of silicon wrapped in wires encased in plastic and metal. But it's the instructions—the software code—that enable a computer to do something wonderful, driving the limitless possibilities of information technology.

Software is everywhere. An inexpensive cell phone has about one million lines of code, while the average car contains nearly one hundred million (Charette, 2005). In this chapter we'll take a peek inside the chips to understand what software is. A lot of terms are associated with software: operating systems, applications, enterprise software, distributed systems, and more. We'll define these terms up front, and put them in a managerial context. A follow-up chapter, Chapter 10 "Software in Flux: Partly Cloudy and Sometimes Free", will focus on changes impacting the software business, including open source software, software as a service (SaaS), and cloud computing. These changes are creating an environment radically different from the software industry that existed in prior decades—confronting managers with a whole new set of opportunities and challenges.

Managers who understand software can better understand the possibilities and impact of technology. They can make better decisions regarding the strategic value of IT and the potential for technology-driven savings. They can appreciate the challenges, costs, security vulnerabilities, legal and compliance issues, and limitations involved in developing and deploying technology solutions. In the next two chapters we will closely examine the software industry and discuss trends, developments and economics—all of which influence decisions managers make about products to select, firms to partner with, and firms to invest in.

Software

When we refer to computer hardware (sometimes just hardware), we're talking about the physical components of information technology—the equipment that you can physically touch, including computers, storage devices, networking equipment, and other peripherals.

Software refers to a computer program or collection of programs—sets of instructions that tell the hardware what to do. Software gets your computer to behave like a Web browser or word processor, makes your iPod play music and video, and enables your bank's ATM to spit out cash.

It's when we start to talk about the categories of software that most people's eyes glaze over. To most folks, software is a big, incomprehensible alphabet soup of acronyms and geeky phrases: OS, VB, SAP, SQL, to name just a few.

Don't be intimidated. The basics are actually pretty easy to understand. But it's not soup; it's more of a layer cake. Think about computer hardware as being at the bottom of the layer cake. The next layer is the **operating system**, the collection of programs that control the hardware. Windows, Mac OS X, and Linux are operating systems. On top of that layer are **applications**—these can range from end-user programs like those in Office, to the complex set of programs that manage a business's inventory, payroll, and accounting. At the top of the cake are users.

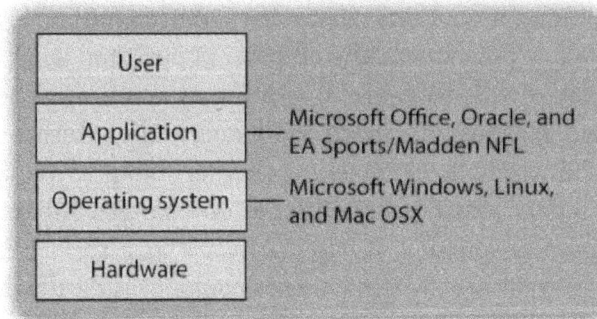

Figure 9.1 The Hardware/Software Layer Cake

The flexibility of these layers gives computers the customization options that managers and businesses demand. Understanding how the layers relate to each other helps you make better decisions on what options are important to your unique business needs, can influence what you buy, and may have implications for everything from competitiveness to cost overruns to security breaches. What follows is a manager's guide to the main software categories with an emphasis on why each is important.

9.2 OPERATING SYSTEMS

Computing hardware needs to be controlled, and that's the role of the operating system. The operating system (sometimes called the "OS") provides a common set of controls for managing computer hardware, making it easier for users to interact with computers and for programmers to write application software. Just about every computing device has an operating system—desktops and laptops, enterprise-class server computers, your mobile phone. Even specialty devices like iPods, video game consoles, and television set top boxes run some form of OS.

Some firms, like Apple and Nintendo, develop their own proprietary OS for their own hardware. Microsoft sells operating systems to everyone from Dell to the ATM manufacturer Diebold (listen for the familiar Windows error beep on some cash machines). And there are a host of specialty firms, such as Wind River (purchased by Intel), that help firms develop operating systems for all sorts of devices that don't necessarily look like a PC, including cars, video editing systems, and fighter jet control panels.

Anyone who has used both a PC and a Mac and has noticed differences across these platforms can get a sense of the breadth of what an operating system does. Even for programs that are otherwise identical for these two systems (like the Firefox browser), subtitle differences are visible. Screen elements like menus, scroll bars, and window borders look different on the Mac than they do in Windows. So do the dialogue boxes that show up when you print or save.

These items look and behave differently because each of these functions touches the hardware, and the team that developed Microsoft Windows created a system distinctly different from their Macintosh counterparts at Apple. Graphical **user interface (UI)** items like scroll bars and menus are displayed on the hardware of the computer display. Files are saved to the hardware of a hard drive or other storage device. Most operating systems also include control panels, desktop file management, and other support programs to work directly with hardware elements like storage devices, displays, printers, and networking equipment. The Macintosh Finder and the Windows Explorer are examples of components of these operating systems. The consistent look, feel, and functionality that operating systems enforce across various programs help make it easier for users to learn new software, which reduces training costs and operator error.

Differences between the Windows and Mac operating systems are evident throughout the user interface, particularly when a program interacts with hardware.

Operating systems are also designed to give programmers a common set of commands to consistently interact with the hardware. These commands make a programmer's job easier by reducing program complexity and making it faster to write software while minimizing the possibility of errors in code. Consider what an OS does for the Wii game developer. Nintendo's Wii OS provides Wii programmers with a set of common standards to use to access the Wiimote, play sounds, draw graphics, save files, and more. Without this, games would be a lot more difficult to write, they'd likely look differently, be less reliable, would cost more, and there would be fewer titles available.

Similarly, when Apple provided developers with a common set of robust, easy-to-use standards for the iPhone and (via the App Store) an easy way for users to install these applications on top of the iPhone/iPod touch OS, software development boomed, and Apple became hands-down the most versatile mobile computing device available[1]. In Apple's case, some *fifty thousand apps* became available through the App Store in less than a year. A good OS and software development platform can catalyze network effects (see Chapter 6 "Understanding Network Effects"). While the OS seems geeky, its effective design has very strategic business implications!

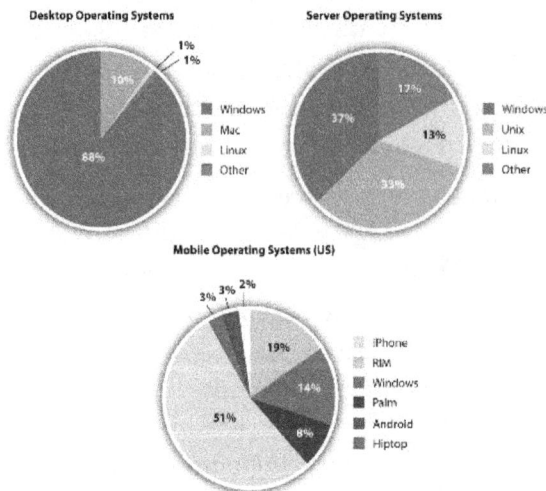

Figure 9.2 Operating System Market Share for Desktop, Server, and Mobile Phones

9.3 APPLICATION SOFTWARE

Operating systems are designed to create a **platform** so that programmers can write additional applications, allowing the computer to do even more useful things. While operating systems control the hardware, *application software* (sometimes referred to as *software applications*, *applications*, or even just *apps*) perform the work that users and firms are directly interested in accomplishing. Think of applications as the place where the users or organization's real work gets done. As we learned in Chapter 6 "Understanding Network Effects", the more application software that is available for a platform (the more games for a video game console, the more apps for your phone), the more valuable it potentially becomes.

Desktop software refers to applications installed on a personal computer—your browser, your Office suite (e.g., word processor, spreadsheet, presentation software), photo editors, and computer games are all desktop software. Enterprise software refers to applications that address the needs of multiple, simultaneous users in an organization or work group. Most companies run various forms of enterprise software programs to keep track of their inventory, record sales, manage payments to suppliers, cut employee paychecks, and handle other functions.

Some firms write their own enterprise software from scratch, but this can be time consuming and costly. Since many firms have similar procedures for accounting, finance, inventory management, and human resource functions, it often makes sense to buy a **software package** (a software product offered commercially by a third party) to support some of these functions. So-called **enterprise resource planning (ERP)** software packages serve precisely this purpose. In the way that Microsoft can sell you a suite of desktop software programs that work together, many companies sell ERP software that coordinates and integrates many of the functions of a business. The leading ERP vendors include the firm's SAP and Oracle, although there are many firms that sell ERP software. A company doesn't have to install all of the modules of an ERP suite, but it might add functions over time—for example, to plug in an accounting program that is able to read data from the firm's previously installed inventory management system. And although a bit more of a challenge to integrate, a firm can also mix and match components, linking software the firm has written with modules purchased from different enterprise software vendors.

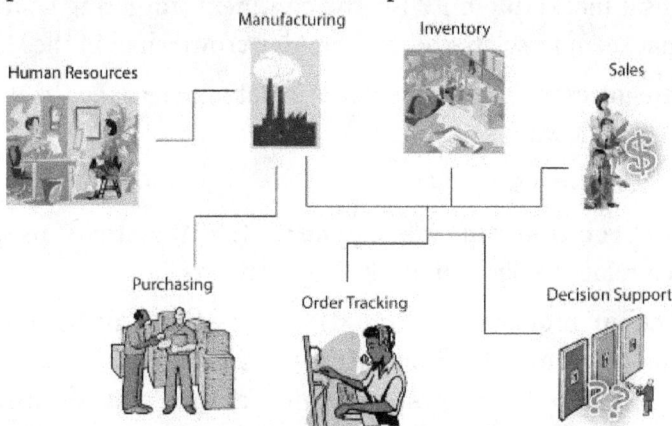

Figure 9.3 ERP in Action1

An ERP system with multiple modules installed can touch many functions of the business:

- *Sales*—A sales rep from Vermont-based SnowboardCo. takes an order for five thousand boards from a French sporting goods chain. The system can verify credit history, apply discounts, calculate price (in euros), and print the order in French.

- *Inventory*—While the sales rep is on the phone with his French customer, the system immediately checks product availability, signaling that one thousand boards are ready to be shipped from the firm's Burlington warehouse, the other four thousand need to be manufactured and can be delivered in two weeks from the firm's manufacturing facility in Guangzhou.

- *Manufacturing*—When the customer confirms the order, the system notifies the Guangzhou factory to ramp up production for the model ordered.

- *Human Resources*—High demand across this week's orders triggers a notice to the Guangzhou hiring manager, notifying her that the firm's products are a hit and that the flood of orders coming in globally mean her factory will have to hire five more workers to keep up.

- *Purchasing*—The system keeps track of raw material inventories, too. New orders trigger an automatic order with SnowboardCo's suppliers, so that raw materials are on hand to meet demand.

- *Order Tracking*—The French customer can log in to track her SnowboardCo order. The system shows her other products that are available, using this as an opportunity to cross-sell additional products.

- *Decision Support*—Management sees the firm's European business is booming and plans a marketing blitz for the continent, targeting board models and styles that seem to sell better for the Alps crowd than in the U.S. market.

- Other categories of enterprise software that managers are likely to encounter include the following:

- 245 Information Systems

- **customer relationship management (CRM)** systems used to support customer-related sales and marketing activities

- **supply chain management (SCM)** systems that can help a firm manage aspects of its value chain, from the flow of raw materials into the firm through delivery of finished products and services at the point-of-consumption

- **business intelligence (BI) systems,** which use data created by other systems to provide reporting and analysis for organizational decision making

Major ERP vendors are now providing products that extend into these and other categories of enterprise application software, as well.

Most enterprise software works in conjunction with a **database management system (DBMS)**, sometimes referred to as a "database system." The database system stores and retrieves the data that an application creates and uses. Think of this as another additional layer in our cake analogy. Although the DBMS is itself considered an application, it's often useful to think of a firm's database systems as sitting above the operating system, but under the enterprise applications. Many ERP systems and enterprise software programs are configured to share the same database system so that an organization's different programs can use a common, shared set of data. This system can be hugely valuable for a company's efficiency. For example, this could allow a separate set of programs that manage an inventory and point-of-sale system to update a single set of data that tells how many products a firm has to sell and how many it has already sold—information that would also be used by the firm's accounting and finance systems to create reports showing the firm's sales and profits.

Firms that don't have common database systems with consistent formats across their enterprise often struggle to efficiently manage their value chain. Common procedures and data formats created by packaged ERP systems and other categories of enterprise software also make it easier for firms to use software to coordinate programs between organizations. This coordination can lead to even more value chain efficiencies. Sell a product? Deduct it from your inventory. When inventory levels get too low, have your computer systems send a message to your supplier's systems so that they can automatically build and ship replacement product to your firm. In many cases these messages are sent without any human interaction, reducing time and errors. And common database systems also facilitate the use of BI systems that provide critical operational and competitive knowledge and empower decision making. For more on CRM and BI systems, and the empowering role of data, see Chapter 11 "The Data Asset: Databases, Business Intelligence, and Competitive Advantage".

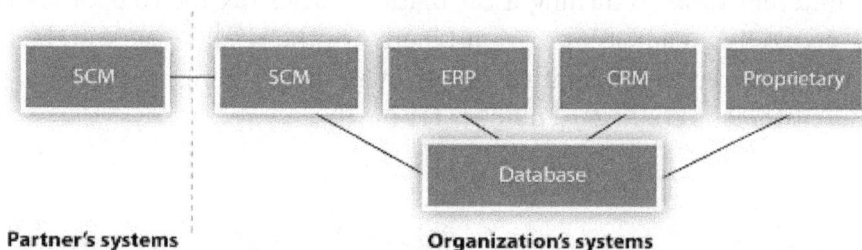

Figure 9.4: An organization's database management system can be set up to work with several applications both within and outside the firm.

9.4 DISTRIBUTED COMPUTING

When computers in different locations can communicate with one another, this is often referred to as **distributed computing**. Distributed computing can yield enormous efficiencies in speed, error reduction, and cost savings and can create entirely new ways of doing business. Designing systems architecture for distributed systems involves many advanced technical topics. Rather than provide an exhaustive decomposition of distributed computing, the examples that follow are meant to help managers understand the bigger ideas behind some of the terms that they are likely to encounter.

Let's start with the term **server**. This is a tricky one because it's frequently used in two ways: (1) in a hardware context a server is a computer that has been configured to support requests from other computers (e.g., Dell sells servers) and (2) in a software context a server is a program that fulfills requests (e.g., the Apache open source Web server). Most of the time, server *software* resides on server-class *hardware*, but you can also set up a PC, laptop, or other small computer to run server software, albeit less powerfully. And you can use mainframe or super-computer-class machines as servers, too.

The World Wide Web, like many other distributed computing services, is what geeks call a *client-server* system. Client-server refers to two pieces of software, a **client** that makes a request, and a server that receives and attempts to fulfill the request. In our WWW scenario, the client is the browser (e.g., Internet Explorer, Firefox, Safari). When you type a Web site's address into the location field of your browser, you're telling the client to "go find the Web server software at the address provided, and tell the server to return the Web site requested."

It is possible to link simple scripting languages to a Web server for performing calculations, accessing databases, or customizing Web sites. But more advanced distributed environments may use a category of software called an **application server**. The application server (or app server) houses business logic for a distributed system. Individual **Web services** served up by the app server are programmed to perform different tasks: returning a calculation ("sales tax for your order will be $11.58"), accessing a database program ("here are the results you searched for"), or even making a request to another server in another organization ("Visa, please verify this customer's credit card number for me").

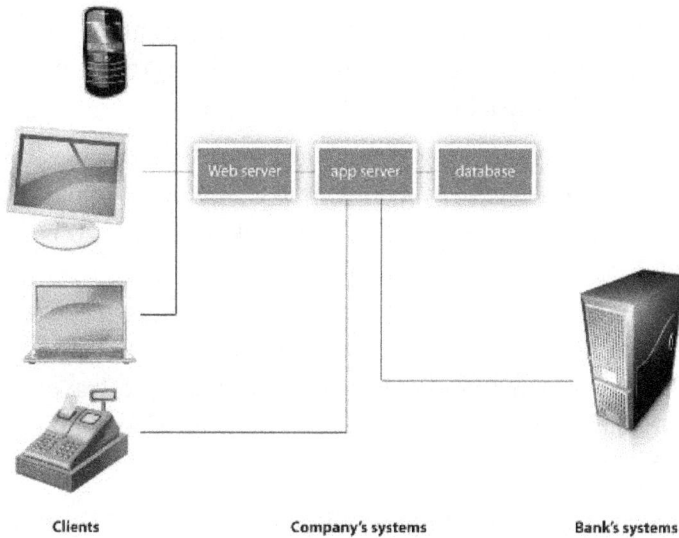

Clients   Company's systems   Bank's systems

Figure 9.5 In this multitiered distributed system, client browsers on various machines (desktop, laptop, mobile) access the system through the Web server. The cash register doesn't use a Web browser, so instead the cash register logic is programmed to directly access the services it needs from the app server. Web services accessed from the app server may be asked to do a variety of functions, including perform calculations, access corporate databases, or even make requests from servers at other firms (for example, to verify a customer's credit card).

Those little chunks of code that are accessed via the application server are sometimes referred to as Web services. The World Wide Web consortium defines *Web services* as software systems designed to support interoperable machine-to-machine interaction over a network[2]. And when computers can talk together (instead of people), this often results in fewer errors, time savings, cost reductions, and can even create whole new ways of doing business! Each Web service defines the standard method for other programs to request it to perform a task and defines the kind of response the calling client can expect back. These standards are referred to as **application programming interfaces (APIs)**.

Look at the advantages that Web services bring a firm like Amazon. Using Web services, the firm can allow the same order entry logic to be used by Web browsers, mobile phone applications, or even by third parties who want to access Amazon product information and place orders with the firm (there's an incentive to funnel sales to Amazon—the firm will give you a cut of any sales that you send Amazon's way). Organizations that have created a robust set of Web services around their processes and procedures are said to have a **service-oriented architecture (SOA)**. Organizing systems like this, with separate applications in charge of client presentation, business logic, and database, makes systems more flexible. Code can be reused, and each layer can be separately maintained, upgraded, or migrated to new hardware—all with little impact on the others.

Web services sound geeky, but here's a concrete example illustrating their power. Southwest Airlines had a Web site where customers could book flights, but many customers also wanted to rent a car or book a hotel, too. To keep customers on Southwest.com, the firm and its hotel and rental car partners created a set of Web services and shared the APIs. Now customers visiting Southwest.com can book a hotel stay and rental car on the same page where they make their flight reservation. This process transforms Southwest.com into a full service travel destination and allows the site to compete head-to-head with the likes of Expedia, Travelocity, and Orbitz (McCarthy, 2002).

Think about why Web services are important from a strategic perspective. By adding hotel and rental car services, Southwest is now able to eliminate the travel agent, along with any fees they might share with the agent. This shortcut allows the firm to capture more profits or pass on savings to customers, securing its position as the first place customers go for low-cost travel. And perhaps most importantly, Southwest can capture key data from visitor travel searches and bookings (something it likely couldn't do if customers went to a site like Expedia or Travelocity). Data is a hugely valuable asset, and this kind of customer data can be used by Southwest to send out custom e-mail messages and other marketing campaigns to bring customers back to the airline. As geeky as they might at first seem, Web services can be very strategic!

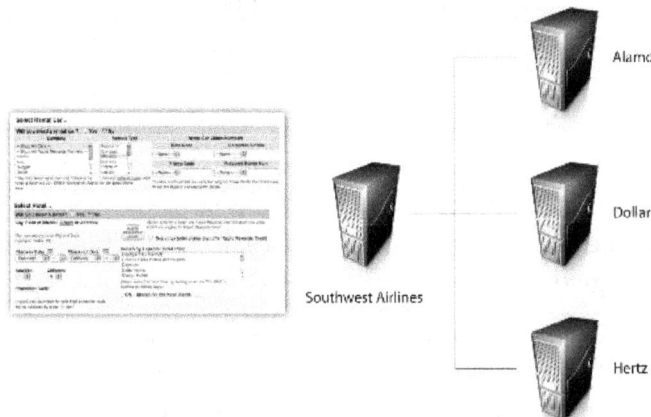

Figure 9.6 Southwest.com uses Web services to allow car rental and hotel firms to book services through Southwest. This process transforms Southwest.com into a full-service online travel agent.

Messaging Standards: An Overview

Two additional terms you might hear within the context of distributed computing are EDI and XML. **EDI (electronic data interchange)** is a set of standards for exchanging information between computer applications. EDI is most often used as a way to send the electronic equivalent of structured documents between different organizations. Using EDI, each element in the electronic document, like a firm name, address, or customer number, is coded so that it can be recognized by the receiving computer program. Eliminating paper documents makes businesses faster and lowers data entry and error costs. One study showed that firms that used EDI decreased their error rates by 82 percent and their cost of producing each document fell by up to 96 percent.

EDI is a very old standard, with roots stretching back to the 1948 Berlin Air Lift. While still in use, a new generation of more-flexible technologies for specifying data standards are taking its place. Chief among the technologies replacing EDI is **extensible markup language (XML)**. XML has lots of uses, but in the context of distributed systems, it allows software developers to create a set of standards for common data elements that, like EDI messages, can be sent between different kinds of computers, different applications, and different organizations. XML is often thought of as easier to code than EDI, and it's more robust because it can be extended—organizations can create formats to represent any kind of data (e.g., a common part number, photos, the complaint field collected by customer support personnel). In fact, most messages sent between Web services are coded in XML (the technology is a key enabler in mashups, discussed in Chapter 7 "Peer Production, Social Media, and Web 2.0"). Many computer programs also use XML as a way to export and import data in a common format that can be used regardless of the kind of computer hardware, operating system, or application program used. And if you design Web sites, you might encounter XML as part of the coding behind the cascading style sheets (CSS) that help maintain a consistent look and feel to the various Web pages in a given Web site.

Connectivity has made our systems more productive and enables entire new strategies and business models. But these wonderful benefits come at the price of increased risk. When systems are more interconnected, opportunities for infiltration and abuse also increase. Think of it this way—each "connection" opportunity is like adding another door to a building. The more doors that have to be defended, the more difficult security becomes. It should be no surprise that the rise of the Internet and distributed computing has led to an explosion in security losses by organizations worldwide.

9.5 WRITING SOFTWARE

So you've got a great idea that you want to express in software—how do you go about creating a program? Programmers write software in a **programming language**. While each language has its strengths and weaknesses, most commercial software is written in C++ (pronounced "see plus plus") or C# (pronounced "see sharp"). Visual Basic (from Microsoft) and Java (from Sun) are also among the more popular of the dozens of programming languages available. Web developers may favor specialty languages like Ruby and Python, while languages like SQL are used in databases.

Most professional programmers use an **integrated development environment (IDE)** to write their code. The IDE includes a text editor, a debugger for sleuthing out errors, and other useful programming tools. The most popular IDE for Windows is Visual Studio, while Apple offers the Xcode IDE. Most IDEs can support several different programming languages. The IDE will also **compile** a programmer's code, turning the higher-level lines of instructions that are readable by humans into lower-level instructions expressed as the patterns of ones and zeros that are readable by a computer's microprocessor.

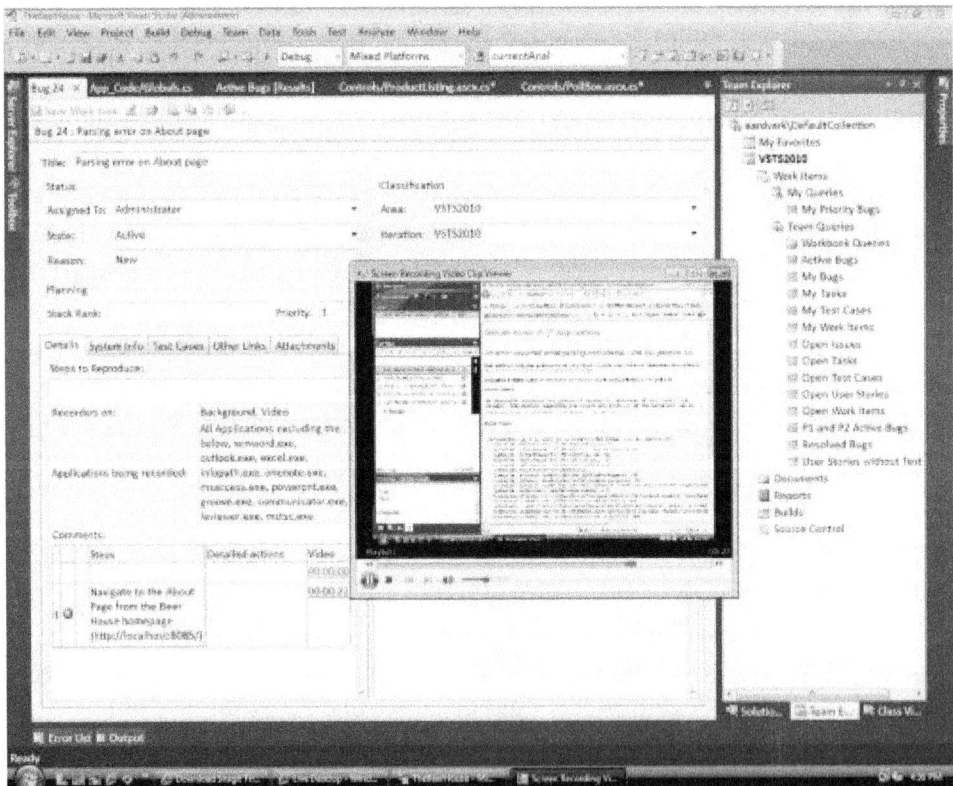

Figure 9.7: Microsoft's Visual Studio IDE supports desktop, server, mobile, and cloud computing software development.

Look at the side of a box of commercial software and you're likely to see system requirements that specify the operating system and processor that the software is designed for (e.g., "this software works on computers with Windows 7 and Intel-compatible processors"). Wouldn't it be great if software could be written once and run everywhere? That's the idea behind **Java**—a programming language developed by Sun Microsystems.

Java programmers don't write code with specific operating system commands (say for Windows, Mac OS X, or Linux), instead they use special Java commands to control their user interface or interact with the display and other hardware. Java programs can run on any computer that has a Java Virtual Machine (JVM), a software layer that interprets Java code so that it can be understood by the operating system and processor of a given computer. Java's platform independence—the ability for developers to "write once, run everywhere"—is its biggest selling point. Many Web sites execute Java applets to run the animation you might see in advertisements or games. Java has also been deployed on over six billion mobile phones worldwide, and is popular among enterprise programmers who want to be sure their programs can scale from smaller hardware up to high-end supercomputers. As long as the machine receiving the Java code has a JVM, then the Java application should run. However, Java has not been popular for desktop applications. Since Java isn't optimized to take advantage of interface elements specific to the Mac or Windows, most Java desktop applications look clunky and unnatural. Java code that runs through the JVM interpreter is also slower than code compiled for the native OS and processor that make up a platform[1].

Scripting languages are the final category of programming tool that we'll cover. Scripting languages typically execute within an application. Microsoft offers a scripting language called VB Script (a derivative of Visual Basic) to automate functions in Office. And most browsers and Web servers support JavaScript, a language that helps make the Web more interactive (despite its name, JavaScript is unrelated to Java). Scripting languages are interpreted within their applications, rather than compiled to run directly by a microprocessor. This distinction makes them slower than the kinds of development efforts found in most commercial software. But most scripting languages are usually easy to use, and are often used both by professional programmers and power users.

1Some offerings have attempted to overcome the speed issues associated with interpreting Java code. Just-in-time compilation stores code in native processor-executable form after each segment is initially interpreted, further helping to speed execution. Other environments allow for Java to be compiled ahead of time so that it can be directly executed by a microprocessor. However, this process eliminates code portability—Java's key selling point. And developers preparing their code for the

JVM actually precompile code into something called Java bytecode, a format that's less human friendly but more quickly interpreted by JVM software.

9.6 TOTAL COST OF OWNERSHIP (TCO): TECH COSTS GO WAY BEYOND THE PRICE TAG

Managers should recognize that there are a whole host of costs that are associated with creating and supporting an organization's information systems. Of course, there are programming costs for custom software as well as purchase, configuration, and licensing costs for packaged software, but there's much, much more.

There are costs associated with design and documentation (both for programmers and for users). There are also testing costs. New programs should be tested thoroughly across the various types of hardware the firm uses, and in conjunction with existing software and systems, *before* being deployed throughout the organization. Any errors that aren't caught can slow down a business or lead to costly mistakes that could ripple throughout an organization and its partners. Studies have shown that errors not caught before deployment could be one hundred times more costly to correct than if they were detected and corrected beforehand (Charette, 2005).

Once a system is "turned on," the work doesn't end there. Firms need to constantly engage in a host of activities to support the system that may also include the following:

- providing training and end user support
- collecting and relaying comments for system improvements
- auditing systems to ensure **compliance** (i.e., that the system operates within the firm's legal constraints and industry obligations)
- providing regular backup of critical data
- planning for redundancy and disaster recovery in case of an outage
- vigilantly managing the moving target of computer security issues

With so much to do, it's no wonder that firms spend 70 to 80 percent of their information systems (IS) budgets just to keep their systems running (Rettig, 2007). The price tag and complexity of these tasks can push some managers to think of technology as being a cost sink rather than a strategic resource. These tasks are often collectively referred to as the **total cost of ownership (TCO)** of an information system. Understanding TCO is critical when making technology investment decisions. TCO is also a major driving force behind the massive tech industry changes discussed in Chapter 10 "Software in Flux: Partly Cloudy and Sometimes Free".

The reason why technology projects fail

Even though information systems represent the largest portion of capital spending at most firms, an astonishing one in three technology development projects fail to be successfully deployed (Dignan, 2007). Imagine if a firm lost its investment in one out of every three land purchases, or when building one in three factories. These statistics are dismal! Writing in *IEEE Spectrum*, risk consultant Robert Charette provides a sobering assessment of the cost of software failures, stating, "The yearly tab for failed and troubled software conservatively runs somewhere from $60 to $70 billion in the United States alone. For that money, you could launch the space shuttle one hundred times, build and deploy the entire 24-satellite Global Positioning System, and develop the Boeing 777 from scratch—and still have a few billion left over" (Charette, 2005).

Why such a bad track record? Sometimes technology itself is to blame, other times it's a failure to test systems adequately, and sometimes it's a breakdown of process and procedures used to set specifications and manage projects. In one example, a multimillion-dollar loss on the NASA Mars Observer was traced back to a laughably simple oversight—Lockheed Martin contractors using English measurements, while the folks at NASA used the metric system (Lloyd, 1999). Yes, a $125 million taxpayer investment was lost because a bunch of rocket scientists failed to pay attention to third grade math. When it comes to the success or failure of technical projects, the devil really is in the details.

Projects rarely fail for just one reason. Project post-mortems often point to a combination of technical, project management, and business decision blunders. The most common factors include the following[2]:

- Unrealistic or unclear project goals
- Poor project leadership and weak executive commitment
- Inaccurate estimates of needed resources
- Badly defined system requirements and allowing "feature creep" during development
- Poor reporting of the project's status
- Poor communication among customers, developers, and users
- Use of immature technology
- Unmanaged risks
- Inability to handle the project's complexity
- Sloppy development and testing practices
- Poor project management

- ◉ Stakeholder politics

- ◉ Commercial pressures (e.g., leaving inadequate time or encouraging corner-cutting)

Managers need to understand the complexity involved in their technology investments, and that achieving success rarely lies with the strength of the technology alone.

But there is hope. Information systems organizations can work to implement procedures to improve the overall quality of their development practices. Mechanisms for quality improvement include **capability maturity model integration (CMMI)**, which gauge an organization's process maturity and capability in areas critical to developing and deploying technology projects, and provides a carefully chosen set of best practices and guidelines to assist quality and process improvement[1] (Kay, 2005).

Firms are also well served to leverage established project planning and software development methodologies that outline critical businesses processes and stages when executing large-scale software development projects. The idea behind these methodologies is straightforward—why reinvent the wheel when there is an opportunity to learn from and follow blueprints used by those who have executed successful efforts. When methodologies are applied to projects that are framed with clear business goals and business metrics, and that engage committed executive leadership, success rates can improve dramatically (Shenhar & Dvir, 2007).

While software development methodologies are the topic of more advanced technology courses, the savvy manager knows enough to inquire about the development methodologies and quality programs used to support large scale development projects, and can use these investigations as further input when evaluating whether those overseeing large scale efforts have what it takes to get the job done.

REFERENCES

Arrington, M., "2008: Rearden Commerce Has a Heck of a Year," TechCrunch, January 13, 2009.

Arrington, M., "Rearden Commerce: Time for the Adults to Come In and Clean House," TechCrunch, April 5, 2007.

Charette, R., "Why Software Fails," IEEE Spectrum, September 2005.

Charette, R., "Why Software Fails," IEEE Spectrum, September 2005.

Dignan, L., "Survey: One in 3 IT Projects Fail; Management OK with It," ZDNet, December 11, 2007. Kay, R., "QuickStudy: Capability Maturity Model Integration (CMMI)," Computerworld, January 24, 2005. Lloyd, R., "Metric Mishap Caused Loss of NASA Orbiter," CNN, September 20, 1999.

Koch, C., "Nike Rebounds: How (and Why) Nike Recovered from Its Supply Chain Disaster," CIO, June 15, 2004.

McCarthy, J., "The Standards Body Politic," InfoWorld, May 17, 2002.

Rettig, C., "The Trouble with Enterprise Software," MIT Sloan Management Review 49, no. 1 (2007): 21–27. Robinson A. and D. Dilts, "OR and ERP," ORMS Today, June 1999.

Rettig, C., "The Trouble with Enterprise Software," MIT Sloan Management Review 49, no. 1 (2007): 21–27.

Schonfeld, E., "At Rearden Commerce, Addiction Is Job One," TechCrunch, May 6, 2008;

Shenhar A. and D. Dvir, Reinventing Project Management: The Diamond Approach to Successful Growth and Innovation (Boston: Harvard Business School Press, 2007).

SOFTWARE IN FLUX: PARTLY CLOUDY AND PARTLY CLOUDY AND OCCASIONALLY FREE

10.1 OPEN SOURCE

Who would have thought a twenty-one-year-old from Finland could start a revolution that continues to threaten the Microsoft Windows empire? But Linus Torvalds did just that. During a marathon six-month coding session, Torvalds created the first version of Linux (Diamond, 2008) marshalling open source revolutionaries like no one before him. Instead of selling his operating system, Torvalds gave it away. Now morphed and modified into scores of versions by hundreds of programmers, **Linux** can be found just about everywhere, and most folks credit Linux as being the most significant product in the OSS arsenal. Today Linux powers everything from cell phones to stock exchanges, set top boxes to supercomputers. You'll find the OS on 30 percent of the servers in corporate America (Lacy, 2006), and supporting most Web servers (including those at Google, Amazon, and Facebook). Linux forms the core of the TiVo operating system, it underpins Google's Android and Chrome OS offerings, and it has even gone interplanetary. Linux has been used to power the Phoenix Lander and to control the Spirit and Opportunity Mars rovers (Brockmeier, 2004; Barrett, 2008). Yes, Linux is even on Mars!

Open source software (OSS) is often described as free. While most OSS can be downloaded for free over the Internet, it's also "free" as in liberated. The source code for OSS products is openly shared. Anyone can look at the source code, change it, and even redistribute it, provided the modified software continues to remain open and free[2]. This openness is in stark contrast to the practice of conventional software firms, who treat their intellectual property as closely guarded secrets, and who almost never provide the source code for their commercial software products. At times, many software industry execs have been downright hostile toward OSS. The former President of SAP once referred to the open source movement as "socialism," while Microsoft's Steve Balmer has called Linux a "cancer" (Fortt, 2007).

But while execs at some firms see OSS as a threat undermining the lifeblood of their economic model, other big- name technology companies are now solidly behind the open source movement. The old notion of open source being fueled on the contributions of loners tooling away for the glory of contributing to better code is now largely inaccurate. The vast majority of people who work on efforts like Linux are now paid to do so by commercially motivated employers (Woods, 2008). Nearly every major hardware firm has paid staff contributing to open source projects, and most firms also work together to fund foundations that set standards and coordinate the release of product revisions and improvements. Such coordination is critical—helping, for example, to ensure that various versions of Linux work alike. Sun Microsystems claims to have eleven thousand engineers contributing to OSS (Preimesberger, 2008). Guido van Rossum, the inventor of the open source Python programming language, works for Google where he continues to coordinate development. IBM programmers work on several open source projects, including Linux. The firm has even deeded a commercially developed programming tool (including an IDE) to the Eclipse foundation, where it's now embraced and supported by dozens of firms.

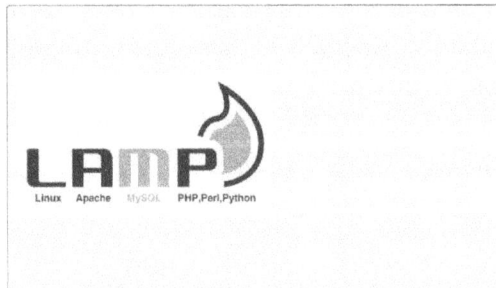

10.2 WHY OPEN SOURCE?

There are many reasons why firms choose open source products over commercial alternatives:

Cost—Free alternatives to costly commercial code can be a tremendous motivator, particularly since conventional software often requires customers to pay for every copy used and to pay more for software that runs on increasingly powerful hardware. Big Lots stores lowered costs by as much as $10 million by finding viable OSS (Castelluccio, 2008) to serve their system needs. Online broker E*TRADE estimates that its switch to open source helped save over $13 million a year (King, 2008). And Amazon claimed in SEC filings that the switch to open source was a key contributor to nearly $20 million in tech savings (Shankland, et. al., 2001). Firms like TiVo, which use OSS in their own products, eliminate a cost spent either developing their own operating system or licensing similar software from a vendor like Microsoft.

Reliability—There's a saying in the open source community, "Given enough eyeballs, all bugs are shallow" (Raymond, 1999). What this means is that the more people who look at a program's code, the greater the likelihood that an error will be caught and corrected. The open source community harnesses the power of legions of geeks who are constantly trawling OSS products, looking to squash bugs and improve product quality. And studies have shown that the quality of popular OSS products outperforms proprietary commercial competitors (Ljungberg, 2000). In one study, Carnegie Mellon University's Cylab estimated the quality of Linux code to be less buggy than commercial alternatives by a factor of two hundred (Castelluccio, 2008)!

Security—OSS advocates also argue that by allowing "many eyes" to examine the code, the security vulnerabilities of open source products come to light more quickly and can be addressed with greater speed and reliability (Wheeler, 2003). High profile hacking contests have frequently demonstrated the strength of OSS products. In one well-publicized 2008 event, laptops running Windows and Macintosh were both hacked (the latter in just two minutes), while a laptop running Linux remained uncompromised (McMillan, 2008). Government agencies and the military often appreciate the opportunity to scrutinize open source efforts to verify system integrity (a particularly sensitive issue among foreign governments leery of legislation like the USA PATRIOT Act of 2001) (Lohr, 2003). Many OSS vendors offer **security focused** (sometimes called *hardened*) versions of their products. These can include systems that monitor the integrity of an OSS distribution, checking file size and other indicators to be sure that code has not been modified and redistributed by bad guys who've added a back door, malicious routines, or other vulnerabilities.

Scalability—Many major OSS efforts can run on everything from cheap commodity hardware to high-end supercomputing. **Scalability** allows a firm to scale from start-up to blue chip without having to significantly rewrite their code, potentially saving big on software development costs. Not only can many forms of OSS be migrated to more powerful hardware, packages like Linux have also been optimized to balance a server's workload among a large number of machines working in tandem. Brokerage firm E*TRADE claims that usage spikes following 2008 U.S. Federal Reserve moves flooded the firm's systems, creating the highest utilization levels in five years. But

E*TRADE credits its scalable open source systems for maintaining performance while competitors' systems struggled (King, 2008).

Agility and Time to Market—Vendors who use OSS as part of product offerings may be able to skip whole segments of the software development process, allowing new products to reach the market faster than if the entire software system had to be developed from scratch, in-house. Motorola has claimed that customizing products built on OSS has helped speed time-to-market for the firm's mobile phones, while the team behind the Zimbra e-mail and calendar effort built their first product in just a few months by using some forty blocks of free code (Guth, 2006).

10.3 OPEN SOURCE SOFTWARE: EXAMPLES

Just about every type of commercial product has an open source equivalent. SourceForge.net lists over two hundred and thirty thousand such products[1]! Many of these products come with the installation tools, support utilities, and full documentation that make them difficult to distinguish from traditional commercial efforts (Woods, 2008). In addition to the LAMP products, some major examples include the following:

- Firefox—a Web browser that competes with Internet Explorer
- OpenOffice—a competitor to Microsoft Office
- Gimp—a graphic tool with features found in Photoshop
- Alfresco—collaboration software that competes with Microsoft Sharepoint and EMC's Documentum
- Marketcetera—an enterprise trading platform for hedge fund managers that competes with FlexTrade and Portware
- Zimbra—open source e-mail software that competes with Outlook server
- MySQL, Ingres, and EnterpriseDB—open source database software packages that each go head-to- head with commercial products from Oracle, Microsoft, Sybase, and IBM
- SugarCRM—customer relationship management software that competes with Salesforce.com and Siebel
- Asterix—an open source implementation for running a PBX corporate telephony system that competes with offerings from Nortel and Cisco, among others
- Free BSD and Sun's OpenSolaris—open source versions of the Unix operating system

Why Give It Away? The Business of Open Source

Open source is a sixty-billion-dollar industry (Asay, 2008), but it has a disproportionate impact on the trillion- dollar IT market. By lowering the cost of computing, open source efforts make more computing options accessible to smaller firms. More reliable, secure computing also lowers costs for all users. OSS also diverts funds that firms would otherwise spend on fixed costs, like operating systems and databases, so that these funds can be spent on innovation or other more competitive initiatives. Think about Google, a firm that some estimate has over 1.4 million servers. Imagine the costs if it had to license software for each of those boxes!

Commercial interest in OSS has sparked an acquisition binge. Red Hat bought open source application server firm JBoss for $350 million. Novell snapped up SUSE Linux for $210 million. And Sun plunked down over $1 billion for open source database provider MySQL (Greenberg, 2008). And with Oracle's acquisition of Sun, one of the world's largest commercial software firms has zeroed in on one of the deepest portfolios of open source products.

But how do *vendors* make money on open source? One way is by selling support and consulting services. While not exactly Microsoft money, Red Hat, the largest purely OSS firm, reported half a billion dollars in revenue in 2008. The firm had two and a half million *paid* subscriptions offering access to software updates and support services (Greenberg, 2008). Oracle, a firm that sells commercial ERP and database products, provides Linux for free, selling high-margin Linux support contracts for as much as five hundred thousand dollars (Fortt, 2007). The added benefit for Oracle? Weaning customers away from Microsoft—a firm that sells many products that compete head-to-head with Oracle's offerings. Service also represents the most important part of IBM's business. The firm now makes more from services than from selling hardware and software (Robertson, 2009). And every dollar saved on buying someone else's software product means more money IBM customers can spend on IBM computers and services. Sun Microsystems was a leader in OSS, even before the Oracle acquisition bid. The firm has used OSS to drive advanced hardware sales, but the firm also sells proprietary products that augment its open source efforts. These products include special optimization, configuration management, and performance tools that can tweak OSS code to work its best (Preimesberger, 2008).

Here's where we also can relate the industry's evolution to what we've learned about standards competition in our earlier chapters. In the pre-Linux days, nearly every major hardware manufacturer made its own, incompatible version of the Unix operating system. These fractured, incompatible markets were each so small that they had difficulty attracting third-party vendors to write application software. Now, much to Microsoft's dismay, all major hardware firms run Linux. That means there's a large, unified market that attracts software developers who might otherwise write for Windows.

To keep standards unified, several Linux-supporting hardware and software firms also back the Linux Foundation, the nonprofit effort where Linus Torvalds serves as a fellow, helping to oversee Linux's evolution. Sharing development expenses in OSS has been likened to going in on a pizza together. Everyone wants a pizza with the same ingredients. The pizza doesn't make you smarter or better. So why not share the cost of a bigger pie instead of buying by the slice (Cohen, 2008)? With OSS, hardware firms spend less money than they would in the brutal, head-to-head competition where each once offered a "me too" operating system that was incompatible with rivals but offered little differentiation. Hardware firms now find their technical talent can be deployed in other value-added services mentioned above: developing commercial software add-ons, offering consulting services, and enhancing hardware offerings.

10.4 CLOUD COMPUTING: IS IT A SCAM OR A HOPE?

Oracle Chairman Larry Ellison, lamenting the buzzword-chasing character of the tech sector, once complained that the computer industry is more fashion-focused than even the women's clothing business (Farber, 2008). Ellison has a point: when a technology term becomes fashionable, the industry hype machine shifts into overdrive. The technology attracts press attention, customer interest, and vendor marketing teams scramble to label their products and services as part of that innovation. Recently, few tech trends have been more fashionable than *cloud computing*.

Like Web 2.0, trying to nail down an exact definition for cloud computing is tough. In fact, it's been quite a spectacle watching industry execs struggle to clarify the concept. HP's Chief Strategy Office "politely refused" when asked by *BusinessWeek* to define the term cloud computing (Hamm, 2008). Richard Stallman, founder of the Free Software Foundation said about cloud computing, "It's worse than stupidity. It's a marketing hype campaign" (McKay, 2009). And Larry Ellison, always ready with a sound bite, offered up this priceless quip, "Maybe I'm an idiot, but I have no idea what anyone is talking about. What is it? It's complete gibberish. It's insane" (Lyons, 2008). Insane, maybe, but also big bucks. By year-end 2008, the various businesses that fall under the rubric of cloud computing had already accounted for an estimated thirty-six-billion-dollar market. That represents a whopping 13 percent of global software sales (Liedtke, 2008)!

When folks talk about cloud computing they're really talking about replacing computing resources—either an organization's or an individual's hardware or software—with *services* provided over the Internet. The name actually comes from the popular industry convention of drawing the Internet or other computer network as a big cloud.

Cloud computing encompasses a bunch of different efforts. We'll concentrate on describing, providing examples, and analyzing the managerial implications of two separate categories of cloud computing: (1) *software as a service (SaaS)*, where a firm subscribes to a third-party software-replacing service that is delivered online, and (2) models often referred to as **utility computing**, *platform as a service, or infrastructure as a service*. Using these latter techniques, an organization develops its own systems, but runs them over the Internet on someone else's hardware. A later section on virtualization will discuss how some organizations are developing their own **private clouds**, pools of computing resources that reside inside an organization and that can be served up for specific tasks as need arrives.

The benefits and risks of SaaS and the utility computing-style efforts are very similar, but understanding the nuances of each effort can help you figure out if and when the cloud makes sense for your organization. The evolution of cloud computing also has huge implications across the industry: from the financial future of hardware and software firms, to cost structure and innovativeness of adopting organizations, to the skill sets likely to be most valued by employers.

10.5 THE SOFTWARE CLOUD: WHY PURCHASE SOFTWARE WHEN YOU CAN RENT?

If open source isn't enough of a threat to firms that sell packaged software, a new generation of products, collectively known as SaaS, claims that you can now get the bulk of your computing done through your Web browser. Don't install software—let someone else run it for you and deliver the results over the Internet.

Software as a service (SaaS) refers to software that is made available by a third party online. You might also see the terms ASP (application service provider) or HSV (hosted software vendor) used to identify this type of offering. SaaS is potentially a very big deal. Firms using SaaS products can dramatically lower several costs associated with the care and feeding of their information systems, including software licenses, server hardware, system maintenance, and IT staff. Most SaaS firms earn money via a usage-based pricing model akin to a monthly subscription. Others offer free services that are supported by advertising, while others promote the sale of upgraded or premium versions for additional fees.

Make no mistake, SaaS is yet another direct assault on traditional software firms. The most iconic SaaS firm is Salesforce.com, an enterprise customer relationship management (CRM) provider. This "un-software" company even sports a logo featuring the word "software" crossed out, *Ghostbusters*-style (Hempel, 2009).

Figure 10.1: The antisoftware message is evident in the logo of SaaS leader Salesforce.com.

Other enterprise-focused SaaS firms compete directly with the biggest names in software. Some of these upstarts are even backed by leading enterprise software executives. Examples include NetSuite (funded in part by Oracle's Larry Ellison—the guy's all over this chapter), which offers a comprehensive SaaS ERP suite; and Workday (launched by founders of Peoplesoft), which has SaaS offerings for managing human resources. Several traditional software firms have countered start-ups by offering SaaS efforts of their own. IBM offers a SaaS version of its Cognos business intelligence products, Oracle offers CRM On Demand, and SAP's Business ByDesign includes a full suite of enterprise SaaS offerings. Even Microsoft has gone SaaS, with a variety of Web- based services that include CRM, Web meeting tools, collaboration, e-mail, and calendaring.

SaaS is also taking on desktop applications. Intuit has online versions of its QuickBooks, TurboTax, and Quicken finance software. Adobe has an online version of Photoshop. Google and Zoho offer office suites that compete with desktop alternatives, prompting Microsoft's own introduction of an online version of Office. And if you store photos on Flickr or Picassa instead of your PC's hard drive, then you're using SaaS, too.

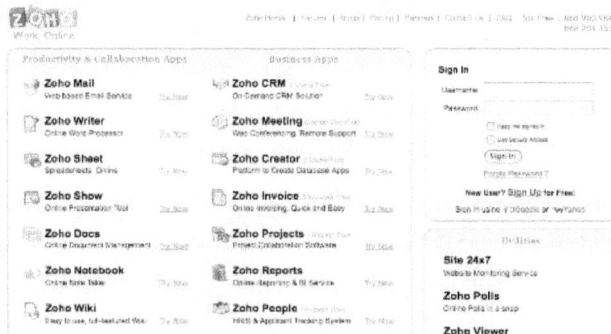

Figure 10.2: A look at Zoho's home page shows the diversity of both desktop and enterprise offerings from this SaaS upstart. Note that the firm makes it services available through browsers, phones, and even Facebook.

10.6 THE BENEFITS OF SAAS

Firms can potentially save big using SaaS. Organizations that adopt SaaS forgo the large upfront costs of buying and installing software packages. For large enterprises, the cost to license, install, and configure products like ERP and CRM systems can easily run into the hundreds of thousands or even millions of dollars. And these costs are rarely a one time fee. Additional costs like annual maintenance contracts have also been rising as rivals fail or get bought up. Less competition among traditional firms recently allowed Oracle and SAP to raise maintenance fees to as much as 20 percent (Lacy, 2008).

Firms that adopt SaaS don't just save on software and hardware, either. There's also the added cost for the IT staff needed to run these systems. Forrester Research estimates that SaaS can bring cost savings of 25 to 60 percent if all these costs are factored in (Quittner, 2008).

There are also accounting and corporate finance implications for SaaS. Firms that adopt software as a service never actually buy a system's software and hardware, so these systems become a variable operating expense. This flexibility helps mitigate the financial risks associated with making a large capital investment in information systems. For example, if a firm pays Salesforce.com sixty-five dollars per month per user for its CRM software, it can reduce payments during a slow season with a smaller staff, or pay more during heavy months when a firm might employ temporary workers. At these rates, SaaS not only looks good to large firms, it makes very sophisticated technology available to smaller firms that otherwise wouldn't be able to afford expensive systems, let alone the IT staff and hardware required to run them.

In addition to cost benefits, SaaS offerings also provide the advantage of being highly scalable. This feature is important because many organizations operate in environments prone to wide variance in usage. Some firms might expect systems to be particularly busy during tax time or the period around quarterly financial reporting deadlines, while others might have their heaviest system loads around a holiday season. A music label might see spikes when an artist drops a new album. Using conventional software, an organization would have to buy enough computing capacity to ensure that it could handle its heaviest anticipated workload. But sometimes these loads are difficult to predict, and if the difference between high workloads and average use is great, a lot of that expensive computer hardware will spend most of its time doing nothing. In SaaS, however, the vendor is responsible for ensuring that systems meet demand fluctuation. Vendors frequently sign a **service level agreement (SLA)** with their customers to ensure a guaranteed uptime and define their ability to meet demand spikes.

When looking at the benefits of SaaS, also consider the potential for higher quality and service levels. SaaS firms benefit from economies of scale that not only lower software and hardware costs, but also potentially boost quality. The volume of customers and diversity of their experiences means that an established SaaS vendor is most likely an expert in dealing with all sorts of critical computing issues. SaaS firms handle backups, instantly deploy upgrades and bug fixes, and deal with the continual burden of security maintenance—all costly tasks that must be performed regularly and with care, although each offers little strategic value to firms that perform these functions themselves in-house. The breadth of a SaaS vendor's customer base typically pushes the firm to evaluate and address new technologies as they emerge, like quickly offering accessibility from mobile platforms like the BlackBerry and iPhone. For all but the savviest of IT shops, an established SaaS vendor can likely leverage its scale and experience to provide better, cheaper, more reliable standard information systems than individual companies typically can.

Software developers who choose to operate as SaaS providers also realize benefits. While a packaged software company like SAP must support multiple versions of its software to accommodate operating systems like Windows, Linux, and various flavors of Unix, an SaaS provider develops, tests, deploys, and supports just one version of the software executing on its own servers.

An argument might also be made that SaaS vendors are more attuned to customer needs. Since SaaS firms run a customer's systems on their own hardware, they have a tighter feedback loop in understanding how products are used (and why they fail)—potentially accelerating their ability to enhance their offerings. And once made, enhancements or fixes are immediately available to customers the next time they log in.

SaaS applications also impact distribution costs and capacity. As much as 30 percent of the price of traditional desktop software is tied to the cost of distribution—pressing CD-ROMs, packaging them in boxes, and shipping them to retail outlets (Drummond, 2001). Going direct to consumers can cut out the middleman, so vendors can charge less or capture profits that they might otherwise share with a store or other distributor. Going direct also means that SaaS applications are available anywhere someone has an Internet connection, making them truly global applications. This feature has allowed many SaaS firms to address highly specialized markets (sometimes called **vertical niches**). For example, the Internet allows a company writing specialized legal software, for example, or a custom package for the pharmaceutical industry, to have a national deployment footprint from day one. Vendors of desktop applications that go SaaS benefit from this kind of distribution, too.

Finally, SaaS allows a vendor to counter the vexing and costly problem of software piracy. It's just about impossible to make an executable, illegal copy of a subscription service that runs on a SaaS provider's hardware.

10.7 SAAS: NOT FREE FROM RISKS

Like any technology, we also recognize there is rarely a silver bullet that solves all problems. A successful manager is able to see through industry hype and weigh the benefits of a technology against its weaknesses and limitations. And there are still several major concerns surrounding SaaS.

The largest concerns involve the tremendous dependence a firm develops with its SaaS vendor. Having all of your eggs in one basket can leave a firm particularly vulnerable. If a traditional software company goes out of business, in most cases its customers can still go on using its products. But if your SaaS vendor goes under, you're hosed. They've got all your data, and even if firms could get their data out, most organizations don't have the hardware, software, staff, or expertise to quickly absorb an abandoned function.

Beware with whom you partner. Any hot technology is likely to attract a lot of start-ups, and most of these start-ups are unlikely to survive. In just a single year, the leading trade association found the number of SaaS vendors dropped from seven hundred members to four hundred fifty (Drummond, 2001). One of the early efforts to collapse was Pandesic, a joint venture between SAP and Intel—two large firms that might have otherwise instilled confidence among prospective customers. In another example, Danish SaaS firm "IT Factory" was declared "Denmark's Best IT Company 2008" by *Computerworld*, only to follow the award one week later with a bankruptcy declaration (Wauters, 2008). Indeed, despite the benefits, the costs of operating as a SaaS vendor can be daunting. NetSuite's founder claimed it "takes ten years and $100 million to do right" (Lacy, 2008) —maybe that's why the firm still wasn't profitable, even a year and a half after going public.

Firms that buy and install packaged software usually have the option of sticking with the old stuff as long as it works, but organizations adopting SaaS may find they are forced into adopting new versions. This fact is important because any radical changes in a SaaS system's user interface or system functionality might result in unforeseen training costs, or increase the chance that a user might make an error.

Keep in mind that SaaS systems are also reliant on a network connection. If a firm's link to the Internet goes down, its link to its SaaS vendor is also severed. Relying on an Internet connection also means that data is transferred to and from a SaaS firm at Internet speeds, rather the potentially higher speeds of a firm's internal network. Solutions to many of these issues are evolving as Internet speeds become faster and Internet service providers become more reliable. There are also several programs that allow for offline use of data that is typically stored in SaaS systems, including Google Gears and Adobe AIR. With these products a user can download a subset of data to be offline (say on a plane flight or other inaccessible location), and then sync the data when the connection is restored. Ultimately, though, SaaS users have a much higher level of dependence on their Internet connections.

And although a SaaS firm may have more security expertise than your organization, that doesn't mean that security issues can be ignored. Any time a firm allows employees to access a corporation's systems and data assets from a remote location, a firm is potentially vulnerable to abuse and infiltration. Some firms may simply be unacceptably uncomfortable with critical data assets existing outside their own network. There may also be contractual or legal issues preventing data from being housed remotely, especially if a SaaS vendor's systems are in another country operating under different laws and regulations. "We're very bound by regulators in terms of client data and country-of-origin issues, so it's very difficult to use the cloud," says Rupert Brown, a chief architect at Merrill Lynch (Gruman, 2008).

SaaS systems are often accused of being less flexible than their installed software counterparts—mostly due to the more robust configuration and programming options available in traditional software packages. It is true that many SaaS vendors have improved system customization options and integration with standard software packages. And at times a lack of complexity can be a blessing—fewer choices can mean less training, faster start-up time, and lower costs associated with system use. But firms with unique needs may find SaaS restrictive.

SaaS offerings usually work well when the bulk of computing happens at the server end of a distributed system because the kind of user interface you can create in a browser isn't as sophisticated as what you can do with a separate, custom-developed desktop program. A comparison of the first few iterations of the Web-based Google office suite, which offers word processing, presentation software, and a spreadsheet, reveals a much more limited feature set than Microsoft's Office desktop software. The bonus, of course, is that an online office suite is accessible anywhere and makes sharing documents a snap. Again, an understanding of trade-offs is key.

Here's another challenge for a firm and its IT staff: SaaS means a greater *consumerization* of technology. Employees, at their own initiative, can go to Socialtext or Google Sites and set up a wiki, WordPress to start blogging, or subscribe to a SaaS offering like Salesforce.com, all without corporate oversight and approval. This work can result in employees operating outside established firm guidelines and procedures, potentially introducing operational inconsistencies or even legal and security concerns.

The consumerization of corporate technology isn't all bad. Employee creativity can blossom with increased access to new technologies, costs might be lower than home grown solutions, and staff could introduce the firm to new tools that might not otherwise be on the radar of the firm's IS Department. But all this creates an environment that requires a level of engagement between a firm's technical staff and the groups that it serves that is deeper than that employed by any prior generation of technology workers. Those working in an organization's information systems group must be sure to conduct regular meetings with representative groups of employees across the firm to understand their pain points and assess their changing technology needs. Non-IT managers should regularly reach out to IT to ensure that their needs are on the tech staff's agenda. Organizations with internal IT-staff R&D functions that scan new technologies and critically examine their relevance and potential impact on the firm can help guide an organization through the promise and peril of new technologies. Now more than ever, IT managers must be deeply knowledgeable about business areas, broadly aware of new technologies, and able to bridge the tech and business worlds. Similarly, any manager looking to advance his or her organization has to regularly consider the impact of new technologies.

10.8 THE HARDWARE CLOUD: THE COUSINS OF UTILITY COMPUTING

While SaaS provides the software *and* hardware to replace an internal information system, sometimes a firm develops its own custom software but wants to pay someone else to run it for them. That's where hardware clouds, utility computing, and related technologies come in. In this model, a firm replaces computing hardware that it might otherwise run on-site with a service provided by a third party online. While the term utility computing was fashionable a few years back (and old timers claim it shares a lineage with terms like hosted computing or even time sharing), now most in the industry have begun referring to this as an aspect of cloud computing, often referred to as **hardware clouds**. Computing hardware used in this scenario exists "in the cloud," meaning somewhere on the Internet. The costs of systems operated in this manner look more like a utility bill—you only pay for the amount of processing, storage, and telecommunications used. Tech research firm Gartner has estimated that 80 percent of corporate tech spending goes toward data center maintenance (Rayport, 2008). Hardware-focused cloud computing provides a way for firms to chip away at these costs.

Major players are spending billions building out huge data centers to take all kinds of computing out of the corporate data center and place it in the cloud. Efforts include Sun's Network.com grid, IBM's Cloud Labs, Amazon's EC2 (Elastic Computing Cloud), Google's App Engine, Microsoft's Azure, and Salesforce.com's Force.com. While cloud vendors typically host your software on their systems, many of these vendors also offer additional tools to help in creating and hosting apps in the cloud. Salesforce.com offers Force.com, which includes not only a hardware cloud but also several cloud-supporting tools, including a programming environment (IDE) to write applications specifically tailored for Web-based delivery. Google's App Engine offers developers a database product called Big Table, while Amazon offers one called Amazon DB. Traditional software firms like Oracle are also making their products available to developers through various cloud initiatives.

Still other cloud computing efforts focus on providing a virtual replacement for operational hardware like storage and backup solutions. These include the cloud-based backup efforts like EMC's Mozy, and corporate storage services like Amazon's Simple Storage Solution (S3). Even efforts like Apple's MobileMe and Microsoft's Live Mesh that sync user data across devices (phone, multiple desktops) are considered part of the cloud craze. The common theme in all of this is leveraging computing delivered over the Internet to satisfy the computing needs of both users and organizations.

Challenges Remain

Hardware clouds and SaaS share similar benefits and risk, and as our discussion of SaaS showed, cloud efforts aren't for everyone. Some additional examples illustrate the challenges in shifting computing hardware to the cloud.

For all the hype about cloud computing, it doesn't work in all situations. From an architectural standpoint, most large organizations run a hodgepodge of systems that include both package applications and custom code written in-house. Installing a complex set of systems on someone else's hardware can be a brutal challenge and in many cases is just about impossible. For that reason we can expect most cloud computing efforts to focus on new software development projects rather than options for old software. Even for efforts that can be custom-built and cloud-deployed, other roadblocks remain. For example, some firms face stringent regulatory compliance issues. To quote one tech industry executive, "How do you demonstrate what you are doing is in compliance when it is done outside?" (Gruman, 2008)

Firms considering cloud computing need to do a thorough financial analysis, comparing the capital and other costs of owning and operating their own systems over time against the variable costs over the same period for moving portions to the cloud. For high-volume, low-maintenance systems, the numbers may show that it makes sense to buy rather than rent. Cloud costs can seem super cheap at first. Sun's early cloud effort offered a flat fee of one dollar per CPU per hour. Amazon's cloud storage rates were twenty-five cents per gigabyte per month. But users often also pay for the number of accesses and the number of data transfers (Preimesberger, 2008). A quarter a gigabyte a month may seem like a small amount, but system maintenance costs often include the need to clean up old files or put them on tape. If unlimited data is stored in the cloud, these costs can add up.

Firms should enter the cloud cautiously, particularly where mission-critical systems are concerned. When one of the three centers supporting Amazon's cloud briefly went dark in 2008, start-ups relying on the service, including Twitter and SmugMug, reported outages. Apple's MobileMe cloud-based product for synchronizing data across computers and mobile devices, struggled for months after its introduction when the cloud repeatedly went down. Vendors with multiple data centers that are able to operate with **fault-tolerant** provisioning, keeping a firm's efforts at more than one location to account for any operating interruptions, will appeal to firms with stricter uptime requirements.

10.9 IMPACT OF CLOUDS ON THE TECHNOLOGY SECTOR

Although still a relatively recent phenomenon, cloud computing's impact across industries is already proving to be broad and significant.

Cloud computing is affecting the competitive dynamics of the hardware, software, and consulting industries. In the past, firms seeking to increase computing capacity invested heavily in expensive, high margin server hardware, creating a huge market for computer manufacturers. But now hardware firms find these markets may be threatened by the cloud. The trend shifting from hardware to services is evident in IBM's quarterly numbers. The firm recently reported its overall earnings were up 12 percent, even though hardware sales were off by 20 percent (Fortt, 2009). What made up the difference? The growth of Big Blue's services business. IBM is particularly well positioned to take advantage of the shift to services because it employs more technology consultants than any other firm in the world, while most of its competitors are forced to partner to offer something comparable. Consulting firm Capgemini's partnership to offer cloud services through Amazon is one such example.

The shift to cloud computing also alters the margin structure for many in the computing industry. While Moore's Law has made servers cheap, deploying SaaS and operating a commercial cloud is still very expensive—much more so than simply making additional copies of conventional, packaged software. Microsoft surprised Wall Street when it announced it would need to pour at least $2 billion more than analysts expected into the year's **server farm** capital spending. The firm's stock— among the world's most widely held—sank 11 percent in a day (Mehta, 2006). As a result, many portfolio managers started paying closer attention to the business implications of the cloud.

Cloud computing can accelerate innovation and therefore changes the desired skills mix and job outlook for IS workers. If cloud computing customers spend less on expensive infrastructure investments, they potentially have more money to reinvest in strategic efforts and innovation. IT careers may change, too. Demand for nonstrategic skills like hardware operations and maintenance are likely to decrease. Organizations will need more business-focused technologists who intimately understand a firm's competitive environment, and can create systems that add value and differentiate the firm from its competition (Fortt, 2009). While these tech jobs require more business training, they're also likely to be more durable and less likely to be outsourced to a third party with a limited understanding of the firm.

By lowering the cost to access powerful systems and software, barriers to entry also decrease. Firms need to think about the strategic advantages they can create, even as technology is easily duplicated. This trend means the potential for more new entrants across industries, and since start-ups can do more with less, it's also influencing entrepreneurship and venture capital. The CTO of SlideShare, a start-up that launched using Amazon's S3 storage cloud, offers a presentation on his firm's site labeled "Using S3 to Avoid VC." Similarly, the CEO of online payments start-up Zuora claims to have saved between half a million and $1 million by using cloud computing: "We have no servers, we run the entire business in the cloud" (Ackerman, 2008). And the sophistication of these tools lowers development time. Enterprise firm Apttus claims it was able to perform the equivalent of six months of development in a couple of weekends by using cloud services. The firm scored its first million-dollar deal in three months, and was break-even in nine months, a ramp-up time that would have been unheard of, had they needed to plan, purchase, and deploy their own data center, and create from scratch the Web services that were provided by its cloud vendor (Rapyort, 2008).

10.10 VIRTUALIZATION: SOFTWARE THAT MAKES ONE COMPUTER ACT LIKE MANY

The reduced costs and increased power of commodity hardware are not the only contributors to the explosion of cloud computing. The availability of increasingly sophisticated software tools has also had an impact. Perhaps the most important software tool in the cloud computing toolbox is **virtualization**. Think of virtualization as being a kind of operating system for operating systems. A server running virtualization software can create smaller compartments in memory that each behave as a separate computer with its own operating system and resources. The most sophisticated of these tools also allow firms to combine servers into a huge pool of computing resources that can be allocated as needed (Lyons, 2008).

Virtualization can generate huge savings. Some studies have shown that on average, conventional data centers run at 15 percent or less of their maximum capacity. Data centers using virtualization software have increased utilization to 80 percent or more (Katz, 2009).This increased efficiency means cost savings in hardware, staff, and real estate. Plus it reduces a firm's IT-based energy consumption, cutting costs, lowering its carbon footprint, and boosting "green cred" (Castro, 2007). Using virtualization, firms can buy and maintain fewer servers, each running at a greater capacity. It can also power down servers until demand increases require them to come online.

While virtualization is a key software building block that makes public cloud computing happen, it can also be used in-house to reduce an organization's hardware needs, and even to create a firm's own private cloud of scalable assets. Bechtel, BT, Merrill Lynch, and Morgan Stanley are among the firms with large private clouds enabled by virtualization (Brodkin, 2008). Another kind of virtualization, **virtual desktops** allow a server to run what amounts to a copy of a PC—OS, applications, and all—and simply deliver an image of what's executing to a PC or other connected device. This allows firms to scale, back up, secure, and upgrade systems far more easily than if they had to maintain each individual PC. One game start-up hopes to remove the high-powered game console hardware attached to your television and instead put the console in the cloud, delivering games to your TV as they execute remotely on superfast server hardware. Virtualization can even live on your desktop. Anyone who's ever run Windows in a window on Mac OS X is using virtualization software; these tools inhabit a chunk of your Mac's memory for running Windows and actually fool this foreign OS into thinking that it's on a PC.

Interest in virtualization has exploded in recent years. VMware, the virtualization software division of storage firm EMC, was the biggest IPO of 2007. But its niche is getting crowded. Microsoft has entered the market, building virtualization into its server offerings. Dell bought a virtualization software firm for $1.54 billion. And there's even an open source virtualization product called Xen (Castro, 2007).

10.11 MAKE, BUY, OR RENT

So now you realize managers have a whole host of options when seeking to fulfill the software needs of their firms. An organization can purchase packaged software from a vendor, use open source offerings, leverage SaaS or other type of cloud computing, outsource development or other IT functions to another firm either domestically or abroad, or a firm can develop all or part of the effort themselves. When presented with all of these options, making decisions about technologies and systems can seem pretty daunting.

First, realize that that for most firms, technology decisions are not binary options for the whole organization in all situations. Few businesses will opt for an IT configuration that is 100 percent in-house, packaged, or SaaS. Being aware of the parameters to consider can help a firm make better, more informed decisions. It's also important to keep in mind that these decisions need to be continuously reevaluated as markets and business needs change. What follows is a summary of some of the key variables to consider.

Competitive Advantage—*Do we rely on unique processes, procedures, or technologies that create vital, differentiating competitive advantage?* If so, then these functions aren't a good candidate to outsource or replace with a package software offering. Amazon.com had originally used recommendation software provided by a third party, and Netflix and Dell both considered third-party software to manage inventory fulfillment. But in all three cases, these firms felt that mastery of these functions was too critical to competitive advantage, so each firm developed proprietary systems unique to the circumstances of each firm.

Security—*Are there unacceptable risks associated with using the packaged software, OSS, cloud solution, or an outsourcing vendor? Are we convinced that the prospective solution is sufficiently secure and reliable? Can we trust the prospective vendor with our code, our data, our procedures and our way of doing business? Are there noncompete provisions for vendor staff that may be privy to our secrets? For off-site work, are there sufficient policies in place for on-site auditing?* If the answers to any of these questions is no, outsourcing might not be a viable option.

Legal and Compliance—*Is our firm prohibited outright from using technologies? Are there specific legal and compliance requirements related to deploying our products or services?* Even a technology as innocuous as instant messaging may need to be deployed in such a way that it complies with laws requiring firms to record and reproduce the electronic equivalent of a paper trail. For example, SEC Rule 17a-4 requires broker dealers to retain client communications for a minimum of three years. HIPAA laws governing health care providers state that electronic communications must also be captured and stored (Shapiro, 2004). While tech has gained a seat in the board room, legal also deserves a seat in systems planning meetings.

Skill, Expertise, and Available Labor—*Can we build it?* The firm may have skilled technologists, but they may not be sufficiently experienced with a new technology. Even if they are skilled, managers much consider the costs of allocating staff away from existing projects for this effort.

Cost—*Is this a cost-effective choice for our firm?* A host of factors must be considered when evaluating the cost of an IT decision. The costs to build, host, maintain, and support an ongoing effort involve labor (software development, quality assurance, ongoing support, training, and maintenance), consulting, security, operations, licensing, energy, and real estate. Any analysis of costs should consider not only the aggregate spending required over the lifetime of the effort but also whether these factors might vary over time.

Time—*Do we have time to build, test, and deploy the system?*

Vendor Issues—Is the vendor reputable and in a sound financial position? Can the vendor guarantee the service levels and reliability we need? What provisions are in place in case the vendor fails or is acquired? Is the vendor certified via the Carnegie Mellon Software Institute or other standards organizations in a way that conveys quality, trust, and reliability?

The list above is a starter. It should also be clear that these metrics are sometimes quite tough to estimate. Welcome to the challenges of being a manager! At times an environment in flux can make an executive feel like he or she is working on a surfboard, constantly being buffeted about by unexpected currents and waves. Hopefully the issues outlined in this chapter will give you the surfing skills you need for a safe ride that avoids the organizational equivalent of a wipeout.

10.12 INTRODUCTION

For many, software has been a magnificent business. It is the two-hundred-billion-dollar-per-year juggernaut (Kirkpatrick, 2004) that placed Microsoft's Bill Gates and Oracle's Larry Ellison among the wealthiest people in the world. Once a successful software product has been written, the economics for a category-leading offering are among the best you'll find in any industry. Unlike physical products assembled from raw materials, the **marginal cost** to produce an additional copy of a software product is effectively zero. Just duplicate, no additional input required. That quality leads to businesses that can gush cash. Microsoft generates one and a half billion dollars a month from Windows and Office alone (Vogelstein, 2006). Network effects and switching cost can also offer a leading software firm a degree of customer preference and lock in that can establish a firm as a standard, and in many cases creates winner-take-all (or at least winner-take-most) markets.

But as great as the business has been, the fundamental model powering the software industry is under assault. **Open source software (OSS)** offerings—free alternatives where anyone can look at and potentially modify a program's code—pose a direct challenge to the assets and advantages cultivated by market leaders. Giants shudder—"How can we compete with free," while others wonder, "How can we make money and fuel innovation on free?" And if free software wasn't enough of a shock, the way firms and users think about software is also changing. A set of services referred to as **cloud computing** is making it more common for a firm to move software out of its own IS shop so that it is run on someone else's hardware. In one variant of this approach known as **software as a service (SaaS)**, users access a *vendor's software* over the Internet, usually by simply starting up a Web browser. With SaaS, you don't need to own the program or install it on your own computer. Hardware clouds can let firms take *their software* and run it on someone else's hardware—freeing them from the burden of buying, managing, and maintaining the physical computing that programs need. Another software technology called **virtualization** can make a single computer behave like many separate machines. This function helps consolidate computing resources and creates additional savings and efficiencies.

These transitions are important. They mean that smaller firms have access to the kinds of burly, sophisticated computing power than only giants had access to in the past. Start-ups can scale quickly and get up and running with less investment capital. Existing firms can leverage these technologies to reduce costs. Got tech firms in your investment portfolio? Understanding what's at work here can inform decisions you make on which stocks to buy or sell. If you make tech decisions for your firm or make recommendations for others, these trends may point to which firms have strong growth and sustainability ahead, or which may be facing troubled times.

REFERENCES

Ackerman, E., "Forecast for Computing: Cloudy," San Jose Mercury News, December 23, 2008. Burrows, P., "Microsoft to Google: Get Off of My Cloud," BusinessWeek, November 21, 2008. Fortt, J., "Goodbye, PC (and Mac). Hello, Services," Fortune, February 4, 2009.

Asay, M., "Open Source Is a $60 Billion Industry," CNET, May 15, 2008.

Asay, M., "Open-Source Database Market Shows Muscles," CNET, February 3, 2009, http://news.cnet.com/ 8301-13505_3-10156188-16.html.

Barrett, S., "Linux on Mars," Science News, Space News, Technology News, June 6, 2008. Brockmeier, J., "NASA Using Linux," Unix Review, March 2004.

Brodkin, J., "Private Clouds Bring IT Mgmt. Challenges," NetworkWorld, December 15, 2008. Castro, K., "The Virtues of Virtualization," BusinessWeek, December 3, 2007.

Castelluccio, M., "Enterprise Open Source Adoption," Strategic Finance, November 2008.

Cohen, S., "Open Source: The Model Is Broken," BusinessWeek, December 1, 2008. Fortt, J., "Why Larry Loves Linux (and He's Not Alone)," Fortune, December 19, 2007. Greenberg, A., "Sun Snaps Up Database Firm, MySQL," Forbes, January 16, 2008.

Diamond, D., "The Good-Hearted Wizard—Linus Torvalds," Virtual Finland, January 2008. Fortt, J., "Why Larry Loves Linux (and He's Not Alone)," Fortune, December 19, 2007.

Drummond, M., "The End of Software as We Know It," Fortune, November 19, 2001. Hempel, J., "Salesforce Hits Its Stride," Fortune, March 2, 2009.

Drummond, M., "The End of Software as We Know It," Fortune, November 19, 2001. Gruman, G., "Early Experiments in Cloud Computing," InfoWorld, April 7, 2008.

Farber, D., "Oracle's Ellison Nails Cloud Computing," CNET, September 26, 2008, http://news.cnet.com/ 8301-13953_3-10052188-80.html?tag=mncol;txt.

Fortt, J., "Tech Execs Get Sexy," Fortune, February 12, 2009.

Grossman, P., "Cloud Computing Begins to Gain Traction on Wall Street," Wall Street and Technology, January 6, 2009.

Gruman, G., "Early Experiments in Cloud Computing," InfoWorld, April 7, 2008.

Guth, R., "Virtual Piecework: Trolling the Web for Free Labor, Software Upstarts Are a New Force," Wall Street Journal, November 13, 2006.

Hamm, S., "Cloud Computing: Eyes on the Skies," BusinessWeek, April 24, 2008.

Katz, R., "Tech Titans Building Boom," IEEE Spectrum 46, no. 2 (February 1, 2009): 40–43. Mehta, S., "Behold the Server Farm," Fortune, July 28, 2006.

Katz, R., "Tech Titans Building Boom," IEEE Spectrum 46, no. 2 (February 1, 2009): 40–43. Lyons, D., "A Mostly Cloudy Computing Forecast," Washington Post, November 4, 2008.

King, R., "Cost-Conscious Companies Turn to Open-Source Software," BusinessWeek, December 1, 2008. Ljungberg, J., "Open Source Movements as a Model for Organizing," European Journal of Information Systems 9, no. 4 (December 2000): 208–16.

Kirkpatrick, D., "How the Open Source World Plans to Smack Down Microsoft and Oracle, and...," Fortune, February 23, 2004.

Kirkpatrick, D., "How the Open Source World Plans to Smack Down Microsoft and Oracle, and...," Fortune, February 23, 2004.

Lacy, L., "Open Warfare in Open Source," BusinessWeek, August 21, 2006. Preimesberger, C., "Sun's 'Open'-Door Policy," eWeek, April 21, 2008.

Lacy, S., "On-Demand Computing: A Brutal Slog," BusinessWeek, July 18, 2008.

Lacy, S., "On-Demand Computing: A Brutal Slog," BusinessWeek, July 18, 2008.

Lacy, S., "Open Warfare in Open Source," BusinessWeek, August 21, 2006. Lyons, D., "Cheapware," Forbes, September 6, 2004.

Liedtke, M., "Cloud Computing: Pie in the Sky Concept or the Next Big Breakthrough on Tech Horizon?" Associated Press Newswires, December 21, 2008.

Lohr, S., "Microsoft to Give Governments Access to Code," New York Times, January 15, 2003. McMillan, R., "Gone in Two Minutes," InfoWorld, March 27, 2008.

Lyons, D., "A Mostly Cloudy Computing Forecast," Washington Post, November 4, 2008. McKay, L., "30,000-Foot Views of the Cloud," Customer Relationship Management, January 2009.

MacMillan, D., P. Burrows, and S. Ante, "Inside the App Economy," BusinessWeek, October 22, 2009. Quittner, J., "How SaaS Helps Cut Small Business Costs," BusinessWeek, December 5, 2008.

Parkinson, J., "Green Data Centers Tackle LEED Certification," SearchDataCenter.com, January 18, 2007. Preimesberger, C., "Sun's 'Open'-Door Policy," eWeek, April 21, 2008.

Preimesberger, C., "Sun's 'Open'-Door Policy," eWeek, April 21, 2008.

Raymond, E., The Cathedral and the Bazaar: Musings on Linux and Open Source by an Accidental Revolutionary (Sebastopol, CA: O'Reilly, 1999).

Rayport, J., "Cloud Computing Is No Pipe Dream," BusinessWeek, December 9, 2008.

Rayport, J., "Cloud Computing Is No Pipe Dream," BusinessWeek, December 9, 2008. Vanderbilt, T., "Data Center Overload," New York Times, June 8, 2009.

Ricadela, A., "Microsoft Wants to 'Kill' Open Source," BusinessWeek, May 15, 2007. Ricadela, A., "The Worth of Open Source? Open Question," BusinessWeek, June 26, 2007.

Robertson, J., "IBM Sees Better-Than-Expected 2009 Profit, Earns US$4.4 Billion in Q4," Associated Press, January 20, 2009, http://humantimes.com/finance/business/sanfrancis/54853.

Schenker, J., "EA Leaps into Free Video Games," BusinessWeek, January 22, 2008.

Shankland, S., "Google's Open-Source Android Now Actually Open," CNET, October 21, 2008, http://news.cnet.com/8301-1001_3-10071093-92.html.

Shankland, S., M. Kane, and R. Lemos, "How Linux Saved Amazon Millions," CNET, October 30, 2001.

Vogelstein, F., "Rebuilding Microsoft," Wired, October 2006.

Wauters, R., "The Extraordinary Rise and Fall of Denmark's IT Factory," TechCrunch, December 2, 2008.

Wheeler, D., Secure Programming for Linux and Unix, 2003, http://www.dwheeler.com/secure-programs/Secure- Programs-HOWTO/index.html.

Woods, D., "The Commercial Bear Hug of Open Source," Forbes, August 18, 2008.

Woods, D., "The Commercial Bear Hug of Open Source," Forbes, August 18, 2008.

THE DATA ASSET BUSINESS INTELLIGENCE, DATABASES, AND COMPETITIVE ADVANTAGE

11.1 INTRODUCTION: AN OVERVIEW

The planet is awash in data. Cash registers ring up transactions worldwide. Web browsers leave a trail of cookie crumbs nearly everywhere they go. And with radio frequency identification (RFID), inventory can literally announce its presence so that firms can precisely journal every hop their products make along the value chain: "I'm arriving in the warehouse," "I'm on the store shelf," "I'm leaving out the front door."

A study by Gartner Research claims that the amount of data on corporate hard drives doubles every six months (Babcock, 2006), while IDC states that the collective number of those bits already exceeds the number of stars in the universe (Mearian, 2008). Wal-Mart alone boasts a data volume well over *125 times* as large as the *entire* print collection of the U.S. Library of Congress[1].

And with this flood of data comes a tidal wave of opportunity. Increasingly standardized corporate data, and access to rich, third-party data sets—all leveraged by cheap, fast computing and easier-to-use software—are collectively enabling a new age of data-driven, fact-based decision making. You're less likely to hear old-school terms like "decision support systems" used to describe what's going on here. The phrase of the day is business intelligence (BI), a catchall term combining aspects of reporting, data exploration and ad hoc queries, and sophisticated data modeling and analysis. Alongside business intelligence in the new managerial lexicon is the phrase analytics, a term describing the extensive use of data, statistical and quantitative analysis, explanatory and predictive models, and fact-based management to drive decisions and actions (Davenport & Harris, 2007).

The benefits of all this data and number crunching are very real, indeed. Data leverage lies at the center of competitive advantage we've studied in the Zara,

Netflix, and Google cases. Data mastery has helped vault Wal- Mart to the top of the *Fortune* 500 list. It helped Harrah's Casino Hotels grow to be twice as profitable as similarly sized Caesars, and rich enough to acquire this rival. And data helped Capital One find valuable customers that competitors were ignoring, delivering ten-year financial performance a full ten times greater than the S&P 500. Data-driven decision making is even credited with helping the Red Sox win their first World Series in eighty- three years and with helping the New England Patriots win three Super Bowls in four years. To quote from a *BusinessWeek* cover story on analytics, "Math Will Rock Your World!" (Baker, 2006)

Sounds great, but it can be a tough slog getting an organization to the point where it has a leveragable data asset. In many organizations data lies dormant, spread across inconsistent formats and incompatible systems, unable to be turned into anything of value. Many firms have been shocked at the amount of work and complexity required to pull together an infrastructure that empowers its managers. But not only can this be done; it must be done. Firms that are basing decisions on hunches aren't managing; they're gambling. And the days of uninformed managerial dice rolling are over.

While we'll study technology in this chapter, our focus isn't as much on the technology itself as it is on what you can do with that technology. Consumer products giant P&G believes in this distinction so thoroughly that the firm renamed its IT function as "Information and Decision Solutions" (Soat, 2007). Solutions drive technology decisions, not the other way around.

In this chapter we'll study the data asset, how it's created, how it's stored, and how it's accessed and leveraged. We'll also study many of the firms mentioned above, and more; providing a context for understanding how managers are leveraging data to create winning models, and how those that have failed to realize the power of data have been left in the dust.

11.2 DATA, INFORMATION, AND KNOWLEDGE

Data refers simply to raw facts and figures. Alone it tells you nothing. The real goal is to turn data into **information**. Data becomes information when it's presented in a context so that it can answer a question or support decision making. And it's when this information can be combined with a manager's **knowledge**—their insight from experience and expertise—that stronger decisions can be made.

Understanding the Structure of Data: Key Terms and Technologies

A **database** is simply a list (or more likely, several related lists) of data. Most organizations have several databases—perhaps even hundreds or thousands. And these various databases might be focused on any combination of functional areas (sales, product returns, inventory, payroll), geographical regions, or business units.

Firms often create specialized databases for recording transactions, as well as databases that aggregate data from multiple sources in order to support reporting and analysis.

Databases are created, maintained, and manipulated using programs called **database management systems (DBMS)**, sometimes referred to as *database software*. DBMS products vary widely in scale and capabilities. They include the single-user, desktop versions of Microsoft Access or Filemaker Pro, Web-based offerings like Intuit QuickBase, and industrial strength products from Oracle, IBM (DB2), Sybase, Microsoft (SQL Server), and others. Oracle is the world's largest database software vendor, and database software has meant big bucks for Oracle cofounder and CEO Larry Ellison. Ellison perennially ranks in the Top 10 of the *Forbes* 400 list of wealthiest Americans.

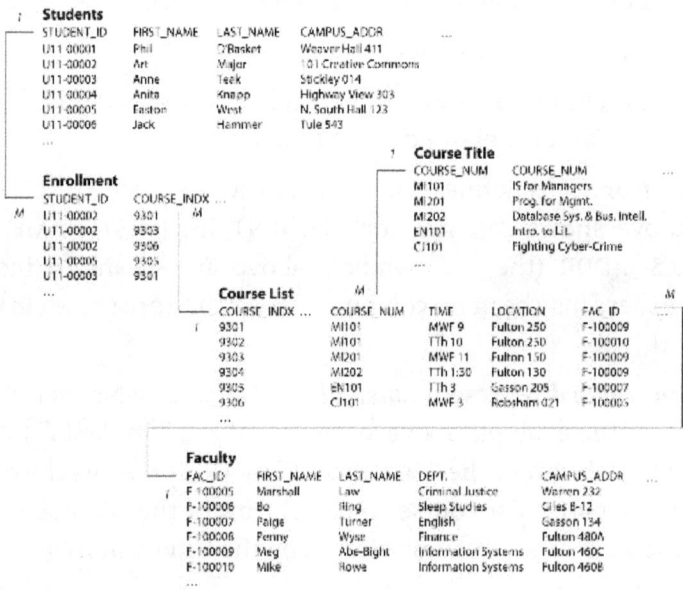

Figure 11.1 A Simplified Relational Database for a University Course Registration System

The acronym SQL (often pronounced *sequel*) also shows up a lot when talking about databases. Structured query language (SQL) is by far the most common language for creating and manipulating databases. You'll find variants of SQL inhabiting everything from lowly desktop software, to high-powered enterprise products. Microsoft's high-end database is even called SQL Server. And of course there's also the open source MySQL (whose stewardship now sits with Oracle as part of the firm's purchase of Sun Microsystems). Given this popularity, if you're going to learn one language for database use, SQL's a pretty good choice. And for a little inspiration, visit Monster.com or another job site and search for jobs mentioning

SQL. You'll find page after page of listings, suggesting that while database systems have been good for Ellison, learning more about them might be pretty good for you, too.

Even if you don't become a database programmer or **database administrator (DBA)**, you're almost surely going to be called upon to dive in and use a database. You may even be asked to help identify your firm's data requirements. It's quite common for nontech employees to work on development teams with technical staff, defining business problems, outlining processes, setting requirements, and determining the kinds of data the firm will need to leverage. Database systems are powerful stuff, and can't be avoided, so a bit of understanding will serve you well.

A complete discourse on technical concepts associated with database systems is beyond the scope of our managerial introduction, but here are some key concepts to help get you oriented, and that all managers should know.

- A **table or file** refers to a list of data.

- A *database* is either a single table or a collection of related tables. The course registration database above depicts five tables.

- A **column or field** defines the data that a table can hold. The "Students" table above shows columns for STUDENT_ID, FIRST_NAME, LAST_NAME, CAMPU.S._ADDR (the "..." symbols above are meant to indicate that in practice there may be more columns or rows than are shown in this simplified diagram).

- A **row or record** represents a single instance of whatever the table keeps track of. In the example above, each row of the "Students" table represents a student, each row of the "Enrollment" table represents the enrollment of a student in a particular course, and each row of the "Course List" represents a given section of each course offered by the University.

- A **key** is the field used to relate tables in a database. Look at how the STUDENT_ID key is used above. There is *one* unique STUDENT_ID for each student, but the STUDENT_ID may appear *many* times in the "Enrollment" table, indicating that each student may be enrolled in many classes. The "1" and "M" in the diagram above indicate the one to many relationships among the keys in these tables.

Databases organized like the one above, where multiple tables are related based on common keys, are referred to as **relational databases**. There are many other database formats (sporting names like *hierarchical*, and *object-oriented*), but relational databases are far and away the most popular. And all SQL databases are relational databases.

We've just scratched the surface for a very basic introduction. Expect that a formal class in database systems will offer you far more detail and better design principles than are conveyed in the elementary example above. But you're already well on your way!

11.3 WHAT SOURCES DO DATA COME FROM?

Organizations can pull together data from a variety of sources. While the examples that follow aren't meant to be an encyclopedic listing of possibilities, they will give you a sense of the diversity of options available for data gathering.

Transaction Processing Systems

For most organizations that sell directly to their customers, **transaction processing systems (TPS)** represent a fountain of potentially insightful data. Every time a consumer uses a point-of-sale system, an ATM, or a service desk, there's a **transaction** (some kind of business exchange) occurring, representing an event that's likely worth tracking.

The cash register is the data generation workhorse of most physical retailers, and the primary source that feeds data to the TPS. But while TPS can generate a lot of bits, it's sometimes tough to match this data with a specific customer. For example, if you pay a retailer in cash, you're likely to remain a mystery to your merchant because your name isn't attached to your money. Grocers and retailers can tie you to cash transactions if they can convince you to use a **loyalty card**. Use one of these cards and you're in effect giving up information about yourself in exchange for some kind of financial incentive. The explosion in retailer cards is directly related to each firm's desire to learn more about you and to turn you into a more loyal and satisfied customer.

Some cards provide an instant discount (e.g., the CVS Pharmacy ExtraCare card), while others allow you to build up points over time (Best Buy's Reward Zone). The latter has the additional benefit of acting as a switching cost. A customer may think "I could get the same thing at Target, but at Best Buy, it'll increase my existing points balance and soon I'll get a cash back coupon."

Enterprise Software (CRM, SCM, and ERP)

Firms increasingly set up systems to gather additional data beyond conventional purchase transactions or Web site monitoring. CRM or customer relationship management systems are often used to empower employees to track and record data at nearly every point of customer contact. Someone calls for a quote? Brings a return back to a store? Writes a complaint e-mail? A well-designed CRM system can capture all these events for subsequent analysis or for triggering follow-up events.

Enterprise software includes not just CRM systems but also categories that touch every aspect of the value chain, including supply chain management (SCM) and enterprise resource planning (ERP) systems. More importantly, enterprise software tends to be more integrated and standardized than the prior era of proprietary systems that many firms developed themselves. This integration helps in combining data across business units and functions, and in getting that data into a form where it can be turned into information (for more on enterprise systems, see Chapter 9 "Understanding Software: A Primer for Managers").

Surveys

Sometimes firms supplement operational data with additional input from surveys and focus groups. Oftentimes, direct surveys can tell you what your cash register can't. Zara store managers informally survey customers in order to help shape designs and product mix. Online grocer FreshDirect (see Chapter 2 "Strategy and Technology: Concepts and Frameworks for Understanding What Separates Winners from Losers") surveys customers weekly and has used this feedback to drive initiatives from reducing packaging size to including star ratings on produce (Braddock, 2009). Many CRM products also have survey capabilities that allow for additional data gathering at all points of customer contact.

External Sources

Sometimes it makes sense to combine a firm's data with bits brought in from the outside. Many firms, for example, don't sell directly to consumers (this includes most drug companies and packaged goods firms). If your firm has partners that sell products for you, then you'll likely rely heavily on data collected by others.

Data bought from sources available to all might not yield competitive advantage on its own, but it can provide key operational insight for increased efficiency and cost savings. And when combined with a firm's unique data assets, it may give firms a high-impact edge.

Consider restaurant chain Brinker, a firm that runs seventeen hundred eateries in twenty-seven countries under the Chili's, On The Border, and Maggiano's brands. Brinker (whose ticker symbol is EAT), supplements their own data with external feeds on weather, employment statistics, gas prices, and other factors, and uses this in predictive models that help the firm in everything from determining staffing levels to switching around menu items (King, 2009).

In another example, Carnival Cruise Lines combines its own customer data with third-party information tracking household income and other key measures. This data plays a key role in a recession, since it helps the firm target limited marketing dollars on those past customers that are more likely to be able to afford to go on a cruise. So far it's been a winning approach. For three years in a row, the firm has experienced double-digit increases in bookings by repeat customers (King, 2009).

11.4 DATA RICH, INFORMATION POOR

Despite being a wash in data, many organizations are data rich but information poor. A survey by consulting firm Accenture found 57 percent of companies reporting that they didn't have a beneficial, consistently updated, companywide analytical capability. Among major decisions, only 60 percent were backed by analytics—40 percent were made by intuition and gut instinct (King, 2009). The big culprit limiting BI initiatives is getting data into a form where it can be used, analyzed, and turned into information. Here's a look at some factors holding back information advantages.

Incompatible Systems

Just because data is collected doesn't mean it can be used. This limit is a big problem for large firms that have **legacy systems**, outdated information systems that were not designed to share data, aren't compatible with newer technologies, and aren't aligned with the firm's current business needs. The problem can be made worse by mergers and acquisitions, especially if a firm depends on operational systems that are incompatible with its partner. And the elimination of incompatible systems isn't just a technical issue. Firms might be under extended agreement with different vendors or outsourcers, and breaking a contract or invoking an escape clause may be costly. Folks working in M&A (the area of investment banking focused on valuing and facilitating mergers and acquisitions) beware—it's critical to uncover these hidden costs of technology integration before deciding if a deal makes financial sense.

Operational Data Can't Always Be Queried

Another problem when turning data into information is that most transactional databases aren't set up to be simultaneously accessed for reporting and analysis. When a customer buys something from a cash register, that action may post a sales record and deduct an item from the firm's inventory. In most TPS systems, requests made to the database can usually be performed pretty quickly—the system adds or modifies the few records involved and it's done—in and out in a flash.

But if a manager asks a database to analyze historic sales trends showing the most and least profitable products over time, they may be asking a computer to look at thousands of transaction records, comparing results, and neatly ordering findings. That's not a quick in-and-out task, and it may very well require significant processing to come up with the request. Do this against the very databases you're using to record your transactions, and you might grind your computers to a halt.

Getting data into systems that can support analytics is where data warehouses and data marts come in, the topic of our next section.

11.5 THE UTILISATION OF DATA MARTS AND WAREHOUSES

Since running analytics against transactional data can bog down a system, and since most organizations need to combine and reformat data from multiple sources, firms typically need to create separate data repositories for their reporting and analytics work—a kind of staging area from which to turn that data into information.

Two terms you'll hear for these kinds of repositories are **data warehouse** and **data mart**. A data warehouse is a set of databases designed to support decision making in an organization. It is structured for fast online queries and exploration. Data warehouses may aggregate enormous amounts of data from many different operational systems.

A data mart is a database focused on addressing the concerns of a specific problem (e.g., increasing customer retention, improving product quality) or business unit (e.g., marketing, engineering).

Marts and warehouses may contain huge volumes of data. For example, a firm may not need to keep large amounts of historical point-of-sale or transaction data in its operational systems, but it might want past data in its data mart so that managers can hunt for patterns and trends that occur over time.

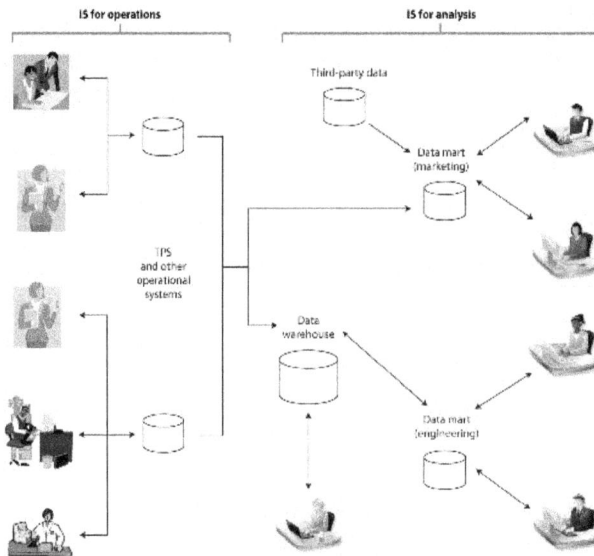

Figure 11.2 Information systems supporting operations (such as TPS) are typically separate, and "feed" information systems used for analytics (such as data warehouses and data marts).

It's easy for firms to get seduced by a software vendor's demonstration showing data at your fingertips, presented in pretty graphs. But as mentioned earlier, getting data in a format that can be used for analytics is hard, complex, and challenging work. Large data warehouses can cost millions and take years to build. Every dollar spent on technology may lead to five to seven more dollars on consulting and other services (King, 2009).

Most firms will face a trade-off—do we attempt a large-scale integration of the whole firm, or more targeted efforts with quicker payoffs? Firms in fast-moving industries or with particularly complex businesses may struggle to get sweeping projects completed in enough time to reap benefits before business conditions change. Most consultants now advise smaller projects with narrow scope driven by specific business goals (Rigby & Ledingham, 2004; King, 2009).

Firms can eventually get to a unified data warehouse but it may take time. Even analytics king Wal-Mart is just getting to that point. In 2007, it was reported that Wal-Mart had seven hundred different data marts and hired Hewlett-Packard for help in bringing the systems together to form a more integrated data warehouse (Havenstein, 2007).

The old saying from the movie *Field of Dreams*, "If you build it, they will come," doesn't hold up well for large- scale data analytics projects. This work should start with a clear vision with business-focused objectives. When senior executives can see objectives illustrated in potential payoff, they'll be able to champion the effort, and experts agree, having an executive champion is a key success factor. Focusing on business issues will also drive technology choice, with the firm better able to focus on products that best fit its needs.

Once a firm has business goals and hoped-for payoffs clearly defined, it can address the broader issues needed to design, develop, deploy, and maintain its system[1]:/p>

- ◉ *Data relevance.* What data is needed to compete on analytics and to meet our current and future goals?

- ◉ *Data sourcing.* Can we even get the data we'll need? Where can this data be obtained from? Is it available via our internal systems? Via third-party data aggregators? Via suppliers or sales partners? Do we need to set up new systems, surveys, and other collection efforts to acquire the data we need?

- ◉ *Data quantity.* How much data is needed?

- ◉ *Data quality.* Can our data be trusted as accurate? Is it clean, complete, and reasonably free of errors? How can the data be made more accurate and valuable for analysis? Will we need to 'scrub,' calculate, and consolidate data so that it can be used?

- ◉ *Data hosting.* Where will the systems be housed? What are the hardware and networking requirements for the effort?

⊙ *Data governance.* What rules and processes are needed to manage data from its creation through its retirement? Are there operational issues (backup, disaster recovery)? Legal issues? Privacy issues? How should the firm handle security and access?

For some perspective on how difficult this can be, consider that an executive from one of the largest U.S. banks once lamented at how difficult it was to get his systems to do something as simple as properly distinguishing between men and women. The company's customer-focused data warehouse drew data from thirty-six separate operational systems—bank teller systems, ATMs, student loan reporting systems, car loan systems, mortgage loan systems, and more. Collectively these legacy systems expressed gender in *seventeen* different ways: "M" or "F"; "m" or "f"; "Male" or "Female"; "MALE" or "FEMALE"; "1" for man, "0" for woman; "0" for man, "1" for woman and more, plus various codes for "unknown." The best math in the world is of no help if the values used aren't any good. There's a saying in the industry, "garbage in, garbage out."

11.6 A TOOLKIT FOR BUSINESS INTELLIGENCE

So far we've discussed where data can come from, and how we can get data into a form where we can use it. But how, exactly, do firms turn that data into information? That's where the various software tools of business intelligence (BI) and analytics come in. Potential products in the business intelligence toolkit range from simple spreadsheets to ultrasophisticated data mining packages leveraged by teams employing "rocket-science" mathematics.

Query and Reporting Tools

The idea behind query and reporting tools is to present users with a subset of requested data, selected, sorted, ordered, calculated, and compared, as needed. Managers use these tools to see and explore what's happening inside their organizations.

Canned reports provide regular summaries of information in a predetermined format. They're often developed by information systems staff and formats can be difficult to alter. By contrast, **ad hoc reporting tools** allow users to dive in and create their own reports, selecting fields, ranges, and other parameters to build their own reports on the fly. **Dashboards** provide a sort of heads-up display of critical indicators, letting managers get a graphical glance at key performance metrics. Some tools may allow data to be exported into spreadsheets. Yes, even the lowly spreadsheet can be a powerful tool for modeling "what if" scenarios and creating additional reports (of course be careful: if data can be easily exported, then it can potentially leave the firm dangerously exposed, raising privacy, security, legal, and competitive concerns).

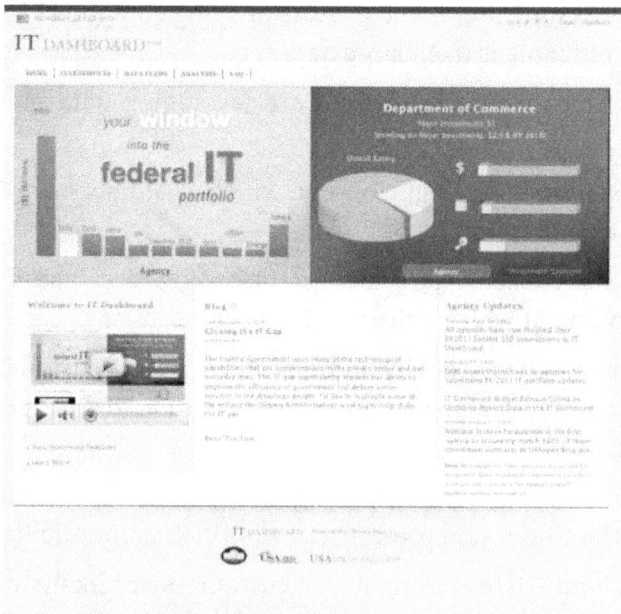

Figure 11.3 The Federal IT Dashboard

The Federal IT dashboard offers federal agencies, and the general public, information about the government's IT investments.

A subcategory of reporting tools is referred to as **online analytical processing (OLAP)** (pronounced "oh-lap"). Data used in OLAP reporting is usually sourced from standard relational databases, but it's calculated and summarized in advance, across multiple dimensions, with the data stored in a special database called a **data cube**. This extra setup step makes OLAP fast (sometimes one thousand times faster than performing comparable queries against conventional relational databases). Given this kind of speed boost, it's not surprising that data cubes for OLAP access are often part of a firm's data mart and data warehouse efforts.

A manager using an OLAP tool can quickly explore and compare data across multiple factors such as time, geography, product lines, and so on. In fact, OLAP users often talk about how they can "slice and dice" their data, "drilling down" inside the data to uncover new insights. And while conventional reports are usually presented as a summarized list of information, OLAP results look more like a spreadsheet, with the various dimensions of analysis in rows and columns, with summary values at the intersection.

Data Mining

While reporting tools can help users explore data, modern data sets can be so large that it might be impossible for humans to spot underlying trends. That's where data mining can help. **Data mining** is the process of using computers to identify hidden patterns and to build models from large data sets.

Some of the key areas where businesses are leveraging data mining include the following:

- ⊙ *Customer segmentation*—figuring out which customers are likely to be the most valuable to a firm.

- ⊙ *Marketing and promotion targeting*—identifying which customers will respond to which offers at which price at what time.

- ⊙ *Market basket analysis*—determining which products customers buy together, and how an organization can use this information to cross-sell more products or services.

- ⊙ *Collaborative filtering*—personalizing an individual customer's experience based on the trends and preferences identified across similar customers.

- ⊙ *Customer churn*—determining which customers are likely to leave, and what tactics can help the firm avoid unwanted defections.

- ⊙ *Fraud detection*—uncovering patterns consistent with criminal activity.

- ⊙ *Financial modeling*—building trading systems to capitalize on historical trends.

- ⊙ *Hiring and promotion*—identifying characteristics consistent with employee success in the firm's various roles.

For data mining to work, two critical conditions need to be present: (1) the organization must have clean, consistent data, and (2) the events in that data should reflect current and future trends. The recent financial crisis provides lessons on what can happen when either of these conditions isn't met.

First lets look at problems with using bad data. A report in the *New York Times* has suggested that in the period leading up to the 2008 financial crisis, some banking executives deliberately deceived risk management systems in order to skew capital-on-hand requirements. This deception let firms load up on risky debt, while carrying less cash for covering losses (Hansell, 2008). Deceive your systems with bad data and your models are worthless. In this case, wrong estimates from bad data left firms grossly overexposed to risk. When debt defaults occurred; several banks failed, and we entered the worst financial crisis since the Great Depression.

Now consider the problem of historical consistency: Computer-driven investment models can be very effective when the market behaves as it has in the past. But models are blind when faced with the equivalent of the "hundred-year flood" (sometimes called *black swans*); events so extreme and unusual that they never showed up in the data used to build the model.

We saw this in the late 1990s with the collapse of the investment firm Long Term Capital Management. LTCM was started by Nobel Prize–winning economists, but when an unexpected Russian debt crisis caused the markets to move in ways not anticipated by its models, the firm lost 90 percent of its value in less than two months. The problem was so bad that the Fed had to step in to supervise the firm's multibillion-dollar bailout. Fast forward a decade to the banking collapse of 2008, and we again see computer-driven trading funds plummet in the face of another unexpected event—the burst of the housing bubble (Wahba, 2008).

Data mining presents a host of other perils, as well. It's possible to **over-engineer** a model, building it with so many variables that the solution arrived at might only work on the subset of data you've used to create it. You might also be looking at a random but meaningless statistical fluke. In demonstrating how flukes occur, one quantitative investment manager uncovered a correlation that at first glance appeared statistically to be a particularly strong predictor for historical prices in the S&P 500 stock index. That predictor? Butter production in Bangladesh (Coy, 1997). Sometimes durable and useful patterns just aren't in your data.

One way to test to see if you're looking at a random occurrence in the numbers is to divide your data, building your model with one portion of the data, and using another portion to verify your results. This is the approach Netflix has used to test results achieved by teams in the Netflix Prize, the firm's million-dollar contest for improving the predictive accuracy of its movie recommendation engine (see Chapter 4 "Netflix: The Making of an E-commerce Giant and the Uncertain Future of Atoms to Bits").

Finally, sometimes a pattern is uncovered but determining the best choice for a response is less clear. As an example, let's return to the data-mining wizards at Tesco. An analysis of product sales data showed several money-losing products, including a type of bread known as "milk loaf." Drop those products, right? Not so fast. Further analysis showed milk loaf was a "destination product" for a loyal group of high-value customers, and that these customers would shop elsewhere if milk loaf disappeared from Tesco shelves. The firm kept the bread as a loss-leader and retained those valuable milk loaf fans (Helm, 2008). Data miner, beware—first findings don't always reveal an optimal course of action.

This last example underscores the importance of recruiting a data mining and business analytics team that possesses three critical skills: information technology (for understanding how to pull together data, and for selecting analysis tools), statistics (for building models and interpreting the strength and validity of results), and business knowledge (for helping set system goals, requirements, and offering deeper insight into what the data really says about the firm's operating environment). Miss one of these key functions and your team could make some major mistakes.

While we've focused on tools in our discussion above, many experts suggest that business intelligence is really an organizational process as much as it is a set of technologies. Having the right team is critical in moving the firm from goal setting through execution and results.

11.7 DATA ASSET IN ACTION: THE RISE OF WAL-MART AND TECHNOLOGY

Wal-Mart demonstrates how a physical product retailer can create and leverage a data asset to achieve world-class supply chain efficiencies targeted primarily at driving down costs.

Wal-Mart isn't just the largest retailer in the world, over the past several years it has popped in and out of the top spot on the *Fortune* 500 list—meaning that the firm has had revenues greater than *any* firm in the United States. Wal-Mart is so big that in three months it sells more than a whole year's worth of sales at number two U.S. retailer, Home Depot[1].

At that size, it's clear that Wal-Mart's key source of competitive advantage is scale. But firms don't turn into giants overnight. Wal-Mart grew in large part by leveraging information systems to an extent never before seen in the retail industry. Technology tightly coordinates the Wal-Mart value chain from tip to tail, while these systems also deliver a mineable data asset that's unmatched in U.S. retail. To get a sense of the firm's overall efficiencies, at the end of the prior decade a McKinsey study found that Wal-Mart was responsible for some 12 percent of the productivity gains in the *entire* U.S. economy (Fishman, 2007). The firm's capacity as a systems innovator is so respected that many senior Wal-Mart IT executives have been snatched up for top roles at Dell, HP, Amazon, and Microsoft. And lest one think that innovation is the province of only those located in the technology hubs of Silicon Valley, Boston, and Seattle, remember that Wal-Mart is headquartered in Bentonville, Arkansas.

A Data-Driven Value Chain

The Wal-Mart efficiency dance starts with a proprietary system called Retail Link, a system originally developed in 1991 and continually refined ever since. Each time an item is scanned by a Wal-Mart cash register, Retail Link not only records the sale, it also automatically triggers inventory reordering, scheduling, and delivery. This process keeps shelves stocked, while keeping inventories at a minimum. An AMR report ranked Wal-Mart as having the seventh best supply chain in the country (the only other retailer in the top twenty was Tesco, at number fifteen) (Friscia, et. al., 2009). The firm's annual **inventory turnover ratio** of 8.5 means that Wal-Mart sells the equivalent of its entire inventory roughly every six weeks (by comparison, Target's turnover ratio is 6.4, Sears' is 3.4, and the average for U.S. retail is less than 2)[2].

Back-office scanners keep track of inventory as supplier shipments come in. Suppliers are rated based on timeliness of deliveries, and you've got to be quick to work with Wal-Mart. In order to avoid a tractor-trailer traffic jam in store parking lots, deliveries are choreographed to arrive at intervals less than ten minutes apart. When Levi's joined Wal-Mart, the firm had to guarantee it could replenish shelves every two days—no prior retailer had required a shorter than five day window from Levi's (Fishman, 2007).

Wal-Mart has been a catalyst for technology adoption among its suppliers. The firm is currently leading an adoption effort that requires partners to leverage RFID technology to track and coordinate inventories. While the rollout has been slow, a recent P&G trial showed RFID boosted sales nearly 20 percent by ensuring that inventory was on shelves and located where it should be (Joseph, 2009).

Data Mining Capability

Wal-Mart also mines its mother lode of data to get its product mix right under all sorts of varying environmental conditions, protecting the firm from "a retailer's twin nightmares: too much inventory, or not enough" (Hays, 2004). For example, the firm's data mining efforts informed buyers that customers stock up on certain products in the days leading up to predicted hurricanes. Bumping up prestorm supplies of batteries and bottled water was a no brainer, but the firm also learned that Pop-Tarts sales spike seven fold before storms hit, and that beer is the top prestorm seller. This insight has lead to truckloads full of six packs and toaster pastries streaming into gulf states whenever word of a big storm surfaces (Hays, 2004).

Data mining also helps the firm tighten operational forecasts, helping to predict things like how many cashiers are needed at a given store at various times of day throughout the year. Data drives the organization, with mined reports forming the basis of weekly sales meetings, as well as executive strategy sessions.

Sharing Data, Keeping Secrets

While Wal-Mart is demanding of its suppliers, it also shares data with them, too. Data can help firms become more efficient so that Wal-Mart can keep dropping prices, and data can help firms uncover patterns that help suppliers sell more. P&G's Gillette unit, for example, claims to have mined Wal-Mart data to develop promotions that increased sales as much as 19 percent. More than seventeen thousand suppliers are given access to their products' Wal-Mart performance across metrics that include daily sales, shipments, returns, purchase orders, invoices, claims and forecasts. And these suppliers collectively interrogate Wal-Mart data warehouses to the tune of twenty-one million queries a year (Evans-Correia, 2006).

While Wal-Mart shares sales data with relevant suppliers, the firm otherwise fiercely guards this asset. Many retailers pool their data by sharing it with information brokers like Information Resources and ACNielsen. This sharing allows smaller firms to pool their data to provide more comprehensive insight on market behavior. But Wal-Mart stopped sharing data with these agencies years ago. The firm's scale is so big, the additional data provided by brokers wasn't adding much value, and it no longer made sense to allow competitors access to what was happening in its own huge chunk of retail sales.

Other aspects of the firm's technology remain under wraps, too. Wal-Mart custom builds large portions of its information systems to keep competitors off its trail. As for infrastructure secrets, the Wal-Mart Data Center in McDonald County, Missouri, was considered so off limits that the county assessor was required to sign a nondisclosure statement before being allowed on-site to estimate property value (McCoy, 2006).

Challenges Abound

But despite success, challenges continue. While Wal-Mart grew dramatically throughout the 1990s, the firm's U.S. business has largely matured. And as a mature business it faces a problem not unlike the example of Microsoft discussed at the end of Chapter 14 "Google: Search, Online Advertising, and Beyond"; Wal-Mart needs to find huge markets or dramatic cost savings in order to boost profits and continue to move its stock price higher.

The firm's aggressiveness and sheer size also increasingly make Wal-Mart a target for criticism. Those low prices come at a price, and the firm has faced accusations of subpar wages and remains a magnet for union activists. Others had identified poor labor conditions at some of the firm's contract manufacturers. Suppliers that compete for Wal-Mart's business are often faced with a catch-22. If they bypass Wal-Mart they miss out on the largest single chunk of world retail sales. But if they sell to Wal-Mart, the firm may demand prices so aggressively low that suppliers end up cannibalizing their own sales at other retailers. Still more criticism comes from local citizen groups that have accused Wal-Mart of ruining the market for mom-and-pop stores (Fishman, 2007).

While some might see Wal-Mart as invincibly standing at the summit of world retail, it's important to note that other megaretailers have fallen from grace. In the 1920s and 1930s, the A&P grocery chain once controlled 80 percent of U.S. grocery sales, at its peak operating five times the number of stores that Wal-Mart has today. But market conditions changed, and the government stepped in to draft antipredatory pricing laws when it felt A&Ps parent was too aggressive.

For all of Wal-Mart's data brilliance, historical data offers little insight on how to adapt to more radical changes in the retail landscape. The firm's data warehouse wasn't able to foretell the rise of Target and other up- market discounters. And yet another major battle is brewing, as Tesco methodically attempts to take its globally honed expertise to U.S. shores. Savvy managers recognize that data use is a vital tool, but not the only tool in management's strategic arsenal.

11.8 DATA ASSET IN USE: HARRAH'S SOLID GOLD CRM FOR THE SERVICE SECTOR

Harrah's Entertainment provides an example of exceptional data asset leverage in the service sector, focusing on how this technology enables world-class service through customer relationship management.

Gary Loveman is a sort of management major trifecta. The CEO of Harrah's Entertainment is a former *operations* professor who has leveraged *information technology* to create what may be the most effective *marketing* organization in the service industry. If you ever needed an incentive to motivate you for cross-disciplinary thinking, Loveman provides it.

Harrah's has leveraged its data-powered prowess to move from an also-ran chain of casinos to become the largest gaming company by revenue. The firm operates some fifty-three casinos, employing more than eighty- five thousand workers on five continents. Brands include Harrah's, Caesars Palace, Bally's, Horseshoe, and Paris Las Vegas. Under Loveman, Harrah's has aggressively swallowed competitors, the firm's $9.4 billion buyout of Caesars Entertainment being its largest deal to date.

Data Asset in Use

Data drives the firm. Harrah's collects customer data on just about everything you might do at their properties—gamble, eat, grab a drink, attend a show, stay in a room. The data's then used to track your preferences and to size up whether you're the kind of customer that's worth pursuing. Prove your worth, and the firm will surround you with top-tier service and develop a targeted marketing campaign to keep wooing you back (Magnini, et. al., 2003).

The ace in the firm's data collection hole is its Total Rewards loyalty card system. Launched over a decade ago, the system is constantly being enhanced by an IT staff of seven hundred, with an annual budget in excess of $100 million (Swabey, 2007). Total Rewards is an **opt-in** loyalty program, but customers consider the incentives to be so good that the card is used by some 80 percent of Harrah's patrons, collecting data on over forty-four million customers (Wagner, 2008; Haugsted, 2007).

Customers signing up for the card provide Harrah's with demographic information such as gender, age, and address. Visitors then present the card for various transactions. Slide it into a slot machine, show it to the restaurant hostess, present it to the parking valet, share your account number with a telephone reservation specialist—every contact point is an opportunity to collect data. Between three hundred thousand and one million customers come through Harrah's doors daily, adding to the firm's data stash and keeping that asset fresh (Hoover, 2007).

Most Valuable Customers

All that data is heavily and relentlessly mined. Customer relationship management should include an assessment to determine which customers are worth having a relationship with. And because Harrah's has so much detailed historical data, the firm can make fairly accurate projections of **customer lifetime value (CLV)**. CLV represents the present value of the likely future income stream generated by an individual purchaser[1]. Once you know this, you can get a sense of how much you should spend to keep that customer coming back. You can size them up next to their peer group and if they fall below expectations you can develop strategies to improve their spending.

The firm tracks over ninety demographic segments, and each responds differently to different marketing approaches. Identifying segments and figuring out how to deal with each involves an iterative model of mining the data to identify patterns, creating a hypothesis (customers in group X will respond to a free steak dinner; group Y will want ten dollars in casino chips), then testing that hypothesis against a control group, turning again to analytics to statistically verify the outcome.

The firm runs hundreds of these small, controlled experiments each year. Loveman says that when marketers suggest new initiatives, "I ask, did we test it first? And if I find out that we just whole-hogged, went after something without testing it, I'll kill 'em. No matter how clever they think it is, we test it" (Nickell, 2002). The former ops professor is known to often quote quality guru W. Edwards Deming, saying, "In God we trust; all others must bring data."

When Harrah's began diving into the data, they uncovered patterns that defied the conventional wisdom in the gaming industry. Big money didn't come from European princes, Hong Kong shipping heirs, or the *Ocean's 11* crowd—it came from locals. The less than 30 percent of customers who spent between one hundred and five hundred dollars per visit accounted for over 80 percent of revenues and nearly 100 percent of profits (Swabey, 2007).

The data also showed that the firm's most important customers weren't the families that many Vegas competitors were trying to woo with Disneyland-style theme casinos—it was Grandma! Harrah's focuses on customers forty- five years and older: twenty-somethings have no money, while thirty-somethings have kids and are too busy. To the premiddle-aged crowd, Loveman says, "God bless you, but we don't need you" (Haugsted, 2007).

The Data-Driven Service: Get Close (but Not Too Close) to Your Customers

The names for reward levels on the Total Rewards card convey increasing customer value—Gold, Diamond, and Platinum. Spend more money at Harrah's and you'll enjoy shorter lines, discounts, free items, and more. And if Harrah's systems determine you're a high-value customer, expect white-glove treatment. The firm will lavish you with attention, using technology to try to anticipate your every need. Customers notice the extra treatment that top-tier Total Rewards members receive and actively work to improve their status.

To illustrate this, Loveman points to the obituary of an Ashville, North Carolina, woman who frequented a casino Harrah's operates on a nearby Cherokee reservation. "Her obituary was published in the Asheville paper and indicated that at the time of her death, she had several grandchildren, she sang in the Baptist choir and she was *a holder of the Harrah's Diamond Total Rewards card*." Quipped Loveman, "When your loyalty card is listed in someone's obituary, I would maintain *you have traction*" (Loveman, 2005).

The degree of customer service pushed through the system is astonishing. Upon check in, a Harrah's customer who enjoys fine dining may find his or her table is reserved, along with tickets for a show afterward. Others may get suggestions or special offers throughout their stay, pushed via text message to their mobile device (Wagner, 2008). The firm even tracks gamblers to see if they're suffering unusual losses, and Harrah's will dispatch service people to intervene with a feel-good offer: "Having a bad day? Here's a free buffet coupon" (Davenport & Harris, 2007).

The firm's CRM effort monitors any customer behavior changes. If a customer who usually spends a few hundred a month hasn't shown up in a while, the firm's systems trigger follow-up contact methods such as sending a letter with a promotion offer, or having a rep make a phone call inviting them back (Loveman, 2005).

Customers come back to Harrah's because they feel that those casinos treat them better than the competition. And Harrah's laser-like focus on service quality and customer satisfaction are embedded into its information systems and operational procedures. Employees are measured on metrics that include speed and friendliness and are compensated based on guest satisfaction ratings. Hourly workers are notoriously difficult to motivate: they tend to be high-turnover, low-wage earners. But at Harrah's, incentive bonuses depend on an entire location's ratings. That encourages strong performers to share tips to bring the new guy up to speed. The process effectively changed the corporate culture at Harrah's from an every-property-for-itself mentality to a collaborative, customer- focused enterprise (Magnini & Honeycutt, 2003).

While Harrah's is committed to learning how to make your customer experience better, the firm is also keenly sensitive to respecting consumer data. The firm has never sold or given away any of its bits to third parties. And the firm admits that some of its efforts to track customers have misfired, requiring special attention to find the sometimes subtitle line between helpful and "too helpful." For example, the firm's CIO has mentioned that customers found it "creepy and Big Brother-ish" when employees tried to greet them by name and talk with them about their past business history at Harrah's, so the firm backed off (Wagner, 2008).

Innovation

Harrah's is constantly tinkering with new innovations that help it gather more data and help push service quality and marketing program success. When the introduction of gaming in Pennsylvania threatened to divert lucrative New York City gamblers from Harrah's Atlantic City properties, the firm launched an interactive billboard in New York's Times Square, allowing passers-by to operate a virtual slot machine using text messages from their cell phones. Players dialing into the video billboard not only control the display, they receive text message offers promoting Harrah's sites in Atlantic City[2].

At Harrah's, tech experiments abound. RFID-enabled poker chips and under-table RFID readers allow pit bosses to track and rate game play far better than they could before. The firm is experimenting with using RFID- embedded bracelets for poolside purchases and Total Rewards tracking for when customers aren't carrying their wallets. The firm has also incorporated drink ordering into gaming machines—why make customers get up to quench their thirst? A break in gambling is a halt in revenue.

The firm was also one of the first to sign on to use Microsoft's Surface technology—a sort of touch-screen and sensor-equipped tabletop. Customers at these tables can play bowling and group pinball games and even pay for drinks using cards that the tables will automatically identify. Tech even helps Harrah's fight card counters and crooks, with facial recognition software scanning casino patrons to spot the bad guys (Lohr, 2007).

Strategy

A walk around Vegas during Harrah's ascendency would find rivals with bigger, fancier casinos. Says Loveman, "We had to compete with the kind of place that God would build if he had the money....The only thing we had was data" (Swabey, 2007).

That data advantage creates intelligence for a high-quality and highly personal customer experience. Data gives the firm a service differentiation edge. The loyalty program also represents a switching cost. And these assets combined to be leveraged across a firm that has gained so much scale that it's now the largest player in its industry, gaining the ability to cross-sell customers on a variety of properties—Vegas vacations, riverboat gambling, locally focused reservation properties, and more.

Harrah's chief marketing officer, David Norton, points out that when Total Rewards started, Harrah's was earning about thirty-six cents on every dollar customers spent gaming—the rest went to competitors. A climb to forty cents would be considered monstrous. By 2005 that number had climbed to forty-five cents, making Harrah's the biggest monster in the industry (Lundquist, 2005). Some of the firm's technology investments have paid back tenfold in just two years—bringing in hundreds of millions of dollars (Swabey, 2007).

The firm's technology has been pretty tough for others to match, too. Harrah's holds several patents covering key business methods and technologies used in its systems. After being acquired by Harrah's, employees of Caesars lamented that they had, for years, unsuccessfully attempted to replicate Harrah's systems without violating the firm's intellectual property (Hoover, 2007).

Challenges

Harrah's efforts to gather data, extract information, and turn this into real profits is unparalleled, but it's not a cure- all. Broader events can often derail even the best strategy. Gaming is a discretionary spending item, and when the economy tanks, gambling is one of the first things consumers will cut. Harrah's has not been immune to the world financial crisis and experienced a loss in 2008.

Also note that if you look up Harrah's stock symbol you won't find it. The firm was **taken private** in January 2008, when buyout firms Apollo Management and TPG Capital paid $30.7 billion for all of the firm's shares. At that time Loveman signed a five-year deal to remain on as CEO, and he's spoken positively about the benefits of being private—primarily that with the distraction of quarterly earnings off the table, he's been able to focus on the long-term viability and health of the business (Knightly, 2009).

But the firm also holds $24 billion in debt from expansion projects and the buyout, all at a time when economic conditions have not been favorable to leveraged firms (Lattman, 2009). A brilliantly successful firm that developed best-in-class customer relationship management in now in a position many consider risky due to debt assumed as part of an overly optimistic buyout occurring at precisely the time when the economy went into a terrible funk. Harrah's awesome risk-reducing, profit-pushing analytics failed to offer any insight on the wisdom (or risk) in the debt and private equity deals.

REFERENCES

Davenport T., and J. Harris, Competing on Analytics: The New Science of Winning (Boston: Harvard Business School Press, 2007).

Mearian, L., "Digital Universe and Its Impact Bigger Than We Thought," Computerworld, March 18, 2008. Soat, J., "P&G's CIO Puts IT at Users' Service," InformationWeek, December 15, 2007.

Harvey, M., "Probe into How Google Mix-Up Caused $1 Billion Run on United," Times Online, September 12, 2008, http://technology.timesonline.co.uk/tol/news/tech_and_web/article4742147.ece.

Appleton, R., "Less Independent Doctors Could Mean More Medical Mistakes," InjuryBoard.com, June 14, 2009. Braddock, R., "Lessons of Internet Marketing from FreshDirect," Wall Street Journal, May 11, 2009.

Capell, K., "Tesco Hits Record Profit, but Lags in U.S.," BusinessWeek, April 21, 2009. Capell, K., "Tesco: 'Wal-Mart's Worst Nightmare,'" BusinessWeek, December 29, 2008.

Davenport T., and J. Harris, "Competing with Multichannel Marketing Analytics," Advertising Age, April 2, 2007. Gefter A., and T. Simonite, "What the Data Miners Are Digging Up about You," CNET, December 1, 2008.

Greenberg, A., "Companies That Profit from Your Data," Forbes, May 14, 2008. Halamka, J., "IT Spending: When Less Is More," BusinessWeek, March 2, 2009.

King, R., "Intelligence Software for Business," BusinessWeek podcast, February 27, 2009. Lowenstein, M., "Tesco: A Retail Customer Divisibility Champion," CustomerThink, October 20, 2002. McCullagh, D., "Q&A: Electronic Health Records and You," CNET/CBSNews.com, May 19, 2009.

Milligan, S., "Business Warms to Democratic Leaders," Boston Globe, May 28, 2009.

Mills, E., "Report: Social Security Numbers Can Be Predicted," CNET, July 6, 2009, http://news.cnet.com/ 8301-1009_3-10280614-83.html.

Mithchell, R., "Why You Should Be Worried about Your Privacy on the Web," Computerworld, May 11, 2009.

Obama, B., President's Speech to the American Medical Association, Chicago, IL, June 15, 2009, http://www.whitehouse.gov/the_press_office/Remarks-by-the-President-to-the-Annual-Conference-of-the-American-Medical-Association.

Swarns, R., "Senator? Terrorist? A Watch List Stops Kennedy at Airport," New York Times, August 20, 2004.

Zhang, J., "Recession Likely to Boost Government Outlays on Health Care," Wall Street Journal, February 24, 2009.

King, R., "Business Intelligence Software's Time Is Now," BusinessWeek, March 2, 2009.

Conry-Murray, A., "The Pain of E-discovery," InformationWeek, June 1, 2009.

Havenstein, H., "HP Nabs Wal-Mart as Data Warehousing Customer," Computerworld, August 1, 2007. King, R., "Intelligence Software for Business," BusinessWeek podcast, February 27, 2009.

Rigby D. and D. Ledingham, "CRM Done Right," Harvard Business Review, November 2004.

Coy, P., "He Who Mines Data May Strike Fool's Gold," BusinessWeek, June 16, 1997. Hansell, S., "How Wall Street Lied to Its Computers," New York Times, September 18, 2008. Helm, B., "Getting Inside the Customer's Mind," BusinessWeek, September 11, 2008.

Lohr, S., "Reaping Results: Data-Mining Goes Mainstream," New York Times, May 20, 2007. McKay, L., "Decisions, Decisions," CRM Magazine, May 1, 2009.

Mulcahy, R., "ABC: An Introduction to Business Intelligence," CIO, March 6, 2007. Wahba, P., "Buffeted 'Quants' Are Still in Demand," Reuters, December 22, 2008.

Evans-Correia, K., "Dillman Replaced as Wal-Mart CIO," SearchCIO, April 6, 2006. Fishman, C., "The Wal-Mart You Don't Know," Fast Company, December 19, 2007.

Friscia, T., K. O'Marah, D. Hofman, and J. Souza, "The AMR Research Supply Chain Top 25 for 2009," AMR Research, May 28, 2009, http://www.amrresearch.com/Content/View.aspx?compURI=tcm:7-43469.

Hays, C., "What Wal-Mart Knows about Customer Habits," New York Times, November 14, 2004. Joseph, D., "Supermarket Strategies: What's New at the Grocer," BusinessWeek, June 8, 2009.

McCoy, M., "Wal-Mart's Data Center Remains Mystery," Joplin Globe, May 28, 2006.

Davenport T. and J. Harris, Competing on Analytics: The New Science of Winning (Boston: Harvard Business School Press, 2007).

Haugsted, L., "Better Take Care of Big Spenders; Harrah's Chief Offers Advice to Cablers," Multichannel News, July 30, 2007.

Hoover, N., "Chief of the Year: Harrah's CIO Tim Stanley," Information Week Research and Reports, 2007. Knightly, A., "Harrah's Boss Speaks," Las Vegas Review-Journal, June 14, 2009.

Lohr, S., "Reaping Results: Data-Mining Goes Mainstream," New York Times, May 20, 2007.

Loveman, G., Speech and Comments, Chief Executive Club of Boston College, January 2005; emphasis added. Lundquist, E., "Harrah's Bets Big on IT," eWeek, July 20, 2005.

Magnini, V., E. Honeycutt, and S. Hodge, "Data Mining for Hotel Firms: Use and Limitations," Cornell Hotel and Restaurant Administration Quarterly, April 2003, http://www.entrepreneur.com/tradejournals/article/ 101938457.html.

Wagner, M., "Harrah's Places Its Bet On IT," InformationWeek, September 16, 2008.

Babcock, C., "Data, Data, Everywhere", InformationWeek, January 9, 2006.

Swabey, P., "Nothing Left to Chance," Information Age, January 18, 2007.

Baker, S., "Math Will Rock Your World," BusinessWeek, January 23, 2006, http://www.businessweek.com/ magazine/content/06_04/b3968001.htm.htm.

Lattman, P., "A Buyout-Shop Breather," Wall Street Journal, May 30, 2009.

Nickell, J., "Welcome to Harrah's," Business 2.0, April 2002.

THE INTERNET AND TELECOMMUNICATIONS: A MANAGER'S GUIDE

12.1 INTRODUCTION: AN OVERVIEW

There's all sorts of hidden magic happening whenever you connect to the Internet. But what really makes it possible for you to reach servers halfway around the world in just a fraction of a second? Knowing this is not only flat-out fascinating stuff; it's also critically important for today's manager to have at least a working knowledge of how the Internet functions.

That's because the Internet is a platform of possibilities and a business enabler. Understanding how the Internet and networking works can help you brainstorm new products and services and understand roadblocks that might limit turning your ideas into reality. Marketing professionals who know how the Internet reaches consumers have a better understanding of how technologies can be used to find and target customers. Finance firms that rely on trading speed to move billions in the blink of an eye need to master Internet infrastructure to avoid being swept aside by more nimble market movers. And knowing how the Internet works helps all managers understand where their firms are vulnerable. In most industries today, if your network goes down then you might as well shut your doors and go home; it's nearly impossible to get anything done if you can't get online. Managers who know the Net are prepared to take the appropriate steps to secure their firms and keep their organization constantly connected.

12.2 INTERNET 101: UNDERSTANDING THE OPERATION OF THE INTERNET

The Internet is a network of networks—millions of them, actually. If the network at your university, your employer, or in your home has Internet access, it connects to an **Internet service provider (ISP)**. Many (but not all) ISPs are big telecommunications companies like Verizon, Comcast, and AT&T. These providers connect to one another, exchanging traffic, and ensuring your messages can get to any other computer that's online and willing to communicate with you.

The Internet has no center and no one owns it. That's a good thing. The Internet was designed to be redundant and fault-tolerant—meaning that if one network, connecting wire, or server stops working, everything else should keep on running. Rising from military research and work at educational institutions dating as far back as the 1960s, the Internet really took off in the 1990s, when graphical Web browsing was invented, and much of the Internet's operating infrastructure was transitioned to be supported by private firms rather than government grants.

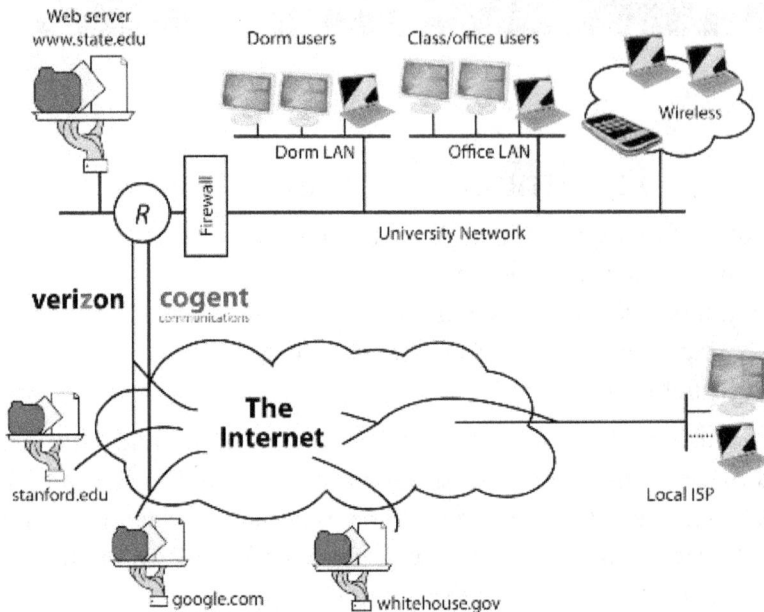

Figure 12.1 The Internet is a network of networks, and these networks are connected together. In the diagram above, the "state.edu" campus network is connected to other networks of the Internet via two ISPs: Cogent and Verizon.

Enough history—let's see how it all works! If you want to communicate with another computer on the Internet then your computer needs to know the answer to three questions: What are you looking for? Where is it? And how do we get there? The computers and software that make up Internet infrastructure can help provide the answers. Let's look at how it all comes together.

The URL: "What Are You Looking For?"

When you type an address into a Web browser (sometimes called a **URL** for *uniform resource locator*), you're telling your browser what you're looking for. Figure 12.2 "Anatomy of a Web Address" describes how to read a typical URL.

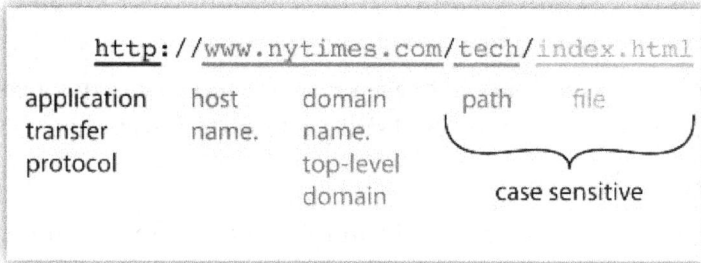

Figure 12.2 Anatomy of a Web Address

The http:// you see at the start of most Web addresses stands for **hypertext transfer protocol**. A **protocol** is a set of rules for communication—sort of like grammar and vocabulary in a language like English. The http protocol defines how Web browser and Web servers communicate and is designed to be independent from the computer's hardware and operating system. It doesn't matter if messages come from a PC, a Mac, a huge mainframe, or a pocket-sized smartphone; if a device speaks to another using a common protocol, then it will be heard and understood.

The Internet supports lots of different applications, and many of these applications use their own application transfer protocol to communicate with each other. The server that holds your e-mail uses something called *SMTP*, or simple mail transfer protocol, to exchange mail with other e-mail servers throughout the world. **FTP**, or file transfer protocol, is used for—you guessed it—file transfer. FTP is how most Web developers upload the Web pages, graphics, and other files for their Web sites. Even the Web uses different protocols. When you surf to an online bank or when you're ready to enter your payment information at the Web site of an Internet retailer, the http at the beginning of your URL will probably change to https (the "s" is for secure). That means that communications between your browser and server will be encrypted for safe transmission. The beauty of the Internet infrastructure is that any savvy entrepreneur can create a new application that rides on top of the Internet.

Hosts and Domain Names

The next part of the URL in our diagram holds the host and domain name. Think of the domain name as the name of the network you're trying to connect to, and think of the host as the computer you're looking for on that network.

Many domains have lots of different hosts. For example, Yahoo!'s main Web site is served from the host named "www" (at the address http://www.yahoo.com), but Yahoo! also runs other hosts including those named "finance" (finance.yahoo.com), "sports" (sports.yahoo.com), and "games" (games.yahoo.com).

Most Web sites are configured to load a default host, so you can often eliminate the host name if you want to go to the most popular host on a site (the default host is almost always named "www"). Another tip: most browsers will automatically add the "http://" for you, too.

Host and domain names are not case sensitive, so you can use a combination of upper and lower case letters and you'll still get to your destination.

Path Name and File Name

Look to the right of the top-level domain and you might see a slash followed by either a path name, a file name, or both. If a Web address has a path and file name, the path maps to a folder location where the file is stored on the server; the file is the name of the file you're looking for.

Most Web pages end in ".html," indicating they are in **hypertext markup language**. While http helps browsers and servers communicate, html is the language used to create and format (render) Web pages. A file, however, doesn't need to be .html; Web servers can deliver just about any type of file: Acrobat documents (.pdf), PowerPoint documents (.ppt or .pptx), Word docs (.doc or .docx), JPEG graphic images (.jpg), and—as we'll see in Chapter 13 "Information Security: Barbarians at the Gateway (and Just About Everywhere Else)"—even malware programs that attack your PC. At some Web addresses, the file displays content for every visitor, and at others (like amazon.com), a file will contain programs that run on the Web server to generate custom content just for you.

You don't always type a path or file name as part of a Web address, but there's always a file lurking behind the scenes. A Web address without a file name will load content from a default page. For example, when you visit "google.com," Google automatically pulls up a page called "index.html," a file that contains the Web page that displays the Google logo, the text entry field, the "Google Search" button, and so on. You might not see it, but it's there.

Butterfingers, beware! Path and file names are case sensitive—amazon.com/books is considered to be different from amazon.com/BOOKS. Mistype your capital letters after the domain name and you might get a 404 error (the very unfriendly Web server error code that means the document was not found).

IP Addresses and the Domain Name System: "Where Is It? And How Do We Get There?"

The IP Address

If you want to communicate, then you need to have a way for people to find and reach you. Houses and businesses have street addresses, and telephones have phone numbers. Every device connected to the Internet has an identifying address, too—it's called an *IP (Internet protocol) address*.

A device gets its **IP address** from whichever organization is currently connecting it to the Internet. Connect using a laptop at your university and your school will assign the laptop's IP address. Connect at a hotel, and the hotel's Internet service provider lends your laptop an IP address. Laptops and other end-user machines might get a different IP address each time they connect, but the IP addresses of servers rarely change. It's OK if you use different IP addresses during different online sessions because services like e-mail and Facebook identify you by your username and password. The IP address simply tells the computers that you're communicating with where they can find you right now. IP addresses can also be used to identify a user's physical location, to tailor search results, and to customize advertising. See Chapter 14 "Google: Search, Online Advertising, and Beyond" to learn more.

IP addresses are usually displayed as a string of four numbers between 0 and 255, separated by three periods. Want to know which IP address your smartphone or computer is using? Visit a Web site like ip-adress.com (one "d"), whatismyipaddress. com, or ipchicken.com.

The Domain Name Service (DNS): The Internet's Phonebook

You can actually type an IP address of a Web site into a Web browser and that page will show up. But that doesn't help users much because four sets of numbers are really hard to remember.

This is where the **domain name service (DNS)** comes in. The domain name service is a distributed database that looks up the host and domain names that you enter and returns the actual IP address for the computer that you want to communicate with. It's like a big, hierarchical set of phone books capable of finding Web servers, e-mail servers, and more. These "phone books" are called *nameservers*—and when they work together to create the DNS, they can get you anywhere you need to go online.

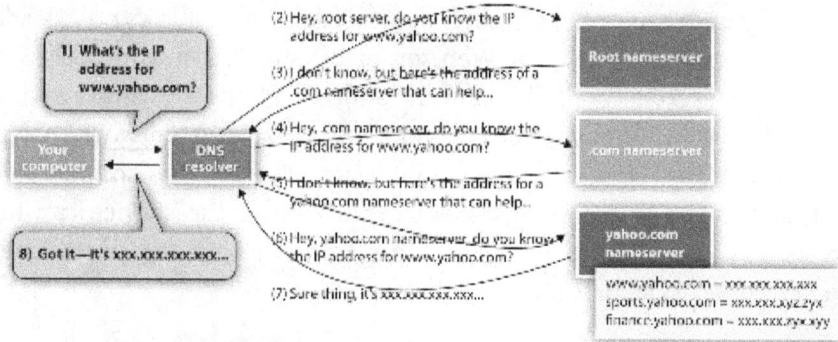

Figure 12.3

When your computer needs to find the IP address for a host or domain name, it sends a message to a DNS resolver, which looks up the IP address starting at the root nameserver. Once the lookup has taken place, that IP address can be saved in a holding space called a cache, to speed future lookups.

To get a sense of how the DNS works, let's imagine that you type www.yahoo. com into a Web browser. Your computer doesn't know where to find that address, but when your computer connected to the network, it learned where to find a service on the network called a DNS resolver. The DNS resolver can look up host/domain name combinations to find the matching IP address using the "phone book" that is the DNS. The resolver doesn't know everything, but it does know where to start a lookup that will eventually give you the address you're looking for. If this is the first time anyone on that network has tried to find "www.yahoo.com," the resolver will contact one of thirteen identical root nameservers. The root acts as a lookup starting place. It doesn't have one big list, but it can point you to a nameserver for the next level, which would be one of the ".com" nameservers in our example. The ".com" nameserver can then find one of the yahoo.com nameservers. The yahoo. com nameserver can respond to the resolver with the IP address for www.yahoo. com, and the resolver passes that information back to your computer. Once your computer knows Yahoo!'s IP address, it's then ready to communicate directly with www.yahoo.com. The yahoo.com nameserver includes IP addresses for all Yahoo!'s public sites: www.yahoo.com, games.yahoo.com, sports.yahoo.com, finance.yahoo. com, and so on.

The system also remembers what it's done so the next time you need the IP address of a host you've already looked up, your computer can pull this out of a storage space called a **cache**, avoiding all those nameserver visits. Caches are periodically cleared and refreshed to ensure that data referenced via the DNS stays accurate.

Distributing IP address lookups this way makes sense. It avoids having one huge, hard-to-maintain, and ever- changing list. Firms add and remove hosts on their own networks just by updating entries in their nameserver. And it allows host IP addresses to change easily, too. Moving your Web server off-site to a hosting provider? Just update your nameserver with the new IP address at the hosting provider, and the world will invisibly find that new IP address on the new network by using the same old, familiar host/domain name combination. The DNS is also fault-tolerant— meaning that if one nameserver goes down, the rest of the service can function. There are exact copies at each level, and the system is smart enough to move on to another nameserver if its first choice isn't responding.

13.3 GETTING WHERE YOU WANT TO GO

TCP/IP: The Internet's Secret Sauce

OK, we know how to read a Web address, we know that every device connected to the Net needs an IP address, and we know that the DNS can look at a Web address and find the IP address of the machine that you want to communicate with. But how does a Web page, an e-mail, or an iTunes download actually get from a remote computer to your desktop?

For our next part of the Internet journey, we'll learn about two additional protocols: TCP and IP. These protocols are often written as TCP/IP and pronounced by reading all five letters in a row, "T-C-P-I-P" (sometimes they're also referred to as the *Internet protocol suite*). TCP and IP are built into any device that a user would use to connect to the Internet—from handhelds to desktops to supercomputers—and together TCP/IP make Internet working happen.

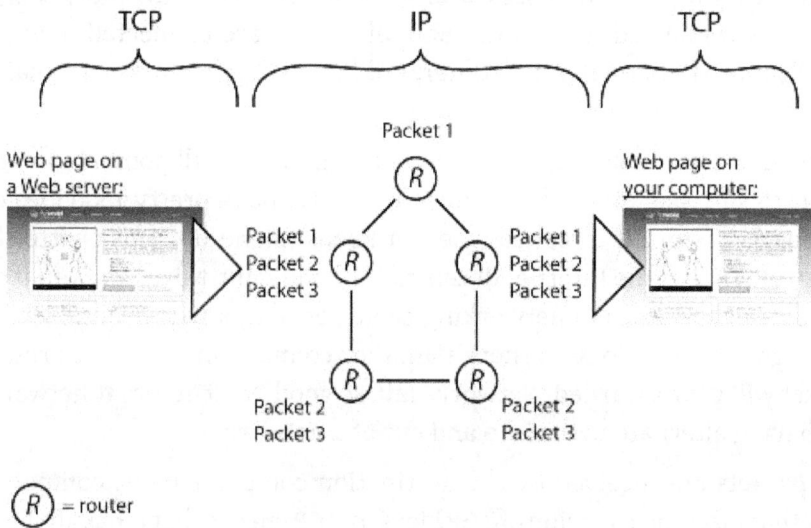

Figure 12.4 TCP/IP in Action

In this example, a server on the left sends a Web page to the user on the right. The application (the Web server) passes the contents of the page to TCP (which is built into the server's operating system). TCP slices the Web page into packets. Then IP takes over, forwarding packets from router to router across the Internet until it arrives at the user's PC. Packets sometimes take different routes, and occasionally arrive out of order. TCP running on the receiving system on the right checks that all packets have arrived, requests that damaged or lost packets be resent, puts them in the right order, and sends a perfect, exact copy of the Web page to your browser.

TCP and IP operate below http and the other application transfer protocols mentioned earlier. **TCP (transmission control protocol)** works its magic at the start and endpoint of the trip—on both your computer and on the destination computer you're communicating with. Let's say a Web server wants to send you a large Web page. The Web server application hands the Web page it wants to send to its own version of TCP. TCP then slices up the Web page into smaller chunks of data called **packets (or datagrams)**. The packets are like little envelopes containing part of the entire transmission—they're labeled with a destination address (where it's going) and a source address (where it came from). Now we'll leave TCP for a second, because TCP on the Web server then hands those packets off to the second half of our dynamic duo, IP.

It's the job of **IP (Internet protocol)** to route the packets to their final destination, and those packets might have to travel over several networks to get to where they're going. The relay work is done via special computers called **routers**, and these routers speak to each other and to other computers using IP (since routers are connected to the Internet, they have IP addresses, too. Some are even named). Every computer on the Internet is connected to a router, and all routers are connected to at least one (and usually more than one) other router, linking up the networks that make up the Internet.

Routers don't have perfect, end-to-end information on all points in the Internet, but they do talk to each other all the time, so a router has a pretty good idea of where to send a packet to get it closer to where it needs to end up. This chatter between the routers also keeps the Internet decentralized and fault-tolerant. Even if one path out of a router goes down (a networking cable gets cut, a router breaks, the power to a router goes out), as long as there's another connection out of that router, then your packet will get forwarded. Networks fail, so good, fault-tolerant network design involves having alternate paths into and out of a network.

Once packets are received by the destination computer (your computer in our example), that machine's version of TCP kicks in. TCP checks that it has all the packets, makes sure that no packets were damaged or corrupted, requests replacement packets (if needed), and then puts the packets in the correct order, passing a perfect copy of your transmission to the program you're communicating with (an e-mail server, Web server, etc.).

This progression—application at the source to TCP at the source (slice up the data being sent), to IP (for forwarding among routers), to TCP at the destination (put the transmission back together and make sure it's perfect), to application at the destination—takes place in both directions, starting at the server for messages coming to you, and starting on your computer when you're sending messages to another computer.

What Connects the Routers and Computers?

Routers are connected together, either via cables or wirelessly. A cable connecting a computer in a home or office is probably copper (likely what's usually called an Ethernet cable), with transmissions sent through the copper via electricity. Long-haul cables, those that carry lots of data over long distances, are usually fiber- optic lines—glass lined cables that transmit light (light is faster and travels farther distances than electricity, but fiber-optic networking equipment is more expensive than the copper-electricity kind). Wireless transmission can happen via Wi-Fi (for shorter distances), or cell phone tower or satellite over longer distances. But the beauty of the Internet protocol suite (TCP/IP) is that it doesn't matter what the actual transmission media are. As long as your routing equipment can connect any two networks, and as long as that equipment "speaks" IP, then you can be part of the Internet.

In reality, your messages likely transfer via lots of different transmission media to get to their final destination. If you use a laptop connected via Wi-Fi, then that wireless connection finds a base station, usually within about three hundred feet. That base station is probably connected to a local area network (LAN) via a copper cable. And your firm or college may connect to fast, long-haul portions of the Internet via fiber-optic cables provided by that firm's Internet service provider (ISP).

Most big organizations have multiple ISPs for redundancy, providing multiple paths in and out of a network. This is so that if a network connection provided by one firm goes down, say an errant backhoe cuts a cable, other connections can route around the problem (see Figure 12.1).

In the United States (and in most deregulated telecommunications markets), Internet service providers come in all sizes, from smaller regional players to sprawling international firms. When different ISPs connect their networking equipment together to share traffic, it's called **peering**. Peering usually takes place at neutral sites called *Internet exchange points* (IXPs), although some firms also have private peering points. Carriers usually don't charge one another for peering. Instead, "the money is made" in the ISP business by charging the end-points in a network—the customer organizations and end users that an ISP connects to the Internet. Competition among carriers helps keep prices down, quality high, and innovation moving forward.

11.4 LAST MILE: GREATER ACCESS AND SPEED

The Internet backbone is made of fiber-optic lines that carry data traffic over long distances. Those lines are pretty speedy. In fact, several backbone providers, including AT&T and Verizon, are rolling out infrastructure with 100 Gbps transmission speeds (that's enough to transmit a two-hour high-definition [HD] movie in about eight seconds)[1] (Spangler, 2010). But when considering overall network speed, remember Amdahl's Law: a system's speed is determined by its slowest component (Gilder, 2000). More often than not, the bottleneck isn't the backbone but the so-called last mile, or the connections that customers use to get online.

High-speed last-mile technologies are often referred to as *broadband Internet access* (or just **broadband**). What qualifies as broadband varies. In 2009, the Federal Communications Commission (FCC) redefined broadband as having a minimum speed of 768 Kbps (roughly fourteen times the speed of those old 56 Kbps modems). Other agencies worldwide may have different definitions. But one thing is clear: a new generation of bandwidth- demanding services requires more capacity. As we increasingly consume Internet services like HD streaming, real-time gaming, video conferencing, and music downloads, we are in fact becoming a bunch of voracious, bit- craving gluttons.

With the pivotal role the United States has played in the creation of the Internet, and in pioneering software, hardware, and telecommunications industries, you might expect the United States to lead the world in last-mile broadband access. Not even close. A recent study ranked the United States twenty-sixth in download speeds, (Lawson, 2010) while others have ranked the United States far behind in speed, availability, and price (Hansell, 2009).

Sounds grim, but help is on the way. A range of technologies and firms are upgrading infrastructure and developing new systems that will increase capacity not just in the United States but also worldwide. Here's an overview of some of the major technologies that can be used to speed the Internet's last mile.

Cable Broadband

Roughly 90 percent of U.S. homes are serviced by a cable provider, each capable of using a thick copper wire to offer broadband access. That wire (called a **coaxial cable** or *coax*) has shielding that reduces electrical interference, allowing cable signals to travel longer distances without degrading and with less chance of interference than conventional telephone equipment.

One potential weakness of cable technology lies in the fact that most residential providers use a system that requires customers to share bandwidth with neighbors. If the guy next door is a BitTorrent-using bandwidth hog, your traffic could suffer (Thompson, 2010).

Cable is fast and it's getting faster. Many cable firms are rolling out a new technology called DOCSIS 3.0 that offers speeds up to and exceeding 50 Mbps (previous high-end speeds were about 16 Mbps and often much less than that). Cable firms are also creating so-called *fiber-copper hybrids* that run higher-speed fiber-optic lines into neighborhoods, then use lower-cost, but still relatively high-speed, copper infrastructure over short distances to homes (Hansell, 2009). Those are fast networks, but they are also very expensive to build, since cable firms are laying entirely new lines into neighborhoods instead of leveraging the infrastructure that they've already got in place.

DSL: Phone Company Copper

Digital subscriber line (DSL) technology uses the copper wire the phone company has already run into most homes. Even as customers worldwide are dropping their landline phone numbers, the wires used to provide this infrastructure can still be used for broadband.

DSL speeds vary depending on the technology deployed. Worldwide speeds may range from 7 Mbps to as much as 100 Mbps (albeit over very short distances) (Hansell, 2009). The Achilles heel of the technology lies in the fact that DSL uses standard copper telephone wiring. These lines lack the shielding used by cable, so signals begin to degrade the further you are from the connecting equipment in telephone company offices. Speeds drop off significantly at less than two miles from a central office or DSL hub. If you go four miles out, the technology becomes unusable. Some DSL providers are also using a hybrid fiber-copper system, but as with cable's copper hybrids, this is expensive to build.

The superspeedy DSL implementations that are popular in Europe and Asia work because foreign cities are densely populated and so many high-value customers can be accessed over short distances. In South Korea, for example, half the population lives in apartments, and most of those customers live in and around Seoul. This density also impacts costs—since so many people live in apartments, foreign carriers run fewer lines to reach customers, digging up less ground or stringing wires across fewer telephone poles. Their U.S. counterparts by contrast need to reach a customer base sprawled across the suburbs, so U.S. firms have much higher infrastructure costs (Hansell, 2009).

There's another company with copper, electricity-carrying cables coming into your home—the electrical utility. BPL, or broadband over power line, technology has been available for years. However, there are few deployments because it is considered to be pricier and less practical than alternatives (King, 2009).

Fiber: A Glass Pipe Filled with Light to Your Doorstep

Fiber to the home (FTTH) is the fastest last-mile technology around. It also works over long distances. Verizon's FiOS technology boasts 50 Mbps download speeds but has tested network upgrades that increase speeds by over six times that (Higginbotham, 2009). The problem with fiber is that unlike cable or DSL copper, fiber to the home networks weren't already in place. That means firms had to build their own fiber networks from scratch.

The cost of this build out can be enormous. Verizon, for example, has spent over $23 billion on its FTTH infrastructure. However, most experts think the upgrade was critical. Verizon has copper into millions of homes, but U.S. DSL is uncompetitive. Verizon's residential landline business was dying as users switch to mobile phone numbers, and while mobile is growing, Verizon Wireless is a joint venture with the United Kingdom's Vodaphone, not a wholly owned firm. This means it shares wireless unit profits with its partner. With FiOS, Verizon now offers pay television, competing with cable's core product. It also offers some of the fastest home broadband services anywhere, and it gets to keep everything it earns.

In 2010, Google also announced plans to bring fiber to the home. Google deems its effort an experiment—it's more interested in learning how developers and users take advantage of ultrahigh-speed fiber to the home (e.g., what kinds of apps are created and used, how usage and time spent online change), rather than becoming a nationwide ISP itself. Google says it will investigate ways to build and operate networks less expensively and plans to share findings with others. The Google network will be "open," allowing other service providers to use Google's infrastructure to resell services to consumers. The firm has pledged to bring speeds of 1 Gbps at competitive prices to at least 50,000 and potentially as many as 500,000 homes. Over 1,100 U.S. communities applied to be part of the Google experimental fiber network (Ingersoll & Kelly, 2010; Rao, 2010).

Wireless

Mobile wireless service from cell phone access providers is delivered via cell towers. While these providers don't need to build a residential wired infrastructure, they still need to secure space for cell towers, build the towers, connect the towers to a backbone network, and license the **wireless spectrum** (or airwave frequency space) for transmission.

We need more bandwidth for mobile devices, too. AT&T now finds that the top 3 percent of its mobile network users gulp up 40 percent of the network's capacity (thanks, iPhone users), and network strain will only increase as more people adopt smartphones. These users are streaming Major League Baseball games, exploring the planet with Google Earth, watching YouTube and Netflix, streaming music through Pandora, and more. Get a bunch of iPhone users in a crowded space, like in a college football stadium on game day, and the result is a network- choking data traffic jam. AT&T estimates that it's not uncommon for 80 percent of game-day iPhone users to take out their phones and surf the Web for stats, snap and upload photos, and more. But cell towers often can't handle the load (Farzad, 2010). If you've ever lost coverage in a crowd, you've witnessed mobile network congestion firsthand. Trying to have enough capacity to avoid congestion traffic jams will cost some serious coin. In the midst of customer complaints, AT&T committed to spending $18 billion on network upgrades to address its wireless capacity problem (Edwards & Kharif, 2010).

Table 12.1 Average Demand Usage by Function

Usage	Demand
Voice Calls	4 MB/hr.
iPhone Browsing	40–60 MB/hr.
Net Radio	60 MB/hr.
YouTube	200–400 MB/hr.
Conventional mobile phones use an estimated 100 MB/month, iPhones 560 MB/month, and iPads almost 1 GB/ month.	

Source: R. Farzad, "The Truth about Bandwidth," BusinessWeek, February 3, 2010.

We're in the midst of transitioning from third generation (*3G*) to fourth generation (*4G*) wireless networks. 3G systems offer access speeds usually less than 2 Mbps (often a lot less) (German, 2010). While variants of 3G wireless might employ an alphabet soup of technologies—EV-DO (evolution data optimized), UMTS (universal mobile telecommunications systems), and HSDPA (high-speed downlink packet link access) among them—3G standards can be narrowed down to two camps: those based on the dominant worldwide standard called *GSM* (global system for mobile communications) and the runner-up standards based on *CDMA* (code division multiplex access). Most of Europe and a good chunk of the rest of the world use GSM. In the United States, AT&T and T-Mobile use GSM-based 3G. Verizon Wireless and Sprint use the CDMA 3G standard. Typically, handsets designed for one network can't be used on networks supporting the other standard. CDMA has an additional limitation in not being able to use voice and data at the same time.

But 3G is being replaced by high-bandwidth 4G (fourth-generation) mobile networks. 4G technologies also fall into two standards camps: LTE (Long Term Evolution) and WiMAX (Worldwide Interoperability for Microwave Access).

LTE looks like the global winner. In the United States, every major wireless firm, except for Sprint, is betting on LTE victory. Bandwidth for the service rivals what we'd consider fast cable a few years back. Average speeds range from 5 to 12 Mbps for downloads and 2 to 5 Mbps for upload, although Verizon tests in Boston and Seattle showed download speeds as high as 50 Mbps and upload speeds reaching 25 Mbps (German, 2010).

Competing with LTE is WiMAX; don't confuse it with Wi-Fi. As with other 3G and 4G technologies, WiMAX needs cell towers and operators need to have licensed spectrum from their respective governments (often paying multibillion-dollar fees to do so). Average download and upload speeds should start out at 3–6 Mbps and 1 Mbps, respectively, although this may go much higher (Lee, 2010).

WiMAX looks like a particularly attractive option for cable firms, offering them an opportunity to get into the mobile phone business and offer a "quadruple play" of services: pay television, broadband Internet, home phone, and mobile. Comcast and Time Warner have both partnered with Clearwire (a firm majority-owned by Sprint), to gain access to WiMAX-based 4G mobile.

4G could also rewrite the landscape for home broadband competition. If speeds increase, it may be possible for PCs, laptops, and set-top boxes (STB) to connect to the Internet wirelessly via 4G, cutting into DSL, cable, and fiber markets.

Satellite Wireless

Wireless systems provided by earth-bound base stations like cell phone towers are referred to as *terrestrial wireless*, but it is possible to provide telecommunications services via satellite. Early services struggled due to a number of problems. For example, the first residential satellite services were only used for downloads, which still needed a modem or some other connection to send any messages from the computer to the Internet. Many early systems also required large antennas and were quite expensive. Finally, some services were based on satellites in geosynchronous earth orbit (GEO). GEO satellites circle the earth in a fixed, or stationary, orbit above a given spot on the globe, but to do so they must be positioned at a distance that is roughly equivalent to the planet's circumference. That means signals travel the equivalent of an around-the-world trip to reach the satellite and then the same distance to get to the user. The "last mile" became the last 44,000 miles at best. And if you used a service that also provided satellite upload as well as download, double that to about 88,000 miles. All that distance means higher latency (more delay) (Ou, 2008).

A firm named O3b Networks thinks it might have solved the challenges that plagued early pioneers. O3b has an impressive list of big-name backers that include HSBC bank, cable magnate John Malone, European aerospace firm SES, and Google.

The name O3b stands for the "Other 3 Billion," of the world's population who lack broadband Internet access, and the firm hopes to provide "fiber-quality" wireless service to more than 150 countries, specifically targeting underserved portions of the developing world. These "middle earth orbit" satellites will circle closer to the earth to reduce latency (only about 5,000 miles up, less than one-fourth the distance of GEO systems). To maintain the lower orbit, O3b's satellites orbit faster than the planet spins, but with plans to launch as many as twenty satellites, the system will constantly blanket regions served. If one satellite circles to the other side of the globe, another one will circle around to take its place, ensuring there's always an O3b "bird" overhead.

Only about 3 percent of the sub-Saharan African population uses the Internet, compared to about 70 percent in the United States. But data rates in the few places served can cost as much as one hundred times the rates of comparable systems in the industrialized world (Lamb, 2008). O3b hopes to change that equation and significantly lower access rates. O3b customers will be local telecommunication firms, not end users. The plan is for local firms to buy O3b's services wholesale and then resell it to customers alongside rivals who can do the same thing, collectively providing more consumer access, higher quality, and lower prices through competition. O3b is a big, bold, and admittedly risky plan, but if it works, its impact could be tremendous.

Wi-Fi and Other Hotspots

Many users access the Internet via **Wi-Fi** (which stands for *wireless fidelity*). Computer and mobile devices have Wi-Fi antennas built into their chipsets, but to connect to the Internet, a device needs to be within range of a *base station* or *hotspot*. The base station range is usually around three hundred feet (you might get a longer range outdoors and with special equipment; and less range indoors when signals need to pass through solid objects like walls, ceilings, and floors). Wi-Fi base stations used in the home are usually bought by end users, then connected to a cable, DSL, or fiber provider.

And now a sort of mobile phone hotspot is being used to overcome limitations in those services, as well. Mobile providers can also be susceptible to poor coverage indoors. That's because the spectrum used by most mobile phone firms doesn't travel well through solid objects. Cell coverage is also often limited in the United States because of a lack of towers, which is a result of the *NIMBY problem* (not in my backyard). People don't want an eighty-foot to four-hundred-foot unsightly tower clouding their local landscape, even if it will give their neighborhood better cell phone coverage (Dechter & Kharif, 2010). To overcome reception and availability problems, mobile telecom services firms have begun offering fentocells. These devices are usually smaller than a box of cereal and can sell for $150 or less (some are free with specific service contracts). Plug a fentocell into a high-speed Internet connection like an in-home cable or fiber service and you can get "five-bar" coverage in a roughly 5,000-square-foot footprint (Mims, 2010). That can be a great solution for someone who has an in-home, high-speed Internet connection, but wants to get phone and mobile data service indoors, too.

Net Neutrality: What's Fair?

Across the world, battle lines are being drawn regarding the topic of Net neutrality. Net neutrality is the principle that all Internet traffic should be treated equally (Honan, 2008). Sometimes access providers have wanted to offer varying (some say "discriminatory") coverage, depending on the service used and bandwidth consumed.

But where regulation stands is currently in flux. In a pivotal U.S. case, the FCC ordered Comcast to stop throttling (blocking or slowing down) subscriber access to the peer-to-peer file sharing service BitTorrent. BitTorrent users can consume a huge amount of bandwidth—the service is often used to transfer large files, both legitimate (like version of the Linux operating system) and pirated (HD movies). Then in spring 2010, a federal appeals court moved against the FCC's position, unanimously ruling that the agency did not have the legal authority to dictate terms to Comcast[4].

On one side of the debate are Internet service firms, with Google being one of the strongest Net neutrality supporters. In an advocacy paper, Google states, "Just as telephone companies are not permitted to tell consumers who they can call or what they can say, broadband carriers should not be allowed to use their market power to control activity online[5]." Many Internet firms also worry that if network providers move away from flat-rate pricing toward usage-based (or metered) schemes, this may limit innovation. Says Google's Vint Cerf (who is considered one of the "fathers of the Internet" for his work on the original Internet protocol suite) "You are less likely to try things out. No one wants a surprise bill at the end of the month" (Jesdanun, 2009). Metered billing may limit the use of everything from iTunes to Netflix; after all, if you have to pay for per-bit bandwidth consumption as well as for the download service, then it's as if you're paying twice.

The counterargument is that if firms are restricted from charging more for their investment in infrastructure and services, then they'll have little incentive to continue to make the kinds of multibillion-dollar investments that innovations like 4G and fiber networks require. Telecom industry executives have railed against Google, Microsoft, Yahoo! and others, calling them free riders who earn huge profits by piggybacking off ISP networks, all while funneling no profits back to the firms that provide the infrastructure. One Verizon vice president said, "The network builders are spending a fortune constructing and maintaining the networks that Google intends to ride on with nothing but cheap servers....It is enjoying a free lunch that should, by any rational account, be the lunch of the facilities providers" (Mohammed, 2006). AT&T's previous CEO has suggested that Google, Yahoo! and other services firms should pay for "preferred access" to the firm's customers. The CEO of Spain's Telefonica has also said the firm is considering charging Google and other Internet service firms for network use (Lunden, 2010).

ISPs also lament the relentlessly increasingly bandwidth demands placed on their networks. Back in 2007, YouTube streamed as much data in three months as the world's radio, cable, and broadcast television channels combined stream in one year (Swanson, 2007), and YouTube has only continued to grow since then. Should ISPs be required to support the strain of this kind of bandwidth hog? And what if this one application clogs network use for other traffic, such as e-mail or Web surfing?

Similarly, shouldn't firms have the right to prioritize some services to better serve customers? Some network providers argue that services like video chat and streaming audio should get priority over, say, e-mail which can afford slight delay without major impact. In that case, there's a pretty good argument that providers should be able to discriminate against services. But improving efficiency and throttling usage are two different things.

Internet service firms say they create demand for broadband business, broadband firms say Google and allies are ungrateful parasites that aren't sharing the wealth. The battle lines on the Net neutrality frontier continue to be drawn, and the eventual outcome will impact consumers, investors, and will likely influence the continued expansion and innovation of the Internet.

Summing Up

Hopefully, this chapter helped reveal the mysteries of the Internet. It's interesting to know how "the cloud" works but it can also be vital. As we've seen, the executive office in financial services firms considers mastery of the Internet infrastructure to be critically important to their competitive advantage. Media firms find the Internet both threatening and empowering. The advancement of last-mile technologies and issues of Net neutrality will expose threats and create opportunity. And a manager who knows how the Internet works will be in a better position to make decisions about how to keep the firm and its customers safe and secure, and be better prepared to brainstorm ideas for winning in a world where access is faster and cheaper, and firms, rivals, partners, and customers are more connected.

REFERENCES

Arnoldy, B., "IP Address Shortage to Limit Internet Access," USA Today, August 3, 2007. Bosker, B., "The 11 Most Expensive Domain Names Ever," The Huffington Post, March 10, 2010. Davis, J., "Secret Geek A-Team Hacks Back, Defends Worldwide Web," Wired, Nov. 24, 2008.

Godin, D., "Cache-Poisoning Attack Snares Top Brazilian Bank," The Register, April 22, 2009. Hutchinson, J., "ICANN, Verisign Place Last Puzzle Pieces in DNSSEC Saga," NetworkWorld, May 2, 2010. Konrad R. and E. Hansen, "Madonna.com Embroiled in Domain Ownership Spat," CNET, August 21, 2000. Kotadia, M., "MikeRoweSoft Settles for an Xbox," CNET, January 26, 2004.

Maney, K., "Tuvalu's Sinking, But Its Domain Is on Solid Ground," USA Today, April 27, 2004. McCullagh, D., "Ethical Treatment of PETA Domain," Wired, August 25, 2001.

Morson, D., "Apple VP Ive Loses Domain Name Bid," MacWorld, May 12, 2009.

Shankland, S., "Google Tries to Break IPv6 Logjam by Own Example," CNET, March 27, 2009.

Streitfeld, D., "Web Site Feuding Enters Constitutional Domain," The Washington Post, September 11, 2000. Ward, M., "Internet Approaches Addressing Limit," BBC News, May 11, 2010.

Berenson, A., "Arrest Over Software Illuminates Wall St. Secret," New York Times, August 23, 2009.

Daimler E. and G. Davis, "'Flash Crash' Proves Diversity Needed in Market Mechanisms," Pittsburgh Post- Gazette, May 29, 2010.

Iati, R., "The Real Story of Trading Software Espionage," Advanced Trading, July 10, 2009.

Schmerken, I.,"High-Frequency Trading Shops Play the Colocation Game," Advanced Trading, October 5, 2009. Timmons, H., "A London Hedge Fund that Opts for Engineers, Not M.B.A.'s," New York Times, August 18, 2006.

Dechter G. and O. Kharif, "How Craig McCaw Built a 4G Network on the Cheap," BusinessWeek, May 24, 2010. Edwards C. and O. Kharif, "Sprint's Bold Play on a 4G Network," BusinessWeek, March 30, 2010.

Farzad, R., "AT&T's iPhone Mess," BusinessWeek, February 3, 2010. Farzad, R., "The Truth about Bandwidth," BusinessWeek, February 3, 2010. German, K., "On Call: Welcome to 4G," CNET, March 9, 2010.

Gilder, G., Telecosm: How Infinite Bandwidth Will Revolutionize Our World (New York: Free Press, 2000). Hansell, S., "The Broadband Gap: Why Is Theirs Faster?" New York Times, March 10, 2009.

Higginbotham, S., "Verizon Tests 10 Gbps to the Home. Yeah, You'll Have to Share," GigaOM, December 17, 2009.

Honan, M., "Inside Net Neutrality," MacWorld, February 12, 2008.

Ingersoll M. and J. Kelly, "Think Big with a Gig: Our Experimental Fiber Network," The Google Blog, February 2, 2010.

Jesdanun, M., "As the Internet Turns 40, Barriers Threaten Growth," Technology Review, August 31, 2009. King, R., "Telecom Companies Scramble for Funding," BusinessWeek, August 3, 2009.

Lamb, G., "O3b Networks: A Far-Out Plan to Deliver the Web," Christian Science Monitor, September 24, 2008. Lawson, S., "US Ranks 26th in New Broadband Index," Computerworld, May 25, 2010.

Lee, N., "Sprint's 4G Plans Explained," CNET, May 19, 2010.

Lunden, I., "Broadband Content Bits: Web Drama Investment, PPL Video Store, Telefonica to Charge?"paidContent:UK, February 11, 2010.

Mims, C., "A Personal Cell Phone Tower," Technology Review, April 7, 2010.

Mohammed, A., "Verizon Executive Calls for End to Google's 'Free Lunch,'" Washington Post, February 7, 2006. Ou, G., "Why Satellite Service Is So Slow," ZDNet, February 23, 2008.

Rao, L., "The Final Tally: More Than 1100 Cities Apply for Google's Fiber Network," TechCrunch, March 27, 2010.

Spangler, T., "Cisco Clarifies 100-Gig AT&T Backbone Claim," Multichannel News, March 9, 2010. Swanson, B., "The Coming Exaflood," Wall Street Journal, January 20, 2007.

Thompson, R., "DSL Internet vs. Cable Internet," High Speed Internet Access Guide, March 23, 2010.

BARBARIANS AT THE INFORMATION SECURITY GATEWAY (AND JUST ABOUT EVERYWHERE ELSE)

13

13.1 INTRODUCTION: AN OVERVIEW

Sitting in the parking lot of a Minneapolis Marshalls, a hacker armed with a laptop and a telescope-shaped antenna infiltrated the store's network via an insecure Wi-Fi base station[1]. The attack launched what would become a billion-dollar-plus nightmare scenario for TJX, the parent of retail chains that include Marshalls, Home Goods, and T. J. Maxx. Over a period of several months, the hacker and his gang stole at least 45.7 million credit and debit card numbers and pilfered driver's licenses and other private information from an additional 450,000 customers (King, 2009).

TJX, at the time a $17.5 billion *Fortune* 500 firm, was left reeling from the incident. The attack deeply damaged the firm's reputation. It burdened customers and banking partners with the time and cost of reissuing credit cards. And TJX suffered under settlement costs, payouts from court-imposed restitution, legal fees, and more. The firm estimated that it spent more than $150 million to correct security problems and settle with consumers affected by the breach, and that was just the tip of the iceberg. Estimates peg TJX's overall losses from this incident at between $1.35 billion and $4.5 billion (Matwyshyn, 2009).

A number of factors led to and amplified the severity of the TJX breach. There was a personnel betrayal: the mastermind was an alleged FBI informant who previously helped bring down a massive credit card theft scheme but then double-crossed the Feds and used insider information to help his gang outsmart the law and carry out subsequent hacks (Goldman, 2009). There was a technology lapse: TJX made itself an easy mark by using WEP, a wireless security technology less secure than the stuff many consumers use in their homes—one known for years to be trivially compromised by the kind of "drive-by" hacking initiated by the perpetrators. And there was a procedural gaffe: retailers were in the process of rolling out a security rubric known as the Payment Card Industry Data Security Standard. Despite an industry deadline, however, TJX had requested and received an extension, delaying the rollout of mechanisms that might have discovered and plugged the hole before the hackers got in (Anthes, 2008).

The massive impact of the TJX breach should make it clear that security must be a top organizational priority. Attacks are on the rise. In 2008, more electronic records were breached than in the previous four years *combined* (King, 2009). While the examples and scenarios presented here are shocking, the good news is that the vast majority of security breaches can be prevented. Let's be clear from the start: no text can provide an approach that will guarantee that you'll be 100 percent secure. And that's not the goal of this chapter. The issues raised in this brief introduction can, however, help make you aware of vulnerabilities; improve your critical thinking regarding current and future security issues; and help you consider whether a firm has technologies, training, policies, and procedures in place to assess risks, lessen the likelihood of damage, and respond in the event of a breach. A constant vigilance regarding security needs to be part of your individual skill set and a key component in your organization's culture. An awareness of the threats and approaches discussed in this chapter should help reduce your chance of becoming a victim.

As we examine security issues, we'll first need to understand what's happening, who's doing it, and what their motivation is. We'll then examine how these breaches are happening with a focus on technologies and procedures. Finally, we'll sum up with what can be done to minimize the risks of being victimized and quell potential damage of a breach for both the individual and the organization.

Particular thanks goes to my Boston College colleague, Professor Sam Ransbotham, whose advice, guidance, and suggestions were invaluable in creating this chapter. Any errors or omissions are entirely my own.

13.2 WHY IS THIS HAPPENING? WHO IS DOING IT? AND WHAT'S THEIR MOTIVATION?

Thieves, vandals, and other bad guys have always existed, but the environment has changed. Today, nearly every organization is online, making any Internet-connected network a potential entry point for the growing worldwide community of computer criminals. Software and hardware solutions are also more complex than ever. Different vendors, each with their own potential weaknesses, provide technology components that may be compromised by misuse, misconfiguration, or mismanagement. Corporations have become data packrats, hoarding information in hopes of turning bits into bucks by licensing databases, targeting advertisements, or cross-selling products. And flatter organizations also mean that lower-level employees may be able to use technology to reach deep into corporate assets—

amplifying threats from operator error, a renegade employee, or one compromised by external forces.

There are a lot of bad guys out there, and motivations vary widely, including the following:

- Account theft and illegal funds transfer
- Stealing personal or financial data
- Compromising computing assets for use in other crimes
- Extortion
- Espionage
- Cyberwarfare
- Terrorism
- Pranksters
- Protest hacking (hacktivism)
- Revenge (disgruntled employees)

Criminals have stolen more than $100 million from U.S. banks in the first three quarters of 2009, and they did it "without drawing a gun or passing a note to a teller" (Kroft, 2009). While some steal cash for their own use, other resell their hacking take to others. There is a thriving cybercrime underworld market in which **data harvesters** sell to **cash-out fraudsters**: criminals who might purchase data from the harvesters in order to buy (then resell) goods using stolen credit cards or create false accounts via identity theft. These collection and resale operations are efficient and sophisticated. Law enforcement has taken down sites like DarkMarket and ShadowCrew, in which card thieves and hacking tool peddlers received eBay-style seller ratings vouching for the "quality" of their wares (Singel, 2008).

Hackers might also infiltrate computer systems to enlist hardware for subsequent illegal acts. A cybercrook might deliberately hop through several systems to make his path difficult to follow, slowing cross-border legal pursuit or even thwarting prosecution if launched from nations without extradition agreements.

In fact, your computer may be up for rent by cyber thieves right now. **Botnets** of zombie computers (networks of infiltrated and compromised machines controlled by a central command) are used for all sorts of nefarious activity. This includes sending spam from thousands of difficult-to-shut-down accounts, launching tough-to-track click fraud efforts or staging what's known as **distributed denial of service (DDoS)** attacks (effectively shutting down Web sites by overwhelming them with a crushing load of seemingly legitimate requests sent simultaneously by thousands of machines). Botnets have been discovered that are capable of sending out 100 billion spam messages a day (Higgins, 2008), and botnets as large as 10 million zombies have been identified. Such systems theoretically control more computing power than the world's fastest supercomputers (Krebs, 2007).

Extortionists might leverage botnets or hacked data to demand payment to avoid retribution. Three eastern European gangsters used a botnet and threatened DDoS to extort $4 million from UK sports bookmakers[1], while an extortion plot against the state of Virginia threatened to reveal names, Social Security numbers, and prescription information stolen from a medical records database (Kroft, 2009). Competition has also lowered the price to inflict such pain. *BusinessWeek* reports that the cost of renting out ten thousand machines, enough to cripple a site like Twitter, has tumbled to just $200 a day (Schectman, 2009).

Corporate espionage might be performed by insiders, rivals, or even foreign governments. Gary Min, a scientist working for DuPont, was busted when he tried to sell information valued at some $400 million, including R&D documents and secret data on proprietary products (Vijayan, 2007). Spies also breached the $300 billion U.S. Joint Strike Fighter project, siphoning off terabytes of data on navigation and other electronics systems (Gorman, et. al., 2009).

Cyberwarfare has become a legitimate threat, with several attacks demonstrating how devastating technology disruptions by terrorists or a foreign power might be. Brazil has seen hacks that cut off power to millions.

The *60 Minutes* news program showed a demonstration by "white hat" hackers that could compromise a key component in an oil refinery, force it to overheat, and cause an explosion. Taking out key components of the vulnerable U.S. power grid may be particularly devastating, as the equipment is expensive, much of it is no longer made in the United States, and some components may take three to four months to replace (Kroft, 2009).

Other threats come from malicious pranksters, like the group that posted seizure-inducing images on Web sites frequented by epilepsy sufferers (Schwartz, 2008). Others are **hacktivists**, targeting firms, Web sites, or even users as a protest measure. In 2009, Twitter was brought down and Facebook and LiveJournal were hobbled as Russian- sympathizing hacktivists targeted the social networking and blog accounts of the Georgian blogger known as Cyxymu. The silencing of millions of accounts was simply collateral damage in a massive DDoS attack meant to mute this single critic of the Russian government (Schectman, 2009).

And as power and responsibility is concentrated in the hands of a few revenge-seeking employees can do great damage. The San Francisco city government lost control of a large portion of its own computer network over a ten-day period when a single disgruntled employee refused to divulge critical passwords Vijayan, 2010).

The bad guys are legion and the good guys often seem outmatched and underresourced. Law enforcement agencies dealing with computer crime are increasingly outnumbered, outskilled, and underfunded. Many agencies are staffed with technically weak personnel who were trained in a prior era's crime fighting techniques. Governments can rarely match the pay scale and stock bonuses offered by private industry. Organized crime networks now have their own R&D labs and are engaged in sophisticated development efforts to piece together methods to thwart current security measures.

13.3 WHERE ARE VULNERABILITIES? UNDERSTANDING THE WEAKNESSES

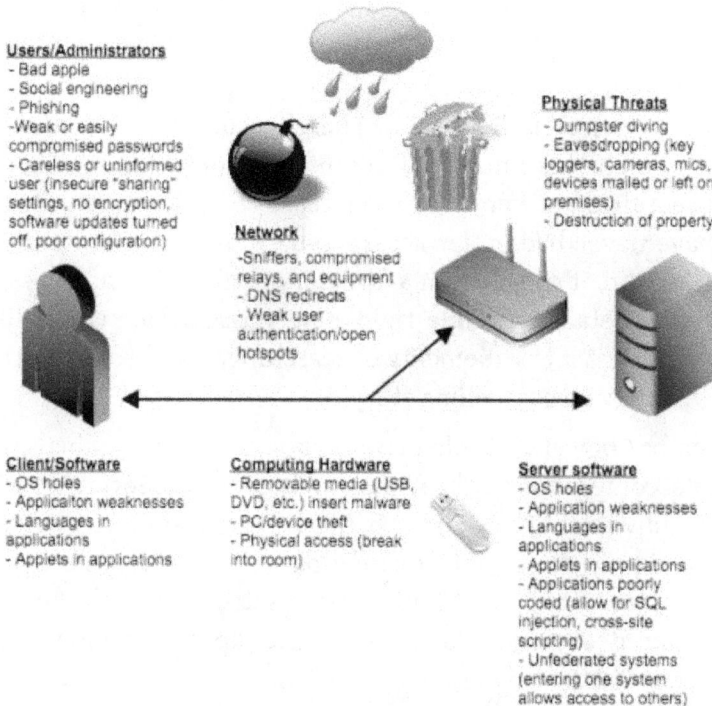

Users/Administrators
- Bad apple
- Social engineering
- Phishing
- Weak or easily compromised passwords
- Careless or uninformed user (insecure "sharing" settings, no encryption, software updates turned off, poor configuration)

Physical Threats
- Dumpster diving
- Eavesdropping (key loggers, cameras, mics, devices mailed or left on premises)
- Destruction of property

Network
- Sniffers, compromised relays, and equipment
- DNS redirects
- Weak user authentication/open hotspots

Client/Software
- OS holes
- Applicaiton weaknesses
- Languages in applications
- Applets in applications

Computing Hardware
- Removable media (USB, DVD, etc.) insert malware
- PC/device theft
- Physical access (break into room)

Server software
- OS holes
- Application weaknesses
- Languages in applications
- Applets in applications
- Applications poorly coded (allow for SQL injection, cross-site scripting)
- Unfederated systems (entering one system allows access to others)

Figure 13.1

This diagram shows only some of the potential weaknesses that can compromise the security of an organization's information systems. Every physical or network "touch point" is a potential vulnerability. Understanding where weaknesses may exist is a vital step toward improved security.

Modern information systems have lots of interrelated components and if one of these components fails, there might be a way in to the goodies. This creates a large attack surface for potential infiltration and compromise, as well as one that is simply vulnerable to unintentional damage and disruption.

User and Administrator Threats Bad Apples

While some of the more sensational exploits involve criminal gangs, research firm Gartner estimates that 70 percent of loss-causing security incidents involve insiders (Mardesich, 2009). Rogue employees can steal secrets, install malware, or hold a firm hostage. Check processing firm Fidelity National Information Services was betrayed when one of its database administrators lifted personal records on 2.3 million of the firm's customers and illegally sold them to direct marketers.

And it's not just firm employees. Many firms hire temporary staffers, contract employees, or outsource key components of their infrastructure. Other firms have been compromised by members of their cleaning or security staff. A contract employee working at Sentry Insurance stole information on 110,000 of the firm's clients (Vijayan, 2007).

Social Engineering

As P. T. Barnum is reported to have said, "There's a sucker born every minute." Con games that trick employees into revealing information or performing other tasks that compromise a firm are known as *social engineering* in security circles. In some ways, crooks have never had easier access to background information that might be used to craft a scam. It's likely that a directory of a firm's employees, their titles, and other personal details is online right now via social networks like LinkedIn and Facebook. With just a few moments of searching, a skilled con artist can piece together a convincing and compelling story.

Data aggregator ChoicePoint sold private information to criminals who posed as legitimate clients, compromising the names, addresses, and Social Security numbers of some 145,000 individuals. In this breach, not a single computer was compromised. Employees were simply duped into turning data over to crooks. Gaffes like that can be painful. ChoicePoint paid $15 million in a settlement with the Federal Trade Commission, suffered customer loss, and ended up abandoning once lucrative businesses (Anthes, 2008).

Phishing

Phishing refers to cons executed through technology. The goal of phishing is to leverage the reputation of a trusted firm or friend to trick the victim into performing an action or revealing information. The cons are crafty. Many have masqueraded as a security alert from a bank or e-commerce site ("Our Web site has been compromised, click to log in and reset your password."), a message from an employer, or even a notice from the government ("Click here to update needed information to receive your tax refund transfer."). Sophisticated con artists will lift logos, mimic standard layouts, and copy official language from legitimate Web sites or prior e-mails.

Gartner estimates that these sorts phishing attacks cost consumers $3.2 billion in 2007 (Avivah, 2007).

Other phishing attempts might dupe a user into unwittingly downloading dangerous software (malware) that can do things like record passwords and keystrokes, provide hackers with deeper access to your corporate network, or enlist your PC as part of a botnet. One attempt masqueraded as a message from a Facebook friend, inviting the recipient to view a video. Victims clicking the link were then told they need to install an updated version of the Adobe Flash plug-in to view the clip. The plug in was really a malware program that gave phishers control of the infected user's computer (Krebs, 2009). Other attempts have populated P2P networks (peer-to-peer file distribution systems such as BitTorrent) with malware-installing files masquerading as video games or other software, movies, songs, and pornography.

So-called spear phishing attacks specifically target a given organization or group of users. In one incident, employees of a medical center received e-mails purportedly from the center itself, indicating that the recipient was being laid off and offering a link to job counseling resources. The link really offered a software payload that recorded and forwarded any keystrokes on the victim's PC (Garretson, 2006). And with this type of phishing, the more you know about a user, the more convincing it is to con them. Phishers using pilfered résumé information from Monster.com crafted targeted and personalized e-mails. The request, seemingly from the job site, advised users to download the "Monster Job Seeker Tool"; this "tool" installed malware that encrypted files on the victim's PC, leaving a ransom note demanding payment to liberate a victim's hard disk (Wilson, 2007).

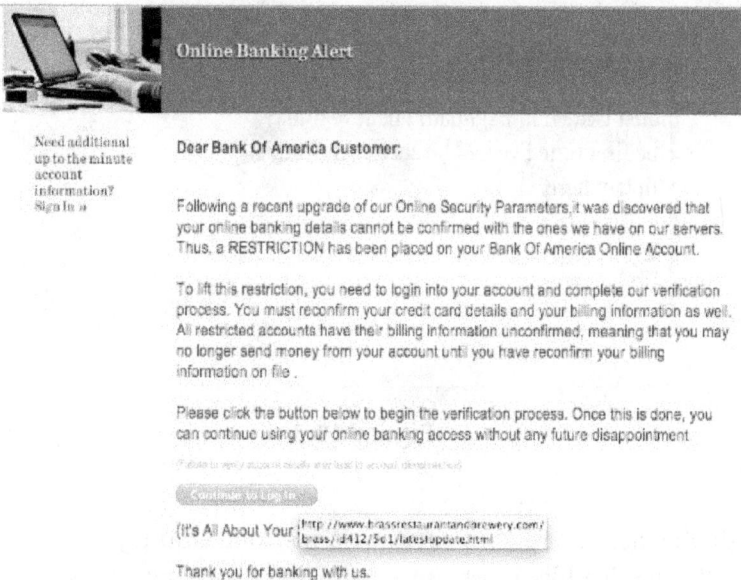

Figure 13.2

This e-mail message looks like it's from Bank of America. However, hovering the cursor above the "Continue to Log In" button reveals the URL without clicking through to the site. Note how the actual URL associated with the link is not associated with Bank of America.

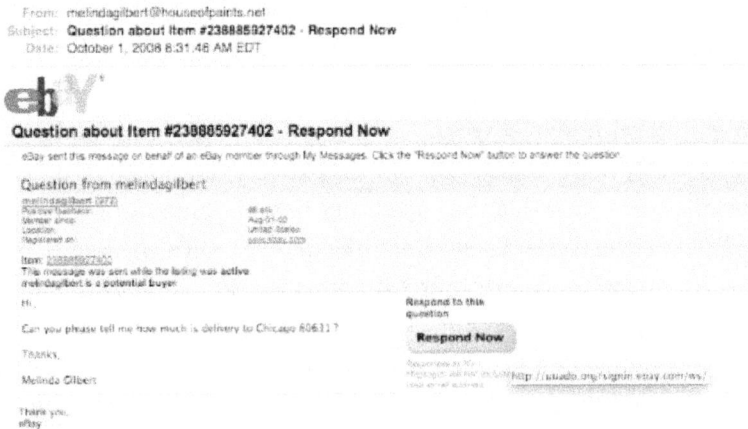

Figure 13.3

This image is from a phishing scheme masquerading as an eBay message. The real destination is a compromised .org domain unassociated with eBay, but the phishers have created a directory at this domain named "signin.ebay.com" in hopes that users will focus on that part of the URL and not recognize they're really headed to a non-eBay site.

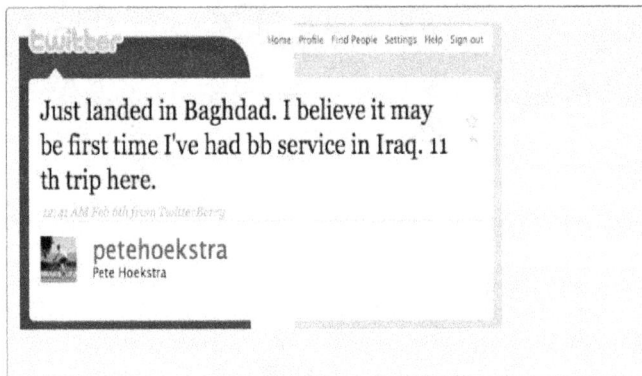

Figure 13.4

Passwords

Many valuable assets are kept secure via just one thin layer of protection—the password. And if you're like most users, your password system is a mess (Manjoo, 2009). With so many destinations asking for passwords, chances are you're using the same password (or easily guessed variants) in a way that means getting just one "key" would open many "doors." The typical Web user has 6.5 passwords, each of which is used at four sites, on average (Summers, 2009). Some sites force users to change passwords regularly, but this often results in insecure compromises. Users make only minor tweaks (e.g., appending the month or year); they write passwords down (in an unlocked drawer or Post-it note attached to the monitor); or they save passwords in personal e-mail accounts or on unencrypted hard drives.

The challenge questions offered by many sites to automate password distribution and reset are often pitifully insecure. What's your mother's maiden name? What elementary school did you attend? Where were you born? All are pretty easy to guess. One IEEE study found acquaintances could correctly answer colleagues' secret questions 28 percent of the time, and those who did not know the person still guessed right at a rate of 17 percent. Plus, within three to six months, 16 percent of study participants forgot answers to *their own* security questions (Lemos, 2009). In many cases, answers to these questions can be easily uncovered online. Chances are, if you've got an account at a site like Ancestry.com, classmates.com, or Facebook, then some of your secret answers have already been exposed—by you! A Tennessee teen hacked into Sarah Palin's personal Yahoo! account (gov.palin@yahoo.com) in part by correctly guessing where she met her husband. A similar attack hit staffers at Twitter, resulting in the theft of hundreds of internal documents, including strategy memos, e-mails, and financial forecasts, many of which ended up embarrassingly posted online (Summers, 2009).

Related to the password problem are issues with system setup and configuration. Many vendors sell software with a common default password. For example, for years, leading database products came with the default account and password combination "scott/tiger." Any firm not changing default accounts and passwords risks having an open door. Other firms are left vulnerable if users set systems for open access— say turning on file sharing permission for their PC. Programmers, take note: well-designed products come with secure default settings, require users to reset passwords at setup, and also offer strong warnings when security settings are made weaker. But unfortunately, there are a lot of legacy products out there, and not all vendors have the insight to design for out-of-the-box security.

Threats from technology (Client and Server Software, Hardware, and Networking)

Malware

Any accessible computing device is a potential target for infiltration by malware. *Malware* (for malicious software) seeks to compromise a computing system without permission. Client PCs and a firm's servers are primary targets, but as computing has spread, malware now threatens nearly any connected system running software, including mobile phones, embedded devices, and a firm's networking equipment.

Some hackers will try to sneak malware onto a system via techniques like phishing. In another high-profile hacking example, infected USB drives were purposely left lying around government offices. Those seemingly abandoned office supplies really contained code that attempted to infiltrate government PCs when inserted by unwitting employees.

Machines are constantly under attack. Microsoft's Internet Safety Enforcement Team claims that the mean time to infection for an unprotected PC is less than five minutes (Markoff, 2008). Oftentimes malware attempts to compromise weaknesses in software—either bugs, poor design, or poor configuration.

Years ago, most attacks centered on weaknesses in the operating system, but now malware exploits have expanded to other targets, including browsers, plug-ins, and scripting languages used by software. *BusinessWeek* reports that Adobe has replaced Microsoft as the primary means by which hackers try to infect or take control of PCs. Even trusted Web sites have become a conduit to deliver malware payloads. More than a dozen sites, including those of the *New York Times*, *USA Today*, and *Nature*, were compromised when seemingly honest advertising clients switched on fake ads that exploit Adobe software (Ricadela, 2009). Some attacks were delivered through Flash animations that direct computers to sites that scan PCs, installing malware payloads through whatever vulnerabilities are discovered. Others circulated via e-mail through PDF triggered payloads deployed when a file was loaded via Acrobat Reader. Adobe is a particularly tempting target, as Flash and Acrobat Reader are now installed on nearly every PC, including Mac and Linux machines.

Malware goes by many names. Here are a few of the more common terms you're likely to encounter[2]. Methods of infection are as follows:

- ⊙ *Viruses.* Programs that infect other software or files. They require an executable (a running program) to spread, attaching to other executables. Viruses can spread via operating systems, programs, or the boot sector or auto-run feature of media such as DVDs or USB drives. Some applications have executable languages (macros) that can also host viruses that run and spread when a file is open.

- ⊙ *Worms.* Programs that take advantage of security vulnerability to automatically spread, but unlike viruses, worms do not require an executable. Some worms scan for and install themselves on vulnerable systems with stunning speed (in an extreme example, the SQL Slammer worm infected 90 percent of vulnerable software worldwide within just ten minutes) (Broersma, 2003).

- *Trojans.* Exploits that, like the mythical Trojan horse, try to sneak in by masquerading as something they're not. The payload is released when the user is duped into downloading and installing the malware cargo, oftentimes via phishing exploits.

While the terms above cover methods for infection, the terms below address the goal of the malware:

- *Botnets or zombie networks.* Hordes of surreptitiously infected computers linked and controlled remotely by a central command. Botnets are used in crimes where controlling many difficult-to- identify PCs is useful, such as when perpetrating click fraud, sending spam, registering accounts that use **CAPTCHAs** (those scrambled character images meant to thwart things like automated account setup or ticket buying), executing "dictionary" password cracking attempts, or launching denial-of- service attacks.

- *Malicious adware.* Programs installed without full user consent or knowledge that later serve unwanted advertisements.

- *Spyware.* Software that surreptitiously monitors user actions, network traffic, or scans for files.

- *Keylogger.* Type of spyware that records user keystrokes. Keyloggers can be either software-based or hardware, such as a recording "dongle" that is plugged in between a keyboard and a PC.

- *Screen capture.* Variant of the keylogger approach. This category of software records the pixels that appear on a user's screen for later playback in hopes of identifying proprietary information.

- *Blended threats.* Attacks combining multiple malware or hacking exploits.

Compromising Web Sites

Some exploits directly target poorly designed and programmed Web sites. Consider the SQL injection technique. It zeros in on a sloppy programming practice where software developers don't validate user input.

It works like this. Imagine that you visit a Web site and are asked to enter your user ID in a field on a Web page (say your user ID is smith). A Web site may be programmed to take the data you enter from the Web page's user ID field (smith), then add it to a database command (creating the equivalent of a command that says "find the account for 'smith'"). The database then executes that command.

But Web sites that don't verify user entries and instead just blindly pass along entered data are vulnerable to attack. Hackers with just a rudimentary knowledge of SQL could type actual code fragments into the user ID field, appending this code to statements executed by the site (see sidebar for a more detailed description). Such modified instructions could instruct the Web site's database software to drop (delete) tables, insert additional data, return all records in a database, or even redirect users to another Web site that will scan clients for weaknesses, then launch further attacks. Security expert Ben Schneier noted a particularly ghastly SQL injection vulnerability in the publicly facing database for the Oklahoma Department of Corrections, where "anyone with basic SQL knowledge could have registered anyone he wanted as a sex offender" (Schneier, 2008).

Not trusting user input is a cardinal rule of programming, and most well-trained programmers know to validate user input. But there's a lot of sloppy code out there, which hackers are all too eager to exploit. IBM identifies SQL injection as the fastest growing security threat, with over half a million attack attempts recorded each day (Wittmann, 2009). Some vulnerable systems started life as quickly developed proofs of concepts, and programmers never went back to add the needed code to validate input and block these exploits. Other Web sites may have been designed by poorly trained developers who have moved on to other projects, by staff that have since left the firm, or where development was outsourced to another firm. As such, many firms don't even know if they suffer from this vulnerability.

SQL injection and other application weaknesses are particularly problematic because there's not a commercial software patch or easily deployed piece of security software that can protect a firm. Instead, firms have to meticulously examine the integrity of their Web sites to see if they are vulnerable[3].

Push-Button Hacking

Not only are the list of technical vulnerabilities well known, hackers have created tools to make it easy for the criminally inclined to automate attacks. Chapter 14 "Google: Search, Online Advertising, and Beyond" outlines how Web sites can interrogate a system to find out more about the software and hardware used by visitors. Hacking toolkits can do the same thing. While you won't find this sort of software for sale on Amazon, a casual surfing of the online underworld (not recommended or advocated) will surface scores of tools that probe systems for the latest vulnerabilities, then launch appropriate attacks. In one example, a $700 toolkit (MPack v. 86) was used to infiltrate a host of Italian Web sites, launching Trojans that infested 15,000 users in just a six-day period5. As an industry executive in BusinessWeek has stated, "The barrier of entry is becoming so low that literally anyone can carry out these attacks" (Schectman, 2009).

Network Threats

The network itself may also be a source of compromise. Recall that the TJX hack happened when a Wi-Fi access point was left open and undetected. A hacker just drove up and performed the digital equivalent of crawling through an open window.

The problem is made more challenging since wireless access points are so inexpensive and easy to install. For less than $100, a user (well intentioned or not) could plug in to an access point that could provide entry for anyone. If a firm doesn't regularly monitor its premises, its network, and its network traffic, it may fall victim.

Other troubling exploits have targeted the very underpinning of the Internet itself. This is the case with so-called DNS cache poisoning. The DNS, or domain name service, is a collection of software that maps an Internet address, such as (http://www.bc.edu), to an IP address, such as 136.167.2.220. 220 (see Chapter 12 "A Manager's Guide to the Internet and Telecommunications" for more detail). DNS cache poisoning exploits can redirect this mapping and the consequences are huge. Imagine thinking that you're visiting your bank's Web site, but instead your network's DNS server has been poisoned so that you really visit a carefully crafted replica that hackers use to steal your log-in credentials and drain your bank account. A DNS cache poisoning attack launched against one of China's largest ISPs redirected users to sites that launched malware exploits, targeting weaknesses in RealPlayer, Adobe Flash, and Microsoft's ActiveX technology, commonly used in browsers (London, 2008).

Physical Threats

A firm doesn't just have to watch out for insiders or compromised software and hardware; a host of other physical threats can grease the skids to fraud, theft, and damage. Most large firms have disaster-recovery plans in place. These often include provisions to backup systems and data to off-site locales, to protect operations and provide a fall back in the case of disaster. Such plans increasingly take into account the potential impact of physical security threats such as terrorism, or vandalism, as well.

Anything valuable that reaches the trash in a recoverable state is also a potential security breach. Hackers and spies sometimes practice **dumpster diving**, sifting through trash in an effort to uncover valuable data or insights that can be stolen or used to launch a security attack. This might include hunting for discarded passwords written on Post-it notes, recovering unshredded printed user account listings, scanning e-mails or program printouts for system clues, recovering tape backups, resurrecting files from discarded hard drives, and more.

Other compromises might take place via **shoulder surfing**, simply looking over someone's shoulder to glean a password or see other proprietary information that might be displayed on a worker's screen.

Firms might also fall victim to various forms of eavesdropping, such as efforts to listen into or record conversations, transmissions, or keystrokes. A device hidden inside a package might sit inside a mailroom or a worker's physical inbox, scanning for open wireless connections, or recording and forwarding conversations (Robertson, 2008). Other forms of eavesdropping can be accomplished via compromised wireless or other network connections, malware keylogger or screen capture programs, as well as hardware devices such as replacement keyboards with keyloggers embedded inside, microphones to capture the slightly unique and identifiable sound of each key being pressed, programs that turn on built-in microphone or cameras that are now standard on many PCs, or even James Bond-style devices using Van Eck techniques that attempt to read monitors from afar by detecting their electromagnetic emissions.

13.4 TAKING ACTION

Taking Action as a User

The weakest link in security is often a careless user, so don't make yourself an easy mark. Once you get a sense of threats, you understand the kinds of precautions you need to take. Security considerations then become more common sense than high tech. Here's a brief list of major issues to consider:

- *Surf smart.* Think before you click—question links, enclosures, download request, and the integrity of Web sites that you visit. Avoid suspicious e-mail attachments and Internet downloads. Be on guard for phishing, and other attempts to con you into letting in malware. Verify anything that looks suspicious before acting. Avoid using public machines (libraries, coffee shops) when accessing sites that contain your financial data or other confidential information.

- *Stay vigilant.* Social engineering con artists and rogue insiders are out there. An appropriate level of questioning applies not only to computer use, but also to personal interactions, be it in person, on the phone, or electronically.

- *Stay updated.* Turn on software update features for your operating system and any application you use (browsers, applications, plug-ins, and applets), and manually check for updates when needed. Malware toolkits specifically scan for older, vulnerable systems, so working with updated programs that address prior concerns lowers your vulnerable attack surface.

- *Stay armed.* Install a full suite of security software. Many vendors offer a combination of products that provide antivirus software that blocks infection, personal firewalls that repel unwanted intrusion, malware scanners that seek out bad code that might already be nesting on your PC, antiphishing software that identifies if you're visiting questionable Web sites, and more. Such tools are increasingly being built into operating systems, browsers, and are deployed at the ISP or service provider (e-mail firm, social network) level. But every consumer should make it a priority to understand the state of the art for personal protection. In the way that you regularly balance your investment portfolio to account tfor economic shifts, or take your car in for an oil change to keep it in top running condition, make it a priority to periodically scan the major trade press or end-user computing sites for reviews and commentary on the latest tools and techniques for protecting yourself (and your firm).

⦿ *Be settings smart.* Don't turn on risky settings like unrestricted folder sharing that may act as an invitation for hackers to drop off malware payloads. Secure home networks with password protection and a firewall. Encrypt hard drives—especially on laptops or other devices that might be lost or stolen. Register mobile devices for location identification or remote wiping. Don't click the "Remember me" or "Save password" settings on public machines, or any device that might be shared or accessed by others. Similarly, if your machine might be used by others, turn off browser settings that auto-fill fields with prior entries—otherwise you make it easy for someone to use that machine to track your entries and impersonate you. And when using public hotspots, be sure to turn on your VPN software to encrypt transmission and hide from network eavesdroppers.

⦿ *Be password savvy.* Change the default password on any new products that you install. Update your passwords regularly. Using guidelines outlined earlier, choose passwords that are tough to guess, but easy for you (and only you) to remember. Federate your passwords so that you're not using the same access codes for your most secure sites. Never save passwords in nonsecured files, e-mail, or written down in easily accessed locations.

⦿ *Be disposal smart.* Shred personal documents. Wipe hard drives with an industrial strength software tool before recycling, donating, or throwing away—remember in many cases "deleted" files can still be recovered. Destroy media such as CDs and DVDs that may contain sensitive information. Erase USB drives when they are no longer needed.

⦿ *Back up.* The most likely threat to your data doesn't come from hackers; it comes from hardware failure (Taylor, 2009). Yet most users still don't regularly back up their systems. This is another do-it- now priority. Cheap, plug-in hard drives work with most modern operating systems to provide continual backups, allowing for quick rollback to earlier versions if you've accidentally ruined some vital work. And services like EMC's Mozy provide monthly, unlimited backup over the Internet for less than what you probably spent on your last lunch (a fire, theft, or similar event could also result in the loss of any backups stored on-site, but Internet backup services can provide off-site storage and access if disaster strikes).

⊙ *Check with your administrator.* All organizations that help you connect to the Internet—your ISP, firm, or school—should have security pages. Many provide free security software tools. Use them as resources. Remember—it's in their interest to keep you safe, too!

Taking Action as an Organization Frameworks, Standards, and Compliance

Developing organizational security is a daunting task. You're in an arms race with adversaries that are tenacious and constantly on the lookout for new exploits. Fortunately, no firm is starting from scratch—others have gone before you and many have worked together to create published best practices.

There are several frameworks, but perhaps the best known of these efforts comes from the International Organization for Standards (ISO), and is broadly referred to as ISO27k or the ISO 27000 series. According to ISO.org, this evolving set of standards provides "a model for establishing, implementing, operating, monitoring, reviewing, maintaining, and improving an Information Security Management System."

Firms may also face compliance requirements—legal or professionally binding steps that must be taken. Failure to do so could result in fine, sanction, and other punitive measures. At the federal level, examples include HIPAA (the Health Insurance Portability and Accountability Act), which regulates health data; the Graham-Leach-Bliley Act, which regulates financial data; and the Children's Online Privacy Protection Act, which regulates data collection on minors. U.S. government agencies must also comply with FISMA (the Federal Information Security Management Act), and there are several initiatives at the other government levels. By 2009, some level of state data breach laws had been passed by over thirty states, while multinationals face a growing number of statues throughout the world. Your legal team and trade associations can help you understand your domestic and international obligations. Fortunately, there are often frameworks and guidelines to assist in compliance. For example, the ISO standards include subsets targeted at the telecommunications and health care industries, and major credit card firms have created the PCI (payment card industry) standards. And there are skilled consulting professionals who can help bring firms up to speed in these areas, and help expand their organizational radar as new issues develop.

Here is a word of warning on frameworks and standards: compliance does not equal security. Outsourcing portions security efforts without a complete, organizational commitment to being secure can also be dangerous. Some organizations simply approach compliance as a necessary evil: a sort of checklist that can reduce the likelihood of a lawsuit or other punitive measure (Davis, 2009). While you want to make sure you're doing everything in your power not to get sued, this isn't the goal.

The goal is taking all appropriate measures to ensure that your firm is secure for your customers, employees, shareholders, and others. Frameworks help shape your thinking and expose things you should do, but security doesn't stop there—this is a constant, evolving process that needs to pervade the organization from the CEO suite and board, down to front line workers and potentially out to customers and partners. And be aware of the security issues associated with any mergers and acquisitions. Bringing in new firms, employees, technologies, and procedures means reassessing the security environment for all players involved.

Education, Audit, and Enforcement

From a people perspective, the security function requires multiple levels of expertise. Operations employees are involved in the day-to-day monitoring of existing systems. A group's R&D function is involved in understanding emerging threats and reviewing, selecting, and implementing updated security techniques. A team must also work on broader governance issues. These efforts should include representatives from specialized security and broader technology and infrastructure functions. It should also include representatives from general counsel, audit, public relations, and human resources. What this means is that even if you're a nontechnical staffer, you may be brought in to help a firm deal with security issues.

Processes and policies will include education and awareness—this is also everyone's business. As the Vice President of Product Development at security firm Symantec puts it, "We do products really well, but the next step is education. We can't keep the Internet safe with antivirus software alone" (Goldman, 2009). Companies should approach information security as a part of their "collective corporate responsibility...regardless of whether regulation requires them to do so[1]."

For a lesson in how important education is, look no further than the head of the CIA. Former U.S. Director of Intelligence John Deutch engaged in shockingly loose behavior with digital secrets, including keeping a daily journal of classified information—some 1,000+ pages—on memory cards he'd transport in his shirt pocket. He also downloaded and stored Pentagon information, including details of covert operations, at home on computers that his family used for routine Internet access (Lewis, 2000).

Employees need to know a firm's policies, be regularly trained, and understand that they will face strict penalties if they fail to meet their obligations. Policies without eyes (audit) and teeth (enforcement) won't be taken seriously. Audits include real-time monitoring of usage (e.g., who's accessing what, from where, how, and why; sound the alarm if an anomaly is detected), announced audits, and surprise spot checks. This function might also stage white hat demonstration attacks—attempts to hunt for and expose weaknesses, hopefully before hackers find them. Frameworks offer guidelines on auditing, but a recent survey found most organizations don't document enforcement procedures in their information security policies, that more than one-third do not audit or monitor user compliance with security policies, and that only 48 percent annually measure and review the effectiveness of security policies (Matwyshyn, 2009).

A firm's technology development and deployment processes must also integrate with the security team to ensure that from the start, applications, databases, and other systems are implemented with security in mind. The team will have specialized skills and monitor the latest threats and are able to advise on precautions necessary to be sure systems aren't compromised during installation, development, testing, and deployment.

What Should Be Safeguarded, and How Much Is Enough?

A worldwide study by PricewaterhouseCoopers and *Chief Security Officer* magazine revealed that most firms don't even know what they need to protect. Only 33 percent of executives responded that their organizations kept accurate inventory of the locations and jurisdictions where data was stored, and only 24 percent kept inventory of all third parties using their customer data (Matwyshyn, 2009). What this means is that most firms don't even have an accurate read on where their valuables are kept, let alone how to protect them.

So information security should start with an inventory-style auditing and risk assessment. Technologies map back to specific business risks. What do we need to protect? What are we afraid might happen? And how do we protect it? Security is an economic problem, involving attack likelihood, costs, and prevention benefits. These are complex trade-offs that must consider losses from theft or resources, systems damage, data loss, disclosure of proprietary information, recovery, downtime, stock price declines, legal fees, government and compliance penalties, and intangibles such as damaged firm reputation, loss of customer and partner confidence, industry damage, promotion of adversary, and encouragement of future attacks.

While many firms skimp on security, firms also don't want to misspend, targeting exploits that aren't likely, while underinvesting in easily prevented methods to thwart common infiltration techniques. Hacker conventions like DefCon can show some really wild exploits. But it's up to the firm to assess how vulnerable it is to these various risks. The local donut shop has far different needs than a military installation, law enforcement agency, financial institution, or firm housing other high-value electronic assets. A skilled risk assessment team will consider these vulnerabilities and what sort of countermeasure investments should take place.

Economic decisions usually drive hacker behavior, too. While in some cases attacks are based on vendetta or personal reasons, in most cases exploit economics largely boils down to

Adversary ROI = Asset value to adversary − Adversary cost.

An adversary's costs include not only the resources, knowledge, and technology required for the exploit, but also the risk of getting caught. Make things tough to get at, and lobbying for legislation that imposes severe penalties on crooks can help raise adversary costs and lower your likelihood of becoming a victim.

Technology's Role

Technical solutions often involve industrial strength variants of the previously discussed issues individuals can employ, so your awareness is already high. Additionally, an organization's approach will often leverage multiple layers of protection and incorporate a wide variety of protective measures.

Patch. Firms must be especially vigilant to pay attention to security bulletins and install software updates that plug existing holes, (often referred to as *patches*). Firms that don't plug known problems will be vulnerable to trivial and automated attacks. Unfortunately, many firms aren't updating all components of their systems with consistent attention. With operating systems automating security update installations, hackers have moved on to application targets. But a major study recently found that organizations took at least twice as long to patch application vulnerabilities as they take to patch operating system holes (Wildstrom, 2009). And remember, software isn't limited to conventional PCs and servers. Embedded systems abound, and connected, yet unpatched devices are vulnerable. Malware has infected everything from unprotected ATM machines (Lilly, 2009) to restaurant point- of-sale systems (McMillan, 2009) to fighter plane navigation systems (Matyszczyk, 2009).

As an example of unpatched vulnerabilities, consider the DNS cache poisoning exploit described earlier in this chapter. The discovery of this weakness was one of the biggest security stories the year it was discovered, and security experts saw this as a major threat. Teams of programmers worldwide raced to provide fixes for the most widely used versions of DNS software. Yet several months after patches were available, roughly one quarter of all DNS servers were still unpatched and exposed[2].

To be fair, not all firms delay patches out of negligence. Some organizations have legitimate concerns about testing whether the patch will break their system or whether the new technology contains a change that will cause problems down the road[3]. And there have been cases where patches themselves have caused problems. Finally, many software updates require that systems be taken down. Firms may have uptime requirements that make immediate patching difficult. But ultimately, unpatched systems are an open door for infiltration.

Lock down hardware. Firms range widely in the security regimes used to govern purchase through disposal system use. While some large firms such as Kraft are allowing employees to select their own hardware (Mac or PC, desktop or notebook, iPhone or BlackBerry) (Wingfield, 2009), others issue standard systems that prevent all unapproved software installation and force file saving to hardened, backed-up, scanned, and monitored servers. Firms in especially sensitive industries such as financial services may regularly reimage the hard drive of end-user PCs, completely replacing all the bits on a user's hard drive with a pristine, current version—effectively wiping out malware that might have previously sneaked onto a user's PC. Other lock-down methods might disable the boot capability of removable media (a common method for spreading viruses via inserted discs or USBs), prevent Wi-Fi use or require VPN encryption before allowing any network transmissions, and more. The cloud helps here, too. (See Chapter 10 "Software in Flux: Partly Cloudy and Sometimes Free".) Employers can also require workers to run all of their corporate applications inside a remote desktop where the actual executing hardware and software is elsewhere (likely hosted as a virtual machine session on the organization's servers), and the user is simply served an image of what is executing remotely. This seals the virtual PC off in a way that can be thoroughly monitored, updated, backed up, and locked down by the firm.

In the case of Kraft, executives worried that the firm's previously restrictive technology policies prevented employees from staying in step with trends. Employees opting into the system must sign an agreement promising they'll follow mandated security procedures. Still, financial services firms, law offices, health care providers, and others may need to maintain stricter control, for legal and industry compliance reasons.

Lock down the network. Network monitoring is a critical part of security, and a host of technical tools can help. Firms employ **firewalls** to examine traffic as it enters and leaves the network, potentially blocking certain types of access, while permitting approved communication. **Intrusion detection systems** specifically look for unauthorized behavior, sounding the alarm and potentially taking action if something seems amiss. Some firms deploy **honeypots**—bogus offerings meant to distract attackers. If attackers take honeypot bait, firms may gain an opportunity to recognize the hacker's exploits, identify the IP address of intrusion, and take action to block further attacks and alert authorities.

Many firms also deploy **blacklists**—denying the entry or exit of specific IP addresses, products, Internet domains, and other communication restrictions. While blacklists block known bad guys, **whitelists** are even more restrictive—permitting communication only with approved entities or in an approved manner.

These technologies can be applied to network technology, specific applications, screening for certain kinds of apps, malware signatures, and hunting for anomalous patterns. The latter is important, as recent malware has become polymorphic, meaning different versions are created and deployed in a way that their signature, a sort of electronic fingerprint often used to recognize malicious code, is slightly altered. This also helps with zero-day exploits, and in situations where whitelisted Web sites themselves become compromised.

Many technical solutions, ranging from network monitoring and response to e-mail screening, are migrating to "the cloud." This can be a good thing—if network monitoring software immediately shares news of a certain type of attack, defenses might be pushed out to all clients of a firm (the more users, the "smarter" the system can potentially become—again we see the power of network effects in action).

Lock down partners. Insist partner firms are compliant, and audit them to ensure this is the case. This includes technology providers and contract firms, as well as value chain participants such as suppliers and distributors. Anyone who touches your network is a potential point of weakness. Many firms will build security expectations and commitments into performance guarantees known as service level agreements (SLAs).

Lock down systems. Audit for SQL injection and other application exploits. The security team must constantly scan exploits and then probe its systems to see if it's susceptible, advising and enforcing action if problems are uncovered. This kind of auditing should occur with all of a firm's partners.

Access controls can also compartmentalize data access on a need-to-know basis. Such tools can not only enforce access privileges, they can help create and monitor audit trails to help verify that systems are not being accessed by the unauthorized, or in suspicious ways.

Audit trails are used for deterring, identifying, and investigating these cases. Recording, monitoring, and auditing access allows firms to hunt for patterns of abuse. Logs can detail who, when, and from where assets are accessed. Giveaways of nefarious activity may include access from unfamiliar IP addresses, from nonstandard times, accesses that occur at higher than usual volumes, and so on. Automated alerts can put an account on hold or call in a response team for further observation of the anomaly.

Single-sign-on tools can help firms offer employees one very strong password that works across applications, is changed frequently (or managed via hardware cards or mobile phone log-in), and can be altered by password management staff.

Multiple administrators should jointly control key systems. Major configuration changes might require approval of multiple staffers, as well as the automatic notification of concerned personnel. And firms should employ a recovery mechanism to regain control in the event that key administrators are incapacitated or uncooperative. This balances security needs with an ability to respond in the event of a crisis. Such a system was not in place in the earlier described case of the rogue

IT staffer who held the city of San Francisco's networks hostage by refusing to give up vital passwords.

Have failure and recovery plans. While firms work to prevent infiltration attempts, they should also have provisions in place that plan for the worst. If a compromise has taken place, what needs to be done? Do stolen assets need to be devalued (e.g., accounts terminated, new accounts issued)? What should be done to notify customers and partners, educate them, and advise them through any necessary responses? Who should work with law enforcement and with the media? Do off-site backups or redundant systems need to be activated? Can systems be reliably restored without risking further damage?

Best practices are beginning to emerge. While postevent triage is beyond the scope of our introduction, the good news is that firms are now sharing data on breaches. Given the potential negative consequences of a breach, organizations once rarely admitted they'd been compromised. But now many are obligated to do so. And the broad awareness of infiltration both reduces organizational stigma in coming forward, and allows firms and technology providers to share knowledge on the techniques used by cybercrooks.

Information security is a complex, continually changing, and vitally important domain. The exploits covered in this chapter seem daunting, and new exploits constantly emerge. But your thinking on key issues should now be broader. Hopefully you've now embedded security thinking in your managerial DNA, and you are better prepared to be a savvy system user and a proactive participant working for your firm's security. Stay safe!

REFERENCES

Anthes, G., "The Grill: Security Guru Ira Winkler Takes the Hot Seat," Computerworld, July 28, 2008. Goldman, D., "Cybercrime: A Secret Underground Economy," CNNMoney, September 17, 2009.

Anthes, G., "The Grill: Security Guru Ira Winkler Takes the Hot Seat," Computerworld, July 28, 2008.

Avivah, L., "Phishing Attacks Escalate, Morph, and Cause Considerable Damage," Gartner, December 12, 2007. Broersma, M., "Slammer—the First 'Warhol' Worm?" CNET, February 3, 2003.

Charney, J., "Commwarrior Cell Phone Virus Marches On," CNET, June 5, 2005. Garretson, C., "Spam that Delivers a Pink Slip," NetworkWorld, November 1, 2006.

Claburn, T., "Payment Card Industry Gets Encryption Religion," InformationWeek, November 13, 2009. Davis, M., "What Will It Take?" InformationWeek, November 23, 2009.

Goldman, D., "Cybercrime: A Secret Underground Economy," CNNMoney, September 17, 2009. King, R., "Lessons from the Data Breach at Heartland," BusinessWeek, July 6, 2009.

Gorman, S., A. Cole, and Y. Dreazen. "Computer Spies Breach Fighter-Jet Project," Wall Street Journal, April 21, 2009.

Higgins, K. J., "SecureWorks Unveils Research on Spamming Botnets," DarkReading, April 9, 2008. Krebs, B., "Storm Worm Dwarfs World's Top Supercomputer," Washington Post, August 31, 2007.

Keizer, G., "Botnet Busts Newest Hotmail CAPTCHA," Computerworld, February 19, 2009. Krebs, B., "'Koobface' Worm Resurfaces on Facebook, MySpace," Washington Post, March 2, 2009. Lemos, R., "Are Your 'Secret Questions' Too Easily Answered?" Technology Review, May 18, 2009. Lemos, R., "Nasty iPhone Worm Hints at the Future," Technology Review, November 29, 2009.

King, R., "Lessons from the Data Breach at Heartland," BusinessWeek, July 6, 2009.

Kroft, S., "Cyberwar: Sabotaging the System," 60 Minutes, November 8, 2009. Schectman, J., "Computer Hacking Made Easy," BusinessWeek, August 13, 2009. Schwartz, M., "The Trolls among Us," New York Times, August 3, 2008.

Lewis, N., "Investigation Of Ex-Chief Of the C.I.A. Is Broadened," New York Times, September 17, 2000. Lilly, P., "Hackers Targeting Windows XP-Based ATM Machines," Maximum PC, June 4, 2009.

London, J., "China Netcom Falls Prey to DNS Cache Poisoning," Computerworld, August 22, 2008. Manjoo, F., "Fix Your Terrible, Insecure Passwords in Five Minutes," Slate, November 12, 2009.

Mardesich, J., "Ensuring the Security of Stored Data," CIO Strategy Center, 2009.

Markoff, J., "A Robot Network Seeks to Enlist Your Computer," New York Times, October 20, 2008.

Matwyshyn, A., Harboring Data: Information Security, Law, and the Corporation (Palo Alto, CA: Stanford University Press, 2009).

Matwyshyn, A., Harboring Data: Information Security, Law, and The Corporation (Palo Alto, CA: Stanford University Press, 2009).

Matyszczyk, C., "French Planes Grounded by Windows Worm," CNET, February 8, 2009.

McMillan, R., "Restaurants Sue Vendors after Point-of-Sale Hack," CIO, December 1, 2009. Taylor, C., "The Tech Catastrophe You're Ignoring," Fortune, October 26, 2009.

Murrell, J., "The iWitness News Roundup: Crime-fighting iPhone," Good Morning Silicon Valley, August 31, 2009.

Ricadela, A., "Can Adobe Beat Back the Hackers?" BusinessWeek, November 19, 2009.

Robertson, J., "Hackers Mull Physical Attacks on a Networked World," San Francisco Chronicle, August 8, 2008. Schectman, J., "Computer Hacking Made Easy," BusinessWeek, August 13, 2009.

Schneier, B., "Oklahoma Data Leak," Schneier on Security, April 18, 2008.

Singel, R., "Underground Crime Economy Health, Security Group Finds," Wired, November 24, 2008. Vijayan, J., "After Verdict, Debate Rages in Terry Childs Case," Computerworld, April 28, 2010.

Steade, S., "It's Shameless How They Flirt," Good Morning Silicon Valley, November 9, 2009. Summers, N., "Building a Better Password," Newsweek, October 19, 2009.

Vance, A., "Times Web Ads Show Security Breach," New York Times, September 14, 2009.

Vijayan, J., "Software Consultant Who Stole Data on 110,000 People Gets Five-Year Sentence," Computerworld, July 10, 2007.

Vijayan, J., "Software Consultant Who Stole Data on 110,000 People Gets Five-Year Sentence," Computerworld, July 10, 2007.

Wildstrom, S., "Massive Study of Net Vulnerabilities: They're Not Where You Think They Are," BusinessWeek, September 14, 2009.

Wilson, T., "Trojan On Monster.com Steals Personal Data," Forbes, August 20, 2007. Wittmann, A., "The Fastest-Growing Security Threat," InformationWeek, November 9, 2009.

Wingfield, N., "It's a Free Country...So Why Can't I Pick the Technology I Use in the Office?" Wall Street Journal, November 15, 2009.

GOOGLE: ONLINE ADVERTISING, SEARCH, AND MORE

14

14.1 INTRODUCTION: AN OVERVIEW

Google has been called a one-trick pony (Li, 2009), but as tricks go, it's got an exquisite one. Google's "trick" is matchmaking—pairing Internet surfers with advertisers and taking a cut along the way. This cut is substantial—about $23 billion in 2009. In fact, as *Wired*'s Steve Levy puts it, Google's matchmaking capabilities may represent "the most successful business idea in history" (Levy, 2009). For perspective, consider that as a ten- year-old firm, and one that had been public for less than five years, Google had already grown to earn more annual advertising dollars than *any* U.S. media company. No television network, no magazine group, no newspaper chain brings in more ad bucks than Google. And none is more profitable. While Google's stated mission is "to organize the world's information and make it universally accessible and useful," advertising drives profits and lets the firm offer most of its services for free.

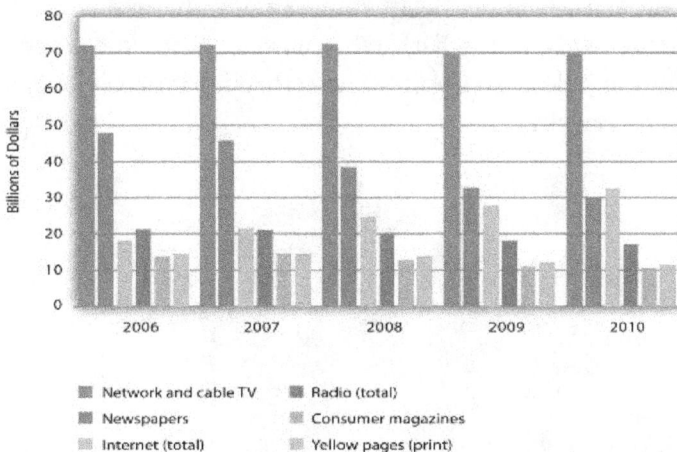

Figure 14.1 U.S. Advertising Spending (by selected media)

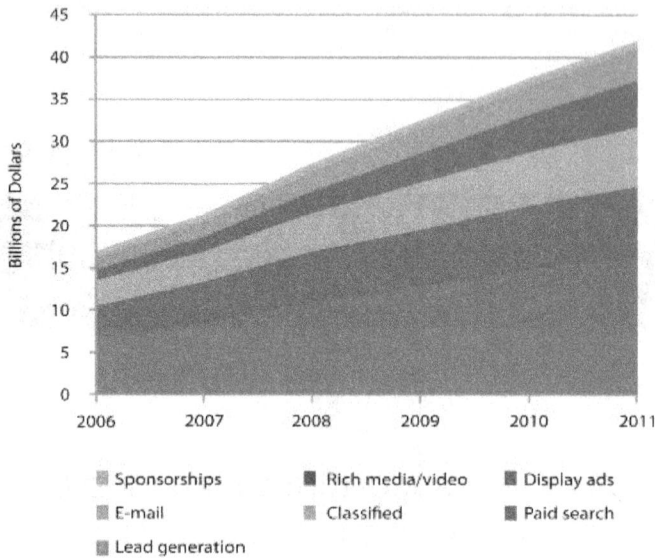

Figure 14.2 U.S. Online Ad Spending (by format)

As more people spend more time online, advertisers are shifting spending away from old channels to the Internet; and Google is swallowing the lion's share of this funds transfer (Pontin, 2009). By some estimates Google has 76 percent of the search advertising business (Sherman, 2009). Add to that Google's lucrative AdSense network that serves ads to sites ranging from small time bloggers to the *New York Times*, plus markets served by Google's acquisition of display ad leader DoubleClick, and the firm controls in the neighborhood of 70 percent of *all* online advertising dollars (Baker, 2008). Google has the world's strongest brand (Rao, 2009) (its name is a verb—*just Google it*). It is regularly voted among the best firms to work for in America (twice topping *Fortune*'s list). While rivals continue to innovate (see Note 14.85 "Search: Google Rules, but It Ain't Over") through Q1 2009, Google continues to dominate the search market.

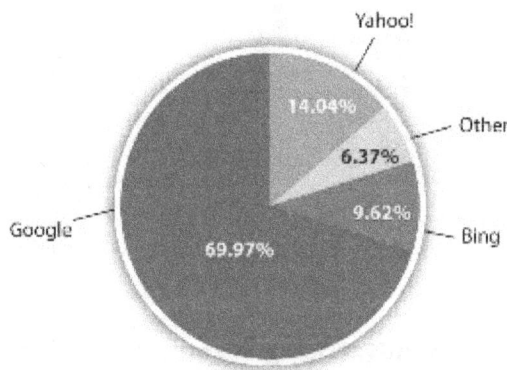

Figure 14.3 U.S. Search Market Share (Volume of Searches, March 2010)1

Wall Street has rewarded this success. The firm's **market capitalization (market cap)**, the value of the firm calculated by multiplying its share price by the number of shares, makes Google the most valuable media company on the planet. By early 2009, Google's market cap was greater than that of News Corp (which includes Fox, MySpace, and the *Wall Street Journal*), Disney (including ABC, ESPN, theme parks, and Pixar), Time Warner (*Fortune, Time, Sports Illustrated*, CNN, and Warner Bros.), Viacom (MTV, VH1, and Nickelodeon), CBS, and the *New York Times*—combined! Not bad for a business started by two twenty-something computer science graduate students. By 2007 that duo, Sergey Brin and Larry Page, were billionaires, tying for fifth on the *Forbes* 400 list of wealthiest Americans.

Studying Google gives us an idea of how quickly technology-fueled market disruptions can happen, and how deeply these disruptions penetrate various industries. We'll also study the underlying technologies that power search, online advertising, and customer profiling. We'll explore issues of strategy, privacy, fraud, and discuss other opportunities and challenges the firm faces going forward.

14.2 SEARCH UNDERSTANDING

Before diving into how the firm makes money, let's first understand how Google's core service, search, works.

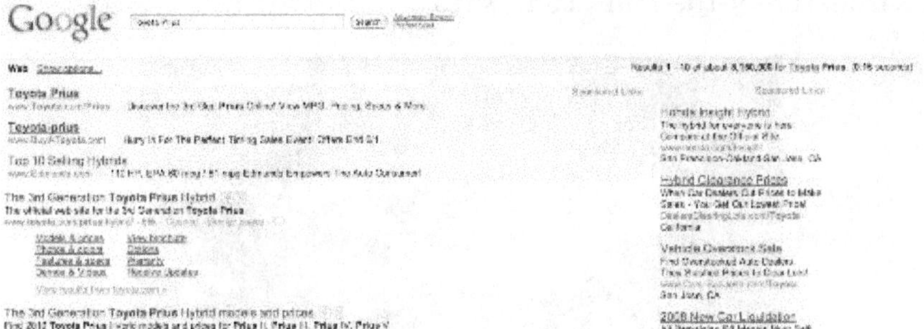

Figure 14.4

Perform a search (or **query**) on Google or another search engine, and the results you'll see are referred to by industry professionals as **organic or natural search**. Search engines use different algorithms for determining the order of organic search results, but at Google the method is called **PageRank** (a bit of a play on words, it ranks Web pages, and was initially developed by Google cofounder Larry Page). Google does not accept money for placement of links in organic search results. Instead, PageRank results are a kind of popularity contest. Web pages that have more pages *linking to them* are ranked higher.

The process of improving a page's organic search results is often referred to as **search engine optimization (SEO)**. SEO has become a critical function for many marketing organizations since if a firm's pages aren't near the top of search results, customers may never discover its site.

Google is a bit vague about the specifics of precisely how PageRank has been refined, in part because many have tried to game the system. In addition to in-bound links, Google's organic search results also consider some two hundred other signals, and the firm's search quality team is relentlessly analyzing user behavior for clues on how to tweak the system to improve accuracy (Levy, 2010). The less scrupulous have tried creating a series of bogus Web sites, all linking back to the pages they're trying to promote (this is called **link fraud,** and Google actively works to uncover and shut down such efforts). We do know that links from some Web sites carry more weight than others. For example, links from Web sites that Google deems as "influential," and links from most ".edu" Web sites, have greater weight in PageRank calculations than links from run-of-the-mill ".com" sites.

Figure 14.5

14.3 UNDERSTANDING THE RISE IN ONLINE AD SPENDING

For several years, Internet advertising has been the only major media ad category to show significant growth. There are three factors driving online ad growth trends: (1) increased user time online, (2) improved measurement and accountability, and (3) targeting.

American teenagers (as well as the average British, Australian, and New Zealander Web surfer) now spend more time on the Internet than watching television[1] (Hendry,

2008)[2]. They're reading fewer print publications, and radio listening among the iPod generation is down 30 percent (Tobias, 2009). So advertisers are simply following the market. Online channels also provide advertisers with a way to reach consumers at work—something that was previously much more difficult to do.

Many advertisers have also been frustrated by how difficult it's been to gauge the effectiveness of traditional ad channels such as TV, print, and radio. This frustration is reflected in the old industry saying, "I know that half of my advertising is working—I just don't know which half." Well, with the Internet, now you know. While measurement technologies aren't perfect, advertisers can now count ad **impressions** (the number of times an ad appears on a Web site), whether a user clicks on an ad, and the product purchases or other Web site activity that comes from those clicks[3]. And as we'll see, many online ad payment schemes are directly linked to ad performance.

Various technologies and techniques also make it easier for firms to target users based on how likely a person is to respond to an ad. In theory a firm can use targeting to spend marketing dollars only on those users deemed to be its best prospects. Let's look at a few of these approaches in action.

14.4 ONLINE SEARCH MARKETING

The practice of running and optimizing search engine ad campaigns is referred to as **search engine marketing (SEM)** (Elliott, 2006). SEM is a hot topic in an increasingly influential field, so it's worth spending some time learning how search advertising works on the Internet's largest search engine.

Roughly two-thirds of Google's revenues come from ads served on its own sites, and the vast majority of this revenue comes from search engine ads[1]. During Google's early years, the firm actually resisted making money through ads. In fact, while at Stanford, Brin and Page even coauthored a paper titled "The Evils of Advertising" (Vise, 2008). But when Yahoo! and others balked at buying Google's search technology (offered for as little as

$500,000), Google needed to explore additional revenue streams. It wasn't until two years after incorporation that Google ran ads alongside organic search results. That first ad, one for "Live Mail Order Lobsters," appeared just minutes after the firm posted a link reading "See Your Ad Here") (Levy, 2009).>

Google has only recently begun incorporating video and image ads into search. For the most part, the ads you'll see to the right (and sometimes top) of Google's organic search results appear as **keyword advertising**, meaning they're targeted based on a user's query. Advertisers bid on the keywords and phrases that they'd like to use to trigger the display of their ad. Linking ads to search was a brilliant move, since the user's search term indicates an overt interest in a given topic. Want to sell hotel stays in Tahiti? Link your ads to the search term "Tahiti Vacation."

Not only are search ads highly targeted, advertisers only pay for results. Text ads appearing on Google search pages are billed on a **pay-per-click (PPC)** basis, meaning that advertisers don't spend a penny unless someone actually clicks on their ad. Note that the term pay-per-click is sometimes used interchangeably with the term **cost-per-click (CPC)**.

If an advertiser wants to display an ad on Google search, they can set up a Google AdWords advertising account in minutes, specifying just a single ad, or multiple ad campaigns that trigger different ads for different keywords. Advertisers also specify what they're willing to pay each time an ad is clicked, how much their overall ad budget is, and they can control additional parameters, such as the timing and duration of an ad campaign.

If no one clicks on an ad, Google doesn't make money, advertisers don't attract customers, and searchers aren't seeing ads they're interested in. So in order to create a winning scenario for everyone, Google has developed a precise ad ranking formula that rewards top performing ads by considering two metrics: the maximum CPC that an advertiser is willing to pay, and the advertisement's quality score—a broad measure of ad performance. Create high quality ads and your advertisements might appear ahead of competition, even if your competitors bid more than you. But if ads perform poorly they'll fall in rankings or even drop from display consideration.

Below is the formula used by Google to determine the rank order of sponsored links appearing on search results pages.

Ad Rank = Maximum CPC × Quality Score

One factor that goes into determining an ad's quality score is the **click-through rate (CTR)** for the ad, the number of users who clicked an ad divided by the number of times the ad was delivered (the impressions). The CTR measures the percentage of people who clicked on an ad to arrive at a destination-site. Also included in a quality score are the overall history of click performance for the keywords linked to the ad, the relevance of an ad's text to the user's query, and Google's automated assessment of the user experience on the **landing page**—the Web site displayed when a user clicks on the ad. Ads that don't get many clicks, ad descriptions that have nothing to do with query terms, and ads that direct users to generic pages that load slowly or aren't strongly related to the keywords and descriptions used in an ad, will all lower an ad's chance of being displayed[2].

When an ad is clicked, advertisers don't actually pay their maximum CPC; Google discounts ads to just one cent more than the minimum necessary to maintain an ad's position on the page. So if you bid one dollar per click, but the ad ranked below you bids ninety cents, you'll pay just ninety-one cents if the ad is clicked. Discounting was a brilliant move. No one wants to get caught excessively overbidding rivals, so discounting helps reduce the possibility of this so-called bidder's remorse. And with this risk minimized, the system actually encouraged higher bids (Levy, 2009)!

Ad ranking and cost-per-click calculations take place as part of an automated auction that occurs *every time* a user conducts a search. Advertisers get a running total of ad performance statistics so that they can monitor the return on their investment and tweak promotional efforts for better results. And this whole system is automated for self- service—all it takes is a credit card, an ad idea, and you're ready to go.

How Much Do Advertisers Pay per Click?

Google rakes in billions on what amounts to pocket change earned one click at a time. Most clicks bring in between thirty cents and one dollar. However, costs can vary widely depending on industry, current competition, and perceived customer value. Table 14.1 "10 Most Expensive Industries for Keyword Ads" shows some of the highest reported CPC rates. But remember, any values fluctuate in real time based on auction participants.

Table 14.1 10 Most Expensive Industries for Keyword Ads

Business/Industry	Keywords in the Top 25	Avg. CPC
Structured Settlements	2	$51.97
Secured Loans	2	$50.67
Buying Endowments	1	$50.35
Mesothelioma Lawyers	5	$50.30
DUI Lawyers 4		$49.78
Conference Call Companies	1	$49.64
Car Insurance Quotes	3	$49.61
Student Loan Consolidation	3	$49.44
Data Recovery	2	$49.43
Remortgages	2	$49.42

Source: X. Becket, "10 Businesses with the Highest Cost Per Click," WebPageFX Weekly, February 20, 2009.

Since rates are based on auctions, top rates reflect what the market is willing to bear. As an example, law firms, which bring in big bucks from legal fees, decisions, and settlement payments often justify higher customer acquisition costs. And firms that see results will keep spending. Los Angeles–based Chase Law Group has said that it brings in roughly 60 percent of its clients through Internet advertising (Mann, 2006).

IP Addresses and Geotargeting

Geotargeting occurs when computer systems identify a user's physical location (sometimes called the *geolocation*) for the purpose of delivering tailored ads or other content. On Google AdWords, for example, advertisers can specify that their ads only appear for Web surfers located in a particular country, state, metropolitan region, or a given distance around a precise locale. They can even draw a custom ad-targeting region on a map and tell Google to only show ads to users detected inside that space.

Ads in Google Search are geotargeted based on **IP address**. Every device connected to the Internet has a unique IP address assigned by the organization connecting the device to the network. Normally you don't see your IP address (a set of four numbers, from 0 to 255, separated by periods; e.g., 136.167.2.220). But the range of IP addresses "owned" by major organizations and Internet service providers (ISPs) is public knowledge. In many cases it's possible to make an accurate guess as to where a computer, laptop, or mobile phone is located simply by cross-referencing a device's current IP address with this public list.

For example, it's known that all devices connected to the Boston College network contain IP addresses starting with the numbers 136.167. If a search engine detects a query coming from an IP address that begins with those two numbers, it can be fairly certain that the person using that device is in the greater Boston area.

Figure 14.6

IP addresses will change depending on how and where you connect to the Internet. Connect your laptop to a hotel's Wi-Fi when visiting a new city, and you're likely to see ads specific to that location. That's because your Internet service provider has changed, and the firm serving your ads has detected that you are using an IP address known to be associated with your new location.

Geotargeting via IP address is fairly accurate, but it's not perfect. For example, some Internet service providers may provide imprecise or inaccurate information on the location of their networks. Others might be so vague that it's difficult to make a best guess at the geography behind a set of numbers (values assigned by a multinational corporation with many locations, for example). And there are other ways locations are hidden, such as when Internet users connect to **proxy servers**, third-party computers that pass traffic to and from a specific address without revealing the address of the connected users.

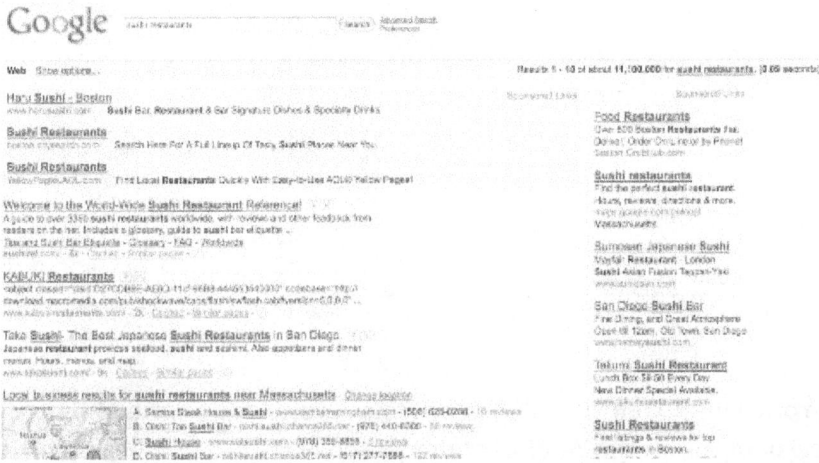

Figure 14.7

In this geotargeting example, the same search term is used at roughly the same time on separate computers located in Silicon Valley area (top) and Boston (bottom). Note how geotargeting impacts results.

14.5 BEYOND SEARCH DISTRIBUTION THROUGH AD NETWORKS

Google runs ads not just in search, but also across a host of Google-owned sites like Gmail, Google News, and Blogger. It will even tailor ads for its map products and for mobile devices. But about 30 percent of Google's revenues come from running ads on Web sites that the firm doesn't even own[1].

Next time you're surfing online, look around the different Web sites that you visit and see how many sport boxes labeled "Ads by Google." Those Web sites are participating in Google's AdSense ad network, which means they're running ads for Google in exchange for a cut of the take. Participants range from small-time bloggers to some of the world's most highly trafficked sites. Google lines up the advertisers, provides the targeting technology, serves the ads, and handles advertiser payment collection. To participate, content providers just sign up online, put a bit of Google-supplied HTML code on their pages, and wait for Google to send them cash (Web sites typically get about seventy to eighty cents for every AdSense dollar that Google collects) (Tedeschi, 2006).

Google originally developed AdSense to target ads based on keywords automatically detected inside the content of a Web site. A blog post on your favorite sports team, for example, might be accompanied by ads from ticket sellers or sports memorabilia vendors. AdSense and similar online ad networks provide advertisers with access to the long tail of niche Web sites by offering both increased opportunities for ad exposure as well as more-refined targeting opportunities.

Figure 14.8

New York Times Web site. The page runs several ads provided by different ad networks. For example, the WebEx banner ad above the article's headline was served by AOL-owned Platform-A/Tacoda. The "Ads by Google" box appeared at the end of the article. Note how the Google ads are related to the content of the *Times* article." style="max-width: 497px;"/>

The images above show advertising embedded around a story on the *New York Times* Web site. The page runs several ads provided by different ad networks. For example, the WebEx banner ad above the article's headline was served by AOL-owned Platform-A/ Tacoda. The "Ads by Google" box appeared at the end of the article. Note how the Google ads are related to the content of the *Times* article.

Running ads on your Web site is by no means a guaranteed path to profits. The Internet graveyard is full of firms that thought they'd be able to sustain their businesses on ads alone. But for many Web sites, ad networks can be like oxygen, sustaining them with revenue opportunities they'd never be able to achieve on their own.

For example, AdSense provided early revenue for the popular social news site Digg, as well as the multimillion- dollar TechCrunch media empire. It supports Disaboom, a site run by physician and quadriplegic Dr. Glen House. And it continues to be the primary revenue generator for AskTheBuilder.com. That site's founder, former builder Tim Carter, had been writing a handyman's column syndicated to some thirty newspapers. The newspaper columns didn't bring in enough to pay the bills, but with AdSense he hit pay dirt, pulling in over $350,000 in ad revenue in just his first year (Rothenberg, 2008)!

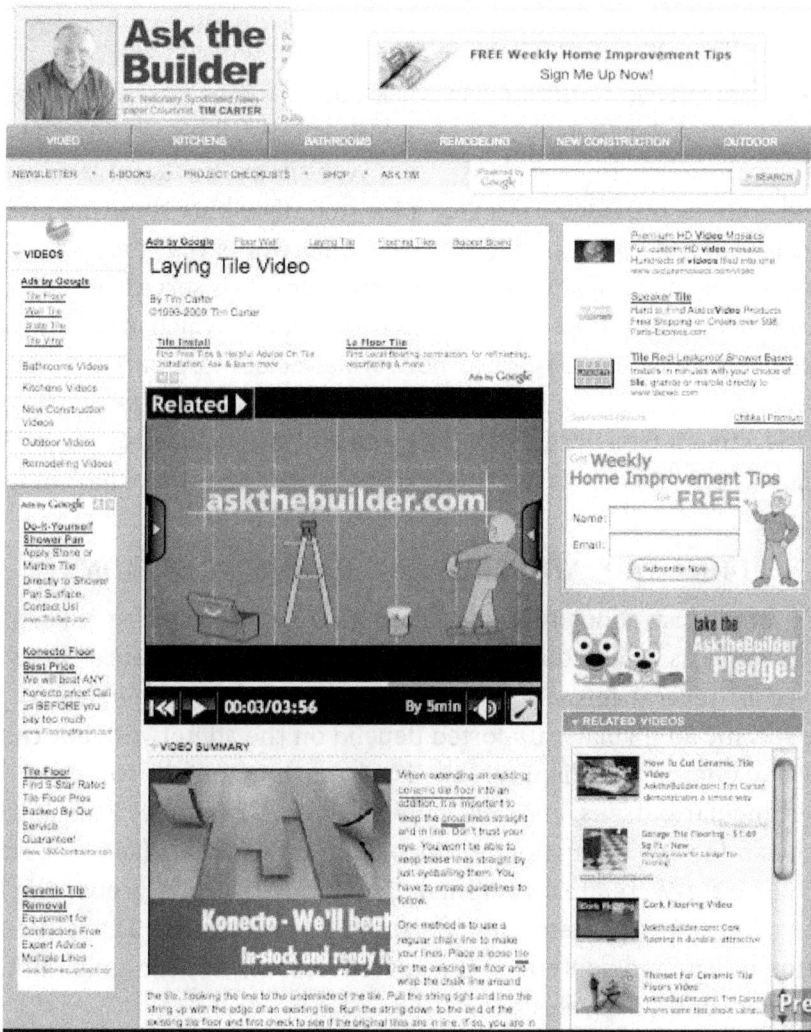

Figure 14.9 Tim Carter's Ask the Builder Web site runs ads from Google and other ad networks. Note different ad formats surrounding the content. Video ads are also integrated into many of the site's video tutorials.

Google launched AdSense in 2003, but Google is by no means the only company to run an ad network, nor was it the first to come up with the idea. Rivals include the Yahoo! Publisher Network, Microsoft's adCenter, and AOL's Platform-A. Others, like Quigo, don't even have a consumer Web site yet manage to consolidate enough advertisers to attract high-traffic content providers such as ESPN, *Forbes*, Fox, and *USA Today*. Advertisers also aren't limited to choosing just one ad network. In fact, many content provider Web sites will serve ads from several ad networks (as well as exclusive space sold by their own sales force), oftentimes mixing several different offerings on the same page.

Network ads and the competitive edge

While advertisers can use multiple ad networks, there are several key strategic factors driving the industry. For Google, its ad network is a distribution play. The ability to reach more potential customers across more Web sites attracts more advertisers to Google. And content providers (the Web sites that distribute these ads) want there to be as many advertisers as possible in the ad networks that they join, since this should increase the price of advertising, the number of ads served, and the accuracy of user targeting. If advertisers attract content providers, which in turn attract more advertisers, then we've just described network effects! More participants bringing in more revenue also help the firm benefit from scale economies—offering a better return on investment from its ad technology and infrastructure. No wonder Google's been on such a tear—the firm's loaded with assets for competitive advantage!

14.6 MORE AD TYPES AND PAYMENT OPTIONS

Online ads aren't just about text ads billed in CPC. Ads running through Google AdSense, through its DoubleClick subsidiary, or on most competitor networks can be displayed in several formats and media types, and can be billed in different ways. The specific ad formats supported depend on the ad network but can include the following: **image (or display) ads** (such as horizontally oriented banners, smaller rectangular buttons, and vertically oriented "skyscraper" ads); **rich media ads** (which can include animation or video); and **interstitials** (ads that run before a user arrives at a Web site's contents). The industry trade group, the **Internet Advertising Bureau (IAB)** sets common standards for display ads so that a single creative (the design and content of the advertisement) can run unmodified across multiple ad networks and Web sites[1].

And there are lots of other ways ads are sold besides cost-per-click. Most graphical display ads are sold according to the number of times the ad appears (the *impression*). Ad rates are quoted in **CPM**, meaning cost per thousand impressions (the M representing the roman numerical for one thousand). Display ads sold on a CPM basis are often used as part of branding campaigns targeted more at creating awareness than generating click-throughs. Such techniques often work best for promoting products like soft drinks, toothpaste, or movies.

Cost-per-action (CPA) ads pay whenever a user clicks through and performs a specified action such as signing up for a service, requesting material, or making a purchase. **Affiliate programs** are a form of cost-per-action, where vendors share a percentage of revenue with Web sites that direct purchasing customers to their online storefronts. Amazon runs the world's largest affiliate program, and referring sites can earn 4 percent to 15 percent of sales generated from these click-throughs. Purists might not consider affiliate programs as advertising (rather than text or banner ads, Amazon's affiliates offer links and product descriptions that point back to Amazon's Web site), but these programs can be important tools in a firm's promotional arsenal.

And rather than buying targeted ads, a firm might sometimes opt to become an exclusive advertiser on a site. For example, a firm could buy access to all ads served on a site's main page; it could secure exclusive access to a region of the page (such as the topmost banner ad); or it may pay to sponsor a particular portion or activity on a Web site (say a parenting forum, or a "click-to-print" button). Such deals can be billed based on a flat rate, CPM, CPC, or any combination of metrics.

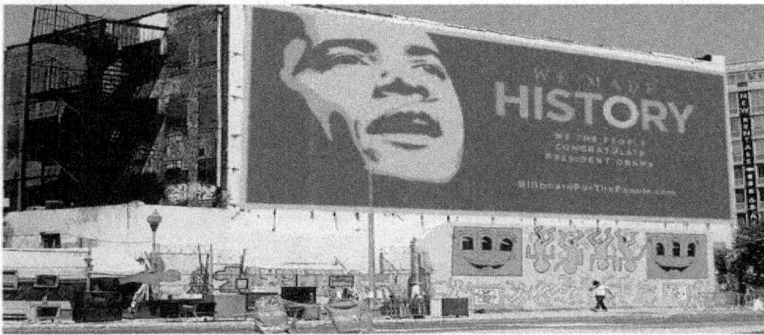

Figure 14.10

14.7 TARGETING BY BEHAVIOUR AND CUSTOMER PROFILING

Advertisers are willing to pay more for ads that have a greater chance of reaching their target audience, and online firms have a number of targeting tools at their disposal. Much of this targeting occurs whenever you visit a Web site, where a behind-the-scenes software dialogue takes place between Web browser and Web server that can reveal a number of pieces of information, including IP address, the type of browser used, the computer type, its operating system, and unique identifiers, called **cookies**.

And remember, *any* server that serves you content can leverage these profiling technologies. You might be profiled not just by the Web site that you're visiting (e.g., nytimes.com), but also by any ad networks that serve ads on that site (e.g., Platform-A, DoubleClick, Google AdSense, Microsoft adCenter).

IP addresses are leveraged extensively in customer profiling. An IP address not only helps with geolocation, it can also indicate a browser's employer or university, which can be further matched with information such as firm size or industry. IBM has used IP targeting to tailor its college recruiting banner ads to specific schools, for example, "There Is Life After Boston College, Click Here to See Why." That campaign garnered click-through rates ranging from 5.0 to 30 percent (Moss, 1999) compared to average rates that are currently well below 1 percent for untargeted banner ads. DoubleClick once even served a banner that included a personal message for an executive at then-client Modem Media. The ad, reading "Congratulations on the twins, John Nardone," was served across hundreds of sites, but was only visible from computers on the Modem Media corporate network (Moss, 1999).

The ability to identify a surfer's computer, browser, or operating system can also be used to target tech ads. For example, Google might pitch its Chrome browser to users detected running Internet Explorer, Firefox, or Safari; while Apple could target those "I'm a Mac" ads just to Windows users.

But perhaps the greatest degree of personalization and targeting comes from cookies. Visit a Web site for the first time, and in most cases, a behind-the-scenes dialogue takes place that goes something like this:

Server: *Have I seen you before?*

Browser: *No.*

Server: *Then take this unique string of numbers and letters (called a cookie). I'll use it to recognize you from now on.*

The cookie is just a line of identifying text assigned and retrieved by a given Web server and stored on your computer by your browser. Upon accepting this cookie your browser has been tagged, like an animal. As you surf around the firm's Web site, that cookie can be used to build a profile associated with your activities. If you're on a portal like Yahoo! you might type in your zip code, enter stocks that you'd like to track, and identify the sports teams you'd like to see scores for. The next time you return to the Web site, your browser responds to the server's *"Have I see you before?"* question with the equivalent of *"Yes, you know me;,"* and it presents the cookie that the site gave you earlier. The site can then match this cookie against your browsing profile, showing you the weather, stock quotes, sports scores, and other info that it thinks you're interested in.

Cookies are used for lots of purposes. Retail Web sites like Amazon use cookies to pay attention to what you've shopped for and bought, tailoring Web sites to display products that the firm suspects you'll be most interested in. Sites also use cookies to keep track of what you put in an online "shopping cart," so if you quit browsing before making a purchase, these items will reappear the next time you visit. And many Web sites also use cookies as part of a "remember me" feature, storing user IDs and passwords. Beware this last one! If you check the "remember me" box on a public

Web browser, the next person who uses that browser is potentially using *your* cookie, and can log in as you!

An organization can't read cookies that it did not give you. So businessweek.com can't tell if you've also got cookies from forbes.com. But you can see all of the cookies in your browser. Take a look and you'll almost certainly see cookies from dozens of Web sites that you've never visited before. These are **third-party cookies** (sometimes called *tracking cookies*), and they are usually served by ad networks or other customer profiling firms.

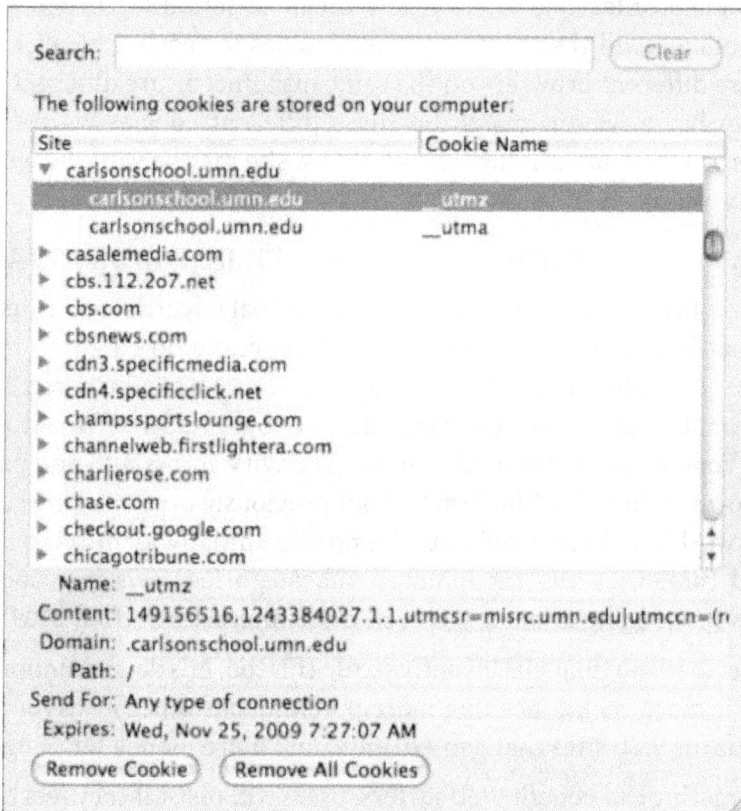

Figure 14.11

The Preferences setting in most Web browsers allows you to see its cookies. This browser has received cookies from several ad networks, media sites, and the University of Minnesota Carlson School of Management.

By serving and tracking cookies in ads shown across partner sites, ad networks can build detailed browsing profiles that include sites visited, specific pages viewed, duration of visit, and the types of ads you've seen and responded to. And that surfing might give an advertising network a better guess at demographics like gender, age, marital status, and more. Visit a new parent site and expect to see diaper ads in the future, even when you're surfing for news or sports scores!

While the Internet offers targeting technologies that go way beyond traditional television, print, and radio offerings, none of these techniques is perfect. Since users are regularly assigned different IP addresses as they connect and disconnect from various physical and Wi-Fi networks, IP targeting can't reliably identify individual users. Cookies also have their weaknesses. They're assigned by browsers and associated with a log-in account profile on that computer. That means that if several people use the same browser on the same computer without logging on to that machine as separate users, then all their Web surfing activity may be mixed into the same cookie profile. (One solution is to create different log-in accounts on that computer. Your PC will then keep separate cookies for each account.) Some users might also use different browsers on the same machine, or use different computers. Unless a firm has a way to match up these different cookies with a single user account or other user- identifying information, a site may be working with multiple, incomplete profiles.

14.8 WHAT DO YOU MEAN BY PROFILING AND PRIVACY?

While AdSense has been wildly successful, contextual advertising has its limits. For example, what kind of useful targeting can firms really do based on the text of a news item on North Korean nuclear testing (Singel, 2009)? So in March 2009, Google announced what it calls "interest-based ads." Google AdSense would now issue a third- party cookie and would track browsing activity across AdSense partner sites, and Google-owned YouTube (the firm had not previously used tracking cookies on its AdSense network). AdSense would build a profile, initially identifying users within thirty broad categories and six hundred subcategories. Says one Google project manager, "We're looking to make ads even more interesting" (Hof, 2009).

Of course, there's a financial incentive to do this too. Ads deemed more interesting should garner more clicks, meaning more potential customer leads for advertisers, more revenue for Web sites that run AdSense, and more money for Google.

But while targeting can benefit Web surfers, users will resist if they feel that they are being mistreated, exploited, or put at risk. Negative backlash might also result in a change in legislation. The U.S. Federal Trade Commission has already called for more transparency and user control in online advertising and for requesting user consent (**opt-in**) when collecting sensitive data (Singel, 2009). Mishandled user privacy could curtail targeting opportunities, limiting growth across the online advertising field. And with less ad support, many of the Internet's free services could suffer.

Google's roll-out of interest-based ads shows the firm's sensitivity to these issues. First, while major rivals have all linked query history to ad targeting, Google steadfastly refuses to do this. Other sites often link registration data (including user-submitted demographics such as gender and age) with tracking cookies, but Google avoids this practice as well.

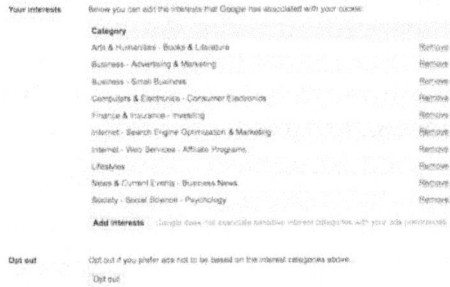

Figure 14.12

Here's an example of one user's interests, as tracked by Google's "Interest-based Ads" and displayed in the firm's "Ad Preferences Manager."

Google has also placed significant control in the hands of users, with options at program launch that were notably more robust than those of its competitors (Hansell, 2009). Each interest-based ad is accompanied by an "Ads by Google" link that will bring users to a page describing Google advertising and which provides access to the company's "Ads Preferences Manager." This tool allows surfers to see any of the hundreds of potential categorizations that Google has assigned to that browser's tracking cookie. Users can remove categorizations, and even add interests if they want to improve ad targeting. Some topics are too sensitive to track, and the technology avoids profiling race, religion, sexual orientation, health, political or trade union affiliation, and certain financial categories (Mithcell, 2009).

Google also allows users to install a cookie that opts them out of interest-based tracking. And since browser cookies can expire or be deleted, the firm has gone a step further, offering a browser **plug-in** that will remain permanent, even if a user's **opt-out** cookie is purged.

14.9 FRAUD, AD NETWORKS, AND SEARCH ENGINES

There's a lot of money to be made online, and this has drawn the attention of criminals and the nefarious. Online fraudsters may attempt to steal from advertisers, harm rivals, or otherwise dishonestly game the system. But bad guys beware—such attempts violate terms-of-service agreements and may lead to prosecution and jail time.

Studying ad-related fraud helps marketers, managers, and technologists understand potential vulnerabilities, as well as the methods used to combat them. This process also builds tech-centric critical thinking, valuation, and risk assessment skills.

Some of the more common types of fraud that are attempted in online advertising include the following:

- *Enriching **click fraud**—when site operators generate bogus ad clicks to earn PPC income.

- *Enriching impression fraud*—when site operators generate false page views (and hence ad impressions) in order to boost their site's CPM earnings.

- *Depleting click fraud*—clicking a rival's ads to exhaust their PPC advertising budget.

- *Depleting impression fraud*—generating bogus impressions to exhaust a rival's CPM ad budget.

- *Rank-based impression fraud*—on-sites where ad rank is based on click performance, fraudsters repeatedly search keywords linked to rival ads or access pages where rival ads appear. The goal is to generate impressions without clicks. This process lowers the performance rank (quality score) of a rival's ads, possibly dropping ads from rank results, and allowing fraudsters to subsequently bid less for the advertising slots previously occupied by rivals.

- *Disbarring fraud*—attempting to frame a rival by generating bogus clicks or impressions that appear to be associated with the rival, in hopes that this rival will be banned from an ad network or punished in search engine listings.

- *Link fraud (also known as spamdexing or link farming)*—creating a series of bogus Web sites, all linking back to a page, in hopes of increasing that page's results in organic search.

- *Keyword stuffing*—packing a Web site with unrelated keywords (sometimes hidden in fonts that are the same color as a Web site's background) in hopes of either luring users who wouldn't normally visit a Web site, or attracting higher-value contextual ads.

Disturbing stuff, but firms are after the bad guys and they've put their best geeks on the case. Widespread fraud would tank advertiser ROI and crater the online advertising market, so Google and rivals are diligently working to uncover and prosecute the crooks.

Busting the Bad Guys

On the surface, enriching click fraud seems the easiest to exploit. Just set up a Web site, run PPC ads on the page, and click like crazy. Each click should ring the ad network cash register, and a portion of those funds will be passed on to the perpetrating site owner—*ka ching!* But remember, each visitor is identified by an IP address, so lots of clicks from a single IP make the bad guys easy to spot.

So organized crime tried to raise the bar, running so-called **click farms** to spread fraud across dozens of IP addresses. *The Times of India* uncovered one such effort where Indian housewives were receiving up to twenty- five cents for each ad click made on fraudster-run Web sites (Vidyasagar, 2004). But an unusually large number of clicks from Indian IP addresses foiled these schemes as well.

Fraudsters then moved on to use **zombie networks**—hordes of surreptitiously infiltrated computers, linked and controlled by rogue software (Mann, 2006). To create zombie networks (sometimes called *bot nets*), hackers exploit security holes, spread viruses, or use so-called phishing techniques to trick users into installing software that will lie dormant, awaiting commands from a central location. The controlling machine then sends out tasks for each zombie, instructing them to visit Web sites and click on ads in a way that mimics real traffic. Zombie bot nets can be massive. Dutch authorities once took down a gang that controlled some 1.5 million machines (Sanders, 2007; Daswani & Stoppleman, 2007).

Scary, but this is where scale, expertise, and experience come in. The more activity an ad network can monitor, the greater the chance that it can uncover patterns that are anomalous. Higher click-through rates than comparable sites? Caught. Too many visits to a new or obscure site? Caught. Clicks that don't fit standard surfing patterns for geography, time, and day? Caught.

Sometimes the goal isn't theft, but sabotage. Google's Ad Traffic Quality Team backtracked through unusual patterns to uncover a protest effort targeted at Japanese credit card firms. Ad clicks were eventually traced to an incendiary blogger who incited readers to search for the Japanese word *kiyashinku* (meaning cashing credit, or credit cards), and to click the credit card firm ads that show up, depleting firm search marketing budgets. Sneaky, but uncovered and shut down, without harm to the advertisers (Jakobsson & Ramzan, 2008).

Search firm and ad network software can use data patterns and other signals to ferret out most other types of fraud, too, including rank-based impression fraud, spamdexing, and keyword stuffing. While many have tried to up the stakes with increasingly sophisticated attacks, large ad networks have worked to match them, increasing their anomaly detection capabilities across all types of fraud (Jakobsson & Ramzan, 2008). Here we see another scale and data-based advantage for Google. Since the firm serves more search results and advertisements than its rivals do, it has vastly more information on online activity. And if it knows more about what's happening online than any other firm, it's likely to be first to shut down anyone who tries to take advantage of the system.

14.10 THE BATTLE STARTS TO TAKE SHAPE

Google has been growing like gangbusters, but the firm's twin engines of revenue growth—ads served on search and through its ad networks—will inevitably mature. And it will likely be difficult for Google to find new growth markets that are as lucrative as these. Emerging advertising outlets such as social networks and mobile have lower click-through rates than conventional advertising, suggesting that Google will have to work harder for less money.

For a look at what can happen when maturity hits, check out Microsoft. The House that Gates Built is more profitable than Google, and continues to dominate the incredibly lucrative markets served by Windows and Office. But these markets haven't grown much for over a decade. In industrialized nations, most Windows and Office purchases come not from growth, but when existing users upgrade or buy new machines. And without substantial year-on-year growth, the stock price doesn't move.

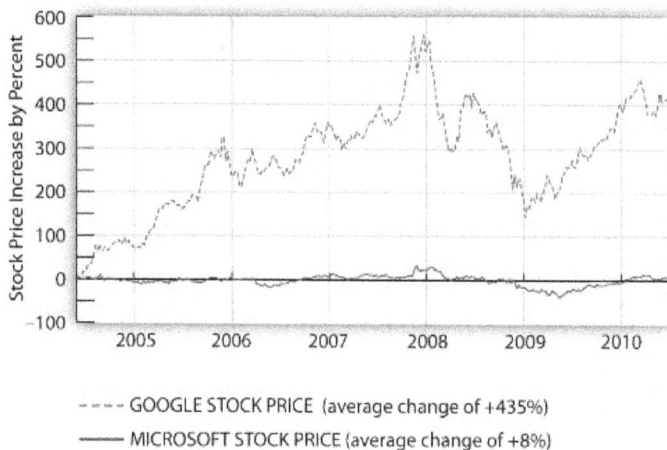

---- GOOGLE STOCK PRICE (average change of +435%)

——— MICROSOFT STOCK PRICE (average change of +8%)

Figure 14.13 A Comparison of Roughly Five Years of Stock Price Change—Google (GOOG) versus Microsoft (MSFT)

For big firms like Microsoft and Google, pushing stock price north requires not just new markets, but *billion- dollar* ones. Adding even $100 million in new revenues doesn't do much for firms bringing in $24 billion and $58 billion a year, respectively. That's why you see Microsoft swinging for the fences, investing in the uncertain, but potentially gargantuan markets of video games, mobile phone software, cloud computing (see Chapter 10 "Software in Flux: Partly Cloudy and Sometimes Free"), music and video, and of course, search and everything else that fuels online ad revenue.

Both Google and Microsoft are on a collision course. But there's also an impressive roster of additional firms circling this space, each with the potential to be competitors, collaborators, merger partners, or all of the above. While wounded and shrinking, Yahoo! is still a powerhouse, ranking ahead of Google in some overall traffic statistics. Google's competition with Apple in the mobile phone business prompted Google CEO Eric Schmidt to resign from Apple's board of directors. Meanwhile, Google's three-quarters-of-a-billion-dollar purchase of the leading mobile advertiser AdMob was quickly followed by Apple snapping up number two mobile ad firm Quattro Wireless for $275 million. Add in eBay, Facebook, Twitter, Amazon, Salesforce.com, Netflix, the video game industry, telecom and mobile carriers, cable firms, and the major media companies, and the next few years have the makings of a big, brutal fight.

Strategic Issues

Google's scale advantages in search and its network effects advantages in advertising were outlined earlier. The firm also leads in search/ad experience and expertise and continues to offer a network reach that's unmatched. But the strength of Google's other competitive resources is less clear.

Within Google's ad network, there are *switching costs* for advertisers and for content providers. Google partners have set up accounts and are familiar with the firm's tools and analytics. Content providers would also need to modify Web sites to replace AdSense or DoubleClick ads with rivals. But choosing Google doesn't cut out the competition. Many advertisers and content providers participate in multiple ad networks, making it easier to shift business from one firm to another. That likely means that Google will have to retain its partners by offering superior value.

Another vulnerability may exist with search consumers. While Google's brand is strong, switching costs for search users are incredibly low. Move from Google.com to Bing.com and you actually save two letters of typing!

Still, there are no signs that Google's search leadership is in jeopardy. So far users have been creatures of habit, returning to Google despite heavy marketing by rivals. And in Google's first decade, no rival has offered technology compelling enough to woo away the googling masses—the firm's share has only increased. Defeating Google with some sort of technical advantage will be difficult, since Web-based innovation can often be quickly imitated. Google now rolls out over 550 tweaks to its search algorithm annually, with many features mimicking or outdoing innovations from rivals (Levy, 2010).

The Google Toolbar helps reinforce search habits among those who have it installed, and Google has paid the Mozilla foundation (the folks behind the Firefox browser) upwards of $66 million a year to serve as its default search option for the open source browser (Shankland, 2008). But Google's track record in expanding reach through distribution deals is mixed. The firm spent nearly $1 billion to have MySpace run AdSense ads, but Google has publicly stated that social network advertising has not been as lucrative as it had hoped (see Chapter 8 "Facebook: Building a Business from the Social Graph"). The firm has also spent nearly $1 billion to have Dell preinstall its computers with the Google browser toolbar and Google desktop search products. But in 2009, Microsoft inked deals that displaced Google on Dell machines, and it also edged Google out in a five-year search contract with Verizon Wireless (Wingfield, 2009).

More advertisements, locations, and formats

Google has been a champion of increased Internet access. But altruism aside, more Net access also means a greater likelihood of ad revenue.

Google's effort to catalyze Internet use worldwide comes through on multiple fronts. In the United States, Google has supported (with varying degrees of success) efforts to offer free Wi-Fi in San Francisco and Mountain View. In early 2010, Google announced it would offer high-speed, fiber-optic Net access to homes in select U.S. cities. The experimental network would offer competitively priced Internet access of up to 1GB per second—that's a speed some one hundred times faster than many Americans have access to today. The networks are meant to be open to other service providers and Google hopes to learn and share insights on how to build high-speed networks more efficiently. Google will also be watching to see how access to ultrahigh-speed networks impacts user behavior and fuels innovation. Globally, Google is also a major backer (along with Liberty Global and HSBC) of the O3b satellite network. O3b stands for "the other three billion" of the world's population who currently lack Internet access. O3b plans to have sixteen satellites circling the globe, blanketing underserved regions with **low latency** (low delay), high-speed Internet access (Malik, 2008). With Moore's Law dropping computing costs as world income levels rise, Google hopes to empower the currently disenfranchised masses to start surfing. Good for global economies, good for living standards, and good for Google.

Another way Google can lower the cost of surfing is by giving mobile phone software away for free. That's the thinking behind the firm's Android offering. With Android, Google provides mobile phone vendors with a Linux-based operating system, supporting tools, standards, and an application marketplace akin to Apple's AppStore. Android itself isn't ad-supported—there aren't Google ads embedded in the OS. But the hope is that if handset manufacturers don't have to write their own software, the cost of wireless mobile devices will go down. And cheaper devices mean that more users will have access to the mobile Internet, adding more ad-serving opportunities for Google and its partner sites.

Developers are now leveraging tailored versions of Android on a wide range of devices, including e-book readers, tablets, televisions, set-top boxes, and automobiles. Google has dabbled in selling ads for television (as well as radio and print), and there may be considerable potential in bringing variants of ad targeting technology, search, and a host of other services across these devices. In 2009, Google also announced the Chrome operating system—a direct strike at challenge to Windows in the Netbook PC market. Powered by a combination of open source Linux and Google's open source Chrome browser, the Chrome OS is specifically designed to provide a lightweight, but consistent user interface for applications that otherwise live in the cloud, preferably residing on Google's server farms (see Chapter 10 "Software in Flux: Partly Cloudy and Sometimes Free").

Google has also successfully lobbied the U.S. government to force wireless telecom carriers to be more open, dismantling what are known in the industry as **walled gardens**. Before Google's lobbying efforts, mobile carriers could act as gatekeepers, screening out hardware providers and software services from their networks. Now, paying customers of carriers that operate over the recently allocated U.S. wireless spectrum will have access to a choice of hardware and less restrictive access to Web sites and services. And Google hopes this expands its ability to compete without obstruction.

YouTube

Then there's Internet video, with Google in the lead here too. It's tough to imagine any peer-produced video site displacing YouTube. Users go to YouTube because there's more content, while amateur content providers go there seeking more users (classic two-sided network effects). This critical advantage was the main reason why, in 2006, Google paid $1.65 billion for what was then just a twenty-month-old start-up.

That popularity comes at a price. Even with falling bandwidth and storage costs, at twenty hours of video uploaded to YouTube *every minute*, the cost to store and serve this content is cripplingly large (Nakashima, 2008). Credit Suisse estimates that in 2009, YouTube will bring in roughly $240 million in ad revenue, pitted against $711 million in operating expenses. That's a shortfall of more than $470 million. Analysts estimate that for YouTube to break even, it would need to achieve an ad CPM of $9.48 on each of the roughly seventy-five billion streams it'll serve up this year. A tough task. For comparison, Hulu (a site that specializes in offering ad-supported streams of television shows and movies) earns CPM rates of thirty dollars and shares about 70 percent of this with copyright holders. Most user-generated content sports CPM rates south of a buck (Wayne, 2009). Some differ with the Credit Suisse report—RampRate pegs the losses at $174 million. In fact, it may be in Google's interest to allow others to think of YouTube as more of a money pit than it really is. That perception might keep rivals away longer, allowing the firm to solidify its dominant position while getting the revenue model right. Even as a public company, Google can keep mum about YouTube specifics. Says the firm's CFO, "We know our cost position, but nobody else does[2]."

The explosion of video uploading is also adding to costs as more cell phones become Net-equipped video cameras. YouTube's mobile uploads were up 400 percent in just the first week following the launch of the video-capturing iPhone 3GS (Kincaid, 2009). Viewing will also skyrocket as mobile devices and television sets ship with YouTube access, adding to revenue potential. The firm is still experimenting with ad models—these include traditional banner and text ads, plus ads transparently layered across the bottom 20 percent of the screen, *preroll* commercials that appear before the selected video, and more. Google has both the money and time to invest in nurturing this market, and it continues to be hesitant in saturating the media with ads that may annoy users and constrain adoption.

Apps and Innovation

In 2007 the firm announced a tagline to sum up its intentions: "search, ads, and apps." Google is king of the first two, but this last item hasn't matured to the point where it impacts the firm's financials.

Experimentation and innovation are deeply ingrained in Google's tech-centric culture, and this has led to a flood of product offerings. Google released more than 360 products in 2008, and another 120 in Q1 2009 (Shiels, 2009). It's also cancelled several along the way, including Jaiku (which couldn't beat Twitter), Google Video (which was superseded by the YouTube acquisition), and a bunch more you've likely not heard of, like Dodgeball, Notebook, Catalog Search, and Mashup Editor (Needleman, 2009).

Google's "Apps" are mostly Web-based software-as-a-service offerings. Apps include an Office-style suite that sports a word processor, presentation tool, and spreadsheet, all served through a browser. While initially clunky, the products are constantly being refined. The spreadsheet product, for example, has been seeing new releases every two weeks, with features such as graphing and pivot tables inching it closer in capabilities to desktop alternatives (Girouard, 2009). And new browser standards, such as HTML 5, will make it even easier for what lives in the browser to mimic what you're currently using on your desktop, even allowing apps to be used offline when Net access isn't available. That'll be critical as long as Internet access is less reliable than your hard drive, but online collaboration is where these products can really excel (no pun intended). Most Google apps allow not only group viewing, but also collaborative editing, common storage, and version control. Google's collaboration push also includes its wiki-like Google Sites tool, and a new platform called Wave, billed as a sort of next-step evolving beyond e-mail and instant messaging.

Unknown is how much money Google will make off all of this. Consumers and small businesses have free access to these products, with usage for up to fifty users funded by in-app ads. But is there much of a market serving ads to people working on spreadsheets? Enterprises can gain additional, ad-free licenses for a fee. While users have been reluctant to give up Microsoft Office, many have individually migrated to Google's Web-based e-mail and calendar tools. Google's enterprise apps group will now do the same thing for organizations, acting as a sort of outsourcer by running e-mail, calendar, and other services for a firm; all while handling upgrades, spam screening, virus protection, backup, and other administrative burdens. Arizona State University, biotech giant Genentech, and auto parts firm Valeo are among the Google partners that have signed on to make the firm's app offerings available to thousands (Coughlin, 2007; Hardy, 2008; Claburn, 2009).

And of course, Microsoft won't let Google take this market without a fight. Office 10 was announced along with a simplified, free, ad-supported, Web-based, online options for Word, Excel, PowerPoint, and OneNote; and Microsoft can also migrate applications like e-mail and calendaring off corporate computers and onto Microsoft's server farms.

It's not until considered in its entirety that one gets a sense of what Google has the potential to achieve. It's possible that increasing numbers of users worldwide will adopt light, cheap netbooks and other devices powered by free Google software (Android, Google's Chrome browser and Chrome OS). Productivity apps, e- mail, calendaring, and collaboration tools will all exist in the cloud, accessible through any browser, with files stored on Google's servers in a way that minimizes hard drive needs. Google will entertain you, help you find the information you need, help you shop, handle payment (Google Checkout), and more. And the firms you engage online may increasingly turn to Google to replace their existing hardware and software infrastructure with corporate computing platforms like Google Apps Engine (see Chapter 10 "Software in Flux: Partly Cloudy and Sometimes Free"). All of this would be based on open standards, but switching costs, scale, and increasing returns from expertise across these efforts could yield enormous advantages.

Studying Google allowed us to learn about search and the infrastructure that powers this critical technology. We've studied the business of ads, covering search advertising, ad networks, and ad targeting in a way that blends strategic and technology issues. And we've covered the ethical, legal, growth, and competitive challenges that Google and its rivals face. Studying Google in this context should not only help you understand what's happening today, it should also help you develop critical thinking skills for assessing the opportunities and threats that will emerge across industries as technologies continue to evolve.

REFERENCES

Baker, L., "Google Now Controls 69% of Online Advertising Market," Search Engine Journal, March 31, 2008.

Casnocha, B., "Success on the Side," The American: The Journal of the American Enterprise Institute, April 24, 2009.

Levy, S., "The Secrets of Googlenomics," Wired, June 2009.

Li, C., "Why Google's One-Trick Pony Struggles to Learn New Tricks," Harvard Business Publishing, May 2009. Pontin, J., "But Who's Counting?" Technology Review, March/April 2009.

Rao, L., "Guess Which Brand Is Now Worth $100 Billion?" TechCrunch, April 30, 2009.

Sherman, C., "Report: Google Leads U.S. Search Advertising Market With 76% Market Share," Search Engine Land, January 20, 2009.

Weldon, D., "Google's Power Play," EnergyDigital, August 30, 2007.

Wolgemuth, L., "Forget the Recession, I Want a Better Chair," U.S. News and World Report, April 28, 2008.

Bruce, S., "Google Says User Data Aids Flu Detection," eHealthInsider, May 25, 2009. Carr, D. F., "How Google Works," Baseline, July 6, 2006.

Katz, R., "Tech Titans Building Boom," IEEE Spectrum 46, no. 2 (February 1, 2009). Levy, S., "Inside the Box," Wired, March 2010.

Liedtke, M., "Google Reigns as World's Most Powerful 10-Year-Old," Associated Press, September 5, 2008. Shankland, S., "Google Unlocks Once-Secret Server," CNET, April 1, 2009.

Wright, A., "Exploring a 'Deep Web' That Google Can't Grasp," New York Times, February 23, 2009.

Hendry, A., "Connected Aussies Spend More Time Online Than Watching TV," Computerworld Australia, May 21, 2008.

Tobias, M., "Newspapers under Siege," Philstar, May 18, 2009.

lliott, S., "More Agencies Investing in Marketing with a Click," New York Times, March 14, 2006. Levy, S., "The Secrets of Googlenomics," Wired, June 2009.

Mann, C., "How Click Fraud Could Swallow the Internet," Wired, January 2006. Olsen, S., "Google, Yahoo Bury the Legal Hatchet," CNET, August 9, 2004.

Vise, D., "Google's Decade," Technology Review, September 12, 2008.

Baker, L., "Google Now Controls 69% of Online Advertising Market," Search Engine Journal, March 31, 2008. Overholt, A., "Search for Tomorrow," Fast Company, December 19, 2007.

Rothenberg, R., "The Internet Runs on Ad Billions," BusinessWeek, April 10, 2008.

Tedeschi, B., "Google's Shadow Payroll Is Not Such a Secret Anymore," New York Times, January 16, 2006.

Moss, M., "These Web Sites Know Who You Are," ZDNet UK, October 13, 1999.

Broache, A., "Judge: Google Must Give Feds Limited Access to Records," CNET, March 17, 2006.

Gold, A., "Keep Your Buzz to Yourself: Google Misjudged Its Users' Right to Privacy," The Harvard Crimson, February 22, 2010.

Gross, G., "Lawmakers Ask for FTC Investigation of Google Buzz," PCWorld, March 29, 2010. Hansell, S., "A Guide to Google's New Privacy Controls," New York Times, March 12, 2009.

Helft, M., "BITS; Google Lets Users See a Bit of Selves" New York Times, November 9, 2009. Hof, R., "Behavioral Targeting: Google Pulls Out the Stops," BusinessWeek, March 11, 2009.

Kincaid, J., "Google Privacy Blunder Shares Your Docs without Permission," TechCrunch, March 7, 2009. Mitchell, R., "What Google Knows about You," Computerworld, May 11, 2009.

Sumagaysay, L., "Not Everyone Likes the (Google Street) View," Good Morning Silicon Valley, May 20, 2009. Singel, R., "Online Behavioral Targeting Targeted by Feds, Critics," Wired News, June 3, 2009.

Daswani N. and M. Stoppleman, "The Anatomy of Clickbot" (paper, Proceedings of the First Conference on First Workshop on Hot Topics in Understanding Botnets, Cambridge, MA, April 11–13, 2007).

Hamner, S., "Pay-per-Click Advertisers Combat Costly Fraud," New York Times, May 12, 2009.

Jakobsson M. and Z. Ramzan, Crimeware: Understanding New Attacks and Defenses (Cupertino, CA: Symantec Press, 2008).

Lafsky, M., "Google and Click Fraud: Behind the Numbers," New York Times, February 27, 2008. Mann, C., "How Click Fraud Could Swallow the Internet," Wired, January 2006.

Sanders, T., "Dutch Botnet Gang Facing Jail," IT News Australia, January 18, 2007. Vidyasagar, N., "India's Secret Army of Online Ad 'Clickers,'" Times of India, May 3, 2004.

Broach, A., "On Capitol Hill, Google and Microsoft Spar over DoubleClick," CNET, September 27, 2007.

Buskirk, E., "Antitrust Probe to Review Hiring Practices at Apple, Google, Yahoo: Report," Wired News, June 3, 2009.

Claburn, T., "Google's Cloud Evangelism Converts Enterprise Customers," InformationWeek, May 13, 2009. Coughlin, S., "Google's E-mail for Universities," BBC News, June 11, 2007.

Girouard, D., "Google Inc. Presentation" (Bank of America and Merrill Lynch 2009 Technology Conference, New York, June 4, 2009).

Hardy, Q., "Google Muscles Further into Business Software," Forbes, February 28, 2008.

Kawamoto D. and A. Broach, "EU Extends Review of Google-DoubleClick Merger," CNET, November 13, 2007. Kincaid, J., "YouTube Mobile Uploads Up 400% Since iPhone 3GS Launch," TechCrunch, June 25, 2009.

Levy, S., "Inside the Box," Wired, March 2010.

Lohr S. and M. Helft, "New Mood in Antitrust May Target Google," New York Times, May 18, 2009. Malik, O., "Google Invests in Satellite Broadband Startup," GigaOM, September 9, 2008.

Montalbano, E., "Forrester: Microsoft Office in No Danger from Competitors," InfoWorld, June 4, 2009. Nakashima, E., "YouTube Ordered to Release User Data," Washington Post, July 4, 2008.

Needleman, R., "Google Killing Jaiku, Dodgeball, Notebook, Other Projects," CNET, January 14, 2009. Shankland, S., "Thanks, Google: Mozilla Revenue Hits $75 Million," CNET, November 19, 2008.

Shiels, M., "Google Unveils 'Smarter Search,'" BBC News, May 13, 2009.

Vogelstein, F., "Why Is Obama's Top Antitrust Cop Gunning for Google?" Wired, July 20, 2009. Wayne, B., "YouTube Is Doomed," Silicon Alley Insider, April 9, 2009.

Wildstrom, S., "Google Book Search and the Dog in the Manger," BusinessWeek, April 18, 2009. Wingfield, N., "Microsoft Wins Key Search Deals," Wall Street Journal, January 8, 2009.

INDEX

A

Across 155

Adjacency 141

Adoption 82

Adversary 259

Amazon 24, 66, 117, 165, 188, 224, 277

Analysis 27, 209

Android 286

Attacks 252

B

Backbone 229

Bandwidth 236

Banner 142, 278

Billion 93, 134-135, 152, 241

Blogger 98

Blogging 98

Blu-ray 56, 85

Bollywood 47

Broadband 230, 234

Browser 277-279, 281, 288

Business 8, 10, 13, 19, 30, 42, 58, 66, 104, 130, 133, 153, 162, 197, 205-206, 212, 218-219

Buyout 217

C

Capital 70

Carroll 117

Channels 24, 54

Chrome 287

Cinematch 48

Command 251

Community 98, 100, 130

Complaints 147

Computers 63, 70-71, 228

Cookies 278-280

Copper 231

Corporate 98, 187

Credits 154

Customers 7, 15, 21-23, 27, 35-36, 44-45, 49, 124, 166, 202, 208, 213-216, 231, 237

D

Databases 199-200

Demand 18, 46

Design 36

Desktop 161, 182

Digital 28, 53

Display 276

Diverse 115

Dollars 142

Domain 223-225, 237

E

Economies 51

Education 257

Electronic 167

E-mail 110, 289

Employees 101, 104, 114, 120-121, 186, 246, 257

Enrollment 200

E-waste 72-75

Exploits 251, 253, 261

F

Facebook 77, 92, 102-105, 117, 123, 133-140, 142-155

Feedback 36

Folding 71

G

Goldcorp 116

Google 10, 20, 67, 87, 110, 122, 136, 141, 149, 186, 224, 232, 236, 265-270, 272-276, 280-281, 284-292

Grocers 16-17

Grocery 15

H

Hacking 243

Hardware 87, 158-159, 177, 179-181, 183, 187-191, 193

Harrah 213-217, 219-220

High-speed 286

I

Impression 282

Interest 109

Investment 21, 78

Iphone 83, 109, 232

K

Kindle 53, 66

L

Laptop 225

Licensing 57

M

Malware 247, 249-251, 254, 260

Market 21, 26, 41, 79-80, 82-83, 85-86, 114-115, 212, 267, 290

Mash-ups 110

Maturity 172

Microsoft 25, 87, 151, 178-179, 195, 199, 284, 289

Mobile 232-235, 285-286

Monsanto 70

Months 35, 37, 62, 82, 190

Multicore 68

Myspace 92, 102, 134, 136, 147

N

Nameserver 226

Netflix 43-58, 209

Netscape 84

Networks 102-104, 142, 222, 228, 233, 236, 274, 276, 279, 283, 286

O

Online 6, 27-28, 30, 45, 96, 98, 119-122,

124, 126, 140, 182, 225, 266, 268-
269, 281, 290

Operations 7, 51

Oracle 179, 199

P

Passwords 249, 255

Patches 259

Patent 25

Patents 25

Paypal 82

Platforms 104

Players 56, 62

Poisoning 253

Policy 120

Popular 46, 97

Porter 14, 30

Postal 50

Predators 147

Prediction 114-115, 129

Private 127, 217

Problems 71, 259

Processors 68

Profiling 277

Profits 26, 35, 57

Projects 171-172, 205

Protection 25

Protocols 227

Providers 232, 285

Public 43, 98, 102

R

Retail 35, 210, 212

Retailer 210

Revenue 141, 151, 274

Rewards 215

Routers 228

S

Satellite 234

Scripting 169

Server 164-165, 191, 224, 227-228, 278

Silicon 67

Software 2, 48, 68, 70-71, 79-80, 86-87,
157-158, 160-161, 163-164, 168-170,
172, 176-188, 190-193, 199, 202, 247,
249-252, 254, 259-260, 283, 289

Standards 167, 233, 256

Starbucks 106, 124-125

Switching 21-22, 78

Systems 7-8, 68, 159-160, 162-163, 167,
170, 183-184, 186-188, 190, 200-206,
208, 210, 215, 234, 258-259, 261

T

Tagging 110

Telephone 231

Television 54, 56

Titles 45-46, 48

Towers 232

Trading 238

Twitter 93, 105-109, 128-129, 131

U

Utility 187

V

Vendors 184

Verizon 231

Version 182

Viruses 250

Visual 168

W

Wal-mart 55, 58, 210-212, 219

Warehouses 204

Wikipedia 100

Windows 86-87, 159, 169

Wireless 232-234

Y

Youtube 93, 114, 118, 287-288, 292

Z

Zuckerberg 133-134, 138, 155

www.ingramcontent.com/pod-product-compliance
Lightning Source LLC
Chambersburg PA
CBHW082004190326
41458CB00010B/3060